OXFORD EDITION

THE PLAYS

OF

OLIVER GOLDSMITH

TOGETHER WITH

THE VICAR OF WAKEFIELD

EDITED, WITH GLOSSARIAL INDEX AND NOTES

BY

C. E. DOBLE, M.A.

WITH THE ASSISTANCE OF

G. OSTLER

WITH FORTY-SIX ILLUSTRATIONS

HENRY FROWDE

LONDON, EDINBURGH, GLASGOW, NEW YORK

TORONTO AND MELBOURNE

1909

OXFORD: HORACE HART

PRINTER TO THE UNIVERSITY

PREFATORY NOTE

THIS volume contains the best-known and most popular of Goldsmith's prose writings, viz. *The Good-Natur'd Man, She Stoops to Conquer*, and *The Vicar of Wakefield*. It is intended to form a supplementary volume to the *Poetical Works* edited by Mr. Austin Dobson for the same Series. The texts of the plays are based on the early editions. In the case of *The Vicar of Wakefield*, the text is that of the second edition, in which Goldsmith made several slight changes, as well as some of more importance, as noted in the Appendix. A few additional corrections have now been made, and the readings of later editions adopted where there seemed sufficient grounds for the change.

Of the editorial matter, the notes have been thrown into the form of a Glossarial Index, as affording a ready means of access to any given subject. In this will be found many parallel passages gathered from Goldsmith's miscellaneous prose works, showing incidentally the frequency with which our author drew upon himself. The passages, in most instances, have been quoted in full, to obviate the necessity of reference to the original. In the Appendix a short history of each of the works in this volume has been given, together with a few notes supplementary to the Glossarial Index.

C. E. DOBLE.

CONTENTS

LIST OF ILLUSTRATIONS

PLATES

ILLUSTRATIONS TO 'THE VICAR OF WAKEFIELD'
By William Mulready, R.A., 1843

THE GOOD-NATUR'D MAN

A COMEDY

AS PERFORMED AT THE

THEATRE-ROYAL, COVENT-GARDEN

[First printed in 1768]

PREFACE

WHEN I undertook to write a comedy, I confess I was strongly prepossessed in favour of the poets of the last age, and strove to imitate them. The term, *genteel comedy*, was then unknown amongst us, and little more was desired by an audience, than nature and humour, in whatever walks of life they were most conspicuous. The author of the following scenes never imagined that more would be expected of him, and therefore to delineate character has been his principal aim. Those who know any thing of composition, are sensible, that in pursuing humour, it will sometimes lead us into the recesses of the mean ; I was even tempted to look for it in the master of a spunging-house ; but in deference to the public taste, grown of late, perhaps, too delicate, the scene of the bailiffs was retrenched in the representation. In deference also to the judgment of a few friends, who think in a particular way, the scene is here restored. The author submits it to the reader in his closet ; and hopes that too much refinement will not banish humour and character from ours, as it has already done from the French theatre. Indeed the French comedy is now become so very elevated and sentimental, that it has not only banished humour and Molière from the stage, but it has banished all spectators too.

Upon the whole, the author returns his thanks to the public for the favourable reception which The Good-Natur'd Man has met with : and to Mr. Colman in particular, for his kindness to it. It may not also be improper to assure any, who shall hereafter write for the theatre, that merit, or supposed merit, will ever be a sufficient passport to his protection.

PROLOGUE

TO THE GOOD-NATUR'D MAN

WRITTEN BY DR. JOHNSON

SPOKEN BY MR. BENSLEY

PREST by the load of life, the weary mind
Surveys the general toil of human kind;
With cool submission joins the lab'ring train,
And social sorrow loses half its pain:
Our anxious bard, without complaint, may share
This bustling season's epidemic care,
Like Cæsar's pilot, dignified by fate,
Tost in one common storm with all the great;
Distrest alike, the statesman and the wit,
When one a borough courts, and one the pit.
The busy candidates for power and fame,
Have hopes, and fears, and wishes, just the same;
Disabled both to combat, or to fly,
Must hear all taunts, and hear without reply.
Uncheck'd, on both loud rabbles vent their rage,
As mongrels bay the lion in a cage.
Th' offended burgess hoards his angry tale,
For that blest year when all that vote may rail;
Their schemes of spite the poet's foes dismiss,
Till that glad night, when all that hate may hiss.
' This day the powder'd curls and golden coat,'
Says swelling Crispin, ' begg'd a cobler's vote.'
' This night, our wit,' the pert apprentice cries,
' Lies at my feet, I hiss him, and he dies.'
The great, 'tis true, can charm the electing tribe;

The bard may supplicate, but cannot bribe.
Yet judg'd by those, whose voices ne'er were sold,
He feels no want of ill-persuading gold ;
But confident of praise, if praise be due,
Trusts without fear, to merit, and to you.

DRAMATIS PERSONAE

MEN.

Mr. Honeywood	MR. POWELL.
Croaker	MR. SHUTER.
Lofty	MR. WOODWARD.
Sir William Honeywood . .	MR. CLARKE.
Leontine	MR. BENSLEY.
Jarvis	MR. DUNSTALL.
Butler	MR. CUSHING.
Bailiff	MR. R. SMITH.
Dubardieu	MR. HOLTAM.
Postboy	MR. QUICK.

WOMEN.

Miss Richland	MRS. BULKLEY.
Olivia	MRS. MATTOCKS.
Mrs Croaker	MRS. PITT.
Garnet	MRS. GREEN.
Landlady	MRS. WHITE.

Scene, LONDON.

THE GOOD-NATUR'D MAN

ACT I

SCENE, AN APARTMENT IN YOUNG HONEYWOOD'S
HOUSE.

Enter Sir William Honeywood, Jarvis.

Sir Will. Good Jarvis, make no apologies for this
honest bluntness. Fidelity like yours is the best excuse
for every freedom.

Jarv. I can't help being blunt, and being very angry
too, when I hear you talk of disinheriting so good, so
worthy a young gentleman as your nephew, my master.
All the world loves him.

Sir Will. Say rather, that he loves all the world; that
is his fault.

Jarv. I am sure there is no part of it more dear to him
than you are, though he has not seen you since he was a
child.

Sir Will. What signifies his affection to me; or how
can I be proud of a place in a heart, where every sharper
and coxcomb find an easy entrance?

Jarv. I grant you that he is rather too good-natur'd;
that he's too much every man's man; that he laughs this
minute with one, and cries the next with another: but
whose instructions may he thank for all this?

Sir Will. Not mine, sure? My letters to him during
my employment in Italy, taught him only that philosophy
which might prevent, not defend his errors.

Jarv. Faith, begging your honour's pardon, I'm sorry

they taught him any philosophy at all ; it has only serv'd to spoil him. This same philosophy is a good horse in the stable, but an arrant jade on a journey. For my own part, whenever I hear him mention the name on't, I'm always sure he's going to play the fool.

Sir Will. Don't let us ascribe his faults to his philosophy, I entreat you. No, Jarvis, his good nature arises rather from his fears of offending the importunate, than his desire of making the deserving happy.

Jarv. What it arises from, I don't know. But to be sure, every body has it that asks it.

Sir Will. Ay, or that does not ask it. I have been now for some time a concealed spectator of his follies, and find them as boundless as his dissipation.

Jarv. And yet, faith, he has some fine name or other for them all. He calls his extravagance, generosity ; and his trusting every body, universal benevolence. It was but last week he went security for a fellow whose face he scarce knew, and that he called an act of exalted mu—mu —munificence ; ay, that was the name he gave it.

Sir Will. And upon that I proceed, as my last effort, though with very little hopes to reclaim him. That very fellow has just absconded, and I have taken up the security. Now, my intention is to involve him in fictitious distress, before he has plung'd himself into real calamity. To arrest him for that very debt, to clap an officer upon him, and then let him see which of his friends will come to his relief.

Jarv. Well, if I could but any way see him thoroughly vexed, every groan of his would be music to me ; yet faith, I believe it impossible. I have tried to fret him myself every morning these three years ; but instead of being angry, he sits as calmly to hear me scold, as he does to his hair-dresser.

Sir Will. We must try him once more, however, and

I'll go this instant to put my scheme into execution : and I don't despair of succeeding, as, by your means, I can have frequent opportunities of being about him without being known.   What a pity it is, Jarvis, that any man's good-will to others should produce so much neglect of himself, as to require correction ?   Yet, we must touch his weaknesses with a delicate hand.   There are some faults so nearly allied to excellence, that we can scarce weed out the vice without eradicating the virtue.

[*Exit.*

Jarv. Well, go thy ways, Sir William Honeywood. It is not without reason that the world allows thee to be the best of men.   But here comes his hopeful nephew ; the strange, good-natur'd, foolish, open-hearted—And yet, all his faults are such that one loves him still the better for them.

Enter Honeywood.

Honeyw. Well, Jarvis, what messages from my friends this morning ?

Jarv. You have no friends.

Honeyw. Well ; from my acquaintance then ?

Jarv. (*Pulling out bills.*) A few of our usual cards of compliment, that's all.   This bill from your tailor; this from your mercer ;   and this from the little broker in Crooked-lane.   He says he has been at a great deal of trouble to get back the money you borrowed.

Honeyw. That I don't know ;   but I'm sure we were at a great deal of trouble in getting him to lend it.

Jarv. He has lost all patience.

Honeyw. Then he has lost a very good thing.

Jarv. There's that ten guineas you were sending to the poor gentleman and his children in the Fleet.   I believe that would stop his mouth, for a while at least.

Honeyw. Ay, Jarvis, but what will fill their mouths in

B 3

the mean time ? Must I be cruel because he happens to be importunate: and, to relieve his avarice, leave them to insupportable distress ?

Jarv. 'Sdeath ! Sir, the question now is how to relieve yourself. Yourself—Havn't I reason to be out of my senses, when I see things going at sixes and sevens ?

Honeyw. Whatever reason you may have for being out of your senses, I hope you'll allow that I'm not quite unreasonable for continuing in mine.

Jarv. You're the only man alive in your present situation that could do so—Every thing upon the waste. There's Miss Richland and her fine fortune gone already, and upon the point of being given to your rival.

Honeyw. I'm no man's rival.

Jarv. Your uncle in Italy preparing to disinherit you ; your own fortune almost spent ; and nothing but pressing creditors, false friends, and a pack of drunken servants that your kindness has made unfit for any other family.

Honeyw. Then they have the more occasion for being in mine.

Jarv. Soh ! What will you have done with him that I caught stealing your plate in the pantry ? In the fact ; I caught him in the fact.

Honeyw. In the fact ? If so I really think that we should pay him his wages and turn him off.

Jarv. He shall be turn'd off at Tyburn, the dog ; we'll hang him, if it be only to frighten the rest of the family.

Honeyw. No, Jarvis ; it's enough that we have lost what he has stolen, let us not add to it the loss of a fellow-creature !

Jarv. Very fine ; well, here was the footman just now, to complain of the butler ; he says he does most work, and ought to have most wages.

Honeyw. That's but just ; though perhaps here comes the butler to complain of the footman.

Jarv. Ay, it's the way with them all, from the scullion to the privy-counsellor. If they have a bad master they keep quarrelling with him ; if they have a good master, they keep quarrelling with one another.

Enter Butler, drunk.

But. Sir, I'll not stay in the family with Jonathan, you must part with him, or part with me, that's the ex-ex-exposition of the matter, Sir.

Honeyw. Full and explicit enough. But what's his fault, good Philip ?

But. Sir, he's given to drinking, Sir, and I shall have my morals corrupted, by keeping such company.

Honeyw. Ha ! ha ! He has such a diverting way—

Jarv. O, quite amusing.

But. I find my wine's a-going, Sir ; and liquors don't go without mouths, Sir ; I hate a drunkard, Sir.

Honeyw. Well, well, Philip, I'll hear you upon that another time, so go to bed now.

Jarv. To bed ! Let him go to the devil !

But. Begging your honour's pardon, and begging your pardon, master Jarvis, I'll not go to bed, nor to the devil neither. I have enough to do to mind my cellar. I forgot, your honour, Mr. Croaker is below. I came on purpose to tell you.

Honeyw. Why didn't you show him up, blockhead ?

But. Shew him up, Sir ! With all my heart, Sir. Up or down, all's one to me. [*Exit.*

Jarv. Ay, we have one or other of that family in this house from morning till night. He comes on the old affair, I suppose. The match between his son that's just return'd from Paris, and Miss Richland, the young lady he's guardian to.

Honeyw. Perhaps so. Mr. Croaker, knowing my

friendship for the young lady, has got it into his head that
I can persuade her to what I please.

Jarv. Ah ! if you loved yourself but half as well as
she loves you, we should soon see a marriage that would
set all things to rights again.

Honeyw. Love me ! Sure, Jarvis, you dream.   No, no ;
her intimacy with me never amounted to more than
friendship—mere friendship.   That she is the most lovely
woman that ever warm'd the human heart with desire,
I own.   But never let me harbour a thought of making
her unhappy, by a connexion with one so unworthy her
merits as I am.   No, Jarvis, it shall be my study to serve
her, even in spite of my wishes ; and to secure her happiness, though it destroys my own.

Jarv. Was ever the like ! I want patience.

Honeyw. Besides, Jarvis, though I could obtain Miss
Richland's consent, do you think I could succeed with
her guardian, or Mrs. Croaker his wife ? who, though
both very fine in their way, are yet a little opposite in
their dispositions, you know.

Jarv. Opposite enough, heaven knows ;   the very
reverse of each other ;   she all laugh and no joke ;   he
always complaining and never sorrowful ;   a fretful poor
soul that has a new distress for every hour in the four
and twenty—

Honeyw. Hush, hush, he 's coming up, he'll hear you.

Jarv. One whose voice is a passing bell—

Honeyw. Well, well, go, do.

Jarv. A raven that bodes nothing but mischief ;   a
coffin and cross bones ; a bundle of rue ; a sprig of deadly
night-shade ; a—(*Honeywood stopping his mouth, at last
pushes him off.*)   [*Exit Jarvis.*

Honeyw. I must own my old monitor is not entirely
wrong.   There is something in my friend Croaker's conversation that quite depresses me.   His very mirth is an

antidote to all gaiety, and his appearance has a stronger effect on my spirits than an undertaker's shop.—Mr. Croaker, this is such a satisfaction—

Enter Croaker.

Croak. A pleasant morning to Mr. Honeywood, and many of them. How is this ? you look most shockingly to-day, my dear friend. I hope this weather does not affect your spirits. To be sure, if this weather continues —I say nothing—But God send we be all better this day three months.

Honeyw. I heartily concur in the wish, though I own not in your apprehensions.

Croak. May be not. Indeed what signifies what weather we have in a country going to ruin like ours ? taxes rising and trade falling. Money flying out of the kingdom, and Jesuits swarming into it. I know at this time no less than an hundred and twenty-seven Jesuits between Charing-cross and Temple-bar.

Honeyw. The Jesuits will scarce pervert you or me, I should hope.

Croak. May be not. Indeed what signifies whom they pervert in a country that has scarce any religion to lose ? I'm only afraid for our wives and daughters.

Honeyw. I have no apprehensions for the ladies, I assure you.

Croak. May be not. Indeed what signifies whether they be perverted or no ? the women in my time were good for something. I have seen a lady drest from top to toe in her own manufactures formerly. But now-a-days the devil a thing of their own manufacture's about them, except their faces.

Honeyw. But, however these faults may be practised abroad, you don't find them at home, either with Mrs. Croaker, Olivia, or Miss Richland.

Croak. The best of them will never be canoniz'd for a saint when she's dead. By the bye, my dear friend, I don't find this match between Miss Richland and my son much relished, either by one side or t'other.

Honeyw. I thought otherwise.

Croak. Ah, Mr. Honeywood, a little of your fine serious advice to the young lady might go far : I know she has a very exalted opinion of your understanding.

Honeyw. But would not that be usurping an authority that more properly belongs to yourself ?

Croak. My dear friend, you know but little of my authority at home. People think, indeed, because they see me come out in a morning thus, with a pleasant face, and to make my friends merry, that all's well within. But I have cares that would break an heart of stone. My wife has so encroached upon every one of my privileges, that I'm now no more than a mere lodger in my own house.

Honeyw. But a little spirit exerted on your side might perhaps restore your authority.

Croak. No, though I had the spirit of a lion ! I do rouse sometimes. But what then ! always haggling and haggling. A man is tired of getting the better before his wife is tired of losing the victory.

Honeyw. It's a melancholy consideration indeed, that our chief comforts often produce our greatest anxieties, and that an increase of our possessions is but an inlet to new disquietudes.

Croak. Ah, my dear friend, these were the very words of poor Dick Doleful to me not a week before he made away with himself. Indeed, Mr. Honeywood, I never see you but you put me in mind of poor—Dick. Ah, there was merit neglected for you ! and so true a friend ; we lov'd each other for thirty years, and yet he never asked me to lend him a single farthing.

Honeyw. Pray what could induce him to commit so rash an action at last ?

Croak. I don't know, some people were malicious enough to say it was keeping company with me ; because we used to meet now and then and open our hearts to each other. To be sure I lov'd to hear him talk, and he lov'd to hear me talk ; poor dear Dick. He us'd to say that Croaker rhym'd to joker : and so we us'd to laugh—Poor Dick. [*Going to cry.*

Honeyw. His fate affects me.

Croak. Ay, he grew sick of this miserable life, where we do nothing but eat and grow hungry, dress and undress, get up and lie down ; while reason, that should watch like a nurse by our side, falls as fast asleep as we do.

Honeyw. To say truth, if we compare that part of life which is to come, by that which we have past, the prospect is hideous.

Croak. Life at the greatest and best is but a froward child, that must be humour'd and coax'd a little till it falls asleep, and then all the care is over.

Honeyw. Very true, Sir, nothing can exceed the vanity of our existence, but the folly of our pursuits. We wept when we came into the world, and every day tells us why.

Croak. Ah, my dear friend, it is a perfect satisfaction to be miserable with you. My son Leontine shan't lose the benefit of such fine conversation. I'll just step home for him. I am willing to show him so much seriousness in one scarce older than himself—And what if I bring my last letter to the *Gazetteer* on the increase and progress of earthquakes ? It will amuse us, I promise you. I there prove how the late earthquake is coming round to pay us another visit, from London to Lisbon, from Lisbon to the Canary Islands, from the Canary Islands to Palmyra, from Palmyra to Constantinople, and so from Constantinople back to London again. [*Exit.*

Honeyw. Poor Croaker ! his situation deserves the utmost pity. I shall scarce recover my spirits these three days. Sure, to live upon such terms is worse than death itself. And yet, when I consider my own situation, a broken fortune, a hopeless passion, friends in distress ; the wish but not the power to serve them—(*pausing and sighing*).

Enter Butler.

But. More company below, sir ; Mrs. Croaker and Miss Richland ; shall I shew them up ? but they're shewing up themselves.   [*Exit.*

Enter Mrs. Croaker and Miss Richland.

Miss Rich. You're always in such spirits.

Mrs. Croak. We have just come, my dear Honeywood, from the auction. There was the old deaf dowager, as usual, bidding like a fury against herself. And then so curious in antiques ! herself the most genuine piece of antiquity in the whole collection.

Honeyw. Excuse me, ladies, if some uneasiness from friendship makes me unfit to share in this good humour : I know you'll pardon me.

Mrs. Croak. I vow he seems as melancholy as if he had taken a dose of my husband this morning. Well, if Richland here can pardon you, I must.

Miss Rich. You would seem to insinuate, madam, that I have particular reasons for being disposed to refuse it.

Mrs. Croak. Whatever I insinuate, my dear, don't be so ready to wish an explanation.

Miss Rich. I own I should be sorry, Mr. Honeywood's long friendship and mine should be misunderstood.

Honeyw. There's no answering for others, madam. But I hope you'll never find me presuming to offer more than the most delicate friendship may readily allow.

Miss Rich. And I shall be prouder of such a tribute from you than the most passionate professions from others.

Honeyw. My own sentiments, madam : friendship is a disinterested commerce between equals ; love, an abject intercourse between tyrants and slaves.

Miss Rich. And, without a compliment, I know none more disinterested, or more capable of friendship, than Mr. Honeywood.

Mrs. Croak. And, indeed, I know nobody that has more friends, at least among the ladies. Miss Fruzz, Miss Odbody, and Miss Winterbottom, praise him in all companies. As for Miss Biddy Bundle, she's his professed admirer.

Miss Rich. Indeed ! an admirer ! I did not know, Sir, you were such a favourite there. But is she seriously so handsome ? Is she the mighty thing talked of ?

Honeyw. The town, madam, seldom begins to praise a lady's beauty, till she's beginning to lose it. (*Smiling.*)

Mrs. Croak. But she's resolved never to lose it, it seems. For, as her natural face decays, her skill improves in making the artificial one. Well, nothing diverts me more than one of those fine, old, dressy things, who thinks to conceal her age, by every where exposing her person ; sticking herself up in the front of a side box : trailing through a minuet at Almack's ; and then, in the public gardens, looking for all the world like one of the painted ruins of the place.

Honeyw. Every age has its admirers, ladies. While you, perhaps, are trading among the warmer climates of youth ; there ought to be some to carry on a useful commerce in the frozen latitudes beyond fifty.

Miss Rich. But, then, the mortifications they must suffer, before they can be fitted out for traffic. I have seen one of them fret a whole morning at her hair-dresser, when all the fault was her face.

Honeyw. And yet, I'll engage, has carried that face at last to a very good market. This good-natur'd town, madam, has husbands, like spectacles, to fit every age, from fifteen to fourscore.

Mrs. Croak. Well, you're a dear good-natur'd creature. But you know you're engaged with us this morning upon a strolling party. I want to shew Olivia the town, and the things ; I believe I shall have business for you for the whole day.

Honeyw. I am sorry, madam, I have an appointment with Mr. Croaker, which it is impossible to put off.

Mrs. Croak. What ! with my husband ! then I'm resolv'd to take no refusal. Nay, I protest you must. You know I never laugh so much as with you.

Honeyw. Why, if I must, I must. I'll swear you have put me into such spirits. Well, do you find jest, and I'll find laugh, I promise you. We'll wait for the chariot in the next room.   [*Exeunt.*

Enter Leontine and Olivia.

Leont. There they go, thoughtless and happy. My dearest Olivia, what would I give to see you capable of sharing in their amusements, and as chearful as they are?

Oliv. How, my Leontine, how can I be chearful, when I have so many terrors to oppress me ? The fear of being detected by this family, and the apprehensions of a censuring world, when I must be detected—

Leont. The world ! my love, what can it say ? At worst it can only say that, being compelled by a mercenary guardian to embrace a life you disliked, you formed a resolution of flying with the man of your choice ; that you confided in his honour, and took refuge in my father's house ; the only one where your's could remain without censure.

Oliv. But consider, Leontine, your disobedience and

my indiscretion ; your being sent to France to bring home a sister ; and, instead of a sister, bringing home——

Leont. One dearer than a thousand sisters. One that I am convinced will be equally dear to the rest of the family, when she comes to be known.

Oliv. And that, I fear, will shortly be.

Leont. Impossible, 'till we ourselves think proper to make the discovery. My sister, you know, has been with her aunt, at Lyons, since she was a child, and you find every creature in the family takes you for her.

Oliv. But mayn't she write, mayn't her aunt write ?

Leont. Her aunt scarce ever writes, and all my sister's letters are directed to me.

Oliv. But won't your refusing Miss Richland, for whom you know the old gentleman intends you, create a suspicion ?

Leont. There, there's my master-stroke. I have resolved not to refuse her ; nay, an hour hence I have consented to go with my father to make her an offer of my heart and fortune.

Oliv. Your heart and fortune !

Leont. Don't be alarm'd, my dearest. Can Olivia think so meanly of my honour, or my love, as to suppose I could ever hope for happiness from any but her ? No, my Olivia, neither the force, nor, permit me to add, the delicacy of my passion, leave any room to suspect me. I only offer Miss Richland a heart, I am convinced she will refuse ; as I am confident, that, without knowing it, her affections are fixed upon Mr. Honeywood.

Oliv. Mr. Honeywood ! You'll excuse my apprehensions ; but when your merits come to be put in the balance—

Leont. You view them with too much partiality. However, by making this offer, I shew a seeming compliance with my father's command ; and perhaps, upon her refusal, I may have his consent to chuse for myself.

Oliv. Well, I submit. And yet, my Leontine, I own, I shall envy her, even your pretended addresses. I consider every look, every expression of your esteem, as due only to me. This is folly perhaps : I allow it : but it is natural to suppose, that merit which has made an impression on one's own heart, may be powerful over that of another.

Leont. Don't, my life's treasure, don't let us make imaginary evils, when you know we have so many real ones to encounter. At worst, you know, if Miss Richland should consent, or my father refuse his pardon, it can but end in a trip to Scotland ; and—

Enter Croaker.

Croak. Where have you been, boy ? I have been seeking you. My friend Honeywood here, has been saying such comfortable things. Ah ! he 's an example indeed. Where is he ? I left him here.

Leont. Sir, I believe you may see him, and hear him too in the next room ; he 's preparing to go out with the ladies.

Croak. Good gracious, can I believe my eyes or my ears ! I'm struck dumb with his vivacity, and stunn'd with the loudness of his laugh. Was there ever such a transformation ! (*a laugh behind the scenes, Croaker mimics it.*) Ha ! ha ! ha ! there it goes : a plague take their balderdash ; yet I could expect nothing less, when my precious wife was of the party. On my conscience, I believe she could spread an horse-laugh through the pews of a tabernacle.

Leont. Since you find so many objections to a wife, Sir, how can you be so earnest in recommending one to me ?

Croak. I have told you, and tell you again, boy, that

Miss Richland's fortune must not go out of the family ; one may find comfort in the money, whatever one does in the wife.

Leont. But, Sir, though, in obedience to your desire, I am ready to marry her ; it may be possible, she has no inclination to me.

Croak. I'll tell you once for all how it stands. A good part of Miss Richland's large fortune consists in a claim upon government, which my good friend, Mr. Lofty, assures me the treasury will allow. One half of this she is to forfeit, by her father's will, in case she refuses to marry you. So, if she rejects you, we seize half her fortune ; if she accepts you, we seize the whole, and a fine girl into the bargain.

Leont. But, Sir, if you will but listen to reason—

Croak. Come, then, produce your reasons. I tell you I'm fix'd, determined, so now produce your reasons. When I'm determined, I always listen to reason, because it can then do no harm.

Leont. You have alleged that a mutual choice was the first requisite in matrimonial happiness.

Croak. Well, and you have both of you a mutual choice. She has her choice—to marry you or lose half her fortune ; and you have your choice—to marry her, or pack out of doors without any fortune at all.

Leont. An only son, Sir, might expect more indulgence.

Croak. An only father, Sir, might expect more obedience; besides, has not your sister here, that never disobliged me in her life, as good a right as you ? He's a sad dog, Livy, my dear, and would take all from you. But he shan't, I tell you he shan't, for you shall have your share.

Oliv. Dear Sir, I wish you'd be convinced that I can never be happy in any addition to my fortune, which is taken from his.

Croak. Well, well, it's a good child, so say no more; but come with me, and we will see something that will give us a great deal of pleasure, I promise you; old Ruggins, the curry-comb maker, lying in state ; I am told he makes a very handsome corpse, and becomes his coffin prodigiously. He was an intimate friend of mine, and these are friendly things we ought to do for each other.

[*Exeunt.*

ACT II

SCENE, CROAKER'S HOUSE.

Miss Richland, Garnet.

Miss Rich. Olivia not his sister ? Olivia not Leontine's sister ? You amaze me !

Garn. No more his sister than I am ; I had it all from his own servant ; I can get any thing from that quarter.

Miss Rich. But how ? Tell me again, Garnet.

Garn. Why, Madam, as I told you before, instead of going to Lyons, to bring home his sister, who has been there with her aunt these ten years ; he never went further than Paris ; there he saw and fell in love with this young lady, by the by, of a prodigious family.

Miss Rich. And brought her home to my guardian, as his daughter ?

Garn. Yes, and his daughter she will be. If he don't consent to their marriage, they talk of trying what a Scotch parson can do.

Miss Rich. Well, I own they have deceived me—And so demurely as Olivia carried it too !—Would you believe it Garnet, I told her all my secrets ; and yet the sly cheat concealed all this from me ?

Garn. And, upon my word, madam, I don't much blame her : she was loth to trust one with her secrets, that was so very bad at keeping her own.

Miss Rich. But, to add to their deceit, the young gentleman, it seems, pretends to make me serious pro-posals. My guardian and he are to be here presently, to open the affair in form. You know I am to lose half my fortune if I refuse him.

Garn. Yet, what can you do ? For being, as you are, in love with Mr. Honeywood, madam—

Miss Rich. How! ideot : what do you mean ? In love with Mr. Honeywood ! Is this to provoke me ?

Garn. That is, madam, in friendship with him ; I meant nothing more than friendship, as I hope to be married ; nothing more.

Miss Rich. Well, no more of this ! As to my guardian, and his son, they shall find me prepared to receive them ; I'm resolved to accept their proposal with seeming pleasure, to mortify them by compliance, and so throw the refusal at last upon them.

Garn. Delicious ! and that will secure your whole fortune to yourself. Well, who could have thought so innocent a face could cover so much 'cuteness !

Miss Rich. Why, girl, I only oppose my prudence to their cunning, and practise a lesson they have taught me against themselves.

Garn. Then you're likely not long to want employment, for here they come, and in close conference.

Enter Croaker, Leontine.

Leont. Excuse me, Sir, if I seem to hesitate upon the point of putting to the lady so important a question.

Croak. Lord ! good Sir, moderate your fears ; you're so plaguy shy, that one would think you had changed sexes. I tell you we must have the half or the whole.

Come, let me see with what spirit you begin ? Well, why don't you ! Eh ! What ? Well then—I must, it seems—Miss Richland, my dear, I believe you guess at our business ; an affair which my son here comes to open, that nearly concerns your happiness.

Miss Rich. Sir, I should be ungrateful not to be pleased with any thing that comes recommended by you.

Croak. How, boy, could you desire a finer opening ? Why don't you begin, I say ?   [*To Leont.*

Leont. 'Tis true, madam, my father, madam, has some intentions—hem—of explaining an affair—which—himself—can best explain, madam.

Croak. Yes, my dear ; it comes entirely from my son ; it's all a request of his own, madam. And I will permit him to make the best of it.

Leont. The whole affair is only this, madam ; my father has a proposal to make, which he insists none but himself shall deliver.

Croak. My mind misgives me, the fellow will never be brought on (*Aside.*) In short, madam, you see before you one that loves you ; one whose whole happiness is all in you.

Miss Rich. I never had any doubts of your regard, Sir : and I hope you can have none of my duty.

Croak. That's not the thing, my little sweeting ; my love ! No, no, another-guess lover than I ; there he stands, madam, his very looks declare the force of his passion—Call up a look, you dog (*Aside.*)—But then, had you seen him, as I have, weeping, speaking soliloquies and blank verse, sometimes melancholy, and sometimes absent—

Miss Rich. I fear, Sir, he's absent now ; or such a declaration would have come most properly from himself.

Croak. Himself ! madam, he would die before he could make such a confession ; and if he had not a channel for his passion through me, it would ere now have drowned his understanding.

Miss Rich. I must grant, Sir, there are attractions in modest diffidence above the force of words. A silent address is the genuine eloquence of sincerity.

Croak. Madam, he has forgot to speak any other language ; silence is become his mother tongue.

Miss Rich. And it must be confessed, Sir, it speaks very powerfully in his favour. And yet I shall be thought too forward in making such a confession ; shan't I, Mr. Leontine ?

Leont. Confusion ! my reserve will undo me. But, if modesty attracts her, impudence may disgust her. I'll try. (*Aside.*) Don't imagine from my silence, madam, that I want a due sense of the honour and happiness intended me. My father, madam, tells me, your humble servant is not totally indifferent to you.—He admires you ; I adore you ; and when we come together, upon my soul I believe we shall be the happiest couple in all St. James's.

Miss Rich. If I could flatter myself, you thought as you speak, Sir—

Leont. Doubt my sincerity, madam ? By your dear self I swear. Ask the brave if they desire glory ? ask cowards, if they covet safety——

Croak. Well, well, no more questions about it.

Leont. Ask the sick, if they long for health ? ask misers, if they love money ? ask——

Croak. Ask a fool, if they can talk nonsense ! What 's come over the boy ? What signifies asking, when there 's not a soul to give you an answer ? If you would ask to the purpose, ask this lady's consent to make you happy.

Miss Rich. Why indeed, Sir, his uncommon ardour almost compels me—forces me to comply. And yet I'm afraid he'll despise a conquest gained with too much ease : won't you, Mr. Leontine ?

Leont. Confusion! (*Aside.*) Oh, by no means, madam, by no means. And yet, madam, you talk'd of force. There is nothing I would avoid so much as compulsion in a thing of this kind. No, madam, I will still be generous, and leave you at liberty to refuse.

Croak. But I tell you, Sir, the lady is not at liberty. It's a match. You see she says nothing. Silence gives consent.

Leont. But, Sir, she talk'd of force. Consider, Sir, the cruelty of constraining her inclinations.

Croak. But I say there's no cruelty. Don't you know, blockhead, that girls have always a roundabout way of saying yes before company? So get you both gone together into the next room, and hang him that interrupts the tender explanation. Get you gone, I say; I'll not hear a word.

Leont. But, Sir, I must beg leave to insist—

Croak. Get off, you puppy, or I'll beg leave to insist upon knocking you down. Stupid whelp! But I don't wonder! the boy takes entirely after his mother.

[*Exeunt Miss Rich. and Leont.*

Enter Mrs. Croaker.

Mrs. Croak. Mr. Croaker, I bring you something, my dear, that I believe will make you smile.

Croak. I'll hold you a guinea of that, my dear.

Mrs. Croak. A letter; and, as I knew the hand, I ventur'd to open it.

Croak. And how can you expect your breaking open my letters should give me pleasure?

Mrs. Croak. Poo, it's from your sister at Lyons, and contains good news; read it.

Croak. What a Frenchified cover is here! That sister of mine has some good qualities, but I could never teach her to fold a letter.

Mrs. Croak. Fold a fiddlestick. Read what it contains.

Croak. (reading.)

' DEAR NICK,

An English gentleman, of large fortune, has for some time made private, though honourable proposals to your daughter Olivia. They love each other tenderly, and I find she has consented, without letting any of the family know, to crown his addresses. As such good offers don't come every day, your own good sense, his large fortune, and family considerations, will induce you to forgive her.

Yours ever,

RACHAEL CROAKER.'

My daughter Olivia privately contracted to a man of large fortune ! This is good news, indeed. My heart never foretold me of this. And yet, how slily the little baggage has carried it since she came home, not a word on 't to the old ones for the world. Yet, I thought I saw something she wanted to conceal.

Mrs. Croak. Well, if they have concealed their amour, they shan't conceal their wedding ; that shall be public, I'm resolv'd.

Croak. I tell thee, woman, the wedding is the most foolish part of the ceremony. I can never get this woman to think of the most serious part of the nuptial engagement.

Mrs. Croak. What, would you have me think of their funeral ? But come, tell me, my dear, don't you owe more to me than you care to confess ? Would you have ever been known to Mr. Lofty, who has undertaken Miss Richland's claim at the treasury, but for me ? Who was it first made him an acquaintance at lady Shabbaroon's rout ? Who got him to promise us his interest ?

Is not he a back-stairs favourite, one that can do what he pleases with those that do what they please ? Is not he an acquaintance that all your groaning and lamentation could never have got us ?

Croak. He is a man of importance, I grant you. And yet what amazes me is, that, while he is giving away places to all the world, he can't get one for himself.

Mrs. Croak. That perhaps may be owing to his nicety. Great men are not easily satisfied.

Enter French Servant.

Serv. An expresse from Monsieur Lofty. He vil be vait upon your honour's instamment. He be only giving four five instruction, read two tree memorial, call upon von ambassadeur. He vil be vid you in one tree minutes.

Mrs. Croak. You see now, my dear. What an extensive department! Well, friend, let your master know, that we are extremely honoured by this honour. Was there any thing ever in a higher stile of breeding ? All messages among the great are now done by express.

Croak. To be sure, no man does little things with more solemnity, or claims more respect than he. But he's in the right on't. In our bad world, respect is given, where respect is claim'd.

Mrs. Croak. Never mind the world, my dear ; you were never in a pleasanter place in your life. Let us now think of receiving him with proper respect, (*a loud rapping at the door,*) and there he is, by the thundering rap.

Croak. Ay, verily, there he is ! as close upon the heels of his own express, as an indorsement upon the back of a bill. Well, I'll leave you to receive him, whilst I go to chide my little Olivia for intending to steal a marriage without mine, or her aunt's consent. I must seem to be angry, or she too may begin to despise my authority.

[*Exit.*

Enter Lofty, speaking to his servant.

Lofty. ' And if the Venetian ambassador, or that teazing creature the Marquis, should call, I'm not at home. Dam'me, I'll be pack-horse to none of them.' My dear madam, I have just snatched a moment.—' And if the expresses to his Grace be ready, let them be sent off ; they're of importance.' Madam, I ask a thousand pardons.

Mrs. Croak. Sir, this honour——

Lofty. ' And, Dubardieu ! if the person calls about the commission, let him know that it is made out. As for Lord Cumbercourt's stale request, it can keep cold : you understand me.' Madam, I ask ten thousand pardons.

Mrs. Croak. Sir, this honour——

Lofty. ' And, Dubardieu ! if the man comes from the Cornish borough, you must do him ; you must do him I say.' Madam, I ask ten thousand pardons. ' And if the Russian ambassador calls : but he will scarce call to-day, I believe.' And now, madam, I have just got time to express my happiness in having the honour of being permitted to profess myself your most obedient humble servant.

Mrs. Croak. Sir, the happiness and honour are all mine ; and yet, I'm only robbing the public while I detain you.

Lofty. Sink the public, madam, when the fair are to be attended. Ah, could all my hours be so charmingly devoted ! Sincerely, don't you pity us poor creatures in affairs ? Thus it is eternally ; solicited for places here, teazed for pensions there, and courted every where. I know you pity me. Yes, I see you do.

Mrs. Croak. Excuse me, Sir, ' Toils of empires pleasures are,' as Waller says.

Lofty. Waller, Waller, is he of the house ?

Mrs. Croak. The modern poet of that name, Sir.

Lofty. Oh, a modern ! We men of business despise the moderns ; and as for the ancients we have no time to read them. Poetry is a pretty thing enough for our wives and daughters ; but not for us. Why now, here I stand that know nothing of books. I say, madam, I know nothing of books ; and yet, I believe, upon a land-carriage fishery, a stamp-act, or a jag-hire, I can talk my two hours without feeling the want of them.

Mrs. Croak. The world is no stranger to Mr. Lofty's eminence in every capacity.

Lofty. I vow to gad, madam, you make me blush. I'm nothing, nothing, nothing in the world ; a mere obscure gentleman. To be sure, indeed, one or two of the present ministers are pleased to represent me as a formidable man. I know they are pleased to bespatter me at all their little dirty levees. Yet, upon my soul, I wonder what they see in me to treat me so ! Measures, not men, have always been my mark ; and I vow, by all that's honourable, my resentment has never done the men, as mere men, any manner of harm—that is as mere men !

Mrs. Croak. What importance, and yet what modesty !

Lofty. Oh, if you talk of modesty, madam ! there I own, I'm accessible to praise : modesty is my foible : it was so, the Duke of Brentford used to say of me. ' I love Jack Lofty,' he used to say : ' no man has a finer knowledge of things ; quite a man of information ; and when he speaks upon his legs, by the Lord he's prodigious, he scouts them ; and yet all men have their faults ; too much modesty is his,' says his Grace.

Mrs. Croak. And yet, I dare say, you don't want assurance when you come to solicit for your friends.

Lofty. O, there indeed I'm in bronze. Apropos ! I have just been mentioning Miss Richland's case to a certain personage ; we must name no names. When I ask, I'm not to be put off, madam. No, no, I take my

friend by the button. A fine girl, Sir ; great justice in
her case. A friend of mine. Borough interest. Business must be done, Mr. Secretary. I say, Mr. Secretary,
her business must be done, Sir. That's my way, madam.

Mrs. Croak. Bless me ! you said all this to the secretary of state, did you ?

Lofty. I did not say the secretary, did I ? Well, curse it,
since you have found me out I will not deny it. It was
to the secretary.

Mrs. Croak. This was going to the fountain head at
once, not applying to the understrappers, as Mr. Honeywood would have had us.

Lofty. Honeywood ! he ! he ! He was, indeed, a fine
solicitor. I suppose you have heard what has just happened to him ?

Mrs. Croak. Poor dear man ; no accident, I hope.

Lofty. Undone, madam, that's all. His creditors have
taken him into custody. A prisoner in his own house.

Mrs. Croak. A prisoner in his own house ! How ! At
this very time ! I'm quite unhappy for him.

Lofty. Why so am I. The man, to be sure, was
immensely good-natur'd. But then I could never find
that he had any thing in him.

Mrs. Croak. His manner, to be sure, was excessive
harmless : some, indeed, thought it a little dull. For
my part, I always concealed my opinion.

Lofty. It can't be concealed, madam ; the man was
dull, dull as the last new comedy ! a poor impracticable
creature ! I tried once or twice to know if he was fit for
business ; but he had scarce talents to be groom-porter
to an orange barrow.

Mrs. Croak. How differently does Miss Richland think
of him ! For, I believe, with all his faults, she loves him.

Lofty. Loves him ! Does she ? You should cure her
of that by all means. Let me see ; what if she were

sent to him this instant, in his present doleful situation ?
My life for it, that works her cure.   Distress is a perfect
antidote to love.   Suppose we join her in the next room ?
Miss Richland is a fine girl, has a fine fortune, and must not
be thrown away.   Upon my honour, madam, I have a
regard for Miss Richland ; and rather than she should be
thrown away, I should think it no indignity to marry her
myself.   [*Exeunt.*

Enter Olivia and Leontine.

Leont. And yet, trust me, Olivia, I had every reason
to expect Miss Richland's refusal, as I did every thing in
my power to deserve it.   Her indelicacy surprises me.

Oliv. Sure, Leontine, there's nothing so indelicate in
being sensible of your merit.   If so, I fear, I shall be the
most guilty thing alive,

Leont. But you mistake, my dear.   The same attention I used to advance my merit with you, I practised to
lessen it with her.   What more could I do ?

Oliv. Let us now rather consider what is to be done.
We have both dissembled too long.—I have always been
ashamed—I am now quite weary of it.   Sure I could
never have undergone so much for any other but you.

Leont. And you shall find my gratitude equal to your
kindest compliance.   Though our friends should totally
forsake us, Olivia, we can draw upon content for the
deficiencies of fortune.

Oliv. Then why should we defer our scheme of humble
happiness, when it is now in our power ?   I may be the
favourite of your father, it is true ; but can it ever be
thought, that his present kindness to a supposed child,
will continue to a known deceiver ?

Leont. I have many reasons to believe it will.   As his
attachments are but few, they are lasting.   His own
marriage was a private one, as ours may be.   Besides,

I have sounded him already at a distance, and find all his answers exactly to our wish. Nay, by an expression or two that dropped from him, I am induced to think he knows of this affair.

Oliv. Indeed ! But that would be an happiness too great to be expected.

Leont. However it be, I'm certain you have power over him ; and I'm persuaded, if you informed him of our situation, that he would be disposed to pardon it.

Oliv. You had equal expectations, Leontine, from your last scheme with Miss Richland, which you find has succeeded most wretchedly.

Leont. And that's the best reason for trying another.

Oliv. If it must be so, I submit.

Leont. As we could wish, he comes this way. Now, my dearest Olivia, be resolute. I'll just retire within hearing, to come in at a proper time, either to share your danger, or confirm your victory.   [*Exit.*

Enter Croaker.

Croak. Yes, I must forgive her ; and yet not too easily, neither. It will be proper to keep up the decorums of resentment a little, if it be only to impress her with an idea of my authority.

Oliv. How I tremble to approach him !—Might I presume, Sir,—if I interrupt you—

Croak. No, child, where I have an affection, it is not a little thing that can interrupt me. Affection gets over little things.

Oliv. Sir, you're too kind. I'm sensible how ill I deserve this partiality. Yet heaven knows, there is nothing I would not do to gain it.

Croak. And you have but too well succeeded, you little hussy you. With those endearing ways of yours, on my conscience, I could be brought to forgive any thing, unless it were a very great offence indeed.

Oliv. But mine is such an offence—When you know my guilt—Yes, you shall know it, though I feel the greatest pain in the confession.

Croak. Why then, if it be so very great a pain, you may spare yourself the trouble ; for I know every syllable of the matter before you begin.

Oliv. Indeed ! Then I'm undone.

Croak. Ay, miss, you wanted to steal a match, without letting me know it, did you ? But I'm not worth being consulted, I suppose, when there's to be a marriage in my own family. No, I am to have no hand in the disposal of my own children. No, I'm nobody. I'm to be a mere article of family lumber ; a piece of crack'd china to be stuck up in a corner.

Oliv. Dear Sir, nothing but the dread of your authority could induce us to conceal it from you.

Croak. No, no, my consequence is no more ; I'm as little minded as a dead Russian in winter, just stuck up with a pipe in his mouth till there comes a thaw—It goes to my heart to vex her.   [*Aside.*

Oliv. I was prepar'd, Sir, for your anger, and despair'd of pardon, even while I presum'd to ask it. But your severity shall never abate my affection, as my punishment is but justice.

Croak. And yet you should not despair neither, Livy. We ought to hope all for the best.

Oliv. And do you permit me to hope, Sir ? Can I ever expect to be forgiven ? But hope has too long deceived me.

Croak. Why then, child, it shan't deceive you now, for I forgive you this very moment, I forgive you all ! and now you are indeed my daughter.

Oliv. O transport ! this kindness overpowers me.

Croak. I was always against severity to our children. We have been young and giddy ourselves, and we can't expect boys and girls to be old before their time.

Oliv. What generosity ! but can you forget the many falsehoods, the dissimulation——

Croak. You did indeed dissemble, you urchin you ; but where 's the girl that won't dissemble for an husband ? My wife and I had never been married, if we had not dissembled a little beforehand.

Oliv. It shall be my future care never to put such generosity to a second trial. And as for the partner of my offence and folly, from his native honour, and the just sense he has of his duty, I can answer for him that——

Enter Leontine.

Leont. Permit him thus to answer for himself (*Kneeling*). Thus, Sir, let me speak my gratitude for this unmerited forgiveness. Yes, Sir, this even exceeds all your former tenderness. I now can boast the most indulgent of fathers. The life he gave, compared to this, was but a trifling blessing.

Croak. And, good Sir, who sent for you, with that fine tragedy face, and flourishing manner ? I don't know what we have to do with your gratitude upon this occasion.

Leont. How, Sir ! Is it possible to be silent, when so much obliged ! Would you refuse me the pleasure of being grateful ! of adding my thanks to my Olivia's ! of sharing in the transports that you have thus occasioned ?

Croak. Lord, Sir, we can be happy enough, without your coming in to make up the party. I don't know what 's the matter with the boy all this day; he has got into such a rhodomontade manner all this morning !

Leont. But, Sir, I that have so large a part in the benefit, is it not my duty to show my joy ? is the being admitted to your favour so slight an obligation ? is the happiness of marrying my Olivia so small a blessing ?

Croak. Marrying Olivia! marrying Olivia; marrying his own sister! Sure, the boy is out of his senses. His own sister !

Leont. My sister !

Oliv. Sister ! How have I been mistaken !   [*Aside.*

Leont. Some curs'd mistake in all this I find.   [*Aside.*

Croak. What does the booby mean ? or has he any meaning ? Eh, what do you mean, you blockhead you ?

Leont. Mean, Sir—why, Sir—only when my sister is to be married, that I have the pleasure of marrying her, Sir, that is, of giving her away, Sir—I have made a point of it.

Croak. O, is that all. Give her away. You have made a point of it. Then you had as good make a point of first giving away yourself, as I'm going to prepare the writings between you and Miss Richland this very minute. What a fuss is here about nothing! Why, what's the matter now ? I thought I had made you at least as happy as you could wish.

Oliv. O ! yes, Sir, very happy.

Croak. Do you foresee any thing, child ? You look as if you did. I think if any thing was to be foreseen, I have as sharp a look out as another : and yet I foresee nothing.
                                                                      [*Exit.*

Leontine, Olivia.

Oliv. What can it mean ?

Leont. He knows something, and yet for my life I can't tell what.

Oliv. It can't be the connexion between us, I'm pretty certain.

Leont. Whatever it be, my dearest, I'm resolved to put it out of fortune's power to repeat our mortification.

I'll haste and prepare for our journey to Scotland this very evening. My friend Honeywood has promised me his advice and assistance. I'll go to him and repose our distresses on his friendly bosom : and I know so much of his honest heart, that if he can't relieve our uneasinesses, he will at least share them.   [*Exeunt.*

ACT III

SCENE, YOUNG HONEYWOOD'S HOUSE.

Bailiff, Honeywood, Follower.

Bailiff. Lookey, Sir, I have arrested as good men as you in my time : no disparagement of you neither. Men that would go forty guineas on a game of cribbage. I challenge the town to show a man in more genteeler practice than myself.

Honeyw. Without all question, Mr. ——. I forget your name, Sir ?

Bail. How can you forget what you never knew ; he ! he ! he !

Honeyw. May I beg leave to ask your name ?

Bail. Yes, you may.

Honeyw. Then, pray, Sir, what is your name ?

Bail. That I didn't promise to tell you. He ! he ! he ! A joke breaks no bones, as we say among us that practise the law.

Honeyw. You may have reason for keeping it a secret, perhaps ?

Bail. The law does nothing without reason. I'm ashamed to tell my name to no man, Sir. If you can shew cause, as why, upon a special capus, that I should prove my name—But, come, Timothy Twitch is my name.

And, now you know my name, what have you to say to
that ?

Honeyw. Nothing in the world, good Mr. Twitch, but
that I have a favour to ask, that's all.

Bail. Ay, favours are more easily asked than granted,
as we say among us that practise the law. I have taken
an oath against granting favours. Would you have me
perjure myself ?

Honeyw. But my request will come recommended in
so strong a manner, as, I believe, you'll have no scruple
(*pulling out his purse*). The thing is only this : I believe
I shall be able to discharge this trifle in two or three days
at farthest ; but as I would not have the affair known for
the world, I have thoughts of keeping you, and your
good friend here, about me till the debt is discharged ;
for which I shall be properly grateful.

Bail. Oh ! that's another maxum, and altogether
within my oath. For certain, if an honest man is to get
any thing by a thing, there's no reason why all things
should not be done in civility.

Honeyw. Doubtless, all trades must live, Mr. Twitch ;
and yours is a necessary one.   (*Gives him money.*)

Bail. Oh ! your honour ; I hope your honour takes
nothing amiss as I does, as I does nothing but my duty
in so doing. I'm sure no man can say I ever give a
gentleman, that was a gentleman, ill usage. If I saw
that a gentleman was a gentleman, I have taken money
not to see him for ten weeks together.

Honeyw. Tenderness is a virtue, Mr. Twitch.

Bail. Ay, Sir, it's a perfect treasure. I love to see a
gentleman with a tender heart. I don't know, but I
think I have a tender heart myself. If all that I have
lost by my heart was put together, it would make a—but
no matter for that.

Honeyw. Don't account it lost, Mr. Twitch. The

ingratitude of the world can never deprive us of the conscious happiness of having acted with humanity ourselves.

Bail. Humanity, Sir, is a jewel. It's better than gold. I love humanity. People may say, that we in our way, have no humanity ; but I'll shew you my humanity this moment. There's my follower here, little Flanigan, with a wife and four children, a guinea or two would be more to him, than twice as much to another. Now, as I can't shew him any humanity myself, I must beg leave you'll do it for me.

Honeyw. I assure you, Mr. Twitch, yours is a most powerful recommendation. (*Giving money to the follower.*)

Bail. Sir, you're a gentleman. I see you know what to do with your money. But, to business : we are to be with you here as your friends, I suppose. But set in case company comes.—Little Flanigan here, to be sure has a good face ; a very good face ; but then, he is a little seedy, as we say among us that practise the law. Not well in clothes. Smoke the pocket-holes.

Honeyw. Well, that shall be remedied without delay.

Enter Servant.

Serv. Sir, Miss Richland is below.

Honeyw. How unlucky ! Detain her a moment. We must improve, my good friend, little Mr. Flanigan's appearance first. Here, let Mr. Flanigan have a suit of my clothes—quick—the brown and silver—Do you hear ?

Serv. That your honour gave away to the begging gentleman that makes verses, because it was as good as new.

Honeyw. The white and gold, then.

Serv. That, your honour, I made bold to sell, because it was good for nothing.

Honeyw. Well, the first that comes to hand then. The

blue and gold.   I believe Mr. Flanigan will look best in blue.   [*Exit Flanigan.*

Bail. Rabbet me, but little Flanigan will look well in any thing.   Ah, if your honour knew that bit of flesh as well as I do, you'd be perfectly in love with him.   There's not a prettier scout in the four counties after a shy-cock than he :   scents like a hound ;   sticks like a weazle. He was master of the ceremonies to the black Queen of Morocco, when I took him to follow me. (*Re-enter Flanigan.*)   Heh, ecod, I think he looks so well, that I don't care if I have a suit from the same place for myself.

Honeyw. Well, well, I hear the lady coming.   Dear Mr. Twitch, I beg you'll give your friend directions not to speak.   As for yourself, I know you will say nothing without being directed.

Bail. Never you fear me ;   I'll show the lady that I have something to say for myself as well as another. One man has one way of talking, and another man has another, that's all the difference between them.

Enter Miss Richland and her Maid.

Miss Rich. You'll be surpris'd, Sir, with this visit. But you know I'm yet to thank you for chusing my little library.

Honeyw. Thanks, madam, are unnecessary ;   as it was I that was obliged by your commands.   Chairs here. Two of my very good friends, Mr. Twitch and Mr. Flanigan.   Pray, gentlemen, sit without ceremony.

Miss Rich. Who can these odd-looking men be !   I fear it is as I was informed.   It must be so.   (*Aside.*)

Bail. (*after a pause.*) Pretty weather, very pretty weather for the time of the year, madam.

Fol. Very good circuit weather in the country.

Honeyw. You officers are generally favourites among the ladies.   My friends, madam, have been upon very disagreeable duty, I assure you. The fair should, in some measure, recompence the toils of the brave !

Miss Rich. Our officers do indeed deserve every favour. The gentlemen are in the marine service, I presume, Sir ?

Honeyw. Why, madam, they do—occasionally serve in the Fleet, madam. A dangerous service !

Miss Rich. I'm told so. And I own, it has often surprised me, that, while we have had so many instances of bravery there, we have had so few of wit at home to praise it.

Honeyw. I grant, madam, that our poets have not written as our soldiers have fought ; but they have done all they could, and Hawke or Amherst could do no more.

Miss Rich. I'm quite displeased when I see a fine subject spoiled by a dull writer.

Honeyw. We should not be so severe against dull writers, madam. It is ten to one, but the dullest writer exceeds the most rigid French critic who presumes to despise him.

Fol. Damn the French, the parle vous, and all that belongs to them.

Miss Rich. Sir !

Honeyw. Ha, ha, ha ! honest Mr. Flanigan. A true English officer, madam ; he 's not contented with beating the French, but he will scold them too.

Miss Rich. Yet, Mr. Honeywood, this does not convince me but that severity in criticism is necessary. It was our first adopting the severity of French taste, that has brought them in turn to taste us.

Bail. Taste us ! By the Lord, madam, they devour us. Give monseers but a taste, and I'll be damn'd but they come in for a bellyful.

Miss Rich. Very extraordinary this !

Fol. But very true. What makes the bread rising ? the parle vous that devour us. What makes the mutton fivepence a pound ? the parle vous that eat it up. What makes the beer threepence-halfpenny a pot ?——

Honeyw. Ah ! the vulgar rogues ; all will be out. (*Aside.*) Right, gentlemen, very right, upon my word, and quite to the purpose. They draw a parallel, madam, between the mental taste and that of our senses. We are injured as much by the French severity in the one, as by French rapacity in the other. That 's their meaning.

Miss Rich. Though I don't see the force of the parallel, yet I'll own, that we should sometimes pardon books, as we do our friends, that have now and then agreeable absurdities to recommend them.

Bail. That 's all my eye. The King only can pardon, as the law says : for, set in case——

Honeyw. I'm quite of your opinion, Sir. I see the whole drift of your argument. Yes, certainly, our presuming to pardon any work, is arrogating a power that belongs to another. If all have power to condemn, what writer can be free ?

Bail. By his habus corpus. His habus corpus can set him free at any time : for, set in case——

Honeyw. I'm oblig'd to you, Sir, for the hint. If, madam, as my friend observes, our laws are so careful of a gentleman's person, sure we ought to be equally careful of his dearer part, his fame.

Fol. Ay, but if so be a man 's nabb'd, you know——

Honeyw. Mr. Flanigan, if you spoke for ever, you could not improve the last observation. For my own part, I think it conclusive.

Bail. As for the matter of that, mayhap—

Honeyw. Nay, Sir, give me leave in this instance to be positive. For where is the necessity of censuring works without genius, which must shortly sink of themselves ? what is it, but aiming our unnecessary blow against a victim already under the hands of justice ?

Bail. Justice ! O, by the elevens, if you talk about justice, I think I am at home there : for, in a course of law—

Honeyw. My dear Mr. Twitch, I discern what you'd be at perfectly ; and I believe the lady must be sensible of the art with which it is introduced. I suppose you perceive the meaning, madam, of his course of law.

Miss Rich. I protest, Sir, I do not. I perceive only that you answer one gentleman before he has finished, and the other before he has well begun.

Bail. Madam, you are a gentlewoman, and I will make the matter out. This here question is about severity and justice, and pardon, and the like of they. Now to explain the thing—.

Honeyw. O ! curse your explanations.   [*Aside.*

Enter Servant.

Serv. Mr. Leontine, Sir, below, desires to speak with you upon earnest business.

Honeyw. That's lucky. (*Aside.*) Dear madam, you'll excuse me and my good friends here, for a few minutes. There are books, madam, to amuse you. Come, gentlemen, you know I make no ceremony with such friends. After you, Sir. Excuse me. Well, if I must. But I know your natural politeness.

Bail. Before and behind, you know.

Fol. Ay, ay, before and behind, before and behind.
            [*Exeunt Honeywood, Bailiff, and Follower.*

Miss Rich. What can all this mean, Garnet ?

Garn. Mean, madam ! why, what should it mean, but what Mr. Lofty sent you here to see ! These people he calls officers are officers sure enough : sheriff's officers ; bailiffs, madam.

Miss Rich. Ay, it is certainly so. Well, though his

perplexities are far from giving me pleasure, yet I own there's something very ridiculous in them, and a just punishment for his dissimulation.

Garn. And so they are. But I wonder, madam, that the lawyer you just employed to pay his debts, and set him free, has not done it by this time. He ought at least to have been here before now. But lawyers are always more ready to get a man into troubles than out of them.

Enter Sir William.

Sir Will. For Miss Richland to undertake setting him free, I own, was quite unexpected. It has totally un-hinged my schemes to reclaim him. Yet it gives me pleasure to find, that among a number of worthless friend-ships, he has made one acquisition of real value; for there must be some softer passion on her side that prompts this generosity. Ha! here before me : I'll endeavour to sound her affections. Madam, as I am the person that have had some demands upon the gentleman of this house, I hope you'll excuse me, if before I enlarged him, I wanted to see yourself.

Miss Rich. The precaution was very unnecessary, Sir. I suppose your wants were only such as my agent had power to satisfy.

Sir Will. Partly, madam. But I was also willing you should be fully apprized of the character of the gentle-man you intended to serve.

Miss Rich. It must come, Sir, with a very ill grace from you. To censure it, after what you have done, would look like malice ; and to speak favourably of a character you have oppressed, would be impeaching your own. And sure, his tenderness, his humanity, his universal friendship may atone for many faults.

Sir Will. That friendship, madam, which is exerted

in too wide a sphere, becomes totally useless. Our bounty, like a drop of water, disappears when diffused too widely. They, who pretend most to this universal benevolence, are either deceivers, or dupes. Men who desire to cover their private ill-nature, by a pretended regard for all ; or men who, reasoning themselves into false feelings, are more earnest in pursuit of splendid, than of useful virtues.

Miss Rich. I am surprised, Sir, to hear one, who has probably been a gainer by the folly of others, so severe in his censure of it.

Sir Will. Whatever I may have gained by folly, madam, you see I am willing to prevent your losing by it.

Miss Rich. Your cares for me, Sir, are unnecessary. I always suspect those services which are denied where they are wanted, and offered, perhaps, in hopes of a refusal. No, Sir, my directions have been given, and I insist upon their being complied with.

Sir Will. Thou amiable woman ! I can no longer contain the expressions of my gratitude : my pleasure. You see before you one, who has been equally careful of his interest ; one, who has for some time been a concealed spectator of his follies, and only punished, in hopes to reclaim them—his uncle !

Miss Rich. Sir William Honeywood ! You amaze me. How shall I conceal my confusion ? I fear, Sir, you'll think I have been too forward in my services. I confess I—

Sir Will. Don't make any apologies, madam. I only find myself unable to repay the obligation. And yet, I have been trying my interest of late to serve you. Having learnt, madam, that you had some demands upon Government, I have, though unasked, been your solicitor there.

Miss Rich. Sir, I'm infinitely obliged to your intentions.

But my guardian has employed another gentleman, who assures him of success.

Sir Will. Who, the important little man that visits here ? Trust me, madam, he 's quite contemptible among men in power, and utterly unable to serve you. Mr. Lofty's promises are much better known to people of fashion, than his person, I assure you.

Miss Rich. How have we been deceived ! As sure as can be, here he comes.

Sir Will. Does he ! Remember I'm to continue un-known. My return to England has not as yet been made public. With what impudence he enters !

Enter Lofty.

Lofty. Let the chariot—let my chariot drive off ; I'll visit to his Grace's in a chair. Miss Richland here before me ! Punctual, as usual, to the calls of humanity. I'm very sorry, madam, things of this kind should happen, especially to a man I have shewn every where, and carried amongst us as a particular acquaintance.

Miss Rich. I find, Sir, you have the art of making the misfortunes of others your own.

Lofty. My dear madam, what can a private man like me do ? One man can't do every thing ; and then, I do so much in this way every day : let me see ; something considerable might be done for him by subscription ; it could not fail if I carried the list. I'll undertake to set down a brace of dukes, two dozen lords, and half the lower house, at my own peril.

Sir Will. And, after all, it 's more than probable, Sir, he might reject the offer of such powerful patronage.

Lofty. Then, madam, what can we do ? You know I never make promises. In truth, I once or twice tried to do something with him in the way of business ; but, as I often told his uncle, Sir William Honeywood, the man was utterly impracticable.

Sir Will. His uncle ! then that gentleman, I suppose, is a particular friend of yours.

Lofty. Meaning me, Sir ?—Yes, madam, as I often said, my dear Sir William, you are sensible I would do any thing, as far as my poor interest goes, to serve your family : but what can be done ? there's no procuring first-rate places for ninth-rate abilities.

Miss Rich. I have heard of Sir William Honeywood ; he's abroad in employment : he confided in your judgment, I suppose.

Lofty. Why, yes, madam, I believe Sir William had some reason to confide in my judgment ; one little reason, perhaps.

Miss Rich. Pray, Sir, what was it ?

Lofty. Why, madam—but let it go no farther—it was I procured him his place.

Sir Will. Did you, Sir ?

Lofty. Either you or I, Sir.

Miss Rich. This, Mr. Lofty, was very kind indeed.

Lofty. I did love him, to be sure ; he had some amusing qualities ; no man was fitter to be a toast-master to a club, or had a better head.

Miss Rich. A better head ?

Lofty. Ay, at a bottle. To be sure he was as dull as a choice spirit : but hang it, he was grateful, very grateful ; and gratitude hides a multitude of faults.

Sir Will. He might have reason, perhaps. His place is pretty considerable, I'm told.

Lofty. A trifle, a mere trifle among us men of business. The truth is, he wanted dignity to fill up a greater.

Sir Will. Dignity of person, do you mean, Sir ? I'm told he's much about my size and figure, Sir.

Lofty. Ay, tall enough for a marching regiment ; but

then he wanted a something—a consequence of form—
a kind of a—I believe the lady perceives my meaning.

Miss Rich. O, perfectly ; you courtiers can do any
thing, I see.

Lofty. My dear madam, all this is but a mere exchange ;
we do greater things for one another every day.   Why,
as thus, now : let me suppose you the first Lord of the
Treasury ; you have an employment in you that I want ;
I have a place in me that you want ; do me here, do you
there : interest of both sides, few words, flat, done and
done, and it's over.

Sir Will. A thought strikes me. (*Aside.*) Now you
mention Sir William Honeywood, madam ; and as he
seems, Sir, an acquaintance of yours ; you'll be glad to
hear he's arriv'd from Italy; I had it from a friend who
knows him as well as he does me, and you may depend
on my information.

Lofty. The devil he is ! If I had known that, we should
not have been quite so well acquainted.   [*Aside.*

Sir Will. He is certainly return'd ; and, as this gentleman is a friend of yours, he can be of signal service to
us, by introducing me to him ; there are some papers
relative to your affairs, that require despatch and his
inspection.

Miss Rich. This gentleman, Mr. Lofty, is a person
employed in my affairs : I know you'll serve us.

Lofty. My dear madam, I live but to serve you.   Sir
William shall even wait upon him, if you think proper to
command it.

Sir Will. That would be quite unnecessary.

Lofty. Well, we must introduce you then.   Call upon
me—let me see—ay, in two days.

Sir Will. Now, or the opportunity will be lost for
ever.

Lofty. Well, if it must be now, now let it be.   But

damn it, that's unfortunate; my Lord Grig's cursed
Pensacola business comes on this very hour, and I'm
engaged to attend—another time—

Sir Will. A short letter to Sir William will do.

Lofty. You shall have it; yet, in my opinion, a letter
is a very bad way of going to work; face to face, that's
my way.

Sir Will. The letter, Sir, will do quite as well.

Lofty. Zounds! Sir, do you pretend to direct me?
direct me in the business of office? Do you know me,
Sir? who am I?

Miss Rich. Dear Mr. Lofty, this request is not so much
his as mine; if my commands—but you despise my power.

Lofty. Delicate creature! your commands could even
controul a debate at midnight: to a power so constitu-
tional, I am all obedience and tranquillity. He shall have
a letter; where is my secretary! Dubardieu! And yet,
I protest I don't like this way of doing business. I think
if I spoke first to Sir William—But you will have it so.

[*Exit with Miss Richland.*

Sir Will. (*alone.*) Ha, ha, ha! This too is one of my
nephew's hopeful associates. O vanity, thou constant
deceiver, how do all thy efforts to exalt, serve but to sink
us! Thy false colourings, like those employed to heighten
beauty, only seem to mend that bloom which they contribute to destroy. I'm not displeased at this interview:
exposing this fellow's impudence to the contempt it
deserves, may be of use to my design; at least, if he
can reflect, it will be of use to himself.

Enter Jarvis.

Sir Will. How now, Jarvis, where's your master, my
nephew?

Jarv. At his wit's ends, I believe: he's scarce gotten
out of one scrape, but he's running his head into another.

Sir Will. How so ?

Jarv. The house has but just been cleared of the bailiffs, and now he's again engaging tooth and nail in assisting old Croaker's son to patch up a clandestine match with the young lady that passes in the house for his sister.

Sir Will. Ever busy to serve others !

Jarv. Aye, any body but himself. The young couple, it seems, are just setting out for Scotland ; and he supplies them with money for the journey.

Sir Will. Money ! how is he able to supply others, who has scarce any for himself ?

Jarv. Why, there it is : he has no money, that's true ; but then, as he never said no to any request in his life, he has given them a bill, drawn by a friend of his upon a merchant in the City, which I am to get changed ; for you must know that I am to go with them to Scotland myself.

Sir Will. How !

Jarv. It seems the young gentleman is obliged to take a different road from his mistress, as he is to call upon an uncle of his that lives out of the way, in order to prepare a place for their reception, when they return ; so they have borrowed me from my master, as the properest person to attend the young lady down.

Sir Will. To the land of matrimony ! A pleasant journey, Jarvis.

Jarv. Ay, but I'm only to have all the fatigues on't.

Sir Will. Well, it may be shorter, and less fatiguing, than you imagine. I know but too much of the young lady's family and connexions, whom I have seen abroad. I have also discovered that Miss Richland is not indifferent to my thoughtless nephew ; and will endeavour, though I fear, in vain, to establish that connexion. But, come, the letter I wait for must be almost finished ; I'll let you farther into my intentions, in the next room.

[*Exeunt.*

ACT IV

SCENE, CROAKER'S HOUSE.

Lofty. Well, sure the devil's in me of late, for running my head into such defiles, as nothing but a genius like my own could draw me from. I was formerly contented to husband out my places and pensions with some degree of frugality ; but, curse it, of late I have given away the whole Court Register in less time than they could print the title page : yet, hang it, why scruple a lie or two to come at a fine girl, when I every day tell a thousand for nothing ? Ha! Honeywood here before me. Could Miss Richland have set him at liberty ?

Enter Honeywood.

Mr. Honeywood, I'm glad to see you abroad again. I find my concurrence was not necessary in your unfortunate affairs. I had put things in a train to do your business ; but it is not for me to say what I intended doing.

Honeyw. It was unfortunate indeed, Sir. But what adds to my uneasiness is, that while you seem to be acquainted with my misfortune, I myself continue still a stranger to my benefactor.

Lofty. How ! not know the friend that served you ?

Honeyw. Can't guess at the person.

Lofty. Inquire.

Honeyw. I have ; but all I can learn is, that he chuses to remain concealed, and that all inquiry must be fruitless.

Lofty. Must be fruitless !

Honeyw. Absolutely fruitless.

Lofty. Sure of that ?

Honeyw. Very sure.

Lofty. Then I'll be damn'd if you shall ever know it from me.

Honeyw. How, Sir !

Lofty. I suppose now, Mr. Honeywood, you think my rent-roll very considerable, and that I have vast sums of money to throw away ; I know you do. The world, to be sure, says such things of me.

Honeyw. The world, by what I learn, is no stranger to your generosity. But where does this tend ?

Lofty. To nothing ; nothing in the world. The town, to be sure, when it makes such a thing as me the subject of conversation, has asserted, that I never yet patronised a man of merit.

Honeyw. I have heard instances to the contrary, even from yourself.

Lofty. Yes, Honeywood, and there are instances to the contrary, that you shall never hear from myself.

Honeyw. Ha ! dear Sir, permit me to ask you but one question.

Lofty. Sir, ask me no questions : I say, Sir, ask me no questions ; I'll be damned if I answer them.

Honeyw. I will ask no farther. My friend ! my benefactor, it is, it must be here, that I am indebted for freedom, for honour. Yes, thou worthiest of men, from the beginning I suspected it, but was afraid to return thanks ; which, if undeserved, might seem reproaches.

Lofty. I protest I do not understand all this, Mr. Honey-wood. You treat me very cavalierly. I do assure you, Sir—Blood, Sir, can't a man be permitted to enjoy the luxury of his own feelings, without all this parade !

Honeyw. Nay, do not attempt to conceal an action that adds to your honour. Your looks, your air, your manner, all confess it.

Lofty. Confess it, Sir ! Torture itself, Sir, shall never bring me to confess it. Mr. Honeywood, I have admitted

you upon terms of friendship. Don't let us fall out ;
make me happy, and let this be buried in oblivion. You
know I hate ostentation ; you know I do. Come, come,
Honeywood, you know I always loved to be a friend,
and not a patron. I beg this may make no kind of distance between us. Come, come, you and I must be
more familiar—Indeed we must.

Honeyw. Heavens ! Can I ever repay such friendship ?
Is there any way ! Thou best of men, can I ever return
the obligation ?

Lofty. A bagatelle, a mere bagatelle ! But I see your
heart is labouring to be grateful. You shall be grateful.
It would be cruel to disappoint you.

Honeyw. How! teach me the manner. Is there any
way ?

Lofty. From this moment you're mine. Yes, my
friend, you shall know it—I'm in love.

Honeyw. And can I assist you ?

Lofty. Nobody so well.

Honeyw. In what manner. I'm all impatience.

Lofty. You shall make love for me.

Honeyw. And to whom shall I speak in your favour ?

Lofty. To a lady with whom you have great interest,
I assure you : Miss Richland.

Honeyw. Miss Richland !

Lofty. Yes, Miss Richland. She has struck the blow
up to the hilt in my bosom, by Jupiter.

Honeyw. Heavens ! was ever any thing more unfortunate ! It is too much to be endured.

Lofty. Unfortunate indeed ! And yet I can endure it,
till you have opened the affair to her for me. Between
ourselves, I think she likes me. I'm not apt to boast,
but I think she does.

Honeyw. Indeed ! But, do you know the person you
apply to ?

Lofty. Yes, I know you are her friend and mine; that's enough. To you, therefore, I commit the success of my passion. I'll say no more, let friendship do the rest. I have only to add, that if at any time my little interest can be of service—but, hang it, I'll make no promises—you know my interest is yours at any time. No apologies, my friend, I'll not be answered, it shall be so.   [*Exit.*

Honeyw. Open, generous, unsuspecting man! He little thinks that I love her too; and with such an ardent passion!—But then it was ever but a vain and hopeless one; my torment, my persecution! What shall I do! Love, friendship, a hopeless passion, a deserving friend! Love, that has been my tormentor; a friend, that has, perhaps, distressed himself, to serve me. It shall be so. Yes, I will discard the fondling hope from my bosom, and exert all my influence in his favour. And yet to see her in the possession of another!—Insupportable! But then to betray a generous, trusting friend!—Worse, worse! Yes, I'm resolv'd. Let me but be the instrument of their happiness, and then quit a country, where I must for ever despair of finding my own.   [*Exit.*

Enter Olivia and Garnet, who carries a milliner's box.

Oliv. Dear me, I wish this journey were over. No news of Jarvis yet? I believe the old peevish creature delays purely to vex me.

Garn. Why, to be sure, madam, I did hear him say a little snubbing, before marriage, would teach you to bear it the better afterwards.

Oliv. To be gone a full hour, though he had only to get a bill changed in the City! How provoking!

Garn. I'll lay my life, Mr. Leontine, that had twice as much to do, is setting off by this time from his inn; and here you are left behind.

Oliv. Well, let us be prepared for his coming, however. Are you sure you have omitted nothing, Garnet ?

Garn. Not a stick, madam—all's here. Yet I wish you could take the white and silver to be married in. It's the worst luck in the world, in any thing but white. I knew one Bett Stubbs, of our town, that was married in red ; and, as sure as eggs is eggs, the bridegroom and she had a miff before morning.

Oliv. No matter. I'm all impatience till we are out of the house.

Garn. Bless me, madam, I had almost forgot the wedding ring !—The sweet little thing—I don't think it would go on my little finger. And what if I put in a gentleman's night-cap, in case of necessity, madam ? But here's Jarvis.

Enter Jarvis.

Oliv. O Jarvis, are you come at last ? We have been ready this half-hour. Now let's be going. Let us fly !

Jarv. Aye, to Jericho ; for we shall have no going to Scotland this bout, I fancy.

Oliv. How ! what's the matter ?

Jarv. Money, money, is the matter, madam. We have got no money. What the plague do you send me of your fool's errand for ? My master's bill upon the City is not worth a rush. Here it is ; Mrs. Garnet may pin up her hair with it.

Oliv. Undone ! How could Honeywood serve us so ! What shall we do ? Can't we go without it ?

Jarv. Go to Scotland without money ! To Scotland without money ! Lord how some people understand geography ! We might as well set sail for Patagonia upon a cork-jacket.

Oliv. Such a disappointment ! What a base insincere

man was your master, to serve us in this manner ? Is this his good nature ?

Jarv. Nay, don't talk ill of my master, madam. I won't bear to hear any body talk ill of him but myself.

Garn. Bless us ! now I think on't madam, you need not be under any uneasiness : I saw Mr. Leontine receive forty guineas from his father just before he set out, and he can't yet have left the inn. A short letter will reach him there.

Oliv. Well remember'd, Garnet; I'll write immediately. How's this! Bless me, my hand trembles so, I can't write a word. Do you write, Garnet; and, upon second thought, it will be better from you.

Garn. Truly, madam, I write and indite but poorly. I never was kute at my larning. But I'll do what I can to please you. Let me see. All out of my own head, I suppose !

Oliv. Whatever you please.

Garn. (*Writing.*) 'Muster Croaker'—Twenty guineas, madam ?

Oliv. Aye, twenty will do.

Garn. ' At the bar of the Talbot till call'd for. Expedition—Will be blown up—All of a flame—Quick despatch —Cupid, the little god of love '—I conclude it, madam, with Cupid : I love to see a love-letter end like poetry.

Oliv. Well, well, what you please, any thing. But how shall we send it ? I can trust none of the servants of this family.

Garn. Odso, madam, Mr. Honeywood's butler is in the next room : he's a dear, sweet man ; he'll do any thing for me.

Jarv. He ! the dog, he'll certainly commit some blunder. He's drunk and sober ten times a day.

Oliv. No matter. Fly, Garnet ; any body we can trust will do. [*Exit Garnet.*] Well, Jarvis, now we can have nothing more to interrupt us. You may take up the things, and carry them on to the inn. Have you no hands, Jarvis ?

Jarv. Soft and fair, young lady. You, that are going to be married, think things can never be done too fast : but we, that are old, and know what we are about, must elope methodically, madam.

Oliv. Well sure, if my indiscretions were to be done over again——

Jarv. My life for it, you would do them ten times over.

Oliv. Why will you talk so ? If you knew how unhappy they make me——

Jarv. Very unhappy, no doubt : I was once just as unhappy when I was going to be married myself. I'll tell you a story about that——

Oliv. A story ! when I'm all impatience to be away. Was there ever such a dilatory creature !——

Jarv. Well, madam, if we must march, why we will march, that's all. Though, odds-bobs, we have still forgot one thing ; we should never travel without—a case of good razors, and a box of shaving powder. But no matter, I believe we shall be pretty well shaved by the way.   [*Going.*

Enter Garnet.

Garn. Undone, undone, madam. Ah, Mr. Jarvis, you said right enough. As sure as death, Mr. Honeywood's rogue of a drunken butler dropp'd the letter before he went ten yards from the door. There's old Croaker has just pick'd it up, and is this moment reading it to himself in the hall.

Oliv. Unfortunate ! we shall be discovered.

Garn. No, madam : don't be uneasy, he can make neither head nor tail of it. To be sure he looks as if he was broke loose from Bedlam about it, but he can't find

what it means for all that.   O lud, he is coming this way
all in the horrors !

Oliv. Then let us leave the house this instant, for fear
he should ask farther questions.   In the mean time,
Garnet, do you write and send off just such another.

[*Exeunt.*

Enter Croaker.

Croak. Death and destruction ! Are all the horrors of
air, fire and water to be levelled only at me ! Am I only to
be singled out for gunpowder-plots, combustibles and conflagration ! Here it is—An incendiary letter dropped at
my door.   ' To muster Croaker, these with speed.'   Aye,
aye, plain enough the direction : all in the genuine incendiary spelling, and as cramp as the devil.   ' With
speed.'   O, confound your speed.   But let me read it
once more. (*Reads.*) ' Mustar Croaker as sone as yowe see
this leve twenty gunnes at the bar of the Talbot tell
called for, or yowe and yower experetion will be all blown
up.'   Ah, but too plain.   Blood and gunpowder in every
line of it.   Blown up ! murderous dog ! All blown up !
Heavens ! what have I and my poor family done, to be all
blown up ! (*Reads.*) ' Our pockets are low, and money we
must have.'   Aye, there's the reason; they'll blow us
up, because they have got low pockets. (*Reads.*) ' It is
but a short time you have to consider ; for if this takes
wind, the house will quickly be all of a flame.'   Inhuman
monsters ! blow us up, and then burn us.   The earthquake at Lisbon was but a bonfire to it. (*Reads.*) ' Make
quick despatch, and so no more at present.   But may
Cupid, the little god of love, go with you wherever you
go.'   The little god of love ! Cupid, the little god of love
go with me ! Go you to the devil, you and your little
Cupid together ; I'm so frightened, I scarce know whether
I sit, stand, or go.   Perhaps this moment I'm treading on

lighted matches, blazing brimstone, and barrels of gun-powder. They are preparing to blow me up into the clouds. Murder ! We shall be all burnt in our beds ; we shall be all burnt in our beds.

Enter Miss Richland.

Miss Rich. Lord, Sir, what's the matter ?

Croak. Murder's the matter. We shall be all blown up in our beds before morning.

Miss Rich. I hope not, Sir.

Croak. What signifies what you hope, madam, when I have a certificate of it here in my hand ? Will nothing alarm my family ? Sleeping and eating, sleeping and eating is the only work from morning till night in my house. My insensible crew could sleep though rock'd by an earthquake ; and fry beef steaks at a volcano.

Miss Rich. But, Sir, you have alarmed them so often already ; we have nothing but earthquakes, famines, plagues, and mad dogs from year's end to year's end. You remember, Sir, it is not above a month ago, you assured us of a conspiracy among the bakers, to poison us in our bread ; and so kept the whole family a week upon potatoes.

Croak. And potatoes were too good for them. But why do I stand talking here with a girl, when I should be facing the enemy without ? Here, John, Nicodemus, search the house. Look into the cellars, to see if there be any combustibles below ; and above, in the apart-ments, that no matches be thrown in at the windows. Let all the fires be put out, and let the engine be drawn out in the yard, to play upon the house in case of necessity.

[*Exit.*

Miss Rich. (*Alone.*) What can he mean by all this ? Yet, why should I enquire, when he alarms us in this manner almost every day ! But Honeywood has desired an interview with me in private. What can he mean ? or, rather, what means this palpitation at his approach ? It is the first time he ever shewed any thing in his conduct that seemed particular. Sure he cannot mean to ——but he's here.

Enter Honeywood.

Honeyw. I presumed to solicit this interview, madam, before I left town, to be permitted——

Miss Rich. Indeed ! Leaving town, Sir ?—

Honeyw. Yes, madam ; perhaps the kingdom. I have presumed, I say, to desire the favour of this interview,—in order to disclose something which our long friendship prompts. And yet my fears—

Miss Rich. His fears ! What are his fears to mine ! (*Aside.*) We have indeed been long acquainted, Sir ; very long. If I remember our first meeting was at the French ambassador's.—Do you recollect how you were pleased to rally me upon my complexion there ?

Honeyw. Perfectly, madam : I presumed to reprove you for painting : but your warmer blushes soon convinced the company, that the colouring was all from nature.

Miss Rich. And yet you only meant it in your goodnatur'd way, to make me pay a compliment to myself. In the same manner you danced that night with the most aukward woman in company, because you saw nobody else would take her out.

Honeyw. Yes ; and was rewarded the next night, by dancing with the finest woman in company, whom every body wished to take out.

Miss Rich. Well, Sir, if you thought so then, I fear your judgment has since corrected the errors of a first impression. We generally show to most advantage at first. Our sex are like poor tradesmen, that put all their best goods to be seen at the windows.

Honeyw. The first impression, madam, did indeed deceive me. I expected to find a woman with all the faults of conscious flattered beauty. I expected to find her vain and insolent. But every day has since taught me that it is possible to possess sense without pride, and beauty without affectation.

Miss Rich. This, Sir, is a style very unusual with Mr. Honeywood ; and I should be glad to know why he thus attempts to increase that vanity, which his own lessons have taught me to despise.

Honeyw. I ask pardon, madam. Yet, from our long friendship, I presumed I might have some right to offer, without offence, what you may refuse without offending.

Miss Rich. Sir ! I beg you'd reflect ; though, I fear, I shall scarce have any power to refuse a request of yours ; yet you may be precipitate : consider, Sir.

Honeyw. I own my rashness ; but as I plead the cause of friendship, of one who loves—Don't be alarmed, madam—who loves you with the most ardent passion, whose whole happiness is placed in you——

Miss Rich. I fear, Sir, I shall never find whom you mean, by this description of him.

Honeyw. Ah, madam, it but too plainly points him out ; though he should be too humble himself to urge his pretensions, or you too modest to understand them.

Miss Rich. Well ; it would be affectation any longer to pretend ignorance ; and I will own, Sir, I have long been prejudiced in his favour. It was but natural to wish to make his heart mine, as he seemed himself ignorant of its value.

Honeyw. I see she always loved him. (*Aside.*) I find, madam, you're already sensible of his worth, his passion. How happy is my friend, to be the favourite of one with such sense to distinguish merit, and such beauty to reward it.

Miss Rich. Your friend, Sir ! What friend ?

Honeyw. My best friend—my friend, Mr. Lofty, madam.

Miss Rich. He, Sir !

Honeyw. Yes, he, madam. He is, indeed, what your warmest wishes might have formed him. And to his other qualities he adds that of the most passionate regard for you.

Miss Rich. Amazement!—No more of this, I beg you, Sir.

Honeyw. I see your confusion, madam, and know how to interpret it. And, since I so plainly read the language of your heart, shall I make my friend happy, by communicating your sentiments ?

Miss Rich. By no means.

Honeyw. Excuse me ; I must ; I know you desire it.

Miss Rich. Mr. Honeywood, let me tell you, that you wrong my sentiments and yourself. When I first applied to your friendship, I expected advice and assistance ; but now, Sir, I see that it is in vain to expect happiness from him, who has been so bad an economist of his own ; and that I must disclaim his friendship who ceases to be a friend to himself.   [*Exit.*

Honeyw. How is this ! she has confessed she loved him, and yet she seemed to part in displeasure. Can I have done any thing to reproach myself with ? No : I believe not : yet after all, these things should not be done by a third person : I should have spared her confusion. My friendship carried me a little too far.

Enter Croaker, with the letter in his hand, and Mrs. Croaker.

Mrs. Croak. Ha ! ha ! ha ! And so, my dear, it's your supreme wish that I should be quite wretched upon this occasion ? ha ! ha !

Croak. (*Mimicking.*) Ha ! ha ! ha ! And so, my dear, it's your supreme pleasure to give me no better consolation ?

Mrs. Croak. Positively, my dear ; what is this incendiary stuff and trumpery to me ? our house may travel through the air like the house of Loretto, for aught I care, if I am to be miserable in it.

Croak. Would to heaven it were converted into a house of correction for your benefit. Have we not every thing to alarm us ? Perhaps this very moment the tragedy is beginning.

Mrs. Croak. Then let us reserve our distress till the rising of the curtain, or give them the money they want, and have done with them.

Croak. Give them my money !—And pray, what right have they to my money ?

Mrs. Croak. And pray, what right then have you to my good humour ?

Croak. And so your good humour advises me to part with my money ? Why then, to tell your good humour a piece of my mind, I'd sooner part with my wife. Here's Mr. Honeywood, see what he'll say to it. My dear Honeywood, look at this incendiary letter dropped at my door. It will freeze you with terror ; and yet lovey here can read it—can read it, and laugh.

Mrs. Croak. Yes, and so will Mr. Honeywood.

Croak. If he does, I'll suffer to be hanged the next minute in the rogue's place, that's all.

Mrs. Croak. Speak, Mr. Honeywood ; is there any thing more foolish than my husband's fright upon this occasion ?

Honeyw. It would not become me to decide, madam ; but doubtless, the greatness of his terrors, now, will but invite them to renew their villany another time.

Mrs. Croak. I told you, he'd be of my opinion.

Croak. How, Sir ! do you maintain that I should lie down, under such an injury, and shew, neither by my tears nor complaints, that I have something of the spirit of a man in me ?

Honeyw. Pardon me, Sir. You ought to make the loudest complaints, if you desire redress. The surest way to have redress, is to be earnest in the pursuit of it.

Croak. Aye, whose opinion is he of now ?

Mrs. Croak. But don't you think that laughing-off our fears is the best way ?

Honeyw. What is the best, madam, few can say ; but I'll maintain it to be a very wise way.

Croak. But we're talking of the best. Surely the best way is to face the enemy in the field, and not wait till he plunders us in our very bed-chamber.

Honeyw. Why, Sir, as to the best, that—that's a very wise way too.

Mrs. Croak. But can any thing be more absurd, than to double our distresses by our apprehensions, and put it in the power of every low fellow, that can scrawl ten words of wretched spelling, to torment us ?

Honeyw. Without doubt, nothing more absurd.

Croak. How ! would it not be more absurd to despise the rattle till we are bit by the snake ?

Honeyw. Without doubt, perfectly absurd.

Croak. Then you are of my opinion ?

Honeyw. Entirely.

Mrs. Croak. And you reject mine ?

Honeyw. Heavens forbid, madam ! No sure, no reasoning can be more just than yours. We ought certainly to despise malice if we cannot oppose it, and not make the incendiary's pen as fatal to our repose as the highwayman's pistol.

Mrs. Croak. O ! then you think I'm quite right ?

Honeyw. Perfectly right.

Croak. A plague of plagues, we can't be both right. I ought to be sorry, or I ought to be glad. My hat must be on my head, or my hat must be off.

Mrs. Croak. Certainly, in two opposite opinions, if one be perfectly reasonable, the other can't be perfectly right.

Honeyw. And why may not both be right, madam ? Mr. Croaker in earnestly seeking redress, and you in waiting the event with good humour ? Pray let me see the letter again. I have it. This letter requires twenty guineas to be left at the bar of the Talbot Inn. If it be indeed an incendiary letter, what if you and I, Sir, go there ; and, when the writer comes to be paid his expected booty, seize him ?

Croak. My dear friend, it's the very thing ; the very thing. While I walk by the door, you shall plant yourself in ambush near the bar ; burst out upon the miscreant like a masqued battery ; extort a confession at once, and so hang him up by surprise.

Honeyw. Yes, but I would not chuse to exercise too much severity. It is my maxim, Sir, that crimes generally punish themselves.

Croak. Well, but we may upbraid him a little, I suppose ?   [*Ironically.*

Honeyw. Aye, but not punish him too rigidly.

Croak. Well, well, leave that to my own benevolence.

Honeyw. Well, I do ; but remember that universal benevolence is the first law of nature.

[*Exeunt Honeywood and Mrs. Croaker.*

Croak. Yes ; and my universal benevolence will hang the dog, if he had as many necks as a hydra.

ACT V

SCENE, AN INN.

Enter Olivia, Jarvis.

Oliv. Well, we have got safe to the Inn, however. Now, if the post-chaise were ready—

Jarv. The horses are just finishing their oats ; and, as they are not going to be married, they chuse to take their own time.

Oliv. You are for ever giving wrong motives to my impatience.

Jarv. Be as impatient as you will, the horses must take their own time ; besides, you don't consider, we have got no answer from our fellow-traveller yet. If we hear nothing from Mr. Leontine, we have only one way left us.

Oliv. What way ?

Jarv. The way home again.

Oliv. Not so. I have made a resolution to go, and nothing shall induce me to break it.

Jarv. Aye ; resolutions are well kept, when they jump with inclination. However, I'll go hasten things without. And I'll call, too, at the bar, to see if any thing should be left for us there. Don't be in such a plaguy hurry, madam, and we shall go the faster, I promise you.

[*Exit Jarvis.*

Enter Landlady.

Land. What ! Solomon, why don't you move ? Pipes and tobacco for the Lamb there.—Will nobody answer ? To the Dolphin ; quick. The Angel has been outrageous this half hour. Did your ladyship call, madam ?

Oliv. No, madam.

Land I find, as you're for Scotland, madam—But that's no business of mine ; married, or not married, I

ask no questions. To be sure we had a sweet little couple
set off from this two days ago for the same place. The
gentleman, for a tailor, was, to be sure, as fine a spoken
tailor, as ever blew froth from a full pot. And the young
lady so bashful, it was near half an hour before we could
get her to finish a pint of rasberry between us.

Oliv. But this gentleman and I are not going to be
married, I assure you.

Land. May be not. That's no business of mine; for
certain, Scotch marriages seldom turn out well. There
was, of my own knowledge, Miss Macfag, that married
her father's footman.—Alack-a-day, she and her husband
soon parted, and now keep separate cellars in Hedge-lane.

Oliv. A very pretty picture of what lies before me !

[*Aside.*

Enter Leontine.

Leont. My dear Olivia, my anxiety, till you were out
of danger, was too great to be resisted. I could not help
coming to see you set out, though it exposes us to a
discovery.

Oliv. May every thing you do prove as fortunate. Indeed, Leontine, we have been most cruelly disappointed.
Mr. Honeywood's bill upon the City has, it seems, been
protested, and we have been utterly at a loss how to
proceed.

Leont. How ! an offer of his own too. Sure, he could
not mean to deceive us.

Oliv. Depend upon his sincerity ; he only mistook the
desire for the power of serving us. But let us think no
more of it. I believe the post-chaise is ready by this.

Land. Not quite yet : and, begging your ladyship's pardon, I don't think your ladyship quite ready for the post-
chaise. The north-road is a cold place, madam. I have
a drop in the house of as pretty rasberry as ever was

tipt over tongue. Just a thimblefull to keep the wind off your stomach. To be sure, the last couple we had here, they said it was a perfect nosegay. Ecod, I sent them both away as good-natured.—Up went the blinds, round went the wheels, and drive away post-boy, was the word.

Enter Croaker.

Croak. Well, while my friend Honeywood is upon the post of danger at the bar, it must be my business to have an eye about me here. I think I know an incendiary's look ; for wherever the devil makes a purchase, he never fails to set his mark. Ha ! who have we here ? My son and daughter ! What can they be doing here !

Land. I tell you, madam, it will do you good ; I think I know by this time what 's good for the north-road. It 's a raw night, madam—Sir—

Leont. Not a drop more, good madam. I should now take it as a greater favour, if you hasten the horses, for I am afraid to be seen myself.

Land. That shall be done. Wha, Solomon ! are you all dead there ? Wha, Solomon, I say ! [*Exit bawling.*

Oliv. Well ! I dread, lest an expedition begun in fear, should end in repentance.—Every moment we stay increases our danger, and adds to my apprehensions.

Leont. There 's no danger, trust me, my dear; there can be none. If Honeywood has acted with honour, and kept my father as he promised, in employment till we are out of danger, nothing can interrupt our journey.

Oliv. I have no doubt of Mr. Honeywood's sincerity, and even his desires to serve us. My fears are from your father's suspicions. A mind so disposed to be alarmed without a cause, will be but too ready when there 's a reason.

Leont. Why, let him when we are out of his power. But believe me, Olivia, you have no great reason to dread his resentment. His repining temper, as it does no manner of injury to himself, so will it never do harm to others. He only frets to keep himself employed, and scolds for his private amusement.

Oliv. I don't know that ; but, I'm sure, on some occasions, it makes him look most shockingly.

Croak. (*Discovering himself.*) How does he look now ?—How does he look now ?

Oliv. Ah !

Leont. Undone !

Croak. How do I look now ? Sir, I am your very humble servant. Madam, I am yours. What, you are going off, are you ? Then, first, if you please, take a word or two from me with you before you go. Tell me first where you are going ? and when you have told me that, perhaps I shall know as little as I did before.

Leont. If that be so, our answer might but increase your displeasure, without adding to your information.

Croak. I want no information from you, puppy : and you too, good madam, what answer have you got ? Eh ! (*A cry without, Stop him.*) I think I heard a noise. My friend Honeywood without—has he seized the incendiary? Ah, no, for now I hear no more on 't.

Leont. Honeywood without ! Then, Sir, it was Mr. Honeywood that directed you hither ?

Croak. No, Sir, it was Mr. Honeywood conducted me hither.

Leont. Is it possible ?

Croak. Possible ! Why he 's in the house now, Sir ; more anxious about me than my own son, Sir.

Leont. Then, Sir, he 's a villain.

Croak. How, sirrah ! a villain, because he takes most care of your father ? I'll not bear it. I tell you I'll not bear it. Honeywood is a friend to the family, and I'll have him treated as such.

Leont. I shall study to repay his friendship as it deserves.

Croak. Ah, rogue, if you knew how earnestly he entered into my griefs, and pointed out the means to detect them, you would love him as I do. (*A cry without, Stop him.*) Fire and fury! they have seized the incendiary: they have the villain, the incendiary in view. Stop him! stop an incendiary! a murderer; stop him!   [*Exit.*

Oliv. O, my terrors! What can this new tumult mean?

Leont. Some new mark, I suppose, of Mr. Honeywood's sincerity. But we shall have satisfaction: he shall give me instant satisfaction.

Oliv. It must not be, my Leontine, if you value my esteem or my happiness. Whatever be our fate, let us not add guilt to our misfortunes—Consider that our innocence will shortly be all that we have left us. You must forgive him.

Leont. Forgive him! Has he not in every instance betrayed us? Forced me to borrow money from him, which appears a mere trick to delay us; promised to keep my father engaged till we were out of danger, and here brought him to the very scene of our escape?

Oliv. Don't be precipitate. We may yet be mistaken.

Enter Postboy, dragging in Jarvis, Honeywood entering soon after.

Post. Aye, master, we have him fast enough. Here is the incendiary dog. I'm entitled to the reward; I'll take my oath I saw him ask for the money at the bar, and then run for it.

Honeyw. Come, bring him along. Let us see him. Let him learn to blush for his crimes. (*Discovering his mistake.*) Death! what's here! Jarvis, Leontine, Olivia! What can all this mean?

Jarv. Why, I'll tell you what it means : that I was an old fool, and that you are my master—that's all.

Honeyw. Confusion !

Leont. Yes, Sir, I find you have kept your word with me. After such baseness, I wonder how you can venture to see the man you have injured ?

Honeyw. My dear Leontine, by my life, my honour—

Leont. Peace, peace, for shame ; and do not continue to aggravate baseness by hypocrisy. I know you, Sir, I know you.

Honeyw. Why, won't you hear me ! By all that's just, I knew not—

Leont. Hear you, Sir ! to what purpose ? I now see through all your low arts ; your ever complying with every opinion; your never refusing any request; your friendship, as common as a prostitute's favours, and as fallacious ; all these, Sir, have long been contemptible to the world, and are now perfectly so to me.

Honeyw. Ha ! ' contemptible to the world ' ! that reaches me. [*Aside.*

Leont. All the seeming sincerity of your professions, I now find, were only allurements to betray ; and all your seeming regret for their consequences only calculated to cover the cowardice of your heart. Draw, villain !

Enter Croaker, out of breath.

Croak. Where is the villain ? Where is the incendiary ? (*Seizing the postboy.*) Hold him fast, the dog : he has the gallows in his face. Come, you dog, confess ; confess all, and hang yourself.

Post. Zounds ! master, what do you throttle me for ?

Croak. (*Beating him.*) Dog, do you resist ; do you resist?

Post. Zounds! master, I'm not he ; there's the man

that we thought was the rogue, and turns out to be one of the company.

Croak. How !

Honeyw. Mr. Croaker, we have all been under a strange mistake here ; I find there is nobody guilty ; it was all an error ; entirely an error of our own.

Croak. And I say, Sir, that you're in an error ; for there's guilt and double guilt, a plot, a damned jesuitical pestilential plot, and I must have proof of it.

Honeyw. Do but hear me.

Croak. What, you intend to bring 'em off, I suppose; I'll hear nothing.

Honeyw. Madam, you seem at least calm enough to hear reason.

Oliv. Excuse me.

Honeyw. Good Jarvis, let me then explain it to you.

Jarv. What signifies explanations when the thing is done ?

Honeyw. Will nobody hear me ? Was there ever such a set, so blinded by passion and prejudice ! (*To the post-boy.*) My good friend, I believe you'll be surprised, when I assure you—

Post. 'Sure me nothing—I'm sure of nothing but a good beating.

Croak. Come then you, madam, if you ever hope for any favour or forgiveness, tell me sincerely all you know of this affair.

Oliv. Unhappily, Sir, I'm but too much the cause of your suspicions : you see before you, Sir, one that with false pretences has stept into your family to betray it : not your daughter—

Croak. Not my daughter !

Oliv. Not your daughter—but a mean deceiver—who —support me, I cannot—

Honeyw. Help, she's going, give her air.

CROAKER THRASHING THE POSTBOY

Croak. Aye, aye, take the young woman to the air ;
I would not hurt a hair of her head, whoseever daughter
she may be—not so bad as that neither.

[*Exeunt all but Croaker.*

Croak. Yes, yes, all's out : I now see the whole affair :
my son is either married, or going to be so, to this lady,
whom he imposed upon me as his sister. Aye, certainly
so ; and yet I don't find it afflicts me so much as one
might think. There's the advantage of fretting away
our misfortunes beforehand, we never feel them when
they come.

Enter Miss Richland and Sir William.

Sir Will. But how do you know, madam, that my
nephew intends setting off from this place.

Miss Rich. My maid assured me he was come to this
inn, and my own knowledge of his intending to leave the
kingdom, suggested the rest. But what do I see, my
guardian here before us ! Who, my dear Sir, could have
expected meeting you here ? to what accident do we
owe this pleasure ?

Croak. To a fool, I believe.

Miss Rich. But to what purpose did you come.

Croak. To play the fool.

Miss Rich. But with whom ?

Croak. With greater fools than myself.

Miss Rich. Explain.

Croak. Why, Mr. Honeywood brought me here, to do
nothing, now I am here ; and my son is going to be
married to I don't know who, that is here : so now you
are as wise as I am.

Miss Rich. Married ! to whom, Sir ?

Croak. To Olivia, my daughter as I took her to be ;
but who the devil she is, or whose daughter she is, I know
no more than the man in the moon.

Sir Will. Then, Sir, I can inform you ; and, though a

stranger, yet you shall find me a friend to your family : it will be enough, at present, to assure you, that both in point of birth and fortune the young lady is at least your son's equal.   Being left by her father Sir James Wood-ville——

Croak. Sir James Woodville ! What, of the West ?

Sir Will. Being left by him, I say, to the care of a mercenary wretch, whose only aim was to secure her fortune to himself, she was sent to France, under pretence of education ; and there every art was tried to fix her for life in a convent, contrary to her inclinations.   Of this I was informed upon my arrival at Paris ; and, as I had been once her father's friend, I did all in my power to frustrate her guardian's base intentions.   I had even meditated to rescue her from his authority, when your son stept in with more pleasing violence, gave her liberty, and you a daughter.

Croak. But I intend to have a daughter of my own chusing, Sir.   A young lady, Sir, whose fortune, by my interest with those who have interest, will be double what my son has a right to expect.   Do you know Mr. Lofty, Sir ?

Sir Will. Yes, Sir ; and know that you are deceived in him.   But step this way, and I'll convince you.

[Croaker and Sir William seem to confer.

Enter Honeywood.

Honeyw. Obstinate man, still to persist in his outrage ! insulted by him, despised by all, I now begin to grow contemptible, even to myself.   How have I sunk by too great an assiduity to please ! How have I over-taxed all my abilities, lest the approbation of a single fool should escape me ! But all is now over ; I have survived my reputation, my fortune, my friendships, and nothing remains henceforward for me but solitude and repent-ance.

Miss Rich. Is it true, Mr. Honeywood, that you are setting off, without taking leave of your friends ? The report is, that you are quitting England. Can it be ?

Honeyw. Yes, madam ; and though I am so unhappy as to have fallen under your displeasure, yet, thank Heaven, I leave you to happiness, to one who loves you, and deserves your love ; to one who has power to procure you affluence, and generosity to improve your enjoyment of it.

Miss Rich. And are you sure, Sir, that the gentleman you mean is what you describe him ?

Honeyw. I have the best assurances of it, his serving me. He does indeed deserve the highest happiness, and that is in your power to confer. As for me, weak and wavering as I have been, obliged by all, and incapable of serving any, what happiness can I find but in solitude ? What hope but in being forgotten ?

Miss Rich. A thousand ! to live among friends that esteem you, whose happiness it will be to be permitted to oblige you.

Honeyw. No, madam, my resolution is fixed. Inferio-rity among strangers is easy ; but among those that once were equals, insupportable. Nay, to shew you how far my resolution can go, I can now speak with calmness of my former follies, my vanity, my dissipation, my weak-ness. I will even confess, that, among the number of my other presumptions, I had the insolence to think of loving you. Yes, madam, while I was pleading the pas-sion of another, my heart was tortur'd with its own. But it is over, it was unworthy our friendship, and let it be forgotten.

Miss Rich. You amaze me !

Honeyw. But you'll forgive it, I know you will ; since

the confession should not have come from me even now,
but to convince you of the sincerity of my intention of—
never mentioning it more.   [*Going.*

Miss Rich. Stay, Sir, one moment—Ha ! he here—

Enter Lofty.

Lofty. Is the coast clear ? None but friends ? I have
followed you here with a trifling piece of intelligence :
but it goes no farther, things are not yet ripe for a discovery. I have spirits working at a certain board ; your
affair at the treasury will be done in less than—a thousand years. Mum !

Miss Rich. Sooner, Sir, I should hope.

Lofty. Why, yes, I believe it may, if it falls into proper
hands, that know where to push and where to parry ;
that know how the land lies—eh, Honeywood !

Miss Rich. It has fallen into yours.

Lofty. Well, to keep you no longer in suspense, your
thing is done. It is done, I say—that's all. I have just
had assurances from Lord Neverout, that the claim has
been examined, and found admissible. *Quietus* is the
word, madam.

Honeyw. But how ! his lordship has been at Newmarket
these ten days.

Lofty. Indeed ! Then Sir Gilbert Goose must have
been most damnably mistaken. I had it of him.

Miss Rich. He ! why Sir Gilbert and his family have
been in the country this month.

Lofty. This month ! it must certainly be so—Sir
Gilbert's letter did come to me from Newmarket, so that
he must have met his lordship there ; and so it came
about. I have his letter about me ; I'll read it to you,
(*Taking out a large bundle.*) That's from Paoli of Corsica,
that from the marquis of Squilachi.—Have you a mind
to see a letter from Count Poniatowski, now King of

Poland—Honest Pon—(*Searching*.) O, Sir, what, are you here too ? I'll tell you what, honest friend, if you have not absolutely delivered my letter to Sir William Honeywood, you may return it. The thing will do without him.

Sir Will. Sir, I have delivered it ; and must inform you, it was received with the most mortifying contempt.

Croak. Contempt ! Mr. Lofty, what can that mean ?

Lofty. Let him go on, let him go on, I say. You'll find it come to something presently.

Sir Will. Yes, Sir, I believe you'll be amazed, if after waiting some time in the anti-chamber, after being surveyed with insolent curiosity by the passing servants, I was at last assured, that Sir William Honeywood knew no such person, and I must certainly have been imposed upon.

Lofty. Good ; let me die ; very good. Ha ! ha ! ha !

Croak. Now, for my life, I can't find out half the goodness of it.

Lofty. You can't. Ha ! ha !

Croak. No, for the soul of me ! I think it was as confounded a bad answer as ever was sent from one private gentleman to another.

Lofty. And so you can't find out the force of the message ? Why, I was in the house at that very time. Ha ! ha ! It was I that sent that very answer to my own letter. Ha ! ha !

Croak. Indeed ! How ? why ?

Lofty. In one word, things between Sir William and me must be behind the curtain. A party has many eyes. He sides with Lord Buzzard, I side with Sir Gilbert Goose. So that unriddles the mystery.

Croak. And so it does, indeed ; and all my suspicions are over.

Lofty. Your suspicions ! What, then, you have been

suspecting, you have been suspecting, have you ?
Mr. Croaker, you and I were friends ; we are friends no
longer. Never talk to me. It's over ; I say, it's over.

Croak. As I hope for your favour I did not mean to
offend. It escaped me. Don't be discomposed.

Lofty. Zounds ! Sir, but I am discomposed, and will
be discomposed. To be treated thus ! Who am I ! Was
it for this I have been dreaded both by ins and outs ?
Have I been libelled in the Gazetteer, and praised in the
St. James's ? have I been chaired at Wildman's, and a
speaker at Merchant-Tailors' Hall ? have I had my hand
to addresses, and my head in the print-shops ; and talk
to me of suspects ?

Croak. My dear Sir, be pacified. What can you have
but asking pardon ?

Lofty. Sir, I will not be pacified—Suspects ! Who am
I ! To be used thus ! Have I paid court to men in favour
to serve my friends ; the lords of the treasury, Sir William
Honeywood, and the rest of the gang, and talk to me of
suspects ! Who am I, I say, who am I !

Sir Will. Since, Sir, you are so pressing for an answer,
I'll tell you who you are. A gentleman, as well acquainted with politics as with men in power; as well acquainted with persons of fashion as with modesty ; with
lords of the treasury as with truth ; and with all, as you
are with Sir William Honeywood. I am Sir William
Honeywood.   [*Discovering his ensigns of the Bath.*

Croak. Sir William Honeywood !

Honeyw. Astonishment ! my uncle !   (*Aside.*)

Lofty. So then, my confounded genius has been all this
time only leading me up to the garret, in order to fling me
out of the window.

Croak. What, Mr. Importance, and are these your
works ! Suspect you ? You, who have been dreaded by
the ins and outs : you, who have had your hand to

addresses, and your head stuck up in print-shops. If you were served right, you should have your head stuck up in a pillory.

Lofty. Aye, stick it where you will ; for by the Lord, it cuts but a very poor figure where it sticks at present.

Sir Will. Well, Mr. Croaker, I hope you now see how incapable this gentleman is of serving you, and how little Miss Richland has to expect from his influence.

Croak. Aye, Sir, too well I see it ; and I can't but say I have had some boding of it these ten days. So I'm resolved, since my son has placed his affections on a lady of moderate fortune, to be satisfied with his choice, and not run the hazard of another Mr. Lofty in helping him to a better.

Sir Will. I approve your resolution ; and here they come to receive a confirmation of your pardon and consent.

Enter Mrs. Croaker, Jarvis, Leontine, and Olivia.

Mrs. Croak. Where's my husband ! Come, come, lovey, you must forgive them. Jarvis here has been to tell me the whole affair ; and I say, you must forgive them. Our own was a stolen match, you know, my dear ; and we never had any reason to repent of it.

Croak. I wish we could both say so. However, this gentleman, Sir William Honeywood, has been beforehand with you in obtaining their pardon. So, if the two poor fools have a mind to marry, I think we can tack them together without crossing the Tweed for it.

[Joining their hands.

Leont. How blest and unexpected ! What what can we say to such goodness ? But our future obedience shall be the best reply. And as for this gentleman, to whom we owe—

Sir Will. Excuse me, Sir, if I interrupt your thanks, as

I have here an interest that calls me. (*Turning to Honey-wood.*) Yes, Sir, you are surprised to see me ; and I own that a desire of correcting your follies led me hither. I saw with indignation the errors of a mind that only sought applause from others ; that easiness of disposition, which though inclined to the right had not courage to condemn the wrong. I saw with regret those splendid errors, that still took name from some neighbouring duty ; your charity, that was but injustice ; your benevolence, that was but weakness ; and your friendship, but credulity. I saw with regret great talents and extensive learning only employed to add sprightliness to error, and encrease your perplexities. I saw your mind with a thousand natural charms : but the greatness of its beauty served only to heighten my pity for its prostitution.

Honeyw. Cease to upbraid me, Sir : I have for some time but too strongly felt the justice of your reproaches. But there is one way still left me. Yes, Sir, I have determined this very hour to quit for ever a place where I have made myself the voluntary slave of all, and to seek among strangers that fortitude which may give strength to the mind, and marshal all its dissipated virtues. Yet ere I depart, permit me to solicit favour for this gentleman ; who, notwithstanding what has happened, has laid me under the most signal obligations. Mr. Lofty——

Lofty. Mr. Honeywood, I'm resolved upon a reformation as well as you. I now begin to find that the man who first invented the art of speaking truth was a much cunninger fellow than I thought him. And to prove that I design to speak truth for the future, I must now assure you, that you owe your late enlargement to another ; as, upon my soul, I had no hand in the matter. So now, if any of the company has a mind for preferment, he may take my place, I'm determined to resign.   [*Exit.*

Honeyw. How have I been deceived !

Sir Will. No, Sir, you have been obliged to a kinder, fairer friend for that favour—to Miss Richland. Would she complete our joy, and make the man she has honoured by her friendship happy in her love, I should then forget all, and be as blest as the welfare of my dearest kinsman can make me.

Miss Rich. After what is past it would be but affectation to pretend to indifference. Yes, I will own an attachment, which I find was more than friendship. And if my intreaties cannot alter his resolution to quit the country, I will even try if my hand has not power to detain him.   [*Giving her hand.*

Honeyw. Heavens ! how can I have deserved all this ? How express my happiness, my gratitude ! A moment like this overpays an age of apprehension.

Croak. Well, now I see content in every face ; but heaven send we be all better this day three months !

Sir Will. Henceforth, nephew, learn to respect yourself. He who seeks only for applause from without, has all his happiness in another's keeping.

Honeyw. Yes, Sir, I now too plainly perceive my errors ; my vanity in attempting to please all by fearing to offend any ; my meanness in approving folly lest fools should disapprove. Henceforth, therefore, it shall be my study to reserve my pity for real distress ; my friendship for true merit ; and my love for her, who first taught me what it is to be happy.

EPILOGUE TO THE GOOD-NATUR'D MAN [1]

SPOKEN BY MRS. BULKLEY

As puffing quacks some caitiff wretch procure
To swear the pill, or drop, has wrought a cure ;
Thus, on the stage, our play-wrights still depend
For Epilogues and Prologues on some friend,
Who knows each art of coaxing up the town,
And makes full many a bitter pill go down.
Conscious of this, our bard has gone about,
And teaz'd each rhyming friend to help him out.
An Epilogue, things can't go on without it ;
It could not fail, would you but set about it.
Young man, cries one (a bard laid up in clover),
Alas, young man, my writing days are over ;
Let boys play tricks, and kick the straw, not I ;
Your brother Doctor there, perhaps, may try.
What I ! dear Sir, the Doctor interposes ;
What, plant my thistle, Sir, among his roses !
No, no, I've other contests to maintain ;
To-night I head our troops at Warwick-lane.
Go ask your manager—Who, me ! Your pardon ;
Those things are not our forte at Covent-garden.
Our author's friends, thus plac'd at happy distance,
Give him good words indeed, but no assistance.

The author, in expectation of an Epilogue from a friend at
Oxford, deferred writing one himself till the very last hour. What
is here offered, owes all its success to the graceful manner of the
actress who spoke it.

As some unhappy wight, at some new play,
At the pit door stands elbowing away,
While oft, with many a smile, and many a shrug,
He eyes the centre, where his friends sit snug ;
His simpering friends, with pleasure in their eyes,
Sink as he sinks, and as he rises rise :
He nods, they nod ; he cringes, they grimace ;
But not a soul will budge to give him place.
Since then, unhelp'd, our bard must now conform
' To 'bide the pelting of this pitt'less storm,'
Blame where you must, be candid where you can,
And be each critick the *Good-natur'd Man.*

SHE STOOPS TO CONQUER

OR

THE MISTAKES OF A NIGHT

A COMEDY

AS ACTED AT THE

THEATRE-ROYAL, COVENT-GARDEN

[First printed in 1773]

DEDICATION

TO SAMUEL JOHNSON, LL.D.

Dear Sir,

By inscribing this slight performance to you, I do not mean so much to compliment you as myself. It may do me some honour to inform the public, that I have lived many years in intimacy with you. It may serve the interests of mankind also to inform them, that the greatest wit may be found in a character, without impairing the most unaffected piety.

I have, particularly, reason to thank you for your partiality to this performance. The undertaking a Comedy, not merely sentimental, was very dangerous; and Mr. Colman, who saw this piece in its various stages, always thought it so. However, I ventured to trust it to the public; and, though it was necessarily delayed till late in the season, I have every reason to be grateful. I am,

Dear Sir,

Your most sincere

Friend and admirer,

OLIVER GOLDSMITH.

PROLOGUE

BY DAVID GARRICK, ESQ.

Enter Mr. Woodward, dressed in black, and holding a Handkerchief to his Eyes.

Excuse me, Sirs, I pray—I can't yet speak—
I'm crying now—and have been all the week.
' 'Tis not alone this mourning suit,' good masters :
' I've that within '—for which there are no plasters !
Pray, would you know the reason why I'm crying ?
The Comic Muse, long sick, is now a-dying !
And if she goes, my tears will never stop ;
For as a play'r, I can't squeeze out one drop ;
I am undone, that 's all—shall lose my bread—
I'd rather, but that 's nothing—lose my head.
When the sweet maid is laid upon the bier,
Shuter and I shall be chief mourners here.
To her a mawkish drab of spurious breed,
Who deals in Sentimentals, will succeed !
Poor Ned and I are dead to all intents ;
We can as soon speak Greek as Sentiments !
Both nervous grown, to keep our spirits up,
We now and then take down a hearty cup.
What shall we do ?—If Comedy forsake us !
They'll turn us out, and no one else will take us.
But, why can't I be moral ?—Let me try—
My heart thus pressing—fix'd my face and eye—
With a sententious look, that nothing means,
(Faces are blocks in sentimental scenes)

Thus I begin—' All is not gold that glitters,
Pleasures seem sweet, but prove a glass of bitters.
When ign'rance enters, folly is at hand :
Learning is better far than house and land.
Let not your virtue trip, who trips may stumble,
And virtue is not virtue, if she tumble.'

  I give it up—morals won't do for me ;
To make you laugh, I must play tragedy.
One hope remains—hearing the maid was ill,
A Doctor comes this night to shew his skill.
To cheer her heart, and give your muscles motion,
He, in Five Draughts prepar'd, presents a potion :
A kind of magic charm—for be assur'd,
If you will swallow it, the maid is cur'd :
But desperate the Doctor, and her case is,
If you reject the dose, and make wry faces !
This truth he boasts, will boast it while he lives,
No pois'nous drugs are mix'd in what he gives.
Should he succeed, you'll give him his degree ;
If not, within he will receive no fee !
The college you, must his pretensions back,
Pronounce him Regular, or dub him Quack.

DRAMATIS PERSONAE

MEN.

Sir Charles Marlow	. MR. GARDNER.
Young Marlow, (his son) . . .	. MR. LEWIS.
Hardcastle	. MR. SHUTER.
Hastings	. MR. DUBELLAMY.
Tony Lumpkin	. MR. QUICK.
Diggory	. MR. SAUNDERS.

WOMEN.

Mrs. Hardcastle	. MRS. GREEN.
Miss Hardcastle	. MRS. BULKLEY.
Miss Neville	. MRS. KNIVETON.
Maid	. MISS WILLEMS.

Landlord, Servants, &c., &c.

SHE STOOPS TO CONQUER

OR

THE MISTAKES OF A NIGHT

ACT I

SCENE, A CHAMBER IN AN OLD-FASHIONED HOUSE.

Enter Mrs. Hardcastle and Mr. Hardcastle.

Mrs. Hard. I vow, Mr. Hardcastle, you're very particular. Is there a creature in the whole country but
ourselves, that does not take a trip to town now and then,
to rub off the rust a little ? There's the two Miss Hoggs,
and our neighbour Mrs. Grigsby, go to take a month's
polishing every winter.

Hard. Ay, and bring back vanity and affectation to
last them the whole year. I wonder why London cannot
keep its own fools at home ! In my time, the follies of
the town crept slowly among us, but now they travel
faster than a stage-coach. Its fopperies come down not
only as inside passengers, but in the very basket.

Mrs. Hard. Ay, your times were fine times indeed ;
you have been telling us of them for many a long year.
Here we live in an old rumbling mansion, that looks for
all the world like an inn, but that we never see company.
Our best visitors are old Mrs. Oddfish, the curate's wife,
and little Cripplegate, the lame dancing-master ; and all
our entertainment your old stories of Prince Eugene and

the Duke of Marlborough. I hate such old fashioned trumpery.

Hard. And I love it. I love every thing that's old: old friends, old times, old manners, old books, old wines; and, I believe, Dorothy, (*Taking her hand*) you'll own I have been pretty fond of an old wife.

Mrs. Hard. Lord, Mr. Hardcastle, you're for ever at your Dorothy's, and your old wives. You may be a Darby, but I'll be no Joan, I promise you. I'm not so old as you'd make me, by more than one good year. Add twenty to twenty, and make money of that.

Hard. Let me see; twenty added to twenty makes just fifty and seven.

Mrs. Hard. It's false, Mr. Hardcastle; I was but twenty when I was brought to bed of Tony, that I had by Mr. Lumpkin, my first husband; and he's not come to years of discretion yet.

Hard. Nor ever will, I dare answer for him. Ay, you have taught him finely.

Mrs. Hard. No matter. Tony Lumpkin has a good fortune. My son is not to live by his learning. I don't think a boy wants much learning to spend fifteen hundred a year.

Hard. Learning, quotha! a mere composition of tricks and mischief.

Mrs. Hard. Humour, my dear: nothing but humour. Come, Mr. Hardcastle, you must allow the boy a little humour.

Hard. I'd sooner allow him an horse-pond. If burning the footmen's shoes, frightening the maids, and worrying the kittens be humour, he has it. It was but yesterday he fastened my wig to the back of my chair, and when I went to make a bow, I popt my bald head in Mrs. Frizzle's face.

Mrs. Hard. And am I to blame? The poor boy was

always too sickly to do any good. A school would be his death. When he comes to be a little stronger who knows what a year or two's Latin may do for him?

Hard. Latin for him. A cat and fiddle. No, no, the ale-house and the stable are the only schools he'll ever go to.

Mrs. Hard. Well, we must not snub the poor boy now, for I believe we shan't have him long among us. Any body that looks in his face may see he's consumptive.

Hard. Ay, if growing too fat be one of the symptoms.

Mrs. Hard. He coughs sometimes.

Hard. Yes, when his liquor goes the wrong way.

Mrs. Hard. I'm actually afraid of his lungs.

Hard. And truly so am I; for he sometimes whoops like a speaking trumpet—(*Tony hallooing behind the scenes.*)— O there he goes—a very consumptive figure, truly.

Enter Tony, crossing the stage.

Mrs. Hard. Tony, where are you going, my charmer? Won't you give papa and I a little of your company, lovee?

Tony. I'm in haste, mother, I cannot stay.

Mrs. Hard. You shan't venture out this raw evening, my dear: You look most shockingly.

Tony. I can't stay, I tell you. The 'Three Pigeons' expects me down every moment. There's some fun going forward.

Hard. Ay; the ale-house, the old place: I thought so.

Mrs. Hard. A low, paltry set of fellows.

Tony. Not so low neither. There's Dick Muggins the exciseman, Jack Slang the horse doctor, little Aminidab that grinds the music box, and Tom Twist that spins the pewter platter.

Mrs. Hard. Pray, my dear, disappoint them for one night at least.

Tony. As for disappointing them I should not so much mind ; but I can't abide to disappoint myself.

Mrs. Hard. (*Detaining him.*) You shan't go.

Tony. I will, I tell you.

Mrs. Hard. I say you shan't.

Tony. We'll see which is strongest, you or I.

[*Exit hauling her out.*

Hard. (*Solus.*) Ay, there goes a pair that only spoil each other. But is not the whole age in a combination to drive sense and discretion out of doors ? There's my pretty darling Kate ! the fashions of the times have almost infected her too. By living a year or two in town, she is as fond of gauze and French frippery as the best of them.

Enter Miss Hardcastle.

Hard. Blessings on my pretty innocence ! drest out as usual, my Kate. Goodness ! What a quantity of superfluous silk hast thou got about thee, girl ! I could never teach the fools of this age, that the indigent world could be clothed out of the trimmings of the vain.

Miss Hard. You know our agreement, Sir. You allow me the morning to receive and pay visits, and to dress in my own manner ; and in the evening I put on my housewife's dress to please you.

Hard. Well, remember I insist on the terms of our agreement ; and, by the by, I believe I shall have occasion to try your obedience this very evening.

Miss Hard. I protest, Sir, I don't comprehend your meaning.

Hard. Then to be plain with you, Kate, I expect the young gentleman I have chosen to be your husband from town this very day. I have his father's letter, in which he informs me his son is set out, and that he intends to follow himself shortly after.

Miss Hard. Indeed ! I wish I had known something of this before. Bless me, how shall I behave ? It's a thousand to one I shan't like him ; our meeting will be so formal, and so like a thing of business, that I shall find no room for friendship or esteem.

Hard. Depend upon it, child, I never will controul your choice ! but Mr. Marlow, whom I have pitched upon, is the son of my old friend, Sir Charles Marlow, of whom you have heard me talk so often. The young gentleman has been bred a scholar, and is designed for an employment in the service of his country. I am told he's a man of an excellent understanding.

Miss Hard. Is he ?

Hard. Very generous.

Miss Hard. I believe I shall like him.

Hard. Young and brave.

Miss Hard. I'm sure I shall like him.

Hard. And very handsome.

Miss Hard. My dear papa, say no more (*kissing his hand*), he's mine, I'll have him.

Hard. And, to crown all, Kate, he's one of the most bashful and reserved young fellows in all the world.

Miss Hard. Eh ! you have frozen me to death again. That word 'reserved' has undone all the rest of his accomplishments. A reserved lover it is said always makes a suspicious husband.

Hard. On the contrary, modesty seldom resides in a breast that is not enriched with nobler virtues. It was the very feature in his character that first struck me.

Miss Hard. He must have more striking features to catch me, I promise you. However, if he be so young, and so every thing as you mention, I believe he'll do still. I think I'll have him.

Hard. Ay, Kate, but there is still an obstacle. It's more than an even wager he may not have you.

Miss Hard. My dear papa, why will you mortify one so ? Well, if he refuses, instead of breaking my heart at his indifference, I'll only break my glass for its flattery, set my cap to some newer fashion, and look out for some less difficult admirer.

Hard. Bravely resolved ! In the mean time I'll go prepare the servants for his reception : as we seldom see company, they want as much training as a company of recruits the first day's muster.   [*Exit.*

Miss Hard. (*Alone.*) Lud, this news of papa's puts me all in a flutter. Young, handsome ; these he put last ; but I put them foremost. Sensible, good-natured ; I like all that. But then reserved and sheepish, that's much against him. Yet can't he be cured of his timidity, by being taught to be proud of his wife ? Yes, and can't I —But I vow I'm disposing of the husband, before I have secured the lover.

Enter Miss Neville.

Miss Hard. I'm glad you're come, Neville, my dear. Tell me, Constance, how do I look this evening ? Is there any thing whimsical about me ? Is it one of my well-looking days, child ? am I in face to-day ?

Miss Nev. Perfectly, my dear. Yet now I look again —bless me !—sure no accident has happened among the canary birds or the gold fishes. Has your brother or the cat been meddling ? or has the last novel been too moving ?

Miss Hard. No ; nothing of all this. I have been threatened—I can scarce get it out—I have been threatened with a lover !

Miss Nev. And his name—

Miss Hard. Is Marlow.

Miss Nev. Indeed !

Miss Hard. The son of Sir Charles Marlow.

Miss Nev. As I live, the most intimate friend of

Mr. Hastings, my admirer. They are never asunder. I believe you must have seen him when we lived in town.

Miss Hard. Never.

Miss Nev. He's a very singular character, I assure you. Among women of reputation and virtue he is the modestest man alive ; but his acquaintance give him a very different character among creatures of another stamp : you understand me.

Miss Hard. An odd character, indeed. I shall never be able to manage him. What shall I do ? Pshaw, think no more of him, but trust to occurrences for success. But how goes on your own affair, my dear ? has my mother been courting you for my brother Tony as usual ?

Miss Nev. I have just come from one of our agreeable tête-à-têtes. She has been saying a hundred tender things, and setting off her pretty monster as the very pink of perfection.

Miss Hard. And her partiality is such, that she actually thinks him so. A fortune like yours is no small temptation. Besides, as she has the sole management of it, I'm not surprised to see her unwilling to let it go out of the family.

Miss Nev. A fortune like mine, which chiefly consists in jewels, is no such mighty temptation. But at any rate if my dear Hastings be but constant, I make no doubt to be too hard for her at last. However, I let her suppose that I am in love with her son, and she never once dreams that my affections are fixed upon another.

Miss Hard. My good brother holds out stoutly. I could almost love him for hating you so.

Miss Nev. It's a good-natured creature at bottom, and I'm sure would wish to see me married to any body but himself. But my aunt's bell rings for our afternoon's walk round the improvements. Allons! Courage is necessary, as our affairs are critical.

Miss Hard. ' Would it were bed-time and all were well.'

[*Exeunt.*

SCENE, AN ALEHOUSE ROOM.

Several shabby fellows with punch and tobacco. Tony at the head of the table, a little higher than the rest : a mallet in his hand.

Omnes. Hurrea! hurrea! hurrea! bravo!

First Fel. Now, gentlemen, silence for a song. The 'squire is going to knock himself down for a song.

Omnes. Ay, a song, a song!

Tony. Then I'll sing you, gentlemen, a song I made upon this alehouse, the Three Pigeons.

SONG.

Let school-masters puzzle their brain,
   With grammar, and nonsense, and learning,
Good liquor, I stoutly maintain,
   Gives *genus* a better discerning.
Let them brag of their heathenish gods,
   Their Lethes, their Styxes, and Stygians, *MILTON*
Their qui's, and their quae's, and their quod's,
   They're all but a parcel of pigeons.
               Toroddle, toroddle, toroll.

When Methodist preachers come down,
   A-preaching that drinking is sinful,
I'll wager the rascals a crown,
   They always preach best with a skinful.
For when you come down with your pence,
   For a slice of their scurvy religion,
I'll leave it to all men of sense,
   But you, my good friend, are the pigeon.
               Toroddle, toroddle, toroll.

Then come put the jorum about,
  And let us be merry and clever,
Our hearts and our liquors are stout,
  Here's the Three Jolly Pigeons for ever.
Let some cry up woodcock or hare,
  Your bustards, your ducks, and your widgeons;
But of all the gay birds in the air,
  Here's a health to the Three Jolly Pigeons.
                    Toroddle, toroddle, toroll.

Omnes. Bravo, bravo!

First Fel. The 'squire has got spunk in him.

Second Fel. I loves to hear him sing, bekeays he never gives us nothing that's low.

Third Fel. O damn any thing that's low, I cannot bear it.

Fourth Fel. The genteel thing is the genteel thing at any time. If so be that a gentleman bees in a concatenation accordingly.

Third Fel. I like the maxum of it, Master Muggins. What, though I am obligated to dance a bear, a man may be a gentleman for all that. May this be my poison, if my bear ever dances but to the very genteelest of tunes; 'Water Parted,' or the minuet in 'Ariadne.'

Second Fel. What a pity it is the 'squire is not come to his own. It would be well for all the publicans within ten miles round of him.

Tony. Ecod, and so it would, Master Slang. I'd then shew what it was to keep choice of company.

Second Fel. O he takes after his own father for that. To be sure old 'squire Lumpkin was the finest gentleman I ever set my eyes on. For winding the straight horn, or beating a thicket for a hare, or a wench, he never had his fellow. It was a saying in the place that he kept the best horses, dogs, and girls in the whole county.

Tony. Ecod, and when I'm of age, I'll be no bastard,

I promise you. I have been thinking of Bett Bouncer and the miller's grey mare to begin with. But come my boys, drink about and be merry, for you pay no reckoning. Well, Stingo, what's the matter ?

Enter Landlord.

Land. There be two gentlemen in a post-chaise at the door. They have lost their way upo' the forest ; and they are talking something about Mr. Hardcastle.

Tony. As sure as can be, one of them must be the gentleman that's coming down to court my sister. Do they seem to be Londoners ?

Land. I believe they may. They look woundily like Frenchmen.

Tony. Then desire them to step this way, and I'll set them right in a twinkling. (*Exit Landlord.*) Gentlemen, as they mayn't be good enough company for you, step down for a moment, and I'll be with you in the squeezing of a lemon. [*Exeunt mob.*

Tony. (*Alone.*) Father-in-law has been calling me whelp and hound this half year. Now if I pleased, I could be so revenged on the old grumbletonian. But then I'm afraid—afraid of what ! I shall soon be worth fifteen hundred a year, and let him frighten me out of that if he can.

Enter Landlord, conducting Marlow and Hastings.

Marl. What a tedious uncomfortable day have we had of it ! We were told it was but forty miles across the country, and we have come above threescore.

Hast. And all, Marlow, from that unaccountable reserve of yours, that would not let us inquire more frequently on the way.

Marl. I own, Hastings, I am unwilling to lay myself under an obligation to every one I meet : and often stand the chance of an unmannerly answer.

Hast. At present, however, we are not likely to receive any answer.

Tony. No offence, gentlemen. But I'm told you have been inquiring for one Mr. Hardcastle in these parts. Do you know what part of the country you are in ?

Hast. Not in the least, Sir, but should thank you for information.

Tony. Nor the way you came ?

Hast. No, Sir, but if you can inform us——

Tony. Why, gentlemen, if you know neither the road you are going, nor where you are, nor the road you came, the first thing I have to inform you is, that—you have lost your way.

Marl. We wanted no ghost to tell us that.

Tony. Pray, gentlemen, may I be so bold as to ask the place from whence you came.

Marl. That's not necessary toward directing us where we are to go.

Tony. No offence ; but question for question is all fair, you know. Pray, gentlemen, is not this same Hardcastle a cross-grain'd, old-fashion'd, whimsical fellow, with an ugly face ; a daughter, and a pretty son ?

Hast. We have not seen the gentleman, but he has the family you mention.

Tony. The daughter, a tall, trapesing, trolloping, talkative maypole—the son, a pretty, well-bred, agreeable youth, that everybody is fond of.

Marl. Our information differs in this. The daughter is said to be well-bred and beautiful ; the son, an aukward booby, reared up and spoiled at his mother's apronstring.

Tony. He-he-hem !—Then gentlemen, all I have to tell you is, that you won't reach Mr. Hardcastle's house this night, I believe.

Hast. Unfortunate !

Tony. It's a damn'd long, dark, boggy, dirty, dangerous way. Stingo, tell the gentlemen the way to Mr. Hard-castle's ! (*Winking upon the Landlord.*) Mr. Hardcastle's, of Quagmire Marsh, you understand me ?

Land. Master Hardcastle's ! Lock-a-daisy, my masters, you're come a deadly deal wrong ! When you came to the bottom of the hill, you should have cross'd down Squash-Lane.

Marl. Cross down Squash-Lane !

Land. Then you were to keep straight forward, 'till you came to four roads.

Marl. Come to where four roads meet !

Tony. Ay ; but you must be sure to take only one of them.

Marl. O Sir, you're facetious.

Tony. Then keeping to the right, you are to go side-ways 'till you come upon Crack-skull common : there you must look sharp for the track of the wheel, and go for-ward 'till you come to farmer Murrain's barn. Coming to the farmer's barn you are to turn to the right, and then to the left, and then to the right about again, till you find out the old mill.

Marl. Zounds, man ! we could as soon find out the longitude !

Hast. What's to be done, Marlow ?

Marl. This house promises but a poor reception ; though perhaps the landlord can accommodate us.

Land. Alack, master, we have but one spare bed in the whole house.

Tony. And to my knowledge, that's taken up by three lodgers already. (*After a pause, in which the rest seem disconcerted.*) I have hit it. Don't you think, Stingo, our landlady could accommodate the gentlemen by the fire-side, with——three chairs and a bolster ?

Hast. I hate sleeping by the fire-side.

Marl. And I detest your three chairs and a bolster.

Tony. You do, do you !—then let me see—what if you go on a mile further, to the Buck's Head ; the old Buck's Head on the hill, one of the best inns in the whole county ?

Hast. O ho ! so we have escaped an adventure for this night, however.

Land. (*Apart to Tony.*) Sure, you ben't sending them to your father's as an inn, be you ?

Tony. Mum, you fool you. Let them find that out. (*To them.*) You have only to keep on straight forward, till you come to a large old house by the road side. You'll see a pair of large horns over the door. That's the sign. Drive up the yard, and call stoutly about you.

Hast. Sir, we are obliged to you. The servants can't miss the way ?

Tony. No, no ; but I tell you though, the landlord is rich, and going to leave off business ; so he wants to be thought a gentleman, saving your presence, he ! he ! he ! He'll be for giving you his company, and ecod, if you mind him, he'll persuade you that his mother was an alderman, and his aunt a justice of peace.

Land. A troublesome old blade to be sure ; but a' keeps as good wines and beds as any in the whole country.

Marl. Well, if he supplies us with these, we shall want no farther connexion. We are to turn to the right, did you say ?

Tony. No, no : straight forward. I'll just step myself, and shew you a piece of the way. (*To the landlord.*) Mum.

Land. Ah, bless your heart, for a sweet, pleasant—— damn'd mischievous son of a whore.   [*Exeunt.*

ACT II

SCENE, AN OLD-FASHIONED HOUSE.

Enter Hardcastle, followed by three or four aukward Servants.

Hard. Well, I hope you are perfect in the table exercise I have been teaching you these three days. You all know your posts and your places, and can shew that you have been used to good company, without ever stirring from home.

Omnes. Ay, ay.

Hard. When company comes, you are not to pop out and stare, and then run in again, like frighted rabbits in a warren.

Omnes. No, no.

Hard. You, Diggory, whom I have taken from the barn, are to make a shew at the side-table; and you, Roger, whom I have advanced from the plough, are to place yourself behind my chair. But you're not to stand so, with your hands in your pockets. Take your hands from your pockets, Roger; and from your head, you blockhead you. See how Diggory carries his hands. They're a little too stiff, indeed, but that's no great matter.

Dig. Ay, mind how I hold them. I learned to hold my hands this way, when I was upon drill for the militia. And so being upon drill——

Hard. You must not be so talkative, Diggory. You must be all attention to the guests. You must hear us talk, and not think of talking; you must see us drink, and not think of drinking—you must see us eat, and not think of eating.

Dig. By the laws, your worship, that's parfectly unpossible. Whenever Diggory sees yeating going forward, ecod, he's always wishing for a mouthful himself.

Hard. Blockhead! Is not a belly-full in the kitchen as good as a belly-full in the parlour? Stay your stomach with that reflection.

Dig. Ecod, I thank your worship, I'll make a shift to stay my stomach with a slice of cold beef in the pantry.

Hard. Diggory, you are too talkative. Then if I happen to say a good thing, or tell a good story at table, you must not all burst out a-laughing, as if you made part of the company.

Dig. Then ecod, your worship must not tell the story of ould grouse in the gun-room : I can't help laughing at that—he! he! he!—for the soul of me. We have laughed at that these twenty years—ha! ha! ha!

Hard. Ha! ha! ha! The story is a good one. Well, honest Diggory, you may laugh at that—but still remember to be attentive. Suppose one of the company should call for a glass of wine, how will you behave? A glass of wine, Sir, if you please, (*To Diggory*)—Eh, why don't you move?

Dig. Ecod, your worship, I never have courage till I see the eatables and drinkables brought upo' the table, and then I'm as bauld as a lion.

Hard. What, will nobody move?

First Serv. I'm not to leave this place.

Second Serv. I'm sure it's no place of mine.

Third Serv. Nor mine, for sartain.

Dig. Wauns, and I'm sure it canna be mine.

Hard. You numbskulls! and so while, like your betters, you are quarrelling for places, the guests must be starved. O you dunces! I find I must begin all over again——But don't I hear a coach drive into the yard? To your posts, you blockheads. I'll go in the mean time, and give my old friend's son a hearty reception at the gate.   [*Exit Hardcastle.*

Dig. By the elevens, my place is gone quite out of my head.

Roger. I know that my place is to be every where.

First Serv. Where the devil is mine ?

Second Serv. My place is to be no where at all ; and so ize go about my business. [*Exeunt servants, running about as if frighted, different ways.*

Enter Servant with candles, shewing in Marlow and Hastings.

Serv. Welcome, gentlemen, very welcome ! This way.

Hast. After the disappointments of the day, welcome once more, Charles, to the comforts of a clean room, and a good fire. Upon my word, a very well-looking house, antique but creditable.

Marl. The usual fate of a large mansion. Having first ruined the master by good house-keeping, it at last comes to levy contributions as an inn.

Hast. As you say, we passengers are to be taxed to pay all these fineries. I have often seen a good side-board, or a marble chimney-piece, though not actually put in the bill, inflame a reckoning confoundedly.

Marl. Travellers, George, must pay in all places : the only difference is, that in good inns you pay dearly for luxuries ; in bad inns you are fleeced and starved.

Hast. You have lived pretty much among them. In truth, I have been often surprised, that you who have seen so much of the world, with your natural good sense, and your many opportunities, could never yet acquire a requisite share of assurance.

Marl. The Englishman's malady. But tell me, George, where could I have learned that assurance you talk of ? My life has been chiefly spent in a college or an inn, in seclusion from that lovely part of the creation that chiefly

teach men confidence. I don't know that I was ever
familiarly acquainted with a single modest woman, except my mother—But among females of another class,
you know—

Hast. Ay, among them you are impudent enough of
all conscience.

Marl. They are of *us*, you know.

Hast. But in the company of women of reputation
I never saw such an ideot, such a trembler; you look for
all the world as if you wanted an opportunity of stealing
out of the room.

Marl. Why, man, that's because I do want to steal out
of the room. Faith, I have often formed a resolution to
break the ice, and rattle away at any rate. But I don't
know how, a single glance from a pair of fine eyes has
totally overset my resolution. An impudent fellow may
counterfeit modesty : But I'll be hanged if a modest man
can ever counterfeit impudence.

Hast. If you could but say half the fine things to them,
that I have heard you lavish upon the bar-maid of an inn,
or even a college bed-maker—

Marl. Why, George, I can't say fine things to them ;
they freeze, they petrify me. They may talk of a comet,
or a burning mountain, or some such bagatelle. But to
me, a modest woman, drest out in all her finery, is the
most tremendous object of the whole creation.

Hast. Ha ! ha ! ha ! At this rate, man, how can you
ever expect to marry ?

Marl. Never, unless, as among kings and princes, my
bride were to be courted by proxy. If, indeed, like an
eastern bridegroom, one were to be introduced to a wife
he never saw before, it might be endured. But to go
through all the terrors of a formal courtship, together
with the episode of aunts, grandmothers, and cousins, and
at last to blurt out the broad staring question of, ' Madam,

will you marry me ?' No, no, that's a strain much above me, I assure you.

Hast. I pity you. But how do you intend behaving to the lady you are come down to visit at the request of your father.

Marl. As I behave to all other ladies. Bow very low. Answer yes or no to all her demands—But for the rest, I don't think I shall venture to look in her face till I see my father's again.

Hast. I'm surprised that one who is so warm a friend can be so cool a lover.

Marl. To be explicit, my dear Hastings, my chief inducement down was to be instrumental in forwarding your happiness, not my own. Miss Neville loves you, the family don't know you, as my friend you are sure of a reception, and let honour do the rest.

Hast. My dear Marlow ! But I'll suppress the emotion. Were I a wretch, meanly seeking to carry off a fortune, you should be the last man in the world I would apply to for assistance. But Miss Neville's person is all I ask, and that is mine, both from her deceased father's consent, and her own inclination.

Marl. Happy man ! You have talents and art to captivate any woman. I'm doom'd to adore the sex, and yet to converse with the only part of it I despise. This stammer in my address, and this aukward prepossessing visage of mine, can never permit me to soar above the reach of a milliner's 'prentice, or one of the duchesses of Drury-lane. Pshaw ! this fellow here to interrupt us !

Enter Hardcastle.

Hard. Gentlemen, once more you are heartily welcome. Which is Mr. Marlow ? Sir, you are heartily welcome. It's not my way, you see, to receive my friends with my back to the fire. I like to give them a hearty reception in the old style, at my gate. I like to see their horses and trunks taken care of.

Marl. (*Aside.*) He has got our names from the servants already. (*To him.*) We approve your caution and hospitality, Sir. (*To Hastings.*) I have been thinking, George, of changing our travelling dresses in the morning. I am grown confoundedly ashamed of mine.

Hard. I beg, Mr. Marlow, you'll use no ceremony in this house.

Hast. I fancy, Charles, you're right : the first blow is half the battle. I intend opening the campaign with the white and gold.

Hard. Mr. Marlow—Mr. Hastings—gentlemen—pray be under no restraint in this house. This is Liberty-hall, gentlemen. You may do just as you please here.

Marl. Yet, George, if we open the campaign too fiercely at first, we may want ammunition before it is over. I think to reserve the embroidery to secure a retreat.

Hard. Your talking of a retreat, Mr. Marlow, puts me in mind of the Duke of Marlborough, when we went to besiege Denain He first summoned the garrison—

Marl. Don't you think the *ventre dor* waistcoat will do with the plain brown ?

Hard. He first summoned the garrison, which might consist of about five thousand men——

Hast. I think not : brown and yellow mix but very poorly.

Hard. I say, gentlemen, as I was telling you, he summoned the garrison, which might consist of about five thousand men——

Marl. The girls like finery.

Hard. Which might consist of about five thousand men, well appointed with stores, ammunition, and other implements of war. 'Now,' says the Duke of Marlborough to George Brooks, that stood next to him—You must have heard of George Brooks—' I'll pawn my dukedom,' says he, ' but I take that garrison without spilling a drop of blood.' So——

Marl. What, my good friend, if you gave us a glass of punch in the mean time, it would help us to carry on the siege with vigour.

Hard. Punch, Sir! (*Aside.*) This is the most unaccountable kind of modesty I ever met with.

Marl. Yes, Sir, punch. A glass of warm punch, after our journey, will be comfortable. This is Liberty-hall, you know.

Hard. Here 's cup, Sir.

Marl. (*Aside.*) So this fellow, in his Liberty-hall, will only let us have just what he pleases.

Hard. (*Taking the cup.*) I hope you'll find it to your mind. I have prepared it with my own hands, and I believe you'll own the ingredients are tolerable. Will you be so good as to pledge me, Sir? Here, Mr. Marlow, here is to our better acquaintance. (*Drinks.*)

Marl. (*Aside.*) A very impudent fellow this! but he 's a character, and I'll humour him a little. Sir, my service to you. (*Drinks.*)

Hast. (*Aside.*) I see this fellow wants to give us his company, and forgets that he 's an innkeeper, before he has learned to be a gentleman.

Marl. From the excellence of your cup, my old friend, I suppose you have a good deal of business in this part of the country. Warm work, now and then at elections, I suppose.

Hard. No, Sir, I have long given that work ove Since our betters have hit upon the expedient of electii each other, there is no business ' for us that sell ale.'

Hast. So, then, you have no turn for politics, I find

Hard. Not in the least. There was a time, indee fretted myself about the mistakes of government, other people ; but finding myself every day grow more angry, and the government growing no better, I left it to mend itself. Since that, I no more trouble my head about Heyder Ally or Ally Cawn, than about Ally Croaker. Sir, my service to you.

Hast. So that with eating above stairs, and drinking below, with receiving your friends within, and amusing them without, you lead a good pleasant bustling life of it.

Hard. I do stir about a great deal, that's certain. Half the differences of the parish are adjusted in this very parlour.

Marl. (*After drinking.*) And you have an argument in your cup, old gentleman, better than any in Westminster-hall.

Hard. Ay, young gentleman, that, and a little philosophy.

Marl. (*Aside.*) Well, this is the first time I e— ——heard of an inn-keeper's philosophy.

Hast. So then, like an experienced general, you attack them on every quarter. If you find their reason manageable, you attack it with your philosophy ; if you find they have no reason, you attack them with this. Here's your health, my philosopher.   (*Drinks.*)

Hard. Good, very good, thank you ; ha ! ha ! ha ! Your generalship puts me in mind of Prince Eugene, when he fought the Turks at the battle of Belgrade. You shall hear.

Marl. Instead of the battle of Belgrade, I believe it's almost time to talk about supper. What has your philosophy got in the house for supper ?

Hard. For supper, Sir ; (*Aside.*) Was ever such a request to a man in his own house !

Marl. Yes, Sir, supper, Sir ; I begin to feel an appetite. I shall make dev'lish work to-night in the larder, I promise you.

Hard. (*Aside.*) Such a brazen dog, sure, never my eyes beheld. (*To him.*) Why, really, Sir, as for supper I can't well tell. My Dorothy, and the cook-maid settle these things between them. I leave these kind of things entirely to them.

Marl. You do, do you.

Hard. Entirely. By the by, I believe they are in actual consultation upon what's for supper this moment in the kitchen.

Marl. Then I beg they'll admit me as one of their privy council. It's a way I have got. When I travel I always chuse to regulate my own supper. Let the cook be called. No offence, I hope, Sir.

Hard. O no, Sir, none in the least ; yet I don't know how : our Bridget, the cook-maid, is not very communicative upon these occasions. Should we send for her, she might scold us all out of the house.

Hast. Let's see your list of the larder then. I ask it as a favour. I always match my appetite to my bill of fare.

Marl. (*To Hardcastle, who looks at them with surprize.*) Sir, he's very right, and it's my way too.

Hard. Sir, you have a right to command here. Here, Roger, bring us the bill of fare for to-night's supper. I believe it's drawn out. Your manner, Mr. Hastings, puts me in mind of my uncle, colonel Wallop. It was a saying of his, that no man was sure of his supper till he had eaten it.

Hast. (*Aside.*) All upon the high rope ! His uncle a colonel ! we shall soon hear of his mother being a justice of the peace. But let's hear the bill of fare.

Marl. (*Perusing.*) What's here ? For the first course ; for the second course ; for the dessert. The devil, Sir, do you think we have brought down the whole Joiners' Company, or the corporation of Bedford, to eat up such a supper ? Two or three little things, clean and comfortable, will do.

Hast. But let 's hear it.

Marl. (*Reading.*) For the first course at the top, a pig, and pruin sauce.

Hast. Damn your pig, I say.

Marl. And damn your pruin sauce, say I.

Hard. And yet, gentlemen, to men that are hungry, pig with pruin sauce is very good eating.

Marl. At the bottom a calf's tongue and brains.

Hast. Let your brains be knock'd out, my good Sir, I don't like them.

Marl. Or you may clap them on a plate by themselves. I do.

Hard. (*Aside*). Their impudence confounds me. (*To them.*) Gentlemen, you are my guests, make what alterations you please. Is there any thing else you wish to retrench or alter, gentlemen ?

Marl. Item. A pork pye, a boiled rabbit and sausages, a Florentine, a shaking pudding, and a dish of tiff—taff—taffety cream.

Hast. Confound your made dishes, I shall be as much at a loss in this house as at a green and yellow dinner at the French ambassador's table. I'm for plain eating.

Hard. I'm sorry, gentlemen, that I have nothing you like, but if there be any thing you have a particular fancy to——

Marl. Why, really, Sir, your bill of fare is so exquisite. that any one part of it is full as good as another. Send us what you please. So much for supper. And now to see that our beds are air'd, and properly taken care of.

Hard. I entreat you'll leave all that to me. You shall not stir a step.

Marl. Leave that to you ! I protest, Sir, you must excuse me, I always look to these things myself.

Hard. I must insist, Sir, you'll make yourself easy on that head.

Marl. You see I'm resolv'd on it. (*Aside.*) A very troublesome fellow this, as ever I met with.

Hard. Well, Sir, I'm resolved at least to attend you. (*Aside.*) This may be modern modesty, but I never saw any thing look so like old-fashion'd impudence.

[*Exeunt Marlow and Hardcastle.*

Hast. (*Alone.*) So I find this fellow's civilities begin to grow troublesome. But who can be angry at those assiduities which are meant to please him ? Ha ! what do I see ? Miss Neville, by all that 's happy !

Enter Miss Neville.

Miss Nev. My dear Hastings ! To what unexpected good fortune ! to what accident, am I to ascribe this happy meeting ?

Hast. Rather let me ask the same question, as I could never have hoped to meet my dearest Constance at an inn.

Miss Nev. An inn ! sure, you mistake ! my aunt, my guardian, lives here. What could induce you to think this house an inn ?

Hast. My friend, Mr. Marlow, with whom I came down, and I have been sent here as to an inn, I assure you. A young fellow whom we accidentally met at a house hard by directed us hither.

Miss Nev. Certainly it must be one of my hopeful cousin's tricks, of whom you have heard me talk so often, ha ! ha ! ha !

Hast. He whom your aunt intends for you ? he of whom I have such just apprehensions ?

Miss Nev. You have nothing to fear from him, I assure you. You'd adore him if you knew how heartily he despises me. My aunt knows it too, and has undertaken to court me for him, and actually begins to think she has made a conquest.

Hast. Thou dear dissembler! You must know, my Constance, I have just seized this happy opportunity of my friend's visit here to get admittance into the family. The horses that carried us down are now fatigued with their journey, but they'll soon be refreshed; and then, if my dearest girl will trust in her faithful Hastings, we shall soon be landed in France, where even among slaves the laws of marriage are respected.

Miss Nev. I have often told you, that though ready to obey you, I yet should leave my little fortune behind with reluctance. The greatest part of it was left me by my uncle, the India director, and chiefly consists in jewels. I have been for some time persuading my aunt to let me wear them. I fancy I'm very near succeeding. The instant they are put into my possession you shall find me ready to make them and myself yours.

Hast. Perish the baubles! Your person is all I desire. In the mean time my friend Marlow must not be let into his mistake. I know the strange reserve of his temper is such, that if abruptly informed of it, he would instantly quit the house before our plan was ripe for execution.

Miss Nev. But how shall we keep him in the deception? Miss Hardcastle is just returned from walking; what if we still continue to deceive him?——This, this way——

[They confer.

Enter Marlow.

Marl. The assiduities of these good people teize me beyond bearing. My host seems to think it ill manners to leave me alone, and so he claps not only himself but his old-fashioned wife on my back. They talk of coming to sup with us too; and then, I suppose, we are to run the gauntlet through all the rest of the family.—What have we got here!

Hast. My dear Charles ! Let me congratulate you !— The most fortunate accident !—Who do you think is just alighted ?

Marl. Cannot guess.

Hast. Our mistresses, boy, Miss Hardcastle and Miss Neville. Give me leave to introduce Miss Constance Neville to your acquaintance. Happening to dine in the neighbourhood, they called on their return to take fresh horses here. Miss Hardcastle has just stept into the next room, and will be back in an instant. Wasn't it lucky ? eh !

Marl. (*Aside.*) I have been mortified enough of all conscience, and here comes something to complete my embarrassment.

Hast. Well, but wasn't it the most fortunate thing in the world ?

Marl. Oh ! yes. Very fortunate—a most joyful encounter—But our dresses, George, you know are in disorder—What if we should postpone the happiness 'till to-morrow ?—To-morrow at her own house—It will be every bit as convenient—and rather more respectful— To-morrow let it be. [*Offering to go.*

Miss Nev. By no means, Sir. Your ceremony will displease her. The disorder of your dress will shew the ardour of your impatience. Besides, she knows you are in the house, and will permit you to see her.

Marl. O ! the devil ! how shall I support it ? hem ! hem ! Hastings, you must not go. You are to assist me, you know. I shall be confoundedly ridiculous. Yet, hang it ! I'll take courage. Hem !

Hast. Pshaw, man ! it's but the first plunge, and all's over. She's but a woman, you know.

Marl. And of all women, she that I dread most to encounter.

Enter Miss Hardcastle, as returned from walking.

Hast. (*Introducing them.*) Miss Hardcastle. Mr. Marlow. I'm proud of bringing two persons of such merit together, that only want to know to esteem each other.

Miss Hard. (*Aside.*) Now, for meeting my modest gentleman with a demure face, and quite in his own manner. (*After a pause, in which he appears very uneasy and disconcerted.*) I'm glad of your safe arrival, Sir.— I'm told you had some accidents by the way.

Marl. Only a few, madam. Yes, we had some. Yes, madam, a good many accidents, but should be sorry— madam—or rather glad of any accidents—that are so agreeably concluded. Hem!

Hast. (*To him.*) You never spoke better in your whole life. Keep it up, and I'll insure you the victory.

Miss Hard. I'm afraid you flatter, Sir. You that have seen so much of the finest company can find little entertainment in an obscure corner of the country.

Marl. (*Gathering courage.*) I have lived, indeed, in the world, madam : but I have kept very little company. I have been but an observer upon life, madam, while others were enjoying it.

Miss Nev. But that, I am told, is the way to enjoy it at last.

Hast. (*To him.*) Cicero never spoke better. Once more, and you are confirmed in assurance for ever.

Marl. (*To him.*) Hem! stand by me then, and when I'm down, throw in a word or two to set me up again.

Miss Hard. An observer, like you, upon life were, I fear, disagreeably employed, since you must have had much more to censure than to approve.

Marl. Pardon me, madam. I was always willing to be amused. The folly of most people is rather an object of mirth than uneasiness.

Hast. (*To him.*) Bravo, bravo. Never spoke so well in your whole life. Well! Miss Hardcastle, I see that you and Mr. Marlow are going to be very good company. I believe our being here will but embarrass the interview.

Marl. Not in the least, Mr. Hastings. We like your company of all things. (*To him.*) Zounds! George, sure you won't go? how can you leave us?

Hast. Our presence will but spoil conversation, so we'll retire to the next room. (*To him.*) You don't consider, man, that we are to manage a little tête-à-tête of our own.   [*Exeunt.*

Miss Hard. (*After a pause.*) But you have not been wholly an observer, I presume, Sir : the ladies, I should hope, have employed some part of your addresses.

Marl. (*Relapsing into timidity.*) Pardon me, madam, I—I—I—as yet have studied—only—to—deserve them.

Miss Hard. And that, some say, is the very worst way to obtain them.

Marl. Perhaps so, madam. But I love to converse only with the more grave and sensible part of the sex.— But I'm afraid I grow tiresome.

Miss Hard. Not at all, Sir ; there is nothing I like so much as grave conversation myself; I could hear it for ever. Indeed I have often been surprised how a man of sentiment could ever admire those light airy pleasures, where nothing reaches the heart.

Marl. It's——a disease——of the mind, madam. In the variety of tastes there must be some who wanting a relish——for——um—a—um.

Miss Hard. I understand you, Sir. There must be some, who, wanting a relish for refined pleasures, pretend to despise what they are incapable of tasting.

Marl. My meaning, madam, but infinitely better expressed. And I can't help observing——a——

Miss Hard. (*Aside.*) Who could ever suppose this

fellow impudent upon such occasions. (*To him.*) You were going to observe, Sir——

Marl. I was observing, madam—I protest, madam, I forget what I was going to observe.

Miss Hard. (*Aside.*) I vow and so do I. (*To him.*) You were observing, Sir, that in this age of hypocrisy—something about hypocrisy, Sir.

Marl. Yes, madam. In this age of hypocrisy there are few who upon strict enquiry do not—a—a—a—

Miss Hard. I understand you perfectly, Sir.

Marl. (*Aside.*) Egad! and that's more than I do myself.

Miss Hard. You mean that in this hypocritical age there are few that do not condemn in public what they practise in private, and think they pay every debt to virtue when they praise it.

Marl. True, madam; those who have most virtue in their mouths, have least of it in their bosoms. But I'm sure I tire you, madam.

Miss Hard. Not in the least, Sir; there's something so agreeable and spirited in your manner, such life and force—pray, Sir, go on.

Marl. Yes, madam, I was saying——that there are some occasions—when a total want of courage, madam, destroys all the——and puts us——upon a—a—a—

Miss Hard. I agree with you entirely, a want of courage upon some occasions assumes the appearance of ignorance, and betrays us when we most want to excel. I beg you'll proceed.

Marl. Yes, madam. Morally speaking, madam—But I see Miss Neville expecting us in the next room. I would not intrude for the world.

Miss Hard. I protest, Sir, I never was more agreeably entertained in all my life. Pray go on.

Marl. Yes, madam, I was—But she beckons us to join

her. Madam, shall I do myself the honour to attend you.

Miss Hard. Well then, I'll follow.

Marl. (*Aside.*) This pretty smooth dialogue has done for me.   [*Exit.*

Miss Hard. (*Alone.*) Ha! ha! ha! Was there ever such a sober sentimental interview? I'm certain he scarce look'd in my face the whole time. Yet the fellow, but for his unaccountable bashfulness, is pretty well too. He has good sense, but then so buried in his fears, that it fatigues one more than ignorance. If I could teach him a little confidence, it would be doing somebody that I know of a piece of service. But who is that somebody? —That, faith, is a question I can scarce answer.   [*Exit.*

Enter Tony and Miss Neville, followed by Mrs. Hardcastle and Hastings.

Tony. What do you follow me for, Cousin Con? I wonder you're not ashamed to be so very engaging.

Miss Nev. I hope, cousin, one may speak to one's own relations, and not be to blame.

Tony. Ay, but I know what sort of a relation you want to make me, though; but it won't do. I tell you, Cousin Con, it won't do; so I beg you'll keep your distance, I want no nearer relationship.

            [*She follows, coquetting him, to the back scene.*

Mrs. Hard. Well! I vow, Mr. Hastings, you are very entertaining. There is nothing in the world I love to talk of so much as London, and the fashions, though I was never there myself.

Hast. Never there! You amaze me! From your air and manner, I concluded you had been bred all your life either at Ranelagh, St. James's, or Tower Wharf.

Mrs. Hard. O! Sir, you're only pleased to say so. We country persons can have no manner at all. I'm in love

with the town, and that serves to raise me above some of
our neighbouring rustics ; but who can have a manner,
that has never seen the Pantheon, the Grotto Gardens,
the Borough, and such places where the nobility chiefly
resort ? All I can do is to enjoy London at second-hand.
I take care to know every tête-à-tête from the Scandalous
Magazine, and have all the fashions, as they come out in
a letter from the two Miss Rickets of Crooked-Lane.
Pray how do you like this head, Mr. Hastings ?

Hast. Extremely elegant and dégagée, upon my word,
madam. Your friseur is a Frenchman, I suppose ?

Mrs. Hard. I protest, I dressed it myself from a print
in the Ladies' Memorandum-book for the last year.

Hast. Indeed ! Such a head in a side-box at the play-
house would draw as many gazers as my Lady May'ress
at a City Ball.

Mrs. Hard. I vow, since inoculation began, there is no
such thing to be seen as a plain woman ; so one must
dress a little particular, or one may escape in the crowd.

Hast. But that can never be your case, madam, in any
dress. (*Bowing.*)

Mrs. Hard. Yet, what signifies my dressing when I
have such a piece of antiquity by my side as Mr. Hardcastle : all I can say will never argue down a single
button from his clothes. I have often wanted him to
throw off his great flaxen wig, and where he was bald, to
plaister it over, like my Lord Pately, with powder.

Hast. You are right, madam ; for, as among the ladies
there are none ugly, so among the men there are none old.

Mrs. Hard. But what do you think his answer was ?
Why, with his usual Gothic vivacity, he said I only
wanted him to throw off his wig to convert it into a tête
for my own wearing.

Hast. Intolerable ! At your age you may wear what
you please, and it must become you.

Mrs. Hard. Pray, Mr. Hastings, what do you take to be the most fashionable age about town ?

Hast. Some time ago, forty was all the mode ; but I'm told the ladies intend to bring up fifty for the ensuing winter.

Mrs. Hard. Seriously? Then I shall be too young for the fashion.

Hast. No lady begins now to put on jewels 'till she's past forty. For instance, Miss there, in a polite circle, would be considered as a child, as a mere maker of samplers.

Mrs. Hard. And yet Mrs. Niece thinks herself as much a woman, and is as fond of jewels as the oldest of us all.

Hast. Your niece, is she ? And that young gentleman, a brother of your's, I should presume ?

Mrs. Hard. My son, Sir. They are contracted to each other. Observe their little sports. They fall in and out ten times a day, as if they were man and wife already. (*To them.*) Well, Tony, child, what soft things are you saying to your Cousin Constance this evening ?

Tony. I have been saying no soft things ; but that it's very hard to be followed about so. Ecod ! I've not a place in the house now that's left to myself, but the stable.

Mrs. Hard. Never mind him, Con, my dear, he's in another story behind your back.

Miss Nev. There's something generous in my cousin's manner. He falls out before faces to be forgiven in private.

Tony. That's a damned confounded—crack.

Mrs. Hard. Ah ! he's a sly one. Don't you think they're like each other about the mouth, Mr. Hastings ? The Blenkinsop mouth to a T. They're of a size too. Back to back, my pretties, that Mr. Hastings may see you. Come Tony.

Tony. You had as good not make me, I tell you.

(*Measuring.*)

Miss Nev. O lud ! he has almost cracked my head.

Mrs. Hard. O, the monster ! For shame, Tony. You a man, and behave so !

Tony. If I'm a man, let me have my fortin. Ecod ! I'll not be made a fool of no longer.

Mrs. Hard. Is this, ungrateful boy, all that I'm to get for the pains I have taken in your education ? I that have rock'd you in your cradle, and fed that pretty mouth with a spoon ! Did not I work that waistcoat to make you genteel ? Did not I prescribe for you every day, and weep while the receipt was operating ?

Tony. Ecod ! you had reason to weep, for you have been dosing me ever since I was born. I have gone through every receipt in the 'Compleat Housewife' ten times over ; and you have thoughts of coursing me through Quincey next spring. But, ecod ! I tell you, I'll not be made a fool of no longer.

Mrs. Hard. Wasn't it all for your good, viper ? Wasn't it all for your good ?

Tony. I wish you'd let me and my good alone then. Snubbing this way when I'm in spirits. If I'm to have any good, let it come of itself ; not to keep dinging it, dinging it into one so.

Mrs. Hard. That 's false ; I never see you when you're in spirits. No, Tony, you then go to the alehouse or kennel. I'm never to be delighted with your agreeable wild notes, unfeeling monster !

Tony. Ecod ! mamma, your own notes are the wildest of the two.

Mrs. Hard. Was ever the like ? But I see he wants to break my heart, I see he does.

Hast. Dear madam, permit me to lecture the young

gentleman a little. I'm certain I can persuade him to his duty.

Mrs. Hard. Well! I must retire. Come, Constance, my love. You see, Mr. Hastings, the wretchedness of my situation; was ever poor woman so plagued with a dear, sweet, pretty, provoking, undutiful boy.

[*Exeunt Mrs. Hardcastle and Miss Neville.*

Hastings, Tony.

Tony. (*Singing.*) ' There was a young man riding by, and fain would have his will. Rang do didlo dee.'——Don't mind her. Let her cry. It's the comfort of her heart. I have seen her and sister cry over a book for an hour together, and they said, they liked the book the better the more it made them cry.

Hast. Then you're no friend to the ladies, I find, my pretty young gentleman?

Tony. That's as I find 'um.

Hast. Not to her of your mother's chusing, I dare answer? And yet she appears to me a pretty, well-tempered girl.

Tony. That's because you don't know her as well as I. Ecod! I know every inch about her; and there's not a more bitter cantanckerous toad in all Christendom.

Hast. (*Aside.*) Pretty encouragement this for a lover!

Tony. I have seen her since the height of *that*. She has as many tricks as a hare in a thicket, or a colt the first day's breaking.

Hast. To me she appears sensible and silent.

Tony. Ay, before company. But when she's with her playmates she's as loud as a hog in a gate.

Hast. But there is a meek modesty about her that charms me.

Tony. Yes, but curb her never so little, she kicks up, and you're flung in a ditch.

Hast. Well, but you must allow her a little beauty.—
Yes, you must allow her some beauty.

Tony. Bandbox! She's all a made-up thing, mun. Ah!
could you but see Bet Bouncer of these parts, you might
then talk of beauty. Ecod, she has two eyes as black as
sloes, and cheeks as broad and red as a pulpit cushion.
She'd make two of she.

Hast. Well, what say you to a friend that would take
this bitter bargain off your hands?

Tony. Anon.

Hast. Would you thank him that would take Miss
Neville, and leave you to happiness and your dear Betsy?

Tony. Ay; but where is there such a friend, for who
would take her?

Hast. I am he. If you but assist me, I'll engage to
whip her off to France, and you shall never hear more of
her

Tony. Assist you! Ecod, I will, to the last drop of my
blood. I'll clap a pair of horses to your chaise that shall
trundle you off in a twinkling, and may be get you a part
of her fortin beside in jewels, that you little dream of.

Hast. My dear 'squire, this looks like a lad of spirit.

Tony. Come along, then, and you shall see more of my
spirit before you have done with me.   (*Singing.*)

> We are the boys
> That fears no noise
> Where the thundering cannons roar.

[*Exeunt.*

ACT III

Enter Hardcastle, alone.

Hard. What could my old friend Sir Charles mean by recommending his son as the modestest young man in town ? To me he appears the most impudent piece of brass that ever spoke with a tongue. He has taken possession of the easy chair by the fire-side already. He took off his boots in the parlour and desired me to see them taken care of. I'm desirous to know how his impudence affects my daughter.—She will certainly be shocked at it.

Enter Miss Hardcastle, plainly dressed.

Hard. Well, my Kate, I see you have changed your dress, as I bid you ; and yet, I believe, there was no great occasion.

Miss Hard. I find such a pleasure, Sir, in obeying your commands, that I take care to observe them without ever debating their propriety.

Hard. And yet, Kate, I sometimes give you some cause, particularly when I recommended my modest gentleman to you as a lover to-day.

Miss Hard. You taught me to expect something extraordinary, and I find the original exceeds the description.

Hard. I was never so surprised in my life ! He has quite confounded all my faculties !

Miss Hard. I never saw any thing like it : and a man of the world too !

Hard. Ay, he learned it all abroad—what a fool was I, to think a young man could learn modesty by travelling. He might as soon learn wit at a masquerade.

Miss Hard. It seems all natural to him.

Hard. A good deal assisted by bad company and a French dancing-master.

Miss Hard. Sure you mistake, papa ! A French

dancing-master could never have taught him that timid look—that aukward address—that bashful manner—

Hard. Whose look ? whose manner, child ?

Miss Hard. Mr. Marlow's : his *mauvaise honte*, his timidity, struck me at the first sight.

Hard. Then your first sight deceived you ; for I think him one of the most brazen first sights that ever astonished my senses.

Miss Hard. Sure, Sir, you rally ! I never saw any one so modest.

Hard. And can you be serious ! I never saw such a bouncing, swaggering puppy since I was born. Bully Dawson was but a fool to him.

Miss Hard. Surprising ! He met me with a respectful bow, a stammering voice, and a look fixed on the ground.

Hard. He met me with a loud voice, a lordly air, and a familiarity that made my blood freeze again.

Miss Hard. He treated me with diffidence and respect ; censured the manners of the age ; admired the prudence of girls that never laughed ; tired me with apologies for being tiresome ; then left the room with a bow, and ' Madam, I would not for the world detain you.'

Hard. He spoke to me as if he knew me all his life before ; asked twenty questions, and never waited for an answer ; interrupted my best remarks with some silly pun ; and when I was in my best story of the Duke of Marlborough and Prince Eugene, he asked if I had not a good hand at making punch. Yes, Kate, he asked your father if he was a maker of punch.

Miss Hard. One of us must certainly be mistaken.

Hard. If he be what he has shewn himself, I'm determined he shall never have my consent.

Miss Hard. And if he be the sullen thing I take him, he shall never have mine.

Hard. In one thing then we are agreed—to reject him.

Miss Hard. Yes. But upon conditions. For if you should find him less impudent, and I more presuming ; if you find him more respectful, and I more importunate—— I don't know——the fellow is well enough for a man— Certainly we don't meet many such at a horse-race in the country.

Hard. If we should find him so——But that's impossible. The first appearance has done my business. I'm seldom deceived in that.

Miss Hard. And yet there may be many good qualities under that first appearance.

Hard. Ay, when a girl finds a fellow's outside to her taste, she then sets about guessing the rest of his furniture. With her a smooth face stands for good sense, and a genteel figure for every virtue.

Miss Hard. I hope, Sir, a conversation begun with a compliment to my good sense, won't end with a sneer at my understanding ?

Hard. Pardon me, Kate. But if young Mr. Brazen can find the art of reconciling contradictions, he may please us both, perhaps.

Miss Hard. And as one of us must be mistaken, what if we go to make farther discoveries ?

Hard. Agreed. But depend on't I'm in the right.

Miss Hard. And depend on't I'm not much in the wrong.   [*Exeunt.*

Enter Tony, running in with a casket.

Tony. Ecod ! I have got them. Here they are. My cousin Con's necklaces, bobs and all. My mother shan't cheat the poor souls out of their fortin neither. O ! my genus, is that you.

Enter Hastings.

Hast. My dear friend, how have you managed with your mother ? I hope you have amused her with pretending love for your cousin, and that you are willing to be reconciled at last ? Our horses will be refreshed in a short time, and we shall soon be ready to set off.

Tony. And here's something to bear your charges by the way (*giving the casket*), your sweetheart's jewels. Keep them, and hang those, I say, that would rob you of one of them.

Hast. But how have you procured them from your mother ?

Tony. Ask me no questions, and I'll tell you no fibs. I procured them by the rule of thumb. If I had not a key to every drawer in mother's bureau, how could I go to the alehouse so often as I do ? An honest man may rob himself of his own at any time.

Hast. Thousands do it every day. But to be plain with you, Miss Neville is endeavouring to procure them from her aunt this very instant. If she succeeds, it will be the most delicate way at least of obtaining them.

Tony. Well, keep them, till you know how it will be. But I know how it will be well enough, she'd as soon part with the only sound tooth in her head.

Hast. But I dread the effects of her resentment, when she finds she has lost them.

Tony. Never you mind her resentment, leave me to manage that. I don't value her resentment the bounce of a cracker. Zounds ! here they are. Morice ! Prance !
                                    [*Exit Hastings.*

Tony, Mrs. Hardcastle, and Miss Neville.

Mrs. Hard. Indeed, Constance, you amaze me. Such a girl as you want jewels ! It will be time enough for jewels, my dear, twenty years hence, when your beauty begins to want repairs.

Miss Nev. But what will repair beauty at forty, will certainly improve it at twenty, madam.

Mrs. Hard. Yours, my dear, can admit of none.   That natural blush is beyond a thousand ornaments.   Besides, child, jewels are quite out at present.   Don't you see half the ladies of our acquaintance, my lady Kill-day-light, and Mrs. Crump, and the rest of them carry their jewels to town, and bring nothing but paste and marcasites back.

Miss Nev. But who knows, madam, but somebody that shall be nameless would like me best with all my little finery about me ?

Mrs. Hard. Consult your glass, my dear, and then see if, with such a pair of eyes, you want any better sparklers. What do you think, Tony, my dear ? does your cousin Con want any jewels in your eyes to set off her beauty ?

Tony. That's as thereafter may be.

Miss Nev. My dear aunt, if you knew how it would oblige me !

Mrs. Hard. A parcel of old-fashioned rose and table cut things.   They would make you look like the court of King Solomon at a puppet-shew.   Besides, I believe, I can't readily come at them.   They may be missing, for aught I know to the contrary.

Tony. (*Apart to Mrs. Hardcastle.*) Then why don't you tell her so at once, as she's so longing for them ? Tell her they're lost.   It's the only way to quiet her.   Say they're lost, and call me to bear witness.

Mrs. Hard. (*Apart to Tony.*) You know, my dear, I'm only keeping them for you.   So if I say they're gone, you'll bear me witness, will you ? He ! he ! he !

Tony. Never fear me.   Ecod ! I'll say I saw them taken out with my own eyes.

Miss Nev. I desire them but for a day, madam.   Just to be permitted to shew them as relics, and then they may be locked up again.

Mrs. Hard. To be plain with you, my dear Constance ! if I could find them you should have them.   They're missing, I assure you. Lost for aught I know ; but we must have patience, wherever they are.

Miss Nev. I'll not believe it ; this is but a shallow pretence to deny me. I know they are too valuable to be so slightly kept, and as you are to answer for the loss—

Mrs. Hard. Don't be alarmed, Constance. If they be lost I must restore an equivalent. But my son knows they are missing, and not to be found.

Tony. That I can bear witness to. They are missing, and not to be found, I'll take my oath on 't.

Mrs. Hard. You must learn resignation, my dear ; for though we lose our fortune, yet we should not lose our patience. See me, how calm I am.

Miss Nev. Ay, people are generally calm at the misfortunes of others.

Mrs. Hard. Now I wonder a girl of your good sense should waste a thought upon such trumpery. We shall soon find them ; and in the mean time you shall make use of my garnets till your jewels be found.

Miss Nev. I detest garnets.

Mrs. Hard. The most becoming things in the world to set off a clear complexion. You have often seen how well they look upon me. You shall have them. [*Exit.*

Miss Nev. I dislike them of all things. You shan't stir.—Was ever any thing so provoking—to mislay my own jewels, and force me to wear her trumpery.

Tony. Don't be a fool. If she gives you the garnets, take what you can get. The jewels are your own already. I have stolen them out of her bureau, and she does not know it. Fly to your spark, he'll tell you more of the matter. Leave me to manage her.

Miss Nev. My dear cousin !

Tony. Vanish. She's here and has missed them already. [*Exit Miss Neville.*] Zounds ! how she fidgets and spits about like a catherine-wheel.

Enter Mrs. Hardcastle.

Mrs. Hard. Confusion! thieves! robbers! we are cheated, plundered, broke open, undone.

Tony. What's the matter, what's the matter, mamma? I hope nothing has happened to any of the good family!

Mrs. Hard. We are robbed. My bureau has been broken open, the jewels taken out, and I'm undone.

Tony. Oh! is that all? Ha! ha! ha! By the laws, I never saw it better acted in my life. Ecod, I thought you was ruined in earnest, ha! ha! ha!

Mrs. Hard. Why, boy, I'm ruined in earnest. My bureau has been broken open, and all taken away.

Tony. Stick to that; ha! ha! ha! stick to that. I'll bear witness you know, call me to bear witness.

Mrs. Hard. I tell you, Tony, by all that's precious, the jewels are gone, and I shall be ruined for ever.

Tony. Sure I know they are gone, and I'm to say so.

Mrs. Hard. My dearest Tony, but hear me. They're gone, I say.

Tony. By the laws, mamma, you make me for to laugh, ha! ha! I know who took them well enough, ha! ha! ha!

Mrs. Hard. Was there ever such a blockhead, that can't tell the difference between jest and earnest? I tell you I'm not in jest, booby.

Tony. That's right, that's right: you must be in a bitter passion, and then nobody will suspect either of us. I'll bear witness that they are gone.

Mrs. Hard. Was there ever such a cross-grain'd brute, that won't hear me? Can you bear witness that you're no better than a fool? Was ever poor woman so beset with fools on one hand, and thieves on the other.

Tony. I can bear witness to that.

Mrs. Hard. Bear witness again, you blockhead you, and I'll turn you out of the room directly. My poor

niece, what will become of her ! Do you laugh, you unfeeling brute, as if you enjoyed my distress ?

Tony. I can bear witness to that.

Mrs. Hard. Do you insult me, monster ? I'll teach
you to vex your mother, I will.

Tony. I can bear witness to that.

[*He runs off, she follows him.*

Enter Miss Hardcastle and Maid.

Miss Hard. What an unaccountable creature is that
brother of mine, to send them to the house as an inn, ha !
ha ! I don't wonder at his impudence.

Maid. But what is more, madam, the young gentleman, as you passed by in your present dress, ask'd me if
you were the bar-maid ? He mistook you for the bar-
maid, madam.

Miss Hard. Did he ? Then as I live I'm resolved to
keep up the delusion. Tell me, Pimple, how do you like
my present dress ? Don't you think I look something like
Cherry in the ' Beaux' Stratagem ' ?

Maid. It 's the dress, madam, that every lady wears
in the country, but when she visits or receives company.

Miss Hard. And are you sure he does not remember
my face or person ?

Maid. Certain of it.

Miss Hard. I vow, I thought so ; for though we spoke
for some time together, yet his fears were such that he
never once looked up during the interview. Indeed, if
he had, my bonnet would have kept him from seeing me.

Maid. But what do you hope from keeping him in his
mistake.

Miss Hard. In the first place I shall be seen, and that
is no small advantage to a girl who brings her face to
market. Then I shall perhaps make an acquaintance,
and that 's no small victory gained over one who never

addresses any but the wildest of her sex. But my chief
aim is to take my gentleman off his guard, and like an
invisible champion of romance, examine the giant's force
before I offer to combat.

Maid. But are you sure you can act your part, and
disguise your voice so that he may mistake that, as he
has already mistaken your person ?

Miss Hard. Never fear me. I think I have got the true
bar cant—Did your honour call ?——Attend the Lion
there.—Pipes and tobacco for the Angel.—The Lamb has
been outrageous this half hour.

Maid. It will do, madam. But he's here. [*Exit Maid.*

Enter Marlow.

Marl. What a bawling in every part of the house.
I have scarce a moment's repose. If I go to the best
room, there I find my host and his story. If I fly to the
gallery, there we have my hostess with her curtesy down
to the ground. I have at last got a moment to myself,
and now for recollection.   [*Walks and muses.*

Miss Hard. Did you call, Sir ? Did your honour call ?

Marl. (*Musing.*) As for Miss Hardcastle, she's too grave
and sentimental for me.

Miss Hard. Did your honour call ?

[*She still places herself before him, he turning away.*

Marl. No, child. (*musing.*) Besides, from the glimpse
I had of her, I think she squints.

Miss Hard. I'm sure, Sir, I heard the bell ring.

Marl. No, no. (*musing.*) I have pleased my father,
however, by coming down, and I'll to-morrow please
myself by returning.   [*Taking out his tablets, and perusing.*

Miss Hard. Perhaps the other gentleman called, Sir ?

Marl. I tell you, no.

Miss Hard. I should be glad to know, Sir. We have
such a parcel of servants.

Marl. No, no, I tell you. (*Looks full in her face.*) Yes, child, I think I did call. I wanted—I wanted—I vow, child, you are vastly handsome.

Miss Hard. O la, Sir, you'll make one asham'd.

Marl. Never saw a more sprightly malicious eye. Yes, yes, my dear, I did call. Have you got any of your—a—what d'ye call it, in the house ?

Miss Hard. No, Sir, we have been out of that these ten days.

Marl. One may call in this house, I find, to very little purpose. Suppose I should call for a taste, just by way of trial, of the nectar of your lips ; perhaps, I might be disappointed in that too.

Miss Hard. Nectar ! nectar ! That 's a liquor there 's no call for in these parts. French, I suppose. We keep no French wines here, Sir.

Marl. Of true English growth, I assure you.

Miss Hard. Then it 's odd I should not know it. We brew all sorts of wines in this house, and I have lived here these eighteen years.

Marl. Eighteen years ! Why one would think, child, you kept the bar before you was born. How old are you ?

Miss Hard. O ! Sir, I must not tell my age. They say women and music should never be dated.

Marl. To guess at this distance you can't be much above forty (*approaching.*) Yet nearer I don't think so much (*approaching.*) By coming close to some women, they look younger still ; but when we come very close indeed—(*attempting to kiss her.*)

Miss Hard. Pray, Sir, keep your distance. One would think you wanted to know one's age as they do horses, by mark of mouth.

Marl. I protest, child, you use me extremely ill. If you keep me at this distance, how is it possible you and I can ever be acquainted.

Miss Hard. And who wants to be acquainted with you? I want no such acquaintance, not I. I'm sure you did not treat Miss Hardcastle that was here awhile ago in this obstropalous manner. I'll warrant me, before her you look'd dash'd and kept bowing to the ground, and talk'd, for all the world, as if you was before a Justice of Peace.

Marl. (*Aside.*) Egad! She has hit it, sure enough. (*To her.*) In awe of her, child? Ha! ha! ha! A mere aukward squinting thing, no, no. I find you don't know me. I laughed and rallied her a little; but I was unwilling to be too severe. No, I could not be too severe, curse me!

Miss Hard. O! then, Sir, you are a favourite, I find, among the ladies?

Marl. Yes, my dear, a great favourite. And yet, hang me, I don't see what they find in me to follow. At the Ladies' Club in town I'm called their agreeable Rattle. Rattle, child, is not my real name, but one I'm known by. My name is Solomons, Mr. Solomons, my dear, at your service.   [*Offering to salute her.*

Miss Hard. Hold, Sir, you are introducing me to your Club, not to yourself. And you're so great a favourite there, you say?

Marl. Yes, my dear. There's Mrs. Mantrap, lady Betty Blackleg, the Countess of Sligo, Mrs. Langhorns, old Miss Biddy Buckskin, and your humble servant, keep up the spirit of the place.

Miss Hard. Then it is a very merry place, I suppose?

Marl. Yes, as merry as cards, supper, wine, and old women can make us.

Miss Hard. And their agreeable Rattle, ha! ha! ha!

Marl. (*Aside.*) Egad! I don't quite like this chit. She seems knowing, methinks. You laugh, child?

Miss Hard. I can't but laugh to think what time they all have for minding their work or their family.

Marl. (*Aside*) All's well ; she don't laugh at me. (*To her.*) Do you ever work, child ?

Miss Hard. Ay, sure. There's not a screen or a quilt in the whole house but what can bear witness to that.

Marl. Odso! then you must shew me your embroidery. I embroider and draw patterns myself a little. If you want a judge of your work you must apply to me.

[*Seizing her hand.*

Miss Hard. Ay, but the colours do not look well by candle-light. You shall see all in the morning.

[*Struggling.*

Marl. And why not now, my angel ? Such beauty fires beyond the power of resistance.——Pshaw ! the father here ! My old luck : I never nick'd seven that I did not throw ames ace three times following. [*Exit Marlow.*

Enter Hardcastle, who stands in surprise.

Hard. So, madam. So I find this is your modest lover. This is your humble admirer that kept his eyes fixed on the ground, and only ador'd at humble distance. Kate, Kate, art thou not ashamed to deceive your father so.

Miss Hard. Never trust me, dear papa, but he's still the modest man I first took him for, you'll be convinced of it as well as I.

Hard. By the hand of my body, I believe his impudence is infectious ! Didn't I see him seize your hand ? Didn't I see him hawl you about like a milk-maid ? and now you talk of his respect and his modesty, forsooth !

Miss Hard. But if I shortly convince you of his modesty, that he has only the faults that will pass off with time, and the virtues that will improve with age, I hope you'll forgive him.

Hard. The girl would actually make one run mad ! I tell you I'll not be convinced. I am convinced. He has scarce been three hours in the house, and he has already encroached on all my prerogatives. You may like his impudence, and call it modesty. But my son-in-law, madam, must have very different qualifications.

Miss Hard. Sir, I ask but this night to convince you.

Hard. You shall not have half the time, for I have thoughts of turning him out this very hour.

Miss Hard. Give me that hour then, and I hope to satisfy you.

Hard. Well, an hour let it be, then. But I'll have no trifling with your father. All fair and open, do you mind me.

Miss Hard. I hope, Sir, you have ever found that I considered your commands as my pride ; for your kindness is such, that my duty as yet has been inclination.

[*Exeunt.*

ACT IV

Enter Hastings and Miss Neville.

Hast. You surprise me ! Sir Charles Marlow expected here this night ? Where have you had your information !

Miss Nev. You may depend upon it. I just saw his letter to Mr. Hardcastle, in which he tells him he intends setting out a few hours after his son.

Hast. Then, my Constance, all must be completed before he arrives. He knows me ; and should he find me here, would discover my name, and perhaps my designs, to the rest of the family.

Miss Nev. The jewels, I hope, are safe.

Hast. Yes, yes. I have sent them to Marlow, who

keeps the keys of our baggage. In the mean time I'll go to prepare matters for our elopement. I have had the 'squire's promise of a fresh pair of horses ; and if I should not see him again, will write him farther directions.

[*Exit.*

Miss Nev. Well ! success attend you. In the mean time I'll go amuse my aunt with the old pretence of a violent passion for my cousin. [*Exit.*

Enter Marlow, followed by a Servant.

Marl. I wonder what Hastings could mean by sending me so valuable a thing as a casket to keep for him, when he knows the only place I have is the seat of a post-coach at an inn-door. Have you deposited the casket with the landlady, as I ordered you. Have you put it into her own hands ?

Serv. Yes, your honour.

Marl. She said she'd keep it safe, did she ?

Serv. Yes, she said she'd keep it safe enough; she ask'd me how I came by it ? and she said she had a great mind to make me give an account of myself. [*Exit Servant.*

Marl. Ha ! ha ! ha ! They're safe, however. What an unaccountable set of beings have we got amongst ! This little bar-maid though runs in my head most strangely, and drives out the absurdities of all the rest of the family. She 's mine, she must be mine, or I'm greatly mistaken.

Enter Hastings.

Hast. Bless me ! I quite forgot to tell her that I intended to prepare at the bottom of the garden. Marlow here, and in spirits too.

Marl. Give me joy, George ! Crown me, shadow me with laurels ! Well, George, after all, we modest fellows don't want for success among the women.

Hast. Some women, you mean. But what success has

your honour's modesty been crowned with now that it grows so insolent upon us ?

Marl. Didn't you see the tempting, brisk, lovely, little thing, that runs about the house with a bunch of keys to its girdle.

Hast. Well, and what then ?

Marl. She 's mine, you rogue you. Such fire, such motion, such eyes, such lips—but, egad ! she would not let me kiss them though.

Hast. But are you sure, so very sure of her ?

Marl. Why, man, she talk'd of shewing me her work above stairs, and I am to approve the pattern.

Hast. But how can you, Charles, go about to rob a woman of her honour ?

Marl. Pshaw ! pshaw ! We all know the honour of the bar-maid of an inn. I don't intend to rob her, take my word for it; there 's nothing in this house I shan't honestly pay for.

Hast. I believe the girl has virtue.

Marl. And if she has, I should be the last man in the world that would attempt to corrupt it.

Hast. You have taken care, I hope, of the casket I sent you to lock up ? It 's in safety ?

Marl. Yes, yes. It 's safe enough. I have taken care of it. But how could you think the seat of a post-coach at an inn door a place of safety ? Ah ! numbskull ! I have taken better precautions for you than you did for yourself——I have——

Hast. What !

Marl. I have sent it to the landlady to keep for you.

Hast. To the landlady !

Marl. The landlady !

Hast. You did ?

Marl. I did. She 's to be answerable for its forth-coming, you know.

Hast. Yes, she'll bring it forth, with a witness.

Marl. Wasn't I right ? I believe you'll allow that I acted prudently upon this occasion ?

Hast. (*Aside.*) He must not see my uneasiness.

Marl. You seem a little disconcerted though, me-thinks. Sure nothing has happened ?

Hast. No, nothing. Never was in better spirits in all my life. And so you left it with the landlady, who, no doubt, very readily undertook the charge.

Marl. Rather too readily. For she not only kept the casket ; but, through her great precaution, was going to keep the messenger too. Ha ! ha ! ha !

Hast. He ! he ! he ! They're safe, however.

Marl. As a guinea in a miser's purse.

Hast. (*Aside.*) So now all hopes of fortune are at an end, and we must set off without it. (*To him.*) Well, Charles, I'll leave you to your meditations on the pretty bar-maid, and, he ! he ! he ! may you be as successful for yourself, as you have been for me. [*Exit.*

Marl. Thank ye, George ! I ask no more. Ha ! ha ! ha !

Enter Hardcastle.

Hard. I no longer know my own house. It's turned all topsey-turvey. His servants have got drunk already. I'll bear it no longer, and yet from my respect for his father, I'll be calm. (*To him.*) Mr. Marlow, your servant. I'm your very humble servant. [*Bowing low.*

Marl. Sir, your humble servant. (*Aside.*) What's to be the wonder now ?

Hard. I believe, Sir, you must be sensible, Sir, that no man alive ought to be more welcome than your father's son, Sir. I hope you think so ?

Marl. I do from my soul, Sir. I don't want much intreaty. I generally make my father's son welcome wherever he goes.

Hard. I believe you do, from my soul, Sir. But though I say nothing to your own conduct, that of your servants is insufferable. Their manner of drinking is setting a very bad example in this house, I assure you.

Marl. I protest, my very good Sir, that is no fault of mine. If they don't drink as they ought, *they* are to blame. I ordered them not to spare the cellar. I did, I assure you. (*To the side scene.*) Here, let one of my servants come up. (*To him.*) My positive directions were, that as I did not drink myself, they should make up for my deficiencies below.

Hard. Then they had your orders for what they do ! I'm satisfied !

Marl. They had, I assure you. You shall hear from one of themselves.

Enter Servant, drunk.

Marl. You, Jeremy ! Come forward, sirrah ! What were my orders ? Were you not told to drink freely, and call for what you thought fit, for the good of the house ?

Hard. (*Aside.*) I begin to lose my patience.

Jer. Please your honour, Liberty and Fleet-street for ever ! Though I'm but a servant, I'm as good as another man. I'll drink for no man before supper, Sir, dammy ! Good liquor will sit upon a good supper, but a good supper will not sit upon——hiccup——upon my conscience, Sir.

Marl. You see, my old friend, the fellow is as drunk as he can possibly be. I don't know what you'd have more, unless you'd have the poor devil soused in a beer-barrel.

Hard. Zounds ! he'll drive me distracted, if I contain myself any longer. Mr. Marlow. Sir ; I have submitted to your insolence for more than four hours, and I see no likelihood of its coming to an end. I'm now resolved to be master here, Sir, and I desire that you and your drunken pack may leave my house directly.

Marl. Leave your house!——Sure you jest, my good friend ? What, when I'm doing what I can to please you.

Hard. I tell you, Sir, you don't please me ; so I desire you'll leave my house.

Marl. Sure you cannot be serious ? at this time o' night, and such a night. You only mean to banter me ?

Hard. I tell you, Sir, I'm serious ! and now that my passions are rouzed, I say this house is mine, Sir ; this house is mine, and I command you to leave it directly.

Marl. Ha ! ha ! ha ! A puddle in a storm. I shan't stir a step, I assure you. (*In a serious tone.*) This your house, fellow ! It's my house. This is my house. Mine, while I chuse to stay. What right have you to bid me leave this house, Sir ? I never met with such impudence, curse me, never in my whole life before.

Hard. Nor I, confound me if ever I did. To come to my house, to call for what he likes, to turn me out of my own chair, to insult the family, to order his servants to get drunk, and then to tell me, ' This house is mine, Sir.' By all that's impudent, it makes me laugh. Ha ! ha ! ha ! Pray, Sir, (*bantering*) as you take the house, what think you of taking the rest of the furniture ? There's a pair of silver candlesticks, and there's a fire-screen, and here's a pair of brazen-nosed bellows, perhaps you may take a fancy to them.

Marl. Bring me your bill, Sir ; bring me your bill, and let's make no more words about it.

Hard. There are a set of prints too. What think you of the Rake's Progress for your own apartment ?

Marl. Bring me your bill, I say ; and I'll leave you and your infernal house directly.

Hard. Then there's a mahogany table that you may see your own face in.

Marl. My bill, I say.

Hard. I had forgot the great chair for your own particular slumbers, after a hearty meal.

Marl. Zounds ! bring me my bill, I say, and let 's hear no more on 't.

Hard. Young man, young man, from your father's letter to me, I was taught to expect a well-bred modest man, as a visitor here, but now I find him no better than a coxcomb and a bully; but he will be down here presently, and shall hear more of it.   [*Exit.*

Marl. How 's this ! Sure I have not mistaken the house. Every thing looks like an inn. The servants cry ' Coming ! ' The attendance is aukward ; the bar-maid, too, to attend us. But she 's here, and will farther inform me. Whither so fast, child ? A word with you.

Enter Miss Hardcastle.

Miss Hard. Let it be short then. I'm in a hurry. (*Aside.*) I believe he begins to find out his mistake. But it 's too soon quite to undeceive him.

Marl. Pray, child, answer me one question. What are you, and what may your business in this house be ?

Miss Hard. A relation of the family, Sir.

Marl. What, a poor relation ?

Miss Hard. Yes, Sir, a poor relation appointed to keep the keys, and to see that the guests want nothing in my power to give them.

Marl. That is, you act as the bar-maid of this inn.

Miss Hard. Inn. O law——what brought that in your head ? One of the best families in the county keep an inn ! Ha ! ha ! ha ! old Mr. Hardcastle's house an inn !

Marl. Mr. Hardcastle's house. Is this Mr. Hardcastle's house, child ?

Miss Hard. Ay, sure. Whose else should it be ?

Marl. So then all 's out, and I have been damnably imposed on. O, confound my stupid head, I shall be laugh'd at over the whole town. I shall be stuck up in caricatura in all the print-shops — The *Dullissimo-Maccaroni*. To mistake this house of all others for an inn, and my father's old friend for an inn-keeper ! What a swaggering puppy must he take me for! What a silly puppy do I find myself! There again, may I be hanged, my dear, but I mistook you for the bar-maid.

Miss Hard. Dear me ! dear me ! I'm sure there's nothing in my behaviour to put me upon a level with one of that stamp.

Marl. Nothing, my dear, nothing. But I was in for a list of blunders, and could not help making you a subscriber. My stupidity saw every thing the wrong way. I mistook your assiduity for assurance, and your simplicity for allurement. But it's over—This house I no more show my face in.

Miss Hard. I hope, Sir, I have done nothing to disoblige you. I'm sure I should be sorry to affront any gentleman who has been so polite, and said so many civil things to me. I'm sure I should be sorry (*pretending to cry*) if he left the family upon my account. I'm sure I should be sorry, people said any thing amiss, since I have no fortune but my character.

Marl. (*Aside.*) By heaven, she weeps. This is the first mark of tenderness I ever had from a modest woman, and it touches me. (*To her.*) Excuse me, my lovely girl, you are the only part of the family I leave with reluctance. But to be plain with you, the difference of our birth, fortune and education makes an honourable connexion impossible ; and I can never harbour a thought of seducing simplicity that trusted in my honour, of bringing ruin upon one, whose only fault was being too lovely.

Miss Hard. (*Aside.*) Generous man ! I now begin to admire him. (*To him.*) But I am sure my family is as good as Miss Hardcastle's, and though I'm poor, that's no great misfortune to a contented mind, and, until this moment, I never thought that it was bad to want fortune.

Marl. And why now, my pretty simplicity ?

Miss Hard. Because it puts me at a distance from one, that if I had a thousand pounds, I would give it all to.

Marl. (*Aside.*) This simplicity bewitches me, so that if I stay I'm undone. I must make one bold effort and leave her. (*To her.*) Your partiality in my favour, my dear, touches me most sensibly, and were I to live for myself alone, I could easily fix my choice. But I owe too much to the opinion of the world, too much to the authority of a father, so that—I can scarcely speak it—it affects me. Farewell.   [*Exit.*

Miss Hard. I never knew half his merit till now. He shall not go, if I have power or art to detain him. I'll still preserve the character in which I *stooped to conquer*, but will undeceive my papa, who, perhaps, may laugh him out of his resolution.   [*Exit.*

Enter Tony, Miss Neville.

Tony. Ay, you may steal for yourselves the next time. I have done my duty. She has got the jewels again, that's a sure thing ; but she believes it was all a mistake of the servants.

Miss Nev. But, my dear cousin, sure you won't forsake us in this distress. If she in the least suspects that I am going off, I shall certainly be locked up, or sent to my aunt Pedigree's, which is ten times worse.

Tony. To be sure, aunts of all kinds are damned bad things. But what can I do ? I have got you a pair of horses that will fly like Whistle-jacket, and I'm sure you can't say but I have courted you nicely before her face. Here she comes, we must court a bit or two more, for fear she should suspect us.

                              [*They retire and seem to fondle.*

Enter Mrs. Hardcastle.

Mrs. Hard. Well, I was greatly fluttered to be sure. But my son tells me it was all a mistake of the servants. I shan't be easy, however, till they are fairly married, and then let her keep her own fortune. But what do I see ! fondling together, as I'm alive. I never saw Tony so sprightly before. Ah ! have I caught you, my pretty doves ! What, billing, exchanging stolen glances and broken murmurs. Ah !

Tony. As for murmurs, mother, we grumble a little now and then, to be sure. But there's no love lost between us.

Mrs. Hard. A mere sprinkling, Tony, upon the flame, only to make it burn brighter.

Miss Nev. Cousin Tony promises to give us more of his company at home. Indeed, he shan't leave us any more. It won't leave us, cousin Tony, will it ?

Tony. O! it's a pretty creature. No, I'd sooner leave my horse in a pound, than leave you when you smile upon one so. Your laugh makes you so becoming.

Miss Nev. Agreeable cousin ? Who can help admiring that natural humour, that pleasant, broad, red, thought-less, (*patting his cheek*) ah ! it's a bold face.

Mrs. Hard. Pretty innocence !

Tony. I'm sure I always loved cousin Con's hazel eyes, and her pretty long fingers, that she twists this way and that over the haspicols, like a parcel of bobbins.

Mrs. Hard. Ah, he would charm the bird from the tree. I never was so happy before. My boy takes after his father, poor Mr. Lumpkin, exactly. The jewels, my dear Con, shall be yours incontinently. You shall have them. Isn't he a sweet boy, my dear ? You shall be married to-morrow, and we'll put off the rest of his educa-tion, like Dr. Drowsy's sermons, to a fitter opportunity.

Enter Diggory.

Dig. Where's the 'squire? I have got a letter for your worship.

Tony. Give it to my mamma. She reads all my letters first.

Dig. I had orders to deliver it into your own hands.

Tony. Who does it come from?

Dig. Your worship mun ask that o' the letter itself.

Tony. I could wish to know, though (*turning the letter, and gazing on it*).

Miss Nev. (*Aside.*) Undone, undone! A letter to him from Hastings. I know the hand. If my aunt sees it we are ruined for ever. I'll keep her employed a little if I can. (*To Mrs. Hardcastle.*) But I have not told you, madam, of my cousin's smart answer just now to Mr. Marlow. We so laugh'd—You must know, madam.—This way a little, for he must not hear us.   [*They confer.*

Tony. (*Still gazing.*) A damn'd cramp piece of penmanship, as ever I saw in my life. I can read your print hand very well. But here there are such handles, and shanks, and dashes, that one can scarce tell the head from the tail. ' To Anthony Lumpkin, Esquire.' It's very odd, I can read the outside of my letters, where my own name is, well enough. But when I come to open it, it's all—— buzz. That's hard, very hard; for the inside of the letter is always the cream of the correspondence.

Mrs. Hard. Ha! ha! ha! Very well, very well. And so my son was too hard for the philosopher.

Miss Nev. Yes, madam; but you must hear the rest, madam. A little more this way, or he may hear us. You'll hear how he puzzled him again.

Mrs. Hard. He seems strangely puzzled now himself, methinks.

Tony. (*Still gazing.*) A damn'd up and down hand, as

if it was disguised in liquor. (*Reading.*) Dear Sir, Ay, that's that. Then there's an M, and a T, and an S, but whether the next be an izzard, or an R, confound me, I cannot tell.

Mrs. Hard. What's that, my dear. Can I give you any assistance ?

Miss Nev. Pray, aunt, let me read it. Nobody reads a cramp hand better than I. (*Twitching the letter from him.*) Do you know who it is from ?

Tony. Can't tell, except from Dick Ginger the feeder.

Miss Nev. Ay, so it is, (*pretending to read*) Dear 'squire, hoping that you're in health, as I am at this present. The gentlemen of the Shake-bag club has cut the gentlemen of the Goose-green quite out of feather. The odds—— um—odd battle——um—long fighting—um—here, here, it's all about cocks and fighting; it's of no consequence, here, put it up, put it up.

[*Thrusting the crumpled letter upon him.*

Tony. But I tell you, miss, it's of all the consequence in the world. I would not lose the rest of it for a guinea. Here, mother, do you make it out. Of no consequence !

[*Giving Mrs. Hardcastle the letter.*

Mrs. Hard. How's this ! (*reads*) ' Dear 'squire, I'm now waiting for Miss Neville, with a post-chaise and pair, at the bottom of the garden, but I find my horses yet unable to perform the journey. I expect you'll assist us with a pair of fresh horses, as you promised. Dispatch is necessary, as the hag (ay the hag) your mother, will otherwise suspect us. Yours, Hastings.' Grant me patience. I shall run distracted. My rage choaks me.

Miss Nev. I hope, madam, you'll suspend your resentment for a few moments, and not impute to me any impertinence, or sinister design, that belongs to another.

Mrs. Hard. (*Curtesying very low.*) Fine-spoken madam, you are most miraculously polite and engaging, and quite the very pink of courtesy and circumspection, madam. (*Changing her tone.*) And you, you great ill-fashioned oaf, with scarce sense enough to keep your mouth shut. Were you, too, joined against me ? But I'll defeat all your plots in a moment. As for you, madam, since you have got a pair of fresh horses ready, it would be cruel to disappoint them. So, if you please, instead of running away with your spark, prepare, this very moment, to run off with me. Your old aunt Pedigree will keep you secure, I'll warrant me. You too, Sir, may mount your horse, and guard us upon the way. Here, Thomas, Roger, Diggory, I'll show you, that I wish you better than you do yourselves.   [*Exit.*

Miss Nev. So now I'm completely ruined.

Tony. Ay, that's a sure thing.

Miss Nev. What better could be expected from being connected with such a stupid fool, and after all the nods and signs I made him ?

Tony. By the laws, miss, it was your own cleverness, and not my stupidity, that did your business. You were so nice and so busy with your Shake-bags and Goosegreens, that I thought you could never be making believe.

Enter Hastings.

Hast. So, Sir, I find by my servant, that you have shown my letter, and betrayed us. Was this well done, young gentleman ?

Tony. Here's another. Ask miss there, who betray'd you ? Ecod, it was her doing, not mine.

Enter Marlow.

Marl. So I have been finely used here among you. Rendered contemptible, driven into ill manners, despised, insulted, laughed at.

Tony. Here's another. We shall have old Bedlam broke loose presently.

Miss Nev. And there, Sir, is the gentleman to whom we all owe every obligation.

Marl. What can I say to him, a mere boy, an ideot, whose ignorance and age are a protection.

Hast. A poor contemptible booby, that would but disgrace correction.

Miss Nev. Yet with cunning and malice enough to make himself merry with all our embarrassments.

Hast. An insensible cub.

Marl. Replete with tricks and mischief.

Tony. Baw! dam'me, but I'll fight you both one after the other——with baskets.

Marl. As for him, he's below resentment. But your conduct, Mr. Hastings, requires an explanation. You knew of my mistakes, yet would not undeceive me.

Hast. Tortured as I am with my own disappointments, is this a time for explanations. It is not friendly, Mr. Marlow.

Marl. But, Sir—

Miss Nev. Mr. Marlow, we never kept on your mistake, till it was too late to undeceive you.

Enter Servant.

Serv. My mistress desires you'll get ready immediately, madam. The horses are putting to. Your hat and things are in the next room. We are to go thirty miles before morning.   [*Exit Servant.*

Miss Nev. Well, well: I'll come presently.

Marl. (*To Hastings.*) Was it well done, Sir, to assist in rendering me ridiculous. To hang me out for the scorn of all my acquaintance. Depend upon it, Sir, I shall expect an explanation.   •

Hast. Was it well done, Sir, if you're upon that subject,

to deliver what I entrusted to yourself, to the care of another, Sir.

Miss Nev. Mr. Hastings. Mr. Marlow. Why will you increase my distress by this groundless dispute ? I implore, I intreat you——

Enter Servant.

Serv. Your cloak, madam. My mistress is impatient.

[*Exit Servant.*

Miss Nev. I come. Pray be pacified. If I leave you thus, I shall die with apprehension.

Enter Servant.

Serv. Your fan, muff, and gloves, madam. The horses are waiting.

Miss Nev. O, Mr. Marlow ! if you knew what a scene of constraint and ill-nature lies before me, I'm sure it would convert your resentment into pity.

Marl. I'm so distracted with a variety of passions, that I don't know what I do. Forgive me, madam. George, forgive me. You know my hasty temper, and should not exasperate it.

Hast. The torture of my situation is my only excuse.

Miss Nev. Well, my dear Hastings, if you have that esteem for me that I think, that I am sure you have, your constancy for three years will but increase the happiness of our future connexion. If—

Mrs. Hard. (*Within.*) Miss Neville. Constance, why Constance, I say.

Miss Nev. I'm coming. Well, constancy, remember, constancy is the word. [*Exit.*

Hast. My heart ! how can I support this. To be so near happiness, and such happiness !

Marl. (*To Tony.*) You see now, young gentleman, the

effects of your folly.   What might be amusement to you,
is here disappointment, and even distress.

Tony. (*From a reverie.*) Ecod, I have hit it.   It's here.
Your hands.   Yours and yours, my poor Sulky.   My
boots there, oh.   Meet me two hours hence at the bottom
of the garden ;   and if you don't find Tony Lumpkin a
more good-natur'd fellow than you thought for, I'll give
you leave to take my best horse, and Bett Bouncer into
the bargain.   Come along.   My boots, ho !   [*Exeunt.*

ACT V

Enter Hastings and Servant.

Hast. You saw the old lady and Miss Neville drive off,
you say.

Serv. Yes, your honour.   They went off in a post-
coach, and the young 'squire went on horseback.   They're
thirty miles off by this time.

Hast. Then all my hopes are over.

Serv. Yes, Sir.   Old Sir Charles is arrived.   He and
the old gentleman of the house have been laughing at
Mr. Marlow's mistake this half hour.   They are coming
this way.

Hast. Then I must not be seen.   So now to my fruitless appointment at the bottom of the garden.   This is
about the time.   [*Exit.*

Enter Sir Charles and Hardcastle.

Hard. Ha ! ha ! ha !   The peremptory tone in which he
sent forth his sublime commands.

Sir Charl. And the reserve with which I suppose he
treated all your advances.

Hard. And yet he might have seen something in me
above a common inn-keeper, too.

Sir Charl. Yes, Dick, but he mistook you for an uncommon inn-keeper, ha ! ha ! ha !

Hard. Well, I'm in too good spirits to think of any thing but joy. Yes, my dear friend, this union of our families will make our personal friendships hereditary, and though my daughter's fortune is but small——

Sir Charl. Why, Dick, will you talk of fortune to me ? My son is possessed of more than a competence already, and can want nothing but a good and virtuous girl to share his happiness and increase it. If they like each other, as you say they do——

Hard. If, man ! I tell you they do like each other. My daughter as good as told me so.

Sir Charl. But girls are apt to flatter themselves, you know.

Hard. I saw him grasp her hand in the warmest manner myself ; and here he comes to put you out of your ifs, I warrant him.

Enter Marlow.

Marl. I come, Sir, once more, to ask pardon for my strange conduct. I can scarce reflect on my insolence without confusion.

Hard. Tut, boy, a trifle. You take it too gravely. An hour or two's laughing with my daughter will set all to rights again. She'll never like you the worse for it.

Marl. Sir, I shall be always proud of her approbation.

Hard. Approbation is but a cold word, Mr. Marlow ; if I am not deceived, you have something more than approbation thereabouts. You take me.

Marl. Really, Sir, I have not that happiness.

Hard. Come, boy, I'm an old fellow, and know what's what as well as you that are younger. I know what has past between you ; but mum.

Marl. Sure, Sir, nothing has past between us but the

most profound respect on my side, and the most distant reserve on her's. You don't think, Sir, that my impudence has been past upon all the rest of the family.

Hard. Impudence ! No, I don't say that—not quite impudence—though girls like to be play'd with, and rumpled a little too sometimes. But she has told no tales, I assure you.

Marl. I never gave her the slightest cause.

Hard. Well, well, I like modesty in its place well enough. But this is over-acting, young gentleman. You may be open. Your father and I will like you the better for it.

Marl. May I die, Sir, if I ever——

Hard. I tell you, she don't dislike you ; and as I'm sure you like her——

Marl. Dear, Sir—I protest, Sir——

Hard. I see no reason why you should not be joined as fast as the parson can tie you.

Marl. But hear me, Sir——

Hard. Your father approves the match, I admire it, every moment's delay will be doing mischief, so—

Marl. But why won't you hear me ? By all that's just and true, I never gave Miss Hardcastle the slightest mark of my attachment, or even the most distant hint to suspect me of affection. We had but one interview, and that was formal, modest, and uninteresting.

Hard. (*Aside.*) This fellow's formal modest impudence is beyond bearing.

Sir Charl. And you never grasp'd her hand, or made any protestations.

Marl. As Heaven is my witness, I came down in obedience to your commands. I saw the lady without emotion, and parted without reluctance. I hope you'll exact no farther proofs of my duty, nor prevent me from leaving a house in which I suffer so many mortifications. [*Exit.*

Sir Charl. I'm astonished at the air of sincerity with which he parted.

Hard. And I'm astonished at the deliberate intrepidity of his assurance.

Sir Charl. I dare pledge my life and honour upon his truth.

Hard. Here comes my daughter, and I would stake my happiness upon her veracity.

Enter Miss Hardcastle.

Hard. Kate, come hither, child. Answer us sincerely and without reserve : has Mr. Marlow made you any professions of love and affection ?

Miss Hard. The question is very abrupt, Sir! But since you require unreserved sincerity, I think he has.

Hard. (*To Sir Charles.*) You see.

Sir Charl. And pray, madam, have you and my son had more than one interview ?

Miss Hard. Yes, Sir, several.

Hard. (*To Sir Charles.*) You see.

Sir Charl. But did he profess any attachment ?

Miss Hard. A lasting one.

Sir Charl. Did he talk of love ?

Miss Hard. Much, Sir.

Sir Charl. Amazing ! And all this formally ?

Miss Hard. Formally.

Hard. Now, my friend, I hope you are satisfied.

Sir Charl. And how did he behave, madam ?

Miss Hard. As most profest admirers do. Said some civil things of my face, talked much of his want of merit, and the greatness of mine; mentioned his heart, gave a short tragedy speech, and ended with pretended rapture.

Sir Charl. Now I'm perfectly convinced indeed. I know his conversation among women to be modest and submissive. This forward canting ranting manner by no means describes him, and, I am confident, he never sate for the picture.

Miss Hard. Then, what, Sir, if I should convince you to your face of my sincerity ? if you and my papa, in about half an hour, will place yourselves behind that screen, you shall hear him declare his passion to me in person.

Sir Charl. Agreed. And if I find him what you describe, all my happiness in him must have an end. [*Exit.*

Miss Hard. And if you don't find him what I describe ——I fear my happiness must never have a beginning.

[*Exeunt.*

SCENE CHANGES TO THE BACK OF THE GARDEN.

Enter Hastings.

Hast. What an ideot am I, to wait here for a fellow, who probably takes a delight in mortifying me. He never intended to be punctual, and I'll wait no longer. What do I see ! It is he ! and perhaps with news of my Constance.

Enter Tony, booted and spattered.

Hast. My honest 'squire ! I now find you a man of your word. This looks like friendship.

Tony. Ay, I'm your friend, and the best friend you have in the world, if you knew but all. This riding, by night, by the by, is cursedly tiresome. It has shook me worse than the basket of a stage-coach.

Hast. But how ? where did you leave your fellow travellers ? Are they in safety ? Are they housed ?

Tony. Five and twenty miles in two hours and a half is no such bad driving. The poor beasts have smoaked for it : rabbit me, but I'd rather ride forty miles after a fox than ten with such varment.

Hast. Well, but where have you left the ladies ? I die with impatience.

Tony. Left them ! Why where should I leave them but where I found them.

Hast. This is a riddle.

Tony. Riddle me this then. What 's that goes round the house, and round the house, and never touches the house ?

Hast. I'm still astray.

Tony. Why, that 's it, mon. I have led them astray. By jingo, there 's not a pond or a slough within five miles of the place but they can tell the taste of.

Hast. Ha ! ha ! ha ! I understand ; you took them in a round, while they supposed themselves going forward, and so you have at last brought them home again.

Tony. You shall hear. I first took them down Feather-bed-lane, where we stuck fast in the mud. I then rattled them crack over the stones of Up-and-down Hill—I then introduced them to the gibbet on Heavy-tree Heath, and from that, with a circumbendibus, I fairly lodged them in the horse-pond at the bottom of the garden.

Hast. But no accident, I hope.

Tony. No, no. Only mother is confoundedly frightened. She thinks herself forty miles off. She 's sick of the journey, and the cattle can scarce crawl. So if your own horses be ready, you may whip off with cousin, and I'll be bound that no soul here can budge a foot to follow you.

Hast. My dear friend, how can I be grateful !

Tony. Ay, now it 's dear friend, noble 'squire. Just now, it was all ideot, cub, and run me through the guts. Damn your way of fighting, I say. After we take a knock in this part of the country, we kiss and be friends. But if you had run me through the guts, then I should be dead, and you might go kiss the hangman.

MR. QUICK IN THE CHARACTER OF TONY LUMPKIN

Hast. The rebuke is just.   But I must hasten to relieve Miss Neville ; if you keep the old lady employed, I promise to take care of the young one.   [*Exit Hastings.*

Tony. Never fear me.   Here she comes.   Vanish ! She's got from the pond, and draggled up to the waist like a mermaid.

Enter Mrs. Hardcastle.

Mrs. Hard. Oh, Tony, I'm killed.   Shook.   Battered to death.   I shall never survive it.   That last jolt that laid us against the quickset hedge has done my business.

Tony. Alack, mamma, it was all your own fault.   You would be for running away by night, without knowing one inch of the way.

Mrs. Hard. I wish we were at home again.   I never met so many accidents in so short a journey.   Drench'd in the mud, overturned in a ditch, stuck fast in a slough, jolted to a jelly, and at last to lose our way.   Whereabouts do you think we are, Tony ?

Tony. By my guess we should come upon Crackskull common, about forty miles from home.

Mrs. Hard. O lud ! O lud ! The most notorious spot in all the country.   We only want a robbery to make a complete night on't.

Tony. Don't be afraid, mamma, don't be afraid.   Two of the five that kept here are hanged, and the other three may not find us.   Don't be afraid.   Is that a man that's galloping behind us ? No ; it's only a tree.   Don't be afraid.

Mrs. Hard. The fright will certainly kill me.

Tony. Do you see any thing like a black hat moving behind the thicket ?

Mrs. Hard. O death !

Tony. No, it's only a cow.   Don't be afraid, mamma; don't be afraid.

Mrs. Hard. As I'm alive, Tony, I see a man coming towards us. Ah! I'm sure on't. If he perceives us we are undone.

Tony. (*Aside.*) Father-in-law, by all that's unlucky, come to take one of his night walks. (*To her.*) Ah, it's a highwayman with pistols as long as my arm. A damn'd ill-looking fellow.

Mrs. Hard. Good Heaven defend us? He approaches.

Tony. Do you hide yourself in that thicket, and leave me to manage him. If there be any danger I'll cough and cry *hem.* When I cough be sure to keep close.

[*Mrs. Hardcastle hides behind a tree in the back Scene.*

Enter Hardcastle.

Hard. I'm mistaken, or I heard voices of people in want of help. Oh, Tony, is that you! I did not expect you so soon back. Are your mother and her charge in safety?

Tony. Very safe, Sir, at my aunt Pedigree's. Hem.

Mrs. Hard. (*From behind.*) Ah death! I find there's danger.

Hard. Forty miles in three hours; sure that's too much, my youngster.

Tony. Stout horses and willing minds make short journeys, as they say. Hem.

Mrs. Hard. (*From behind.*) Sure he'll do the dear boy no harm.

Hard. But I heard a voice here; I should be glad to know from whence it came.

Tony. It was I, Sir, talking to myself, Sir. I was saying that forty miles in four hours was very good going. Hem. As to be sure it was. Hem. I have got a sort of cold by being out in the air. We'll go in, if you please. Hem.

Hard. But if you talk'd to yourself, you did not answer

yourself. I'm certain I heard two voices, and am resolved (*Raising his voice*) to find the other out.

Mrs. Hard. (*From behind.*) Oh! he's coming to find me out. Oh!

Tony. What need you go, Sir, if I tell you. Hem. I'll lay down my life for the truth—hem—I'll tell you all, Sir.

[*Detaining him.*

Hard. I tell you, I will not be detained. I insist on seeing. It's in vain to expect I'll believe you.

Mrs. Hard. (*Running forward from behind.*) O lud! he'll murder my poor boy, my darling. Here, good gentleman, whet your rage upon me. Take my money, my life, but spare that young gentleman, spare my child, if you have any mercy.

Hard. My wife! as I'm a christian. From whence can she come? or what does she mean.

Mrs. Hard. (*Kneeling.*) Take compassion on us, good Mr. Highwayman. Take our money, our watches, all we have, but spare our lives. We will never bring you to justice, indeed we won't, good Mr. Highwayman.

Hard. I believe the woman's out of her senses. What, Dorothy, don't you know me?

Mrs. Hard. Mr. Hardcastle, as I'm alive! My fears blinded me. But who, my dear, could have expected to meet you here, in this frightful place, so far from home? What has brought you to follow us?

Hard. Sure, Dorothy, you have not lost your wits? So far from home, when you are within forty yards of your own door. (*To him.*) This is one of your old tricks, you graceless rogue, you. (*To her.*) Don't you know the gate, and the mulberry-tree; and don't you remember the horse-pond, my dear?

Mrs. Hard. Yes, I shall remember the horse-pond as long as I live; I have caught my death in it. (*To Tony.*)

And is it to you, you graceless varlet, I owe all this ? I'll teach you to abuse your mother, I will.

Tony. Ecod, mother, all the parish says you have spoil'd me, and so you may take the fruits on 't.

Mrs. Hard. I'll spoil you, I will.

[*Follows him off the stage. Exit.*

Hard. There 's morality, however, in his reply. [*Exit.*

Enter Hastings and Miss Neville.

Hast. My dear Constance, why will you deliberate thus. If we delay a moment, all is lost for ever. Pluck up a little resolution, and we shall soon be out of the reach of her malignity.

Miss Nev. I find it impossible. My spirits are so sunk with the agitations I have suffered, that I am unable to face any new danger. Two or three years' patience will at last crown us with happiness.

Hast. Such a tedious delay is worse than inconstancy. Let us fly, my charmer. Let us date our happiness from this very moment. Perish fortune ! Love and content will encrease what we possess beyond a monarch's revenue. Let me prevail !

Miss Nev. No, Mr. Hastings ; no. Prudence once more comes to my relief, and I will obey its dictates. In the moment of passion fortune may be despised, but it ever produces a lasting repentance. I'm resolved to apply to Mr. Hardcastle's compassion and justice for redress.

Hast. But though he had the will, he has not the power to relieve you.

Miss Nev. But he has influence, and upon that I am resolved to rely.

Hast. I have no hopes. But since you persist, I must reluctantly obey you.

[*Exeunt.*

SCENE CHANGES.

Enter Sir Charles and Miss Hardcastle.

Sir Charl. What a situation am I in ! If what you say appears, I shall then find a guilty son.   If what he says be true, I shall then lose one, that, of all others, I most wish'd for a daughter.

Miss Hard. I am proud of your approbation, and to shew I merit it, if you place yourselves as I directed, you shall hear his explicit declaration.   But he comes.

Sir Charl. I'll to your father, and keep him to the appointment.   [*Exit Sir Charles.*

Enter Marlow.

Marl. Though prepar'd for setting out, I come once more to take leave, nor did I, till this moment, know the pain I feel in the separation.

Miss Hard. (*In her own natural manner.*) I believe these sufferings cannot be very great, Sir, which you can so easily remove.   A day or two longer, perhaps, might lessen your uneasiness, by shewing the little value of what you now think proper to regret.

Marl. (*Aside.*) This girl every moment improves upon me. (*To her.*) It must not be, madam.   I have already trifled too long with my heart.   My very pride begins to submit to my passion.   The disparity of education and fortune, the anger of a parent, and the contempt of my equals, begin to lose their weight ;   and nothing can restore me to myself, but this painful effort of resolution.

Miss Hard. Then go, Sir.   I'll urge nothing more to detain you.   Though my family be as good as hers you came down to visit, and my education, I hope, not inferior, what are these advantages without equal affluence ?   I must remain contented with the slight approbation of imputed merit ; I must have only the mockery of your addresses, while all your serious aims are fixed on fortune.

Enter Hardcastle and Sir Charles from behind.

Sir Charl. Here, behind this screen.

Hard. Ay, ay, make no noise. I'll engage my Kate covers him with confusion at last.

Marl. By heavens, madam, fortune was ever my smallest consideration. Your beauty at first caught my eye ; 'for who could see that without emotion. But every moment that I converse with you, steals in some new grace, heightens the picture, and gives it stronger expression. What at first seemed rustic plainness, now appears refined simplicity. What seem'd forward assurance, now strikes me as the result of courageous innocence and conscious virtue.

Sir Charl. What can he mean ? He amazes me !

Hard. I told you how it would be. Hush !

Marl. I am now determined to stay, madam, and I have too good an opinion of my father's discernment, when he sees you, to doubt his approbation.

Miss Hard. No, Mr. Marlow, I will not, cannot detain you. Do you think I could suffer a connexion, in which there is the smallest room for repentance ? Do you think I would take the mean advantage of a transient passion, to load you with confusion ? Do you think I could ever relish that happiness, which was acquired by lessening yours ?

Marl. By all that's good, I can have no happiness but what's in your power to grant me. Nor shall I ever feel repentance, but in not having seen your merits before. I will stay, even contrary to your wishes ; and though you should persist to shun me, I will make my respectful assiduities atone for the levity of my past conduct.

Miss Hard. Sir, I must entreat you'll desist. As our acquaintance began, so let it end, in indifference. I might have given an hour or two to levity ; but seriously, Mr. Marlow, do you think I could ever submit to a connexion, where I must appear mercenary and you imprudent ? Do you think I could ever catch at the confident addresses of a secure admirer ?

Marl. (*Kneeling.*) Does this look like security ? Does this look like confidence ? No, madam, every moment that shews me your merit, only serves to encrease my diffidence and confusion. Here let me continue——

Sir Charl. I can hold it no longer. Charles, Charles, how hast thou deceived me ! Is this your indifference, your uninteresting conversation ?

Hard. Your cold contempt ; your formal interview ? What have you to say now ?

Marl. That I'm all amazement ? What can it mean ?

Hard. It means that you can say and unsay things at pleasure. That you can address a lady in private, and deny it in public ; that you have one story for us, and another for my daughter !

Marl. Daughter !—This lady your daughter !

Hard. Yes, Sir, my only daughter. My Kate, whose else should she be ?

Marl. Oh, the devil !

Miss Hard. Yes, Sir, that very identical tall, squinting lady you were pleased to take me for, (*Curtseying*) she that you addressed as the mild, modest, sentimental man of gravity, and the bold forward agreeable Rattle of the ladies' club. Ha ! ha ! ha !

Marl. Zounds, there's no bearing this ; it's worse than death.

Miss Hard. In which of your characters, Sir, will you give us leave to address you ? As the faultering gentleman, with looks on the ground, that speaks just to be heard, and hates hypocrisy; or the loud confident creature, that keeps it up with Mrs. Mantrap, and old Miss Biddy Buckskin, till three in the morning. Ha! ha! ha!

Marl. O, curse on my noisy head. I never attempted to be impudent yet, that I was not taken down. I must be gone.

Hard. By the hand of my body, but you shall not. I see it was all a mistake, and I am rejoiced to find it. You shall not, Sir, I tell you. I know she'll forgive you. Won't you forgive him, Kate? We'll all forgive you. Take courage, man.   [*They retire, she tormenting him, to the back scene.*

Enter Mrs. Hardcastle, Tony.

Mrs. Hard. So, so, they're gone off. Let them go, I care not.

Hard. Who gone?

Mrs. Hard. My dutiful niece and her gentleman, Mr. Hastings, from town. He who came down with our modest visitor here.

Sir Charl. Who, my honest George Hastings? As worthy a fellow as lives, and the girl could not have made a more prudent choice.

Hard. Then, by the hand of my body, I'm proud of the connexion.

Mrs. Hard. Well, if he has taken away the lady, he has not taken her fortune; that remains in this family to console us for her loss.

Hard. Sure, Dorothy, you would not be so mercenary?

Mrs. Hard. Ay, that's my affair, not yours.

Hard. But you know if your son, when of age, refuses to marry his cousin, her whole fortune is then at her own disposal.

Mrs. Hard. Ay, but he's not of age, and she has not thought proper to wait for his refusal.

Enter Hastings and Miss Neville.

Mrs. Hard. (*Aside.*) What, returned so soon ! I begin not to like it.

Hast. (*To Hardcastle.*) For my late attempt to fly off with your niece, let my present confusion be my punishment. We are now come back, to appeal from your justice to your humanity. By her father's consent I first paid her my addresses, and our passions were first founded in duty.

Miss Nev. Since his death, I have been obliged to stoop to dissimulation to avoid oppression. In an hour of levity, I was ready even to give up my fortune to secure my choice. But I'm now recover'd from the delusion, and hope from your tenderness what is denied me from a nearer connexion.

Mrs. Hard. Pshaw, pshaw, this is all but the whining end of a modern novel.

Hard. Be it what it will, I'm glad they're come back to reclaim their due. Come hither, Tony, boy. Do you refuse this lady's hand whom I now offer you.

Tony. What signifies my refusing. You know I can't refuse her till I'm of age, father.

Hard. While I thought concealing your age, boy, was likely to conduce to your improvement, I concurred with your mother's desire to keep it secret. But since I find she turns it to a wrong use, I must now declare you have been of age these three months.

Tony. Of age ! Am I of age, father ?

Hard. Above three months.

Tony. Then you'll see the first use I'll make of my liberty. (*Taking Miss Neville's hand.*) Witness all men by these presents, that I Anthony Lumpkin, esquire, of BLANK place, refuse you, Constantia Neville, spinster, of no place at all, for my true and lawful wife. So Constance

Neville may marry whom she pleases, and Tony Lumpkin is his own man again.

Sir Charl. O brave 'squire.

Hast. My worthy friend !

Mrs. Hard. My undutiful offspring !

Marl. Joy, my dear George, I give you joy sincerely. And could I prevail upon my little tyrant here to be less arbitrary, I should be the happiest man alive, if you would return me the favour.

Hast. (*To Miss Hardcastle.*) Come, madam, you are now driven to the very last scene of all your contrivances. I know you like him, I'm sure he loves you, and you must and shall have him.

Hard. (*Joining their hands.*) And I say so too. And, Mr. Marlow, if she makes as good a wife as she has a daughter, I don't believe you'll ever repent your bargain. So now to supper. To-morrow we shall gather all the poor of the parish about us, and the Mistakes of the Night shall be crown'd with a merry morning ; so, boy, take her, and as you have been mistaken in the mistress, my wish is, that you may never be mistaken in the wife.

[*Exeunt omnes.*

EPILOGUE

By Dr. GOLDSMITH

SPOKEN BY Mrs. BULKLEY

IN THE CHARACTER OF

Miss HARDCASTLE

WELL, having stoop'd to conquer with success,
And gain'd a husband without aid from dress,
Still, as a bar-maid, I could wish it too,
As I have conquer'd him, to conquer you :
And let me say, for all your resolution,
That pretty bar-maids have done execution.
Our life is all a play, compos'd to please,
' We have our exits and our entrances.'
The first act shows the simple country maid,
Harmless and young, of every thing afraid ;
Blushes when hir'd, and with unmeaning action,
' I hopes as how to give you satisfaction.'
Her second act displays a livelier scene—
Th' unblushing bar-maid of a country inn,
Who whisks about the house, at market caters,
Talks loud, coquets the guests, and scolds the waiters.
Next the scene shifts to town, and there she soars,
The chop-house toast of ogling *connoisseurs.*
On 'squires and cits she there displays her arts,
And on the gridiron broils her lovers' hearts—
And as she smiles, her triumphs to compleat,
E'en Common Councilmen forget to eat.
The fourth act shows her wedded to the 'squire,
And madam now begins to hold it higher ;

Pretends to taste, at Operas cries caro,
And quits her Nancy Dawson, for Che Faro :
Doats upon dancing, and in all her pride
Swims round the room, the Heinel of Cheapside :
Ogles and leers with artificial skill,
Till having lost in age the power to kill,
She sits all night at cards, and ogles at spadille.
Such, through our lives the eventful history—
The fifth and last act still remains for me.
The bar-maid now for your protection prays,
Turns female Barrister, and pleads for Bayes.

EPILOGUE[1]

TO BE SPOKEN IN THE CHARACTER OF
TONY. LUMPKIN

By J. CRADOCK, Esq.

WELL—now all's ended—and my comrades gone,
Pray what becomes of mother's nonly son ?
A hopeful blade !—in town I'll fix my station,
And try to make a bluster in the nation ;
As for my cousin Neville, I renounce her,
Off—in a crack—I'll carry big Bett Bouncer.

Why should not I in the great world appear ?
I soon shall have a thousand pounds a year !
No matter what a man may here inherit,
In London—'gad, they've some regard to spirit.
I see the horses prancing up the streets,
And big Bett Bouncer bobs to all she meets ;
Then hoiks to jigs and pastimes ev'ry night—
Not to the play—they say it a'n't polite ;
To Sadler's Wells perhaps, or operas go,
And once by chance, to the *roratorio*.
Thus here and there, for ever up and down,
We'll set the fashions too to half the town ;
And then at auctions—money ne'er regard,
Buy pictures like the great, ten pounds a yard :
Zounds, we shall make these London gentry say,
We know what's damn'd genteel as well as they.

---

[1] This came too late to be spoken.

SCENE FROM

THE GRUMBLER

A FARCE

PLAYED AT COVENT GARDEN THEATRE, MAY 8TH, 1773

DRAMATIS PERSONÆ

Sourby (*the Grumbler*) . . .	MR. QUICK.
Octavio (*his Son*)	MR. DAVIS.
Wentworth (*Brother-in-law to Sourby*)	MR. OWENSON.
Dancing Master (*called Signior Capriole in the Bills*)	MR. KING.
Scamper (*Servant*)	MR. SAUNDERS.
Clarissa (*in love with Octavio*) . .	MISS HELME.
Jenny (*her Maid*)	MISS PEARCE.

SCENE FROM THE GRUMBLER

*Enter Scamper (Sourby's servant) to Sourby, and his
intended wife's maid Jenny.*

Scamper. Sir, a gentleman would speak with you.

Jenny. Good! Here comes Scamper; he'll manage
you, I'll warrant me. (*Aside.*)

Sourby. Who is it?

Scamper. He says his name is Monsieur Ri—Ri—Stay,
Sir, I'll go and ask him again.

Sourby. (*Pulling him by the ears.*) Take that, sirrah,
by the way.

Scamper. Ahi! Ahi! [*Exit.*

Jenny. Sir, you have torn off his hair, so that he
must now have a wig: you have pulled his ears off;
but there are none of them to be had for money.

Sourby. I'll teach him—'Tis certainly Mr. Rigaut, my
notary; I know who it is, let him come in. Could he
find no time but this to bring me money? Plague take
the blockhead!

Enter Dancing-Master and his Fiddler.

Sourby. This is not my man. Who are you, with your
compliments?

Dancing Master. (*Bowing often.*) I am called Rigaudon, Sir, at your service.

Sourby. (*To Jenny.*) Have not I seen that face some-
where before?

Jenny. There are a thousand people like one another.

Sourby. Well, Mr. Rigaudon, what is your business?

Dancing Master. To give you this letter from Madame Clarissa.

Sourby. Give it to me—I would fain know who taught Clarissa to fold a letter thus. What contains it ?

Jenny. (*Aside, while he unfolds the letter.*) A lover, I believe, never complained of that before.

Sourby. (*Reads.*) ' Everybody says I am to marry the most brutal of men. I would disabuse them ; and for that reason you and I must begin the ball to-night.' She is mad !

Dancing Master. Go on, pray, Sir.

Sourby. (*Reads.*) ' You told me you cannot dance ; but I have sent you the first man in the world.' (*Sourby looks at him from head to foot.*)

Dancing Master. Oh Lord, Sir.

Sourby. (*Reads.*) ' Who will teach you in less than an hour enough to serve your purpose.' I learn to dance !

Dancing Master. Finish, if you please.

Sourby. ' And if you love me, you will learn the Allemande.' The Allemande ! I, the Allemande ! Mr. the first man in the world, do you know you are in some danger here ?

Dancing Master. Come, Sir, in a quarter of an hour, you shall dance to a miracle !

Sourby. Mr. Rigaudon, do you know I will send you out of the window if I call my servants ?

Dancing Master. (*Bidding his man play.*) Come, brisk, this little prelude will put you in humour ; you must be held by the hand ; or have you some steps of your own ?

Sourby. Unless you put up that d—d fiddle, I'll beat it about your ears.

Dancing Master. Zounds, Sir ! if you are thereabouts, you shall dance presently—I say presently.

Sourby. Shall I dance, villain ?

Dancing Master. Yes. By the heavens above shall you dance. I have orders from Clarissa to make you dance. She has paid me, and dance you shall ; first, let him go out. [*He draws his sword, and puts it under his arm.*

Sourby. Ah ! I'm dead. What a madman has this woman sent me !

Jenny. I see I must interpose. Stay you there, Sir ; let me speak to him ; Sir, pray do us the favour to go and tell the lady, that it's disagreeable to my master.

Dancing Master. I will have him dance.

Sourby. The rascal ! the rascal !

Jenny. Consider, if you please, my master is a grave man.

Dancing Master. I'll have him dance.

Jenny. You may stand in need of him.

Sourby. (*Taking her aside.*) Yes, tell him that when he will, without costing him a farthing, I'll bleed and purge him his bellyfull.

Dancing Master. I have nothing to do with that ; I'll have him dance, or have his blood.

Sourby. The rascal ! (*muttering.*)

Jenny. Sir, I can't work upon him ; the madman will not hear reason ; some harm will happen—we are alone.

Sourby. 'Tis very true.

Jenny. Look on him ; he has an ill look.

Sourby. He has so (*trembling*).

Dancing Master. Make haste, I say, make haste.

Sourby. Help ! neighbours ! murder !

Jenny. Aye, you may cry for help ; do you know that all your neighbours would be glad to see you robbed and your throat cut ? Believe me, Sir, two Allemande steps may save your life.

Sourby. But if it should come to be known, I should be taken for a fool.

Jenny. Love excuses all follies ; and I have heard say that when Hercules was in love, he spun for Queen Omphale.

Sourby. Yes, Hercules spun, but Hercules did not dance the Allemande.

Jenny. Well, you must tell him so ; the gentleman will teach you another.

Dancing Master. Will you have a minuet, Sir ?

Sourby. A minuet ; no.

Dancing Master. The loure.

Sourby. The loure ; no.

Dancing Master. The passay !

Sourby. The passay ; no.

Dancing Master. What then ? the trocanny, the tricotez, the rigadon ? Come, choose, choose.

Sourby. No, no, no, I like none of these.

Dancing Master. You would have a grave, serious dance, perhaps ?

Sourby. Yes, a serious one, if there be any—but a very serious dance.

Dancing Master. Well, the courante, the hornpipe, the brocane, the saraband ?

Sourby. No, no, no !

Dancing Master. What the devil then will you have ? But make haste, or—death !

Sourby. Come on then, since it must be so ; I'll learn a few steps of the—the——

Dancing Master. What of the—the——

Sourby. I know not what.

Dancing Master. You mock me, Sir ; you shall dance the Allemande, since Clarissa will have it so, or——

[*He leads him about, the fiddle playing the Allemande.*

Sourby. I shall be laughed at by the whole town

if it should be known. I am determined, for this frolic, to deprive Clarissa of that invaluable blessing, the possession of my person.

Dancing Master. Come, come, Sir, move, move. (*Teaching him.*)

Sourby. Cockatrice !

Dancing Master. One, two, three ! (*Teaching.*)

Sourby. A d—d, infernal——

Enter Wentworth.

Oh ! brother, you are come in good time to free me from this cursed bondage.

Wentworth. How ! for shame, brother, at your age to be thus foolish.

Sourby. As I hope for mercy—

Wentworth. For shame, for shame—practising at sixty what should have been finished at six ?

Dancing Master. He's not the only grown gentleman I have had in hand.

Wentworth. Brother, brother, you'll be the mockery of the whole city.

Sourby. Eternal babbler ! hear me ; this curs'd, confounded villain will make me dance perforce.

Wentworth. Perforce !

Sourby. Yes ; by order, he says, of Clarissa ; but since I now find she is unworthy, I give her up—renounce her for ever.

[Prior sums up the rest of the play thus :—' The young couple enter immediately after this declaration, and finding no farther obstruction to their union, the piece finishes with the consent of the Grumbler, " in the hope," as he says, " that they are possessed of mutual requisites to be the plague of each other." '—ED.]

THE

VICAR

OF

WAKEFIELD:

A TALE.

Suppofed to be written by HIMSELF.

Sperate miferi, cavete fælices.

VOL. I.

SALISBURY:

Printed by B. COLLINS,

For F. NEWBERY, in Pater-Nofter-Row, London.

MDCCLXVI.

ADVERTISEMENT

THERE are an hundred faults in this Thing, and an hundred things might be said to prove them beauties. But it is needless. A book may be amusing with numerous errors, or it may be very dull without a single absurdity. The hero of this piece unites in himself the three greatest characters upon earth ; he is a priest, an husbandman, and the father of a family. He is drawn as ready to teach, and ready to obey, as simple in affluence, and majestic in adversity. In this age of opulence and refinement, whom can such a character please ? Such as are fond of high life, will turn with disdain from the simplicity of his country fireside. Such as mistake ribaldry for humour, will find no wit in his harmless conversation ; and such as have been taught to deride religion, will laugh at one, whose chief stores of comfort are drawn from futurity.

OLIVER GOLDSMITH.

CONTENTS

—and chose my wife, as she did her wedding-gown.—PAGE 187.

CHAPTER I

The description of the family of Wakefield, in which a kindred
likeness prevails as well of minds as of persons.

I WAS ever of opinion, that the honest man who married
and brought up a large family, did more service than
he who continued single and only talked of population.
From this motive, I had scarce taken orders a year before
I began to think seriously of matrimony, and chose my
wife, as she did her wedding-gown, not for a fine glossy
surface, but such qualities as would wear well. To do
her justice, she was a good-natured notable woman ; and

as for breeding, there were few country ladies who could shew more. She could read any English book without much spelling ; but for pickling, preserving, and cookery none could excel her. She prided herself also upon being an excellent contriver in housekeeping ; though I could never find that we grew richer with all her contrivances.

However, we loved each other tenderly, and our fondness encreased as we grew old. There was, in fact, nothing that could make us angry with the world or each other. We had an elegant house, situated in a fine country, and a good neighbourhood. The year was spent in a moral or rural amusement, in visiting our rich neighbours, and relieving such as were poor. We had no revolutions to fear, nor fatigues to undergo ; all our adventures were by the fire-side, and all our migrations from the blue bed to the brown.

As we lived near the road, we often had the traveller or stranger visit us to taste our gooseberry-wine, for which we had great reputation ; and I profess with the veracity of an historian, that I never knew one of them find fault with it. Our cousins too, even to the fortieth remove, all remembered their affinity, without any help from the Herald's office, and came very frequently to see us. Some of them did us no great honour by these claims of kindred; as we had the blind, the maimed, and the halt amongst the number. However, my wife always insisted that as they were the same *flesh and blood*, they should sit with us at the same table. So that if we had not very rich, we generally had very happy friends about us ; for this remark will hold good through life, that the poorer the guest, the better pleased he ever is with being treated : and as some men gaze with admiration at the colours of a tulip, or the wing of a butterfly, so I was by nature an admirer of happy human faces. However, when any one of our relations was found to be a person of a very bad

WAKEFIELD

character, a troublesome guest, or one we desired to get rid of, upon his leaving my house, I ever took care to lend him a riding-coat, or a pair of boots, or sometimes an horse of small value, and I always had the satisfaction of finding he never came back to return them. By this the house was cleared of such as we did not like; but never was the family of Wakefield known to turn the traveller or the poor dependant out of doors.

Thus we lived several years in a state of much happiness, not but that we sometimes had those little rubs which Providence sends to enhance the value of its favours. My orchard was often robbed by school-boys, and my wife's custards plundered by the cats or the children. The 'Squire would sometimes fall asleep in the most pathetic parts of my sermon, or his lady return my wife's civilities at church with a mutilated courtesy. But we soon got over the uneasiness caused by such accidents, and usually in three or four days began to wonder how they vext us.

My children, the offspring of temperance, as they were educated without softness, so they were at once well formed and healthy; my sons hardy and active, my daughters beautiful and blooming. When I stood in the midst of the little circle, which promised to be the supports of my declining age, I could not avoid repeating the famous story of Count Abensberg, who, in Henry II's progress through Germany, while other courtiers came with their treasures, brought his thirty-two children, and presented them to his sovereign as the most valuable offering he had to bestow. In this manner, though I had but six, I considered them as a very valuable present made to my country, and consequently looked upon it as my debtor. Our eldest son was named George, after his uncle, who left us ten thousand pounds. Our second child, a girl, I intended to call after her aunt Grissel; but my wife, who during her pregnancy had been reading romances, insisted upon her being called Olivia. In less than another year we had another daughter, and now I was determined that Grissel should be her name; but a rich relation taking a fancy to stand godmother, the girl was, by her directions, called Sophia: so that we had two romantic names in the family; but I solemnly protest I had no hand in it. Moses was our next, and after an interval of twelve years, we had two sons more.

It would be fruitless to deny exultation when I saw my little ones about me; but the vanity and the satisfaction of my wife were even greater than mine. When our visitors would say, 'Well, upon my word, 'Mrs. Primrose, you have the finest children in the whole 'country:'—'Ay, neighbour,' she would answer, 'they 'are as heaven made them, handsome enough, if they be 'good enough; for handsome is that handsome does.' And then she would bid the girls hold up their heads; who, to conceal nothing, were certainly very handsome. Mere outside is so very trifling a circumstance with me, that I should scarce have remembered to mention it, had it not been a general topic of conversation in the country. Olivia, now about eighteen, had that luxuriancy of beauty, with which painters generally draw Hebe; open, sprightly, and commanding. Sophia's features were not so striking at first; but often did more certain execution; for they were soft, modest, and alluring. The one vanquished by a single blow, the other by efforts successfully repeated.

The temper of a woman is generally formed from the turn of her features, at least it was so with my daughters. Olivia wished for many lovers, Sophia to secure one. Olivia was often affected from too great a desire to please. Sophia even represt excellence from her fears to offend.

The one entertained me with her vivacity when I was gay, the other with her sense when I was serious. But these qualities were never carried to excess in either, and I have often seen them exchange characters for a whole day together. A suit of mourning has transformed my coquet into a prude, and a new set of ribbands has given her younger sister more than natural vivacity. My eldest son George was bred at Oxford, as I intended him for one of the learned professions. My second boy Moses, whom I designed for business, received a sort of miscellaneous education at home. But it is needless to attempt describing the particular characters of young people that had seen but very little of the world. In short, a family likeness prevailed through all; and properly speaking, they had but one character, that of being all equally generous, credulous, simple, and inoffensive.

—— This, as may be expected, produced a dispute attended with some acrimony.—PAGE 195.

CHAPTER II

Family misfortunes. The loss of fortune only serves to encrease the pride of the worthy.

THE temporal concerns of our family were chiefly committed to my wife's management; as to the spiritual I took them entirely under my own direction. The profits of my living, which amounted to but thirty-five pounds a year, I made over to the orphans and widows of the clergy of our diocese; for having a fortune of my own, I was careless of temporalities, and felt a secret pleasure in doing my duty without reward. I also set a resolution of keeping no curate, and of being acquainted with every man in the parish, exhorting the married men to temperance, and the bachelors to matrimony ; so that in a few years it was a common saying, that there were three strange wants at Wakefield, a parson wanting pride, young men wanting wives, and ale-houses wanting customers.

Matrimony was always one of my favourite topics, and I wrote several sermons to prove its happiness ; but there was a peculiar tenet which I made a point of supporting : for I maintained with Whiston, that it was unlawful for a priest of the church of England, after the death of his first wife, to take a second, or to express it in one word, I valued myself upon being a strict monogamist.

I was early initiated into this important dispute, on which so many laborious volumes have been written. I published some tracts upon the subject myself, which, as they never sold, I have the consolation of thinking were read only by the happy *few*. Some of my friends called this my weak side ; but alas ! they had not like me made it the subject of long contemplation. The more I reflected upon it, the more important it appeared. I even went a step beyond Whiston in displaying my principles : as he had engraven upon his wife's tomb that she was the *only* wife of William Whiston ; so I wrote a similar epitaph for my wife, though still living, in which I extolled her prudence, economy, and obedience till death ; and having got it copied fair, with an elegant frame, it was placed over the chimney-piece, where it answered several very useful purposes. It admonished my wife of her duty to me, and my fidelity to her ; it inspired her with a passion for fame, and constantly put her in mind of her end.

It was thus, perhaps, from hearing marriage so often recommended, that my eldest son, just upon leaving college, fixed his affections upon the daughter of a neighbouring clergyman, who was a dignitary in the church, and in circumstances to give her a large fortune : but fortune was her smallest accomplishment. Miss Arabella Wilmot was allowed by all (except my two daughters) to be completely pretty. Her youth, health, and innocence, were still heightened by a complexion so transparent and such an happy sensibility of look, as even age could not gaze on with indifference. As Mr. Wilmot knew that I could make a very handsome settlement on my son, he was not averse to the match ; so both families lived together in all that harmony which generally precedes an expected alliance. Being convinced by experience that the days of courtship are the most happy of our lives, I was willing enough to lengthen the period ; and the various amusements which the young couple every day shared in each other's company, seemed to encrease their passion. We were generally awaked in the morning by music, and on fine days rode a hunting. The hours between breakfast and dinner the ladies devoted to dress and study : they usually read a page, and then gazed at themselves in the glass, which even philosophers might own often presented the page of greatest beauty. At dinner my wife took the lead ; for as she always insisted upon carving everything herself, it being her mother's way, she gave us upon these occasions the history of every dish. When we had dined, to prevent the ladies leaving us, I generally ordered the table to be removed ; and sometimes, with the music-master's assistance, the girls would give us a very agreeable concert. Walking out, drinking tea, country dances, and forfeits shortened the rest of the day, without the assistance of cards, as I hated all manner of gaming, except backgammon, at which my old friend and I sometimes took a two-penny hit. Nor can I here pass over an ominous circumstance that happened the last time we played together ; I only wanted to fling a quatre, and yet I threw deuce ace five times running.

Some months were elapsed in this manner, till at last it was thought convenient to fix a day for the nuptials of the young people, who seemed earnestly to desire it. During the preparations for the wedding, I need not describe the busy importance of my wife, nor the sly looks of my daughters : in fact, my attention was fixed on another object, the completing a tract which I intended shortly to publish in defence of my favourite principle. As I looked upon this as a master-piece, both for argument and style, I could not in the pride of my heart avoid shewing it to my old friend Mr. Wilmot, as I made no doubt of receiving his approbation ; but not till too late I discovered that he was most violently attached to the contrary opinion, and with good reason; for he was at that time actually courting a fourth wife. This, as may be expected, produced a dispute attended with some acrimony, which threatened to interrupt our intended alliance : but on the day before that appointed for the ceremony, we agreed to discuss the subject at large.

It was managed with proper spirit on both sides : he asserted that I was heterodox, I retorted the charge : he replied, and I rejoined. In the mean time, while the controversy was hottest, I was called out by one of my relations, who, with a face of concern, advised me to give up the dispute, at least till my son's wedding was over. 'How,' cried I, 'relinquish the cause of truth, and let 'him be a husband, already driven to the very verge of 'absurdity. You might as well advise me to give up 'my fortune, as my argument.' 'Your fortune,' returned my friend, 'I am now sorry to inform you, is 'almost nothing. The merchant in town, in whose hands 'your money was lodged, has gone off, to avoid a statute 'of bankruptcy, and is thought not to have left a shilling 'in the pound. I was unwilling to shock you or the 'family with the account till after the wedding : but

' now it may serve to moderate your warmth in the argu-
' ment ; for, I suppose, your own prudence will enforce
' the necessity of dissembling, at least till your son has
' the young lady's fortune secure.'——' Well,' returned
I, ' if what you tell me be true, and if I am to be a beggar,
' it shall never make me a rascal, or induce me to disavow
' my principles. I'll go this moment and inform the
' company of my circumstances : and as for the argu-
' ment, I even here retract my former concessions in the
' old gentleman's favour, nor will I allow him now to be
' a husband in any sense of the expression.'

It would be endless to describe the different sensations
of both families when I divulged the news of our misfortune : but what others felt was slight to what the lovers
appeared to endure. Mr. Wilmot, who seemed before
sufficiently inclined to break off the match, was by this
blow soon determined : one virtue he had in perfection,
which was prudence ; too often the only one that is left
us at seventy-two.

—— she must have certainly perished had not my companion, perceiving her danger, instantly plunged in to her relief.—Page 204.

CHAPTER III

A migration. The fortunate circumstances of our lives are generally found at last to be of our own procuring.

THE only hope of our family now was, that the report of our misfortune might be malicious or premature: but a letter from my agent in town soon came with a confirmation of every particular. The loss of fortune to myself alone would have been trifling; the only uneasiness I felt was for my family, who were to be humble without an education to render them callous to contempt.

Near a fortnight had passed before I attempted to restrain their affliction; for premature consolation is but the remembrancer of sorrow. During this interval, my

thoughts were employed on some future means of supporting them ; and at last a small Cure of fifteen pounds
a year was offered me in a distant neighbourhood, where
I could still enjoy my principles without molestation.
With this proposal I joyfully closed, having determined
to encrease my salary by managing a little farm.

Having taken this resolution, my next care was to get
together the wrecks of my fortune ; and, all debts col-
lected and paid, out of fourteen thousand pounds we had
but four hundred remaining. My chief attention, therefore, was now to bring down the pride of my family to
their circumstances ; for I well knew that aspiring
beggary is wretchedness itself. ' You cannot be ignorant,
' my children,' cried I, ' that no prudence of ours could
' have prevented our late misfortune ; but prudence may
' do much in disappointing its effects. We are now poor,
' my fondlings, and wisdom bids us conform to our
' humble situation. Let us then, without repining, give
' up those splendours with which numbers are wretched,
' and seek in humbler circumstances that peace with which
' all may be happy. The poor live pleasantly without our
' help, why then should we learn to live without
' theirs ? No, my children, let us from this moment give
' up all pretensions to gentility ; we have still enough left
' for happiness if we are wise, and let us draw upon
' content for the deficiencies of fortune.'

As my eldest son was bred a scholar, I determined to
send him to town, where his abilities might contribute to
our support and his own. The separation of friends and
families is, perhaps, one of the most distressful circumstances attendant on penury. The day soon arrived on
which we were to disperse for the first time. My son,
after taking leave of his mother and the rest, who mingled
their tears with their kisses, came to ask a blessing from
me. This I gave him from my heart, and which, added to

GEORGE'S DEPARTURE

five guineas, was all the patrimony I had now to bestow.
' You are going, my boy,' cried I, ' to London on foot in
' the manner Hooker, your great ancestor, travelled there
' before you. Take from me the same horse that was
' given him by the good bishop Jewel, this staff ; and
' take this book too, it will be your comfort on the way :
' these two lines in it are worth a million, *I have been
' young, and now am old ; yet never saw I the righteous man
' forsaken, or his seed begging their bread.* Let this be your
' consolation as you travel on. Go, my boy, whatever
' be thy fortune let me see thee once a year ; still keep
' a good heart, and farewell.' As he was possest of integrity and honour, I was under no apprehensions from
throwing him naked into the amphitheatre of life ; for
I knew he would act a good part whether vanquished or
victorious.

His departure only prepared the way for our own,
which arrived a few days afterwards. The leaving a
neighbourhood in which we had enjoyed so many hours
of tranquillity, was not without a tear, which scarce fortitude itself could suppress. Besides, a journey of seventy
miles to a family that had hitherto never been above ten
from home, filled us with apprehension ; and the cries of
the poor, who followed us for some miles, contributed to
encrease it. The first day's journey brought us in safety
within thirty miles of our future retreat, and we put up
for the night at an obscure inn in a village by the way.
When we were shewn a room, I desired the landlord, in
my usual way, to let us have his company, with which he
complied, as what he drank would encrease the bill next
morning. He knew, however, the whole neighbourhood
to which I was removing, particularly 'Squire Thornhill,
who was to be my landlord, and who lived within a few
miles of the place. This gentleman he described as one
who desired to know little more of the world than its

pleasures, being particularly remarkable for his attachment to the fair sex. He observed that no virtue was
able to resist his arts and assiduity, and that scarce
a farmer's daughter within ten miles round but what had
found him successful and faithless. Though this account
gave me some pain, it had a very different effect upon my
daughters, whose features seemed to brighten with the
expectation of an approaching triumph ; nor was my
wife less pleased and confident of their allurements and
virtue. While our thoughts were thus employed, the
hostess entered the room to inform her husband, that the
strange gentleman, who had been two days in the house,
wanted money, and could not satisfy them for his reckoning. ' Want money ! ' replied the host, ' that must be
' impossible ; for it was no later than yesterday he paid
' three guineas to our beadle to spare an old broken
' soldier that was to be whipped through the town for
' dog-stealing.' The hostess, however, still persisting in
her first assertion, he was preparing to leave the room,
swearing that he would be satisfied one way or another,
when I begged the landlord would introduce me to a
stranger of so much charity as he described. With this
he complied, shewing in a gentleman who seemed to be
about thirty, drest in clothes that once were laced. His
person was well formed, and his face marked with the
lines of thinking. He had something short and dry in
his address, and seemed not to understand ceremony,
or to despise it. Upon the landlord's leaving the room,
I could not avoid expressing my concern to the stranger
at seeing a gentleman in such circumstances, and offered
him my purse to satisfy the present demand. ' I take it
' with all my heart, Sir,' replied he, ' and am glad that
' a late oversight in giving what money I had about me,
' has shewn me that there are still some men like you.
' I must, however, previously intreat being informed of

WAKEFIELD BRIDGE

' the name and residence of my benefactor, in order to
' repay him as soon as possible.'   In this I satisfied him
fully, not only mentioning my name and late misfortunes,
but the place to which I was going to remove.   ' This,'
cried he, ' happens still more luckily than I hoped for, as
' I am going the same way myself, having been detained
' here two days by the floods, which I hope by to-morrow
' will be found passable.'   I testified the pleasure I should
have in his company, and my wife and daughters joining
in intreaty, he was prevailed upon to stay supper.   The
stranger's conversation, which was at once pleasing and
instructive, induced me to wish for a continuance of it ;
but it was now high time to retire and take refreshment
against the fatigues of the following day.

The next morning we all set forward together : my
family on horseback, while Mr. Burchell, our new companion, walked along the foot-path by the road-side,
observing with a smile, that as we were ill mounted, he
would be too generous to attempt leaving us behind.
As the floods were not yet subsided, we were obliged to
hire a guide, who trotted on before, Mr. Burchell and
I bringing up the rear.   We lightened the fatigues of the
road with philosophical disputes, which he seemed to
understand perfectly.   But what surprised me most was,
that though he was a money-borrower, he defended his
opinions with as much obstinacy as if he had been my
patron.   He now and then also informed me to whom the
different seats belonged that lay in our view as we
travelled the road.   ' That,' cried he, pointing to a very
magnificent house which stood at some distance, ' belongs
' to Mr. Thornhill, a young gentleman who enjoys a large
' fortune, though entirely dependent on the will of his
' uncle, Sir William Thornhill, a gentleman who, content
' with a little himself, permits his nephew to enjoy the
' rest, and chiefly resides in town.'   ' What ! ' cried I, ' is

' my young landlord then the nephew of a man whose
' virtues, generosity, and singularities are so universally
' known ? I have heard Sir William Thornhill represented
' as one of the most generous, yet whimsical men in the
' kingdom ;   a man of consummate benevolence.'——
' Something, perhaps, too much so,' replied Mr. Burchell,
' at least he carried benevolence to an excess when young ;
' for his passions were then strong, and as they were all
' upon the side of virtue, they led it up to a romantic ex-
' treme.   He early began to aim at the qualifications of
' the soldier and scholar ; was soon distinguished in the
' army, and had some reputation among men of learning.
' Adulation ever follows the ambitious ; for such alone
' receive most pleasure from flattery.   He was surrounded
' with crowds, who shewed him only one side of their
' character ; so that he began to lose a regard for private
' interest in universal sympathy.   He loved all mankind ;
' for fortune prevented him from knowing that there were
' rascals.   Physicians tell us of a disorder in which the
' whole body is so exquisitely sensible, that the slightest
' touch gives pain : what some have thus suffered in their
' persons, this gentleman felt in his mind.   The slightest
' distress, whether real or fictitious, touched him to the
' quick, and his soul laboured under a sickly sensibility
' of the miseries of others.   Thus disposed to relieve, it
' will be easily conjectured, he found numbers disposed
' to solicit : his profusions began to impair his fortune,
' but not his good-nature ; that, indeed, was seen to
' encrease as the other seemed to decay : he grew im-
' provident as he grew poor :   and though he talked
' like a man of sense, his actions were those of a fool.
' Still, however, being surrounded with importunity, and
' no longer able to satisfy every request that was made
' him, instead of *money* he gave *promises*.   They were all
' he had to bestow, and he had not resolution enough

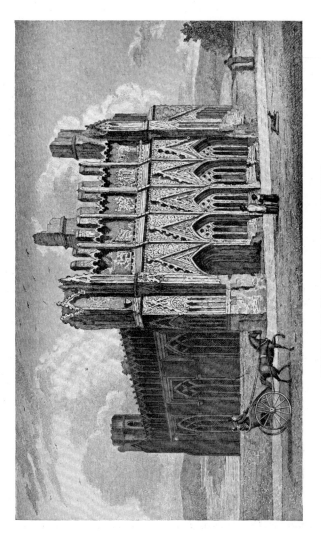

CHANTRY ON THE BRIDGE AT WAKEFIELD

'to give any man pain by a denial. By this he drew
'round him crowds of dependents, whom he was sure to
'disappoint, yet wished to relieve. These hung upon
'him for a time, and left him with merited reproaches
'and contempt. But in proportion as he became con-
'temptible to others, he became despicable to himself.
'His mind had leaned upon their adulation, and that
'support taken away, he could find no pleasure in the
'applause of his heart, which he had never learnt to
'reverence. The world now began to wear a different
'aspect ; the flattery of his friends began to dwindle into
'simple approbation. Approbation soon took the more
'friendly form of advice, and advice when rejected pro-
'duced their reproaches. He now therefore found that
'such friends as benefits had gathered round him, were
'little estimable ; he now found that a man's own heart
'must be ever given to gain that of another. I now
'found, that——that——I forget what I was going to
'observe : in short, Sir, he resolved to respect himself,
'and laid down a plan of restoring his falling fortune.
'For this purpose, in his own whimsical manner, he
'travelled through Europe on foot, and now, though he
'has scarce attained the age of thirty, his circumstances
'are more affluent than ever. At present, his bounties
'are more rational and moderate than before ; but still
'he preserves the character of an humorist, and finds
'most pleasure in eccentric virtues.'

My attention was so much taken up by Mr. Burchell's
account, that I scarce looked forward as he went along,
till we were alarmed by the cries of my family, when turning, I perceived my youngest daughter in the midst of
a rapid stream, thrown from her horse, and struggling
with the torrent. She had sunk twice, nor was it in my
power to disengage myself in time to bring her relief.
My sensations were even too violent to permit my

attempting her rescue : she must have certainly perished had not my companion, perceiving her danger, instantly plunged in to her relief, and, with some difficulty, brought her in safety to the opposite shore. By taking the current a little farther up, the rest of the family got safely over, where we had an opportunity of joining our acknowledgments to her's. Her gratitude may be more readily imagined than described : she thanked her deliverer more with looks than words, and continued to lean upon his arm, as if still willing to receive assistance. My wife also hoped one day to have the pleasure of returning his kindness at her own house. Thus, after we were refreshed at the next inn, and had dined together, as Mr. Burchell was going to a different part of the country, he took leave ; and we pursued our journey : my wife observing as he went, that she liked him extremely, and protesting, that if he had birth and fortune to entitle him to match into such a family as ours, she knew no man she would sooner fix upon. I could not but smile to hear her talk in this lofty strain ; but I was never much displeased with those harmless delusions that tend to make us more happy.

SANDAL CASTLE, NEAR WAKEFIELD

—— These harmless people had several ways of being good company ; while one played, the other would sing some soothing ballad.—PAGE 207.

CHAPTER IV

A proof that even the humblest fortune may grant happiness, which depends not on circumstances but constitution.

THE place of our retreat was in a little neighbourhood, consisting of farmers, who tilled their own grounds, and were equal strangers to opulence and poverty. As they had almost all the conveniences of life within themselves, they seldom visited towns or cities, in search of superfluity. Remote from the polite, they still retained the primæval simplicity of manners ; and frugal by habit, they scarce knew that temperance was a virtue. They wrought with chearfulness on days of labour ; but observed festivals as intervals of idleness and pleasure. They kept up the Christmas carol, sent true love-knots on Valentine morning, ate pancakes on Shrove-tide, shewed their wit on the first of April, and religiously cracked nuts on Michaelmas eve. Being apprized of our approach, the whole neighbourhood came out to meet their minister, drest in their finest clothes, and preceded by a pipe and tabor. A feast also was provided for our reception, at which we sate chearfully down ; and what the conversation wanted in wit, was made up in laughter.

Our little habitation was situated at the foot of a sloping hill, sheltered with a beautiful underwood behind, and a prattling river before : on one side a meadow, on the other a green. My farm consisted of about twenty acres of excellent land, having given an hundred pound for my predecessor's good-will. Nothing could exceed the neatness of my little enclosures : the elms and hedge-rows appearing with inexpressible beauty. My house consisted of but one story, and was covered with thatch, which gave it an air of great snugness ; the walls on the inside were nicely white-washed, and my daughters undertook to adorn them with pictures of their own designing. Though the same room served us for parlour and kitchen, that only made it the warmer. Besides, as it was kept with the utmost neatness, the dishes, plates, and coppers being well scoured, and all disposed in bright rows on the shelves, the eye was agreeably relieved, and did not want richer furniture. There were three other apartments, one for my wife and me, another for our two daughters, within our own, and the third, with two beds, for the rest of the children.

The little republic to which I gave laws, was regulated in the following manner : by sun-rise we all assembled in our common apartment ; the fire being previously kindled by the servant. After we had saluted each other with proper ceremony, for I always thought fit to keep up some mechanical forms of good breeding, without which freedom ever destroys friendship, we all bent in gratitude to that Being who gave us another day. This duty being performed, my son and I went to pursue our usual industry abroad, while my wife and daughters employed themselves in providing breakfast, which was always ready at a certain time. I allowed half an hour for this meal, and an hour for dinner ; which time was taken up in innocent mirth between my wife and daughters, and in philosophical arguments between my son and me.

As we rose with the sun, so we never pursued our labours after it was gone down, but returned home to the expecting family ; where smiling looks, a neat hearth, and pleasant fire were prepared for our reception. Nor were we without guests : sometimes farmer Flamborough, our talkative neighbour, and often the blind piper, would pay us a visit, and taste our gooseberry-wine ; for the making of which we had lost neither the receipt nor the reputation. These harmless people had several ways of being good company; while one played, the other would sing some soothing ballad, Johnny Armstrong's Last Good Night, or The Cruelty of Barbara Allen. The night was concluded in the manner we began the morning, my youngest boys being appointed to read the lessons of the day, and he that read loudest, distinctest, and best, was to have an halfpenny on Sunday to put in the poor's box.

When Sunday came, it was indeed a day of finery, which all my sumptuary edicts could not restrain. How well soever I fancied my lectures against pride had con-quered the vanity of my daughters ; yet I still found them secretly attached to all their former finery : they still loved laces, ribbands, bugles and catgut ; my wife herself retained a passion for her crimson paduasoy, because I formerly happened to say it became her.

The first Sunday in particular their behaviour served to mortify me : I had desired my girls the preceding night to be drest early the next day ; for I always loved to be at church a good while before the rest of the congregation. They punctually obeyed my directions ; but when we were to assemble in the morning at breakfast, down came my wife and daughters, drest out in all their former splendour : their hair plastered up with pomatum, their faces patched to taste, their trains bundled up in an heap behind, and rustling at every motion. I could not help smiling at their vanity, particularly that of my wife, from whom I expected more discretion. In this exigence, therefore, my only resource was to order my son, with an important air, to call our coach. The girls were amazed at the command ; but I repeated it with more solemnity than before.——' Surely, my dear, you jest,' cried my wife, ' we can walk it perfectly well : we want ' no coach to carry us now.' ' You mistake, child, returned I, ' we do want a coach ; for if we walk to ' church in this trim, the very children in the parish will ' hoot after us.'——' Indeed,' replied my wife, ' I always ' imagined that my Charles was fond of seeing his children ' neat and handsome about him.'—' You may be as neat ' as you please,' interrupted I, ' and I shall love you the ' better for it ; but all this is not neatness, but frippery. ' These rufflings, and pinkings, and patchings will only ' make us hated by all the wives of our neighbours. No, ' my children,' continued I, more gravely, ' those gowns ' may be altered into something of a plainer cut ; for ' finery is very unbecoming in us, who want the means of ' decency. I do not know whether such flouncing and ' shredding is becoming even in the rich, if we consider, ' upon a moderate calculation, that the nakedness of the

'indigent world may be clothed from the trimmings of
'the vain.'

This remonstrance had the proper effect ; they went
with great composure, that very instant, to change their
dress ; and the next day I had the satisfaction of finding
my daughters, at their own request, employed in cutting
up their trains into Sunday waistcoats for Dick and Bill,
the two little ones ; and what was still more satisfactory,
the gowns seemed improved by this curtailing.

—— At last, a young gentleman of more genteel appearance than the rest,
came forward, and for a while regarding us, instead of pursuing the chace,
stopt short, and giving his horse to a servant who attended, approached us with
a careless superior air.—PAGE 211.

CHAPTER V

A new and great acquaintance introduced. What we place most
hopes upon, generally proves most fatal.

AT a small distance from the house, my predecessor
had made a seat, overshaded by an hedge of haw-
thorn and honeysuckle. Here, when the weather was
fine and our labour soon finished, we usually sat together,
to enjoy an extensive landscape in the calm of the
evening. Here too we drank tea, which was now become
an occasional banquet; and as we had it but seldom,
it diffused a new joy, the preparations for it being made

with no small share of bustle and ceremony. On these occasions our two little ones always read for us, and they were regularly served after we had done. Sometimes, to give a variety to our amusements, the girls sang to the guitar ; and while they thus formed a little concert, my wife and I would stroll down the sloping field, that was embellished with blue bells and centaury, talk of our children with rapture, and enjoy the breeze that wafted both health and harmony.

In this manner we began to find that every situation in life may bring its own peculiar pleasures : every morning waked us to a repetition of toil ; but the evening repaid it with vacant hilarity.

It was about the beginning of autumn, on a holiday, for I kept such as intervals of relaxation from labour, that I had drawn out my family to our usual place of amusement, and our young musicians began their usual concert. As we were thus engaged, we saw a stag bound nimbly by, within about twenty paces of where we were sitting, and by its panting it seemed prest by the hunters. We had not much time to reflect upon the poor animal's distress, when we perceived the dogs and horsemen come sweeping along at some distance behind, and making the very path it had taken. I was instantly for returning in with my family ; but either curiosity, or surprise, or some more hidden motive, held my wife and daughters to their seats. The huntsman, who rode foremost, passed us with great swiftness, followed by four or five persons more, who seemed in equal haste. At last, a young gentleman of more genteel appearance than the rest, came forward, and for a while regarding us, instead of pursuing the chace, stopt short, and giving his horse to a servant who attended, approached us with a careless superior air. He seemed to want no introduction, but was going to salute my daughters, as one certain of a kind reception ; but they had early learnt the lesson of looking presumption out of countenance. Upon which he let us know his name was Thornhill, and that he was owner of the estate that lay for some extent round us. He again therefore offered to salute the female part of the family, and such was the power of fortune and fine clothes, that he found no second repulse. As his address, though confident, was easy, we soon became more familiar ; and perceiving musical instruments lying near, he begged to be favoured with a song. As I did not approve of such disproportioned acquaintances, I winked upon my daughters in order to prevent their compliance ; but my hint was counteracted by one from their mother ; so that, with a chearful air, they gave us a favourite song of Dryden's. Mr. Thornhill seemed highly delighted with their performance and choice, and then took up the guitar himself. He played but very indifferently ; however, my eldest daughter repaid his former applause with interest, and assured him that his tones were louder than even those of her master. At this compliment he bowed, which she returned with a curtesy. He praised her taste, and she commended his understanding : an age could not have made them better acquainted ; while the fond mother, too, equally happy, insisted upon her landlord's stepping in, and tasting a glass of her gooseberry. The whole family seemed earnest to please him : my girls attempted to entertain him with topics they thought most modern, while Moses, on the contrary, gave him a question or two from the ancients, for which he had the satisfaction of being laughed at : my little ones were no less busy, and fondly stuck close to the stranger. All my endeavours could scarce keep their dirty fingers from handling and tarnishing the lace on his clothes, and lifting up the flaps of his pocket-holes, to see what was there. At the approach of evening he took leave ; but not till he had requested permission to renew his visit, which as he was our landlord, we most readily agreed to.

As soon as he was gone, my wife called a council on the conduct of the day. She was of opinion, that it was a most fortunate hit; for that she had known even stranger things than that brought to bear. She hoped again to see the day in which we might hold up our heads with the best of them; and concluded, she protested she could see no reason why the two Miss Wrinklers should marry great fortunes, and her children get none. As this last argument was directed to me, I protested I could see no reason for it neither, nor why Mr. Simkins got the ten thousand pound prize in the lottery, and we sate down with a blank. ' I protest, Charles,' cried my wife, ' this ' is the way you always damp my girls and me when we ' are in spirits. Tell me, Sophy, my dear, what do you ' think of our new visitor? Don't you think he seemed " to be good-natured? '—' Immensely so indeed, Mamma,' replied she. ' I think he has a great deal to say upon ' every thing, and is never at a loss; and the more trifling ' the subject the more he has to say.'—' Yes,' cried Olivia, ' he is well enough for a man; but for my part, ' I don't much like him, he is so extremely impudent ' and familiar; but on the guitar he is shocking.' These two last speeches I interpreted by contraries. I found by this, that Sophia internally despised, as much as Olivia secretly admired him.——' Whatever may be your ' opinions of him, my children,' cried I, ' to confess the ' truth, he has not prepossest me in his favour. Dispro- ' portioned friendships ever terminate in disgust; and ' I thought, notwithstanding all his ease, that he seemed ' perfectly sensible of the distance between us. Let us ' keep to companions of our own rank. There is no ' character more contemptible than a man that is a for- ' tune-hunter; and I can see no reason why fortune-

'hunting women should not be contemptible too. Thus,
'at best, we shall be contemptible if his views are honour-
'able ; but if they be otherwise ! I should shudder but
'to think of that ! It is true I have no apprehensions
'from the conduct of my children, but I think there are
'some from his character.'—I would have proceeded,
but for the interruption of a servant from the 'Squire,
who, with his compliments, sent us a side of venison, and
a promise to dine with us some days after. This well-
timed present pleaded more powerfully in his favour,
than any thing I had to say could obviate. I therefore
continued silent, satisfied with just having pointed out
danger, and leaving it to their own discretion to avoid
it. That virtue which requires to be ever guarded, is
scarce worth the centinel.

—— I could not avoid, however, observing the assiduity of Mr. Burchell in assisting my daughter Sophia in her part of the task.—Page 217.

CHAPTER VI

The happiness of a country fireside.

AS we carried on the former dispute with some degree of warmth, in order to accommodate matters it was universally agreed that we should have a part of the venison for supper, and the girls undertook the task with alacrity. 'I am sorry,' cried I, 'that we have no neighbour or 'stranger to take a part in this good chear : feasts of 'this kind acquire a double relish from hospitality.'— 'Bless me,' cried my wife, 'here comes our good friend 'Mr. Burchell, that saved our Sophia, and that run you 'down fairly in the argument.'—'Confute me in argu-

' ment, child ! ' cried I. ' You mistake there, my dear,
' I believe there are but few that can do that : I never
' dispute your abilities at making a goose-pye, and I beg
' you'll leave argument to me.'—As I spoke, poor
Mr. Burchell entered the house, and was welcomed by
the family, who shook him heartily by the hand, while
little Dick officiously reached him a chair.

I was pleased with the poor man's friendship, for two
reasons : because I knew that he wanted mine, and
I knew him to be friendly as far as he was able. He
was known in our neighbourhood by the character of
the poor Gentleman that would do no good when he
was young, though he was not yet thirty. He would
at intervals talk with great good sense ; but in general
he was fondest of the company of children, whom he
used to call harmless little men. He was famous, I found,
for singing them ballads, and telling them stories ; and
seldom went out without something in his pockets for
them, a piece of gingerbread, or an halfpenny whistle.
He generally came for a few days into our neighbourhood
once a year, and lived upon the neighbours' hospitality.
He sate down to supper among us, and my wife was not
sparing of her gooseberry-wine. The tale went round ;
he sang us old songs, and gave the children the story
of the Buck of Beverland, with the history of Patient
Grissel, the adventures of Catskin, and then Fair Rosamond's Bower Our cock, which always crew at eleven,
now told us it was time for repose ; but an unforeseen
difficulty started about lodging the stranger ; all our
beds were already taken up, and it was too late to send
him to the next alehouse. In this dilemma, little Dick
offered him his part of the bed, if his brother Moses
would let him lie with him ; ' And I,' cried Bill, ' will
' give Mr. Burchell my part, if my sisters will take me
' to theirs.'—' Well done, my good children,' cried I,

' hospitality is one of the first Christian duties. The
' beast retires to its shelter, and the bird flies to its nest ;
' but helpless man can only find refuge from his fellow-
' creature. The greatest stranger in this world, was He
' that came to save it. He never had an house, as if
' willing to see what hospitality was left remaining
' amongst us. Deborah, my dear,' cried I, to my wife,
' give those boys a lump of sugar each, and let Dick's
' be the largest because he spoke first.'

In the morning early I called out my whole family to
help at saving an after-growth of hay, and our guest
offering his assistance, he was accepted among the number.
Our labours went on lightly ; we turned the swath to
the wind. I went foremost, and the rest followed in due
succession. I could not avoid, however, observing the
assiduity of Mr. Burchell in assisting my daughter Sophia
in her part of the task. When he had finished his own,
he would join in her's, and enter into a close conversation : but I had too good an opinion of Sophia's understanding, and was too well convinced of her ambition, to
be under any uneasiness from a man of broken fortune.
When we were finished for the day, Mr. Burchell was
invited as on the night before ; but he refused, as he
was to lie that night at a neighbour's, to whose child he
was carrying a whistle. When gone, our conversation at
supper turned upon our late unfortunate guest. ' What
' a strong instance,' said I, ' is that poor man of the
' miseries attending a youth of levity and extravagance.
' He by no means wants sense, which only serves to aggra-
' vate his former folly. Poor forlorn creature, where are
' now the revellers, the flatterers, that he could once
' inspire and command ? Gone, perhaps, to attend the
' bagnio pander, grown rich by his extravagance. They
' once praised him, and now they applaud the pander :
' their former raptures at his wit are now converted into

'sarcasms at his folly : he is poor, and perhaps deserves
'poverty ; for he has neither the ambition to be inde-
'pendent, nor the skill to be useful.' Prompted perhaps
by some secret reasons, I delivered this observation with
too much acrimony, which my Sophia gently reproved.
'Whatsoever his former conduct may have been, Papa,
'his circumstances should exempt him from censure now.
'His present indigence is a sufficient punishment for
'former folly, and I have heard my Papa himself say,
'that we should never strike one unnecessary blow at
'a victim over whom Providence holds the scourge of
'its resentment.'—'You are right, Sophy,' cried my son
Moses, 'and one of the ancients finely represents so
'malicious a conduct, by the attempts of a rustic to
'flay Marsyas whose skin, the fable tells us, had been
'wholly stript off by another. Besides, I don't know if
'this poor man's situation be so bad as my father would
'represent it. We are not to judge of the feelings of
'others by what we might feel if in their place. How-
'ever dark the habitation of the mole to our eyes, yet
'the animal itself finds the apartment sufficiently light-
'some. And to confess a truth, this man's mind seems
'fitted to his station ; for I never heard any one more
'sprightly than he was to-day, when he conversed with
'you.' This was said without the least design ; however, it excited a blush, which she strove to cover by
an affected laugh, assuring him, that she scarce took
any notice of what he said to her ; but that she believed
he might once have been a very fine gentleman. The
readiness with which she undertook to vindicate herself,
and her blushing, were symptoms I did not internally
approve ; but I represt my suspicions.

As we expected our landlord the next day, my wife
went to make the venison pasty. Moses sate reading,
while I taught the little ones : my daughters seemed

equally busy with the rest ; and I observed them for a good while cooking something over the fire. I at first supposed they were assisting their mother ; but little Dick informed me in a whisper, that they were making a *wash* for the face. Washes of all kinds I had a natural antipathy to ; for I knew that instead of mending the complexion they spoiled it. I therefore approached my chair by sly degrees to the fire, and grasping the poker, as if it wanted mending, seemingly by accident, over-turned the whole composition, and it was too late to begin another.

— This effectually raised the laugh against poor Moses.—PAGE 222.

CHAPTER VII

A town wit described. The dullest fellows may learn to be
comical for a night or two.

WHEN the morning arrived on which we were to
entertain our young landlord, it may be easily
supposed what provisions were exhausted to make an
appearance. It may also be conjectured that my wife
and daughters expanded their gayest plumage upon this
occasion. Mr. Thornhill came with a couple of friends,
his chaplain and feeder. The servants, who were numerous, he politely ordered to the next alehouse, but my
wife, in the triumph of her heart, insisted on entertaining
them all; for which, by the by, our family was pinched
for three weeks after. As Mr. Burchell had hinted to us
the day before, that he was making some proposals of
marriage to Miss Wilmot, my son George's former mistress, this a good deal damped the heartiness of his

reception : but accident, in some measure, relieved our embarrassment ; for one of the company happening to mention her name, Mr. Thornhill observed with an oath, that he never knew any thing more absurd than calling such a fright a beauty : ' For strike me ugly,' continued he, ' if I should not find as much pleasure in choosing ' my mistress by the information of a lamp under the ' clock at St. Dunstan's.' At this he laughed, and so did we :—the jests of the rich are ever successful. Olivia too could not avoid whispering loud enough to be heard, that he had an infinite fund of humour.

After dinner, I began with my usual toast, the Church ; for this I was thanked by the chaplain, as he said the Church was the only mistress of his affections.——' Come, ' tell us honestly, Frank,' said the 'Squire, with his usual archness, ' suppose the Church, your present mistress, ' drest in lawn sleeves, on one hand, and Miss Sophia, ' with no lawn about her, on the other, which would you ' be for ? ' ' For both, to be sure,' cried the chaplain.— ' Right, Frank,' cried the 'Squire, ' for may this glass ' suffocate me but a fine girl is worth all the priestcraft ' in the Creation. For what are tithes and tricks but an ' imposition, all a confounded imposture, and I can prove ' it.'——' I wish you would,' cried my son Moses, ' and ' I think,' continued he, ' that I should be able to answer ' you.'—' Very well, Sir,' cried the 'Squire, who immediately smoked him, and winking on the rest of the company, to prepare us for the sport, ' if you are for a cool ' argument upon that subject, I am ready to accept the ' challenge. And first, whether are you for managing it ' analogically or dialogically ? ' ' I am for managing it ' rationally,' cried Moses, quite happy at being permitted to dispute. ' Good again,' cried the 'Squire, ' and firstly, ' of the first. I hope you'll not deny that whatever is, ' is. If you don't grant me that I can go no further.'——

' Why,' returned Moses, ' I think I may grant that, and
' make the best of it.'—' I hope too,' returned the other,
' you'll grant that a part is less than the whole.' ' I grant
' that too,' cried Moses, ' it is but just and reasonable.'
——' I hope,' cried the 'Squire, ' you will not deny, that
' the two angles of a triangle are equal to two right
' ones.'—' Nothing can be plainer,' returned t'other, and
looked round with his usual importance.—' Very well,'
cried the 'Squire, speaking very quick, ' the premises
' being thus settled, I proceed to observe, that the con-
' catenation of self-existence, proceeding in a reciprocal
' duplicate ratio, naturally produces a problematical
' dialogism, which in some measure proves that the
' essence of spirituality may be referred to the second
' predicable.'——' Hold, hold,'——cried the other, ' I
' deny that : Do you think I can thus tamely submit
' to such heterodox doctrines ? '—' What,' replied the
'Squire, as if in a passion, ' not submit ! Answer me one
' plain question : Do you think Aristotle right when he
' says, that relatives are related ? ' ' Undoubtedly,'
replied the other. ' If so then,' cried the 'Squire, ' answer
' me directly to what I propose : Whether do you judge
' the analytical investigation of the first part of my
' enthymem deficient secundum quoad, or quoad minus,
' and give me your reasons, give me your reasons, I say,
' directly.'——' I protest,' cried Moses, ' I don't rightly
' comprehend the force of your reasoning ; but if it be
' reduced to one simple proposition, I fancy it may then
' have an answer.'——' O Sir,' cried the 'Squire, ' I am
' your most humble servant, I find you want me to
' furnish you with argument and intellects too. No, Sir,
' there I protest you are too hard for me.' This effectually
raised the laugh against poor Moses, who sate the only
dismal figure in a group of merry faces : nor did he offer
a single syllable more during the whole entertainment.

But though all this gave me no pleasure, it had a very different effect upon Olivia, who mistook it for humour, though but a mere act of the memory. She thought him therefore a very fine gentleman ; and such as consider what powerful ingredients a good figure, fine clothes, and fortune are in that character, will easily forgive her. Mr. Thornhill, notwithstanding his real ignorance, talked with ease, and could expatiate upon the common topics of conversation with fluency. It is not surprising then that such talents should win the affections of a girl, who by education was taught to value an appearance in herself, and consequently to set a value upon it in another.

Upon his departure, we again entered into a debate upon the merits of our young landlord. As he directed his looks and conversation to Olivia, it was no longer doubted but that she was the object that induced him to be our visitor. Nor did she seem to be much displeased at the innocent raillery of her brother and sister upon this occasion. Even Deborah herself seemed to share the glory of the day, and exulted in her daughter's victory as if it were her own. ' And now, my dear,' cried she to me, ' I'll fairly own, that it was I that instructed ' my girls to encourage our landlord's addresses. I had ' always some ambition, and you now see that I was ' right ; for who knows how this may end ? ' ' Aye, ' who knows that indeed,' answered I, with a groan : ' for my part I don't much like it ; and I could have " been better pleased with one that was poor and honest, ' than this fine gentleman with his fortune and infidelity ; ' for depend on't, if he be what I suspect him, no free- ' thinker shall ever have a child of mine.'

' Sure, father,' cried Moses, ' you are too severe in this ; ' for Heaven will never arraign him for what he thinks, ' but for what he does. Every man has a thousand ' vicious thoughts, which arise without his power to

'suppress. Thinking freely of religion may be involun-
'tary with this gentleman : so that allowing his senti-
'ments to be wrong, yet as he is purely passive in his
'assent, he is no more to be blamed for his errors, than
'the governor of a city without walls for the shelter he
'is obliged to afford an invading enemy.'

'True, my son,' cried I ; 'but, if the governor invites
'the enemy there, he is justly culpable. And such is
'always the case with those who embrace error. The
'vice does not lie in assenting to the proofs they see ;
'but in being blind to many of the proofs that offer.
'So that, though our erroneous opinions be involuntary
'when formed, yet as we have been wilfully corrupt, or
'very negligent in forming them, we deserve punishment
'for our vice, or contempt for our folly.'

My wife now kept up the conversation, though not the
argument : she observed, that several very prudent men
of our acquaintance were free-thinkers, and made very
good husbands ; and she knew some sensible girls that
had skill enough to make converts of their spouses :
'And who knows, my dear,' continued she, 'what Olivia
'may be able to do. The girl has a great deal to say
'upon every subject, and to my knowledge is very well
'skilled in controversy.'

'Why, my dear, what controversy can she have read ? '
cried I. 'It does not occur to me that I ever put such
'books into her hands : you certainly over-rate her
'merit.' 'Indeed, Papa,' replied Olivia, 'she does not .'
'I have read a great deal of controversy. I have read
'the disputes between Thwackum and Square ; the
'controversy between Robinson Crusoe and Friday the
'savage, and I am now employed in reading the con-
'troversy in Religious Courtship.' 'Very well,' cried
I, 'that's a good girl, I find you are perfectly qualified
'for making converts, and so go help your mother to
'make the gooseberry-pye.'

—— So loud a report, and so near, startled my daughters: and I could perceive that Sophia in the fright had thrown herself into Mr. Burchell's arms for protection.—PAGE 234.

CHAPTER VIII

An amour, which promises little good fortune, yet may be productive of much.

THE next morning we were again visited by Mr. Burchell, though I began, for certain reasons, to be displeased with the frequency of his return; but I could not refuse him my company and fire-side. It is true his labour more than requited his entertainment; for he wrought among us with vigour, and either in the meadow or at the hay-rick put himself foremost. Besides, he had always something amusing to say that lessened our toil, and was at once so out of the way, and yet so sensible, that I loved, laughed at, and pitied him. My only dislike arose from an attachment he discovered to my daughter : he would in a jesting manner, call her his little mistress, and when he bought each of the girls a set of ribbands, her's was the finest. I knew not how, but he every day seemed to become more amiable, his wit to improve, and his simplicity to assume the superior airs of wisdom.

Our family dined in the field, and we sate, or rather reclined, round a temperate repast, our cloth spread upon the hay, while Mr. Burchell gave cheerfulness to the feast. To heighten our satisfaction, two blackbirds answered each other from opposite hedges, the familiar red-breast came and pecked the crumbs from our hands, and every sound seemed but the echo of tranquillity. ' I never sit thus,' says Sophia, ' but I think of the two lovers so ' sweetly described by Mr. Gay, who were struck dead in ' each other's arms. There is something so pathetic in ' the description, that I have read it an hundred times ' with new rapture.'——' In my opinion,' cried my son, ' the finest strokes in that description are much below ' those in the Acis and Galatea of Ovid. The Roman ' poet understands the use of *contrast* better, and upon ' that figure artfully managed, all strength in the pathetic ' depends.'——' It is remarkable,' cried Mr. Burchell, ' that both the poets you mention have equally con- ' tributed to introduce a false taste into their respective ' countries, by loading all their lines with epithet. Men ' of little genius found them most easily imitated in their ' defects ; and English poetry, like that in the latter ' empire of Rome, is nothing at present but a combination ' of luxuriant images, without plot or connexion ; a string ' of epithets that improve the sound, without carrying ' on the sense. But perhaps, madam, while I thus repre-

MR. BURCHELL READING THE BALLAD OF
THE HERMIT

' hend others, you'll think it just that I should give them
' an opportunity to retaliate, and indeed I have made
' this remark, only to have an opportunity of introducing
' to the company a ballad, which, whatever be its other
' defects, is I think at least free from those I have
' mentioned.'

A BALLAD

I.

' TURN, gentle Hermit of the dale,
 And guide my lonely way,
To where yon taper cheers the vale
 With hospitable ray.

II.

' For here forlorn and lost I tread,
 With fainting steps and slow ;
Where wilds, immeasurably spread,
 Seem length'ning as I go.'

III.

' Forbear, my son,' the Hermit cries,
 ' To tempt the dangerous gloom ;
For yonder faithless phantom flies
 To lure thee to thy doom.

IV.

' Here to the houseless child of want
 My door is open still ;
And though my portion is but scant,
 I give it with good will.

V.

' Then turn to-night, and freely share
 Whate'er my cell bestows ;
My rushy couch and frugal fare,
 My blessing and repose.

VI.

'No flocks that range the valley free,
  To slaughter I condemn ;
Taught by that Power that pities me,
  I learn to pity them :

VII.

'But from the mountain's grassy side
  A guiltless feast I bring ;
A scrip with herbs and fruits supply'd,
  And water from the spring.

VIII.

'Then, pilgrim, turn, thy cares forego ;
  All earth-born cares are wrong ;
Man wants but little here below,
  Nor wants that little long.'

IX.

Soft as the dew from Heav'n descends,
  His gentle accents fell :
The modest stranger lowly bends,
  And follows to the cell.

X.

Far in a wilderness obscure
  The lonely mansion lay ;
A refuge to the neighb'ring poor
  And strangers led astray.

XI.

No stores beneath its humble thatch
  Requir'd a master's care ;
The wicket, op'ning with a latch,
  Receiv'd the harmless pair.

XII.

And now, when busy crowds retire
  To take their ev'ning rest,
The Hermit trimm'd his little fire,
  And cheer'd his pensive guest :

XIII.

And spread his vegetable store,
  And gayly prest, and smil'd ;
And skill'd in legendary lore
  The ling'ring hours beguil'd.

XIV.

Around in sympathetic mirth
  Its tricks the kitten tries,
The cricket chirrups in the hearth,
  The crackling faggot flies.

XV.

But nothing could a charm impart
  To soothe the stranger's woe ;
For grief was heavy at his heart,
  And tears began to flow.

XVI.

His rising cares the Hermit spied,
  With answ'ring care opprest :
' And whence, unhappy youth,' he cried,
  ' The sorrows of thy breast ?

XVII.

' From better habitations spurn'd,
  Reluctant dost thou rove ?
Or grieve for friendship unreturn'd,
  Or unregarded love ?

XVIII.

' Alas ! the joys that fortune brings,
    Are trifling and decay ;
And those who prize the paltry things,
    More trifling still than they.

XIX.

' And what is friendship but a name,
    A charm that lulls to sleep :
A shade that follows wealth or fame,
    But leaves the wretch to weep ?

XX.

' And love is still an emptier sound,
    The modern fair one's jest :
On earth unseen, or only found
    To warm the turtle's nest.

XXI.

' For shame, fond youth, thy sorrows hush,
    And spurn the sex,' he said :
But while he spoke, a rising blush
    His love-lorn guest betray'd.

XXII.

Surpris'd he sees new beauties rise,
    Swift mantling to the view ;
Like colours o'er the morning skies,
    As bright, as transient too.

XXIII.

The bashful look, the rising breast,
    Alternate spread alarms :
The lovely stranger stands confest
    A maid in all her charms.

XXIV.

'And ah ! forgive a stranger rude,
  A wretch forlorn,' she cried ;
'Whose feet unhallow'd thus intrude
  Where Heav'n and you reside.

XXV.

'But let a maid thy pity share,
  Whom love has taught to stray :
Who seeks for rest, but finds despair
  Companion of her way.

XXVI.

'My father liv'd beside the Tyne,
  A wealthy Lord was he :
And all his wealth was mark'd as mine,
  He had but only me.

XXVII.

'To win me from his tender arms,
  Unnumber'd suitors came ;
Who praised me for imputed charms,
  And felt or feign'd a flame.

XXVIII.

'Each hour a mercenary crowd
  With richest proffers strove :
Among the rest young Edwin bow'd,
  But never talk'd of love.

XXIX.

'In humble, simplest habit clad,
  No wealth nor power had he ;
Wisdom and worth were all he had,
  But these were all to me.

XXX.

'And when, beside me in the dale,
  He carol'd lays of love,
His breath lent fragrance to the gale,
  And music to the grove.

XXXI.

'The blossom opening to the day,
  The dews of Heav'n refin'd,
Could nought of purity display
  To emulate his mind.

XXXII.

'The dew, the blossom on the tree,
  With charms inconstant shine ;
Their charms were his, but woe to me,
  Their constancy was mine.

XXXIII.

'For still I try'd each fickle art,
  Importunate and vain ;
And while his passion touch'd my heart,
  I triumph'd in his pain.

XXXIV.

'Till quite dejected with my scorn,
  He left me to my pride ;
And sought a solitude forlorn,
  In secret where he died.

XXXV.

'But mine the sorrow, mine the fault,
  And well my life shall pay ;
I'll seek the solitude he sought,
  And stretch me where he lay.

XXXVI.

' And there forlorn, despairing, hid,
    I'll lay me down and die ;
'Twas so for me that Edwin did,
    And so for him will I.'

XXXVII.

' Forbid it Heav'n ! ' the Hermit cried,
    And clasp'd her to his breast :
The wond'ring fair one turn'd to chide,—
    'Twas Edwin's self that prest.

XXXVIII.

' Turn, Angelina, ever dear,
    My charmer turn to see
Thy own, thy long-lost Edwin here,
    Restor'd to love and thee.

XXXIX.

' Thus let me hold thee to my heart,
    And ev'ry care resign :
And shall we never, never part,
    My life,—my all that 's mine ?

XL.

' No, never from this hour to part,
    We'll live and love so true ;
The sigh that rends thy constant heart,
    Shall break thy Edwin's too.'

While this ballad was reading, Sophia seemed to mix
an air of tenderness with her approbation. But our
tranquillity was soon disturbed by the report of a gun
just by us, and immediately after a man was seen

bursting through the hedge, to take up the game he had killed. This sportsman was the 'Squire's chaplain, who had shot one of the blackbirds that so agreeably entertained us. So loud a report, and so near, startled my daughters : and I could perceive that Sophia in the fright had thrown herself into Mr. Burchell's arms for protection. The gentleman came up, and asked pardon for having disturbed us, affirming that he was ignorant of our being so near. He therefore sate down by my youngest daughter, and sportsman-like, offered her what he had killed that morning. She was going to refuse, but a private look from her mother soon induced her to correct the mistake, and accept his present, though with some reluctance. My wife, as usual, discovered her pride in a whisper, observing, that Sophy had made a conquest of the chaplain, as well as her sister had of the 'Squire. I suspected, however, with more probability, that her affections were placed upon a different object. The chaplain's errand was to inform us, that Mr. Thornhill had provided music and refreshments, and intended that night giving the young ladies a ball by moonlight, on the grass-plot before our door. ' Nor can I deny,' continued he, ' but I have an interest in being first to deliver ' this message, as I expect for my reward to be honoured ' with Miss Sophy's hand as a partner.' To this my girl replied, that she should have no objection, if she could do it with honour ; ' But here,' continued she, ' is a gentle- ' man,' looking at Mr. Burchell, ' who has been my com- ' panion in the task for the day, and it is fit he should ' share in its amusements.' Mr. Burchell returned her a compliment for her intentions ; but resigned her up to the chaplain, adding that he was to go that night five miles, being invited to an harvest supper. His refusal appeared to me a little extraordinary, nor could I conceive how so sensible a girl as my youngest, could thus prefer a man of broken fortune to one whose expectations were much greater. But as men are most capable of distinguishing merit in women, so the ladies often form the truest judgments of us. The two sexes seem placed as spies upon each other, and are furnished with different abilities, adapted for mutual inspection.

— and when got about half-way home, perceived the procession marching
slowly forward towards the church.—PAGE 245.

CHAPTER IX

Two ladies of great distinction introduced.   Superior finery ever
seems to confer superior breeding.

MR. BURCHELL had scarce taken leave, and Sophia
consented to dance with the chaplain, when my
little ones came running out to tell us that the 'Squire was
come with a crowd of company.   Upon our return, we
found our landlord, with a couple of under gentlemen and
two young ladies richly drest, whom he introduced as

women of very great distinction and fashion from town. We happened not to have chairs enough for the whole company : but Mr. Thornhill immediately proposed that every gentleman should sit in a lady's lap. This I positively objected to, notwithstanding a look of disapprobation from my wife. Moses was therefore dispatched to borrow a couple of chairs ; and as we were in want of ladies to make up a set at country dances, the two gentlemen went with him in quest of a couple of partners. Chairs and partners were soon provided. The gentlemen returned with my neighbour Flamborough's rosy daughters, flaunting with red top-knots. But an unlucky circumstance was not adverted to; though the Miss Flamboroughs were reckoned the very best of dancers in the parish, and understood the jig and the round-about to perfection, yet they were totally unacquainted with country dances. This at first discomposed us : however, after a little shoving and dragging, they at last went merrily on. Our music consisted of two fiddles, with a pipe and tabor. The moon shone bright, Mr. Thornhill and my eldest daughter led up the ball, to the great delight of the spectators ; for the neighbours, hearing what was going forward, came flocking about us. My girl moved with so much grace and vivacity, that my wife could not avoid discovering the pride of her heart, by assuring me, that though the little chit did it so cleverly, all the steps were stolen from herself. The ladies of the town strove hard to be equally easy, but without success. They swam, sprawled, languished, and frisked ; but all would not do : the gazers indeed owned that it was fine ; but neighbour Flamborough observed, that Miss Livy's feet seemed as pat to the music as its echo. After the dance had continued about an hour, the two ladies, who were apprehensive of catching cold, moved to break up the ball. One of them, I thought, expressed her sentiments upon this occasion in a very coarse manner, when she observed, that by the *living jingo, she was all of a muck of sweat*. Upon our return to the house, we found a very elegant cold supper, which Mr. Thornhill had ordered to be brought with him. The conversation at this time was more reserved than before. The two ladies threw my girls quite into the shade ; for they would talk of nothing but high life, and high-lived company ; with other fashionable topics, such as pictures, taste, Shakespear, and the musical glasses. 'Tis true they once or twice mortified us sensibly by slipping out an oath ; but that appeared to me as the surest symptom of their distinction, (though I am since informed that swearing is perfectly unfashionable). Their finery, however, threw a veil over any grossness in their conversation. My daughters seemed to regard their superior accomplishments with envy ; and what appeared amiss was ascribed to tip-top quality breeding. But the condescension of the ladies was still superior to their other accomplishments. One of them observed that had Miss Olivia seen a little more of the world, it would greatly improve her. To which the other added, that a single winter in town would make little Sophia quite another thing. My wife warmly assented to both, adding, that there was nothing she more ardently wished than to give her girls a single winter's polishing. To this I could not help replying, that their breeding was already superior to their fortune ; and that greater refinement would only serve to make their poverty ridiculous, and give them a taste for pleasures they had no right to possess.—' And what pleasures,' cried Mr. Thornhill, ' do they not deserve to possess, who have so much in ' their power to bestow ? As for my part,' continued he, ' my fortune is pretty large, love, liberty and pleasure ' are my maxims ; but curse me if a settlement of half ' my estate could give my charming Olivia pleasure, it

'should be hers ; and the only favour I would ask in
'return would be to add myself to the benefit.' I was
not such a stranger to the world as to be ignorant that
this was the fashionable cant to disguise the insolence
of the basest proposal ; but I made an effort to suppress
my resentment. 'Sir,' cried I, 'the family which you
'now condescend to favour with your company, has
'been bred with as nice a sense of honour as you. Any
'attempts to injure that, may be attended with very
'dangerous consequences. Honour, Sir, is our only
'possession at present, and of that last treasure we must
'be particularly careful.'—I was soon sorry for the
warmth with which I had spoken this, when the young
gentleman, grasping my hand, swore he commended my
spirit, though he disapproved my suspicions. 'As to
'your present hint,' continued he, 'I protest nothing was
'farther from my heart than such a thought. No, by all
'that 's tempting, the virtue that will stand a regular
'siege was never to my taste ; for all my amours are
'carried by a coup de main.'

The two ladies, who affected to be ignorant of the
rest, seemed highly displeased with this last stroke of
freedom, and began a very discreet and serious dialogue
upon virtue ; in this my wife, the chaplain, and I soon
joined ; and the 'Squire himself was at last brought to
confess a sense of sorrow for his former excesses. We
talked of the pleasures of temperance, and of the sunshine
in the mind unpolluted with guilt. I was so well pleased,
that my little ones were kept up beyond the usual time to
be edified by so much good conversation. Mr. Thornhill
even went beyond me, and demanded if I had any objection to giving prayers. I joyfully embraced the proposal,
and in this manner the night was passed in a most comfortable way, till at last the company began to think of
returning. The ladies seemed very unwilling to part with

my daughters ; for whom they had conceived a particular affection, and joined in a request to have the pleasure of their company home. The 'Squire seconded the proposal, and my wife added her entreaties ; the girls too looked upon me as if they wished to go. In this perplexity I made two or three excuses, which my daughters as readily removed ; so that at last I was obliged to give a peremptory refusal ; for which we had nothing but sullen looks and short answers the whole day ensuing.

—— But previously **I** should have mentioned the very impolite behaviour
of Mr. Burchell, who during this discourse, sate with his face turned to the fire,
and at the conclusion of every sentence would cry out *fudge !*—PAGE 249.

CHAPTER X

The family endeavours to cope with their betters.   The miseries
of the poor when they attempt to appear above their circumstances.

I NOW began to find that all my long and painful
lectures upon temperance, simplicity, and contentment,
were entirely disregarded.   The distinctions lately paid us
by our betters awaked that pride which I had laid asleep,
but not removed.   Our windows again, as formerly,
were filled with washes for the neck and face.   The sun
was dreaded as an enemy to the skin without doors, and
the fire as a spoiler of the complexion within.   My wife
observed, that rising too early would hurt her daughters'
eyes, that working after dinner would redden their noses,

and she convinced me that the hands never looked so
white as when they did nothing. Instead therefore of
finishing George's shirts, we now had them new modelling
their old gauzes, or flourishing upon cat-gut. The poor
Miss Flamboroughs, their former gay companions, were
cast off as mean acquaintance, and the whole conversation ran upon high life, and high-lived company, with
pictures, taste, Shakespear, and the musical glasses.

But we could have borne all this, had not a fortune-
telling gipsey come to raise us into perfect sublimity.
The tawny sybil no sooner appeared, than my girls came
running to me for a shilling a piece to cross her hand
with silver. To say the truth, I was tired of being always
wise, and could not help gratifying their request, because
I loved to see them happy. I gave each of them a
shilling ; though, for the honour of the family, it must
be observed that they never went without money themselves, as my wife always generously let them have
a guinea each, to keep in their pockets ; but with strict
injunctions never to change it. After they had been
closeted up with the fortune-teller for some time, I knew
by their looks, upon their returning, that they had been
promised something great.—' Well my girls, how have
' you sped ? Tell me, Livy, has the fortune-teller given
' thee a penny-worth ? '—' I protest, Papa,' says the
girl, ' I believe she deals with somebody that 's not
' right ; for she positively declared, that I am to be
' married to a 'Squire in less than a twelvemonth ! '—
' Well, now Sophy, my child,' said I, ' and what sort of
' a husband are you to have ? ' ' Sir,' replied she, ' I am
' to have a Lord soon after my sister has married the
' 'Squire.'——' How,' cried I, ' is that all you are to have
' for your two shillings ! Only a Lord and a 'Squire for
' two shillings ! You fools, I could have promised you
' a Prince and a Nabob for half the money.'

This curiosity of theirs, however, was attended with very serious effects : we now began to think ourselves designed by the stars to something exalted, and already anticipated our future grandeur.

It has been a thousand times observed, and I must observe it once more, that the hours we pass with happy prospects in view, are more pleasing than those crowned with fruition. In the first case, we cook the dish to our own appetite ; in the latter, nature cooks it for us. It is impossible to repeat the train of agreeable reveries we called up for our entertainment. We looked upon our fortunes as once more rising ; and as the whole parish asserted that the 'Squire was in love with my daughter, she was actually so with him ; for they persuaded her into the passion. In this agreeable interval, my wife had the most lucky dreams in the world, which she took care to tell us every morning, with great solemnity and exactness. It was one night a coffin and cross bones, the sign of an approaching wedding ; at another time she imagined her daughters' pockets filled with farthings, a certain sign they would shortly be stuffed with gold. The girls themselves had their omens. They felt strange kisses on their lips ; they saw rings in the candle, purses bounced from the fire, and true love-knots lurked in the bottom of every tea-cup.

Towards the end of the week we received a card from the town ladies ; in which, with their compliments, they hoped to see all our family at church the Sunday following. All Saturday morning I could perceive, in consequence of this, my wife and daughters in close conference together, and now and then glancing at me with looks that betrayed a latent plot. To be sincere, I had strong suspicions that some absurd proposal was preparing for appearing with splendour the next day. In the evening they began their operations in a very regular manner, and my wife undertook to conduct the siege. After tea, when I seemed in spirits, she began thus——'I fancy, 'Charles, my dear, we shall have a great deal of good com-'pany at our church to-morrow.'—'Perhaps we may, 'my dear,' returned I, 'though you need be under no 'uneasiness about that, you shall have a sermon whether 'there be or not.'——'That is what I expect,' returned she ; 'but I think, my dear, we ought to appear there as 'decently as possible, for who knows what may happen?' 'Your precautions,' replied I, 'are highly commendable. 'A decent behaviour and appearance in church is what 'charms me. We should be devout and humble, chear-'ful and serene.'—'Yes,' cried she, 'I know that ; but 'I mean we should go there in as proper a manner as 'possible; not altogether like the scrubs about us.' 'You are quite right, my dear' returned I, 'and I was 'going to make the very same proposal. The proper 'manner of going is, to go there as early as possible, to 'have time for meditation before the service begins.'— 'Phoo, Charles,' interrupted she, 'all that is very true ; 'but not what I would be at. I mean we should go there 'genteelly. You know the church is two miles off, and 'I protest I don't like to see my daughters trudging up 'to their pew all blowzed and red with walking, and 'looking for all the world as if they had been winners 'at a smock race. Now, my dear, my proposal is this : 'there are our two plow horses, the Colt that has been 'in our family these nine years, and his companion 'Blackberry, that has scarce done an earthly thing 'for this month past. They are both grown fat and 'lazy. Why should not they do something as well as 'we ? And let me tell you, when Moses has trimmed 'them a little, they will cut a very tolerable figure.'

To this proposal I objected, that walking would be twenty times more genteel than such a paltry conveyance,

as Blackberry was wall-eyed, and the Colt wanted a tail :
that they had never been broke to the rein ; but had an
hundred vicious tricks ; and that we had but one saddle
and pillion in the whole house. All these objections
however, were over-ruled ; so that I was obliged to
comply. The next morning I perceived them not a little
busy in collecting such materials as might be necessary
for the expedition ; but as I found it would be a business
of time, I walked on to the church before, and they
promised speedily to follow. I waited near an hour in
the reading desk for their arrival ; but not finding them
come as expected, I was obliged to begin, and went
through the service, not without some uneasiness at
finding them absent. This was encreased when all was
finished, and no appearance of the family. I therefore
walked back by the horse-way, which was five miles round,
though the foot-way was but two, and when got about
half-way home, perceived the procession marching slowly
forward towards the church ; my son, my wife, and the
two little ones exalted on one horse, and my two daughters
upon the other. I demanded the cause of their delay ;
but I soon found by their looks they had met with
a thousand misfortunes on the road. The horses had at
first refused to move from the door, till Mr. Burchell
was kind enough to beat them forward for about two
hundred yards with his cudgel. Next, the straps of my
wife's pillion broke down, and they were obliged to stop
to repair them before they could proceed. After that,
one of the horses took it into his head to stand still, and
neither blows nor entreaties could prevail with him to
proceed. He was just recovering from this dismal situation when I found them ; but perceiving every thing
safe, I own their present mortification did not much
displease me, as it would give me many opportunities of
future triumph, and teach my daughters more humility.

—— We all followed him several paces from the door, bawling after him good luck, good luck, till we could see him no longer.—PAGE 254.

CHAPTER XI

The family still resolve to hold up their heads.

MICHAELMAS eve happening on the next day, we were invited to burn nuts and play tricks at neighbour Flamborough's. Our late mortifications had humbled us a little, or it is probable we might have rejected such an invitation with contempt : however, we suffered ourselves to be happy. Our honest neighbour's goose and dumplings were fine, and the lamb's-wool, even in the opinion of my wife, who was a connoisseur, was excellent. It is true, his manner of telling stories was not quite so well. They were very long, and very dull, and all about himself, and we had laughed at them ten times before : however, we were kind enough to laugh at them once more.

Mr. Burchell, who was of the party, was always fond of seeing some innocent amusement going forward, and set the boys and girls to blind man's buff. My wife too was persuaded to join in the diversion, and it gave me pleasure to think she was not yet too old. In the mean time, my neighbour and I looked on, laughed at every feat, and praised our own dexterity when we were young. Hot cockles succeeded next, questions and commands followed that, and last of all, they sat down to hunt the slipper. As every person may not be acquainted with this primaeval pastime, it may be necessary to observe, that the company at this play plant themselves in a ring upon the ground all except one who stands in the middle, whose business it is to catch a shoe, which the company shove about under their hams from one to another, something like a weaver's shuttle. As it is impossible, in this case, for the lady who is up to face all the company at once, the great beauty of the play lies in hitting her a thump with the heel of the shoe on that side least capable of making a defence. It was in this manner that my eldest daughter was hemmed in, and thumped about, all blowzed, in spirits, and bawling for fair play, fair play, with a voice that might deafen a ballad singer, when, confusion on confusion, who should enter the room but our two great acquaintances from town, Lady Blarney and Miss Carolina Wilhelmina Amelia Skeggs ! Description would but beggar, therefore it is unnecessary to describe this new mortification. Death ! To be seen by ladies of such high breeding in such vulgar attitudes !

Nothing better could ensue from such a vulgar play of Mr. Flamborough's proposing. We seemed stuck to the ground for some time, as if actually petrified with amazement.

The two ladies had been at our house to see us, and finding us from home, came after us hither, as they were uneasy to know what accident could have kept us from church the day before. Olivia undertook to be our prolocutor, and delivered the whole in a summary way, only saying, ' We were thrown from our horses.' At which account the ladies were greatly concerned ; but being told the family received no hurt, they were extremely glad : but being informed that we were almost killed by the fright, they were vastly sorry ; but hearing that we had a very good night, they were extremely glad again. Nothing could exceed their complaisance to my daughters ; their professions the last evening were warm, but now they were ardent. They protested a desire of having a more lasting acquaintance. Lady Blarney was particularly attached to Olivia; Miss Carolina Wilhelmina Amelia Skeggs (I love to give the whole name) took a greater fancy to her sister. They supported the conversation between themselves, while my daughters sate silent, admiring their exalted breeding. But as every reader, however beggarly himself, is fond of high-lived dialogues, with anecdotes of Lords, Ladies, and Knights of the Garter, I must beg leave to give him the concluding part of the present conversation.

' All that I know of the matter,' cried Miss Skeggs, ' is
' this, that it may be true, or it may not be true : but
' this I can assure your Ladyship, that the whole rout was
' in amaze ; his Lordship turned all manner of colours,
' my Lady fell into a sound, but Sir Tomkyn, drawing his
' sword, swore he was her's to the last drop of his blood.'

' Well,' replied our Peeress, ' this I can say, that the

' Duchess never told me a syllable of the matter, and
' I believe her Grace would keep nothing a secret from
' me. This you may depend on as fact, that the next
' morning my Lord Duke cried out three times to his
' valet de chambre, " Jernigan, Jernigan, Jernigan, bring
' " me my garters." '

But previously I should have mentioned the very
impolite behaviour of Mr. Burchell, who during this discourse, sate with his face turned to the fire, and at the
conclusion of every sentence would cry out *fudge*, an
expression which displeased us all, and in some measure
damped the rising spirit of the conversation.

' Besides, my dear Skeggs,' continued our Peeress,
' there is nothing of this in the copy of verses that
' Dr. Burdock made upon the occasion.' *Fudge!*

' I am surprized at that,' cried Miss Skeggs ; ' for he
' seldom leaves any thing out, as he writes only for his
' own amusement. But can your Ladyship favour me
' with a sight of them ? ' *Fudge!*

' My dear creature,' replied our Peeress, ' do you think
' I carry such things about me ? Though they are very
' fine to be sure, and I think myself something of a judge ;
' at least I know what pleases myself. Indeed I was
' ever an admirer of all Doctor Burdock's little pieces ;
' for except what he does, and our dear Countess at
' Hanover-Square, there 's nothing comes out but the
' most lowest stuff in nature ; not a bit of high life
' among them.' *Fudge!*

' Your Ladyship should except,' says t'other, ' your
' own things in the Lady's Magazine. I hope you'll say
' there 's nothing low-lived there ? But I suppose we
' are to have no more from that quarter ? ' *Fudge!*

' Why, my dear,' says the Lady, ' you know my reader
' and companion has left me, to be married to Captain
' Roach, and as my poor eyes won't suffer me to write

'myself, I have been for some time looking out for
'another. A proper person is no easy matter to find,
'and to be sure thirty pounds a year is a small stipend
'for a well-bred girl of character, that can read, write,
'and behave in company ; as for the chits about town,
'there is no bearing them about one.' *Fudge!*

'That I know,' cried Miss Skeggs, 'by experience.
'For of the three companions I had this last half year,
'one of them refused to do plain-work an hour in the day,
'another thought twenty-five guineas a year too small
'a salary, and I was obliged to send away the third,
'because I suspected an intrigue with the chaplain.
'Virtue, my dear Lady Blarney, virtue is worth any
'price ; but where is that to be found ?' *Fudge!*

My wife had been for a long time all attention to this
discourse ; but was particularly struck with the latter
part of it. Thirty pounds and twenty-five guineas a
year made fifty-six pounds five shillings English money,
all which was in a manner going a-begging, and might
easily be secured in the family. She for a moment studied
my looks for approbation ; and, to own a truth, I was of
opinion, that two such places would fit our two daughters
exactly. Besides, if the 'Squire had any real affection
for my eldest daughter, this would be the way to make
her every way qualified for her fortune. My wife therefore was resolved that we should not be deprived of
such advantages for want of assurance, and undertook
to harangue for the family. 'I hope,' cried she, 'your
'Ladyships will pardon my present presumption. It is
'true, we have no right to pretend to such favours ; but
'yet it is natural for me to wish putting my children
'forward in the world. And I will be bold to say my
'two girls have had a pretty good education, and capa-
'city, at least the country can't shew better. They can
'read, write, and cast accompts ; they understand their

' needle, breadstitch, cross and change, and all manner
' of plain-work ; they can pink, point, and frill ; and
' know something of music ; they can do up small
' clothes, work upon catgut ; my eldest can cut paper,
' and.my youngest has a very pretty manner of telling
' fortunes upon the cards.' *Fudge!*

When she had delivered this pretty piece of eloquence,
the two ladies looked at each other a few minutes in
silence, with an air of doubt and importance. At last,
Miss Carolina Wilhelmina Amelia Skeggs condescended to
observe, that the young ladies, from the opinion she
could form of them from so slight an acquaintance,
seemed very fit for such employments : ' But a thing
' of this kind, Madam,' cried she, addressing my spouse,
' requires a thorough examination into characters, and
' a more perfect knowledge of each other. Not, madam,'
continued she, ' that I in the least suspect the young
' ladies' virtue, prudence, and discretion ; but there is
' a form in these things, Madam, there is a form.'

My wife approved her suspicions very much, observing,
that she was very apt to be suspicious herself ; but
referred her to all the neighbours for a character : but
this our Peeress declined as unnecessary, alleging that
her cousin Thornhill's recommendation would be sufficient, and upon this we rested our petition.

—— By this time I began to have a most hearty contempt for the poor animal myself, and was almost ashamed at the approach of every customer.—PAGE 264.

CHAPTER XII

Fortune seems resolved to humble the family of Wakefield. Mortifications are often more painful than real calamities.

WHEN we were returned home, the night was dedicated to schemes of future conquest. Deborah exerted much sagacity in conjecturing which of the two girls was likely to have the best place, and most opportunities of seeing good company. The only obstacle to our preferment was in obtaining the 'Squire's recommendation; but he had already shewn us too many instances of his friendship to doubt of it now. Even in bed my wife kept up the usual theme : ' Well, faith, my ' dear Charles, between ourselves, I think we have made ' an excellent day's work of it.'——' Pretty well,' cried I, not knowing what to say.——' What, only pretty ' well ! ' returned she. ' I think it is very well. Suppose ' the girls should come to make acquaintances of taste ' in town ! This I am assured of, that London is the ' only place in the world for all manner of husbands. ' Besides, my dear, stranger things happen every day : ' and as ladies of quality are so taken with my daughters, ' what will not men of quality be ! *Entre nous*, I protest ' I like my Lady Blarney vastly, so very obliging. How-' ever, Miss Carolina Wilhelmina Amelia Skeggs has my ' warm heart. But yet, when they came to talk of places ' in town, you saw at once how I nailed them. Tell me, ' my dear, don't you think I did for my children there ? ' ——' Ay,' returned I, not knowing well what to think of the matter, ' Heaven grant they may be both the ' better for it this day three months ! ' This was one of those observations I usually made to impress my wife with an opinion of my sagacity : for if the girls succeeded, then it was a pious wish fulfilled ; but if any thing unfortunate ensued, then it might be looked upon as a prophecy. All this conversation, however, was only preparatory to another scheme, and indeed I dreaded as much. This was nothing less than, that as we were now to hold up our heads a little higher in the world, it would be proper to sell the Colt, which was grown old, at a neighbouring fair, and buy us a horse that would carry single or double upon an occasion, and make a pretty appearance at church or upon a visit. This at first I opposed stoutly ; but it was as stoutly defended. However, as I weakened, my antagonists gained strength, till at last it was resolved to part with him.

As the fair happened on the following day, I had intentions of going myself ; but my wife persuaded me that
I had got a cold, and nothing could prevail upon her to
permit me from home. ' No, my dear,' said she, ' our
' son Moses is a discreet boy, and can buy and sell to very
' good advantage ; you know all our great bargains are
' of his purchasing. He always stands out and higgles,
' and actually tires them till he gets a bargain.'

As I had some opinion of my son's prudence, I was
willing enough to entrust him with this commission ; and
the next morning I perceived his sisters mighty busy in
fitting out Moses for the fair ; trimming his hair, brushing
his buckles, and cocking his hat with pins. The business
of the toilet being over, we had at last the satisfaction of
seeing him mounted upon the Colt, with a deal box before
him to bring home groceries in. He had on a coat made
of that cloth they call thunder and lightning, which,
though grown too short, was much too good to be thrown
away. His waistcoat was of gosling green, and his sisters
had tied his hair with a broad black ribband. We all
followed him several paces from the door, bawling after
him good luck, good luck, till we could see him no longer.

He was scarce gone, when Mr. Thornhill's butler came
to congratulate us upon our good fortune, saying, that
he overheard his young master mention our names with
great commendation.

Good fortune seemed resolved not to come alone.
Another footman from the same family followed, with
a card for my daughters, importing, that the two ladies
had received such pleasing accounts from Mr. Thornhill
of us all, that, after a few previous enquiries, they
hoped to be perfectly satisfied. ' Ay,' cried my wife,
' I now see it is no easy matter to get into the families
' of the great ; but when one once gets in, then, as Moses
' says, one may go sleep.' To this piece of humour,

for she intended it for wit, my daughters assented with
a loud laugh of pleasure. In short, such was her satisfaction at this message, that she actually put her hand in her
pocket, and gave the messenger seven-pence halfpenny.

This was to be our visiting-day. The next that came
was Mr. Burchell, who had been at the fair. He brought
my little ones a pennyworth of gingerbread each, which
my wife undertook to keep for them, and give them by
letters at a time. He brought my daughters also a
couple of boxes, in which they might keep wafers, snuff,
patches, or even money, when they got it. My wife was
usually fond of a weasel-skin purse, as being the most
lucky; but this by the by. We had still a regard for
Mr. Burchell, though his late rude behaviour was in some
measure displeasing; nor could we now avoid communicating our happiness to him, and asking his advice:
although we seldom followed advice, we were all ready
enough to ask it. When he read the note from the two
ladies, he shook his head, and observed, that an affair of
this sort demanded the utmost circumspection.——This
air of diffidence highly displeased my wife. 'I never
'doubted, Sir,' cried she, 'your readiness to be against
'my daughters and me. You have more circumspection
'than is wanted. However, I fancy when we come to ask
'advice, we will apply to persons who seem to have made
'use of it themselves.'——'Whatever my own conduct
'may have been, Madam,' replied he, 'is not the present
'question; though as I have made no use of advice
'myself, I should in conscience give it to those that will.'
——As I was apprehensive this answer might draw on
a repartee, making up by abuse what it wanted in wit,
I changed the subject, by seeming to wonder what could
keep our son so long at the fair, as it was now almost night-
fall.——'Never mind our son,' cried my wife, 'depend
'upon it he knows what he is about. I'll warrant we'll

'never see him sell his hen of a rainy day. I have seen
'him buy such bargains as would amaze one. I'll tell
'you a good story about that, that will make you split
'your sides with laughing——But as I live, yonder comes
'Moses, without an horse, and the box at his back.'

As she spoke, Moses came slowly on foot, and sweating
under the deal box, which he had strapt round his shoulders like a pedlar.—'Welcome, welcome, Moses; well,
'my boy, what have you brought us from the fair?'——
'I have brought you myself,' cried Moses, with a sly
look, and resting the box on the dresser.—'Ah, Moses,'
cried my wife, 'that we know, but where is the horse?'
'I have sold him,' cried Moses, 'for three pounds five
'shillings and two-pence.'——'Well done, my good boy,'
returned she, 'I knew you would touch them off. Be-
'tween ourselves, three pounds five shillings and two-
'pence is no bad day's work. Come let us have it then.'
——'I have brought back no money,' cried Moses again,
'I have laid it all out in a bargain, and here it is,' pulling
out a bundle from his breast : 'here they are ; a groce of
'green spectacles, with silver rims and shagreen cases.'
——'A groce of green spectacles!' repeated my wife in
a faint voice. 'And you have parted with the Colt, and
'brought us back nothing but a groce of green paltry
'spectacles!'—'Dear mother,' cried the boy, 'why won't
'you listen to reason? I had them a dead bargain, or
'I should not have bought them. The silver rims alone
'will sell for double the money.'—'A fig for the silver
'rims,' cried my wife in a passion : 'I dare swear they
'won't sell for above half the money at the rate of broken
'silver, five shillings an ounce.' 'You need be under no
'uneasiness,' cried I, 'about selling the rims ; for they
'are not worth sixpence, for I perceive they are only
'copper varnished over.'—'What,' cried my wife, 'not
'silver, the rims not silver!' 'No,' cried I, 'no more

'silver than your saucepan.'—'And so,' returned she,
'we have parted with the Colt, and have only got a groce
'of green spectacles, with copper rims and shagreen cases!
'A murrain take such trumpery. The blockhead has
'been imposed upon, and should have known his com-
'pany better.'—'There, my dear,' cried I, 'you are
'wrong, he should not have known them at all.'—'Marry,
'hang the idiot,' returned she, 'to bring me such stuff;
'if I had them I would throw them in the fire.' 'There
'again you are wrong, my dear,' cried I; 'for though
'they be copper, we will keep them by us, as copper
'spectacles, you know, are better than nothing.'

By this time the unfortunate Moses was undeceived.
He now saw that he had indeed been imposed upon by a
prowling sharper, who, observing his figure, had marked
him for an easy prey. I therefore asked the circumstances
of his deception. He sold the horse, it seems, and walked
the fair in search of another. A reverend looking man
brought him to a tent, under pretence of having one to
sell. 'Here,' continued Moses, 'we met another man, very
'well drest, who desired to borrow twenty pounds upon
'these, saying, that he wanted money, and would dis-
'pose of them for a third of the value. The first gentle-
'man, who pretended to be my friend, whispered me to
'buy them, and cautioned me not to let so good an offer
'pass. I sent for Mr. Flamborough, and they talked
'him up as finely as they did me, and so at last we were
'persuaded to buy the two groce between us.'

—— There seemed indeed something applicable to both sides in this letter, and its censures might as well be referred to those to whom it was written, as to us; but the malicious meaning was obvious, and we went no farther.—Page 271.

CHAPTER XIII

Mr. Burchell is found to be an enemy; for he has the confidence to give disagreeable advice.

OUR family had now made several attempts to be fine; but some unforeseen disaster demolished each as soon as projected. I endeavoured to take the advantage of every disappointment, to improve their good sense in proportion as they were frustrated in ambition. 'You 'see, my children,' cried I, 'how little is to be got by 'attempts to impose upon the world, in coping with our 'betters. Such as are poor and will associate with none

'but the rich, are hated by those they avoid, and despised
'by those they follow.   Unequal combinations are always
'disadvantageous to the weaker side : the rich having
'the pleasure, and the poor the inconveniences that
'result from them.   But come, Dick, my boy, and repeat
'the fable that you were reading to-day, for the good of
'the company.'

'Once upon a time,' cried the child, 'a Giant and a
'Dwarf were friends, and kept together.   They made a
'bargain that they would never forsake each other, but
'go seek adventures.   The first battle they fought was
'with two Saracens, and the Dwarf, who was very
'courageous, dealt one of the champions a most angry
'blow.   It did the Saracen very little injury, who lifting
'up his sword, fairly struck off the poor Dwarf's arm.
'He was now in a woeful plight ; but the Giant coming
'to his assistance, in a short time left the two Saracens
'dead on the plain, and the Dwarf cut off the dead man's
'head out of spite.   They then travelled on to another
'adventure.   This was against three bloody-minded
'Satyrs, who were carrying away a damsel in distress.
'The Dwarf was not quite so fierce now as before ; but
'for all that, struck the first blow, which was returned
'by another, that knocked out his eye ; but the Giant was
'soon up with them, and had they not fled, would cer-
'tainly have killed them every one.   They were all very
'joyful for this victory, and the damsel who was relieved
'fell in love with the Giant and married him.   They now
'travelled far, and farther than I can tell, till they met
'with a company of robbers.   The Giant, for the first
'time, was foremost now ; but the Dwarf was not far
'behind.   The battle was stout and long.   Wherever
'the Giant came all fell before him ; but the Dwarf had
'like to have been killed more than once.   At last the
'victory declared for the two adventurers ; but the

'Dwarf lost his leg. The Dwarf was now without an
'arm, a leg, and an eye, while the Giant was without a
'single wound. Upon which he cried out to his little
'companion, My little hero, this is glorious sport ; let us
'get one victory more, and then we shall have honour
'for ever. No, cries the Dwarf, who was by this time
'grown wiser, no, I declare off ; I'll fight no more : for
'I find in every battle that you get all the honour and
'rewards, but all the blows fall upon me.'

I was going to moralize this fable, when our attention
was called off to a warm dispute between my wife and
Mr. Burchell, upon my daughters' intended expedition
to town. My wife very strenuously insisted upon the
advantages that would result from it ; Mr. Burchell, on
the contrary, dissuaded her with great ardour, and I stood
neuter. His present dissuasions seemed but the second
part of those which were received with so ill a grace in
the morning. The dispute grew high, while poor
Deborah, instead of reasoning stronger, talked louder,
and at last was obliged to take shelter from a defeat in
clamour. The conclusion of her harangue, however, was
highly displeasing to us all : she knew, she said, of some
who had their own secret reasons for what they advised ;
but, for her part, she wished such to stay away from her
house for the future.—'Madam,' cried Burchell, with
looks of great composure, which tended to inflame her
the more, 'as for secret reasons, you are right : I have
'secret reasons, which I forbear to mention, because you
'are not able to answer those of which I make no secret :
'but I find my visits here are become troublesome : I'll
'take my leave therefore now, and perhaps come once
'more to take a final farewell when I am quitting the
'country.' Thus saying, he took up his hat, nor could
the attempts of Sophia, whose looks seemed to upbraid
his precipitancy, prevent his going.

When gone, we all regarded each other for some minutes with confusion. My wife, who knew herself to be the cause, strove to hide her concern with a forced smile, and an air of assurance, which I was willing to reprove : ' How, woman,' cried I to her, ' is it thus we ' treat strangers ? Is it thus we return their kindness ? ' Be assured, my dear, that these were the harshest words, ' and to me the most unpleasing, that have escaped your ' lips ! '—' Why would he provoke me then ? ' replied she ; ' but I know the motives of his advice perfectly ' well. He would prevent my girls from going to town, ' that he may have the pleasure of my youngest daughter's ' company here at home. But whatever happens, she ' shall chuse better company than such low-lived fellows ' as he.'—' Low-lived, my dear, do you call him ? ' cried I ; ' it is very possible we may mistake this man's ' character, for he seems upon some occasions the most ' finished gentleman I ever knew.——Tell me, Sophia, my ' girl, has he ever given you any secret instances of his ' attachment ! '—' His conversation with me, Sir,' replied my daughter, ' has ever been sensible, modest, and ' pleasing. As to aught else, no, never. Once, indeed, ' I remember to have heard him say he never knew a ' woman who could find merit in a man that seemed poor.' ' Such my dear,' cried I, ' is the common cant of all the ' unfortunate or idle. But I hope you have been taught ' to judge properly of such men, and that it would be even ' madness to expect happiness from one who has been ' so very bad an economist of his own. Your mother and ' I have now better prospects for you. The next winter, ' which you will probably spend in town, will give you ' opportunities of making a more prudent choice.'

What Sophia's reflections were upon this occasion I can't pretend to determine ; but I was not displeased at the bottom, that we were rid of a guest from whom

I had much to fear. Our breach of hospitality went to my conscience a little; but I quickly silenced that monitor by two or three specious reasons, which served to satisfy and reconcile me to myself. The pain which conscience gives the man who has already done wrong, is soon got over. Conscience is a coward, and those faults it has not strength enough to prevent, it seldom has justice enough to accuse.

—— Then the poor woman would sometimes tell the 'Squire, that she thought him and Olivia extremely of a size, and would bid both stand up to see which was tallest.—PAGE 277.

CHAPTER XIV

Fresh mortifications, or a demonstration that seeming calamities may be real blessings.

THE journey of my daughters to town was now resolved upon, Mr. Thornhill having kindly promised to inspect their conduct himself, and inform us by letter of their behaviour. But it was thought indispensably necessary that their appearance should equal the greatness of their expectations, which could not be done without expence. We debated therefore in full council what were the easiest methods of raising money, or more properly speaking, what we could most conveniently sell. The deliberation was soon finished ; it was found that our remaining horse was utterly useless for the plough, without his companion, and equally unfit for the road, as wanting an eye ; it was therefore determined that we should dispose of him for the purposes above mentioned, at the neighbouring fair, and, to prevent imposition, that I should go with him myself. Though this was one of the first mercantile transactions of my life, yet I had no doubt about acquitting myself with reputation. The opinion a man forms of his own prudence is measured by that of the company he keeps ; and as mine was mostly in the family way, I had conceived no unfavourable sentiments of my worldly wisdom. My wife, however, next morning, at parting, after I had got some paces from the door, called me back, to advise me, in a whisper, to have all my eyes about me.

I had, in the usual forms, when I came to the fair, put my horse through all his paces ; but for some time had no bidders. At last a chapman approached, and, after he had for a good while examined the horse round, finding him blind of one eye, he would have nothing to say to him : a second came up ; but observing he had a spavin, declared he would not take him for the driving home : a third perceived he had a windgall, and would bid no money : a fourth knew by his eye that he had the botts : a fifth wondered what a plague I could do at the fair with a blind, spavined, galled hack, that was only fit to be cut up for a dog-kennel. By this time I began to have a most hearty contempt for the poor animal myself, and was almost ashamed at the approach of every customer ; for though I did not entirely believe all the fellows told me, yet I reflected that the number of witnesses was

a strong presumption they were right, and St. Gregory,
upon Good Works, professes himself to be of the same
opinion.

I was in this mortifying situation, when a brother
clergyman, an old acquaintance, who had also business at
the fair, came up, and shaking me by the hand, proposed
adjourning to a public-house and taking a glass of whatever we could get. I readily closed with the offer, and
entering an ale-house, we were shewn into a little back
room, where there was only a venerable old man, who
sat wholly intent over a large book, which he was reading.
I never in my life saw a figure that prepossessed me more
favourably. His locks of silver grey venerably shaded
his temples, and his green old age seemed to be the result
of health and benevolence. However, his presence did not
interrupt our conversation; my friend and I discoursed on
the various turns of fortune we had met; the Whistonian
controversy, my last pamphlet, the arch-deacon's reply,
and the hard measure that was dealt me. But our attention was in a short time taken off by the appearance of
a youth, who, entering the room, respectfully said something softly to the old stranger. 'Make no apologies,
' my child,' said the old man, ' to do good is a duty we
' owe to all our fellow creatures : take this, I wish it were
' more ; but five pounds will relieve your distress, and
' you are welcome.' The modest youth shed tears of
gratitude, and yet his gratitude was scarce equal to
mine. I could have hugged the good old man in my
arms, his benevolence pleased me so. He continued to
read, and we resumed our conversation, until my companion, after some time, recollecting that he had business
to transact in the fair, promised to be soon back : adding,
that he always desired to have as much of Dr. Primrose's
company as possible. The old gentleman hearing my
name mentioned, seemed to look at me with attention for

some time, and when my friend was gone, most respectfully demanded if I was in any way related to the great
Primrose, that courageous Monogamist, who had been
the bulwark of the Church. Never did my heart feel
sincerer rapture than at that moment. 'Sir,' cried I,
'the applause of so good a man, as I am sure you are,
'adds to that happiness in my breast which your benevo-
'lence has already excited. You behold before you, Sir,
'that Dr. Primrose, the Monogamist, whom you have
'been pleased to call great. You here see that unfor-
'tunate Divine, who has so long, and it would ill become
'me to say, successfully, fought against the Deuterogamy
'of the age.' 'Sir,' cried the stranger, struck with awe,
'I fear I have been too familiar ; but you'll forgive my
'curiosity, Sir : I beg pardon.' 'Sir,' cried I, grasping
his hand, 'you are so far from displeasing me by your
'familiarity, that I must beg you'll accept my friendship,
'as you already have my esteem.'——'Then with
'gratitude I accept the offer,' cried he, squeezing me by
the hand, 'thou glorious pillar of unshaken orthodoxy ;
'and do I behold—' I here interrupted what he was going
to say ; for though, as an author, I could digest no small
share of flattery, yet now my modesty would permit no
more. However, no lovers in romance ever cemented a
more instantaneous friendship. We talked upon several
subjects : at first I thought he seemed rather devout
than learned, and began to think he despised all human
doctrines as dross. Yet this no way lessened him in my
esteem ; for I had for some time begun privately to harbour such an opinion myself. I therefore took occasion
to observe, that the world in general began to be blame-
ably indifferent as to doctrinal matters, and followed
human speculations too much——'Ay, Sir,' replied he,
as if he had reserved all his learning to that moment, 'Ay,
'Sir, the world is in its dotage, and yet the cosmogony, or

'creation of the world has puzzled philosophers of all
'ages. What a medley of opinions have they not
'broached upon the creation of the world ? Sanchonia-
'thon, Manetho, Berosus, and Ocellus Lucanus have all
'attempted it in vain. The latter has these words,
'*Anarchon ara kai atelutaion to pan,* which imply that all
'things have neither beginning nor end. Manetho also,
'who lived about the time of Nebuchadon-Asser, Asser
'being a Syriac word usually applied as a surname to the
'kings of that country, as Teglat Phael-Asser, Nabon-
'Asser, he, I say, formed a conjecture equally absurd ;
'for as we usually say, *ek to biblion kubernetes,* which
'implies that books will never teach the world ; so he
'attempted to investigate—But, Sir, I ask pardon, I am
'straying from the question.'——That he actually was ;
nor could I for my life see how the creation of the world
had any thing to do with the business I was talking of ;
but it was sufficient to shew me that he was a man of
letters, and I now reverenced him the more. I was
resolved, therefore, to bring him to the touchstone ; but
he was too mild and too gentle to contend for victory.
Whenever I made any observation that looked like a
challenge to controversy, he would smile, shake his head,
and say nothing ; by which, I understood he could say
much, if he thought proper. The subject therefore
insensibly changed from the business of antiquity to
that which brought us both to the fair ; mine I told him
was to sell an horse, and very luckily, indeed, his was to
buy one for one of his tenants. My horse was soon produced, and in fine we struck a bargain. Nothing now
remained but to pay me, and he accordingly pulled out
a thirty pound note, and bid me change it. Not being
in a capacity of complying with his demand, he ordered
his footman to be called up, who made his appearance in
a very genteel livery. 'Here Abraham,' cried he, 'go

'and get gold for this ; you'll do it at neighbour Jackson's
'or any where.' While the fellow was gone, he entertained me with a pathetic harangue on the great scarcity
of silver, which I undertook to improve, by deploring
also the great scarcity of gold ; so that by the time Abraham returned, we had both agreed that money was never
so hard to be come at as now. Abraham returned to inform us, that he had been over the whole fair, and could
not get change, though he had offered half a crown for
doing it. This was a very great disappointment to us
all ; but the old gentleman, having paused a little, asked
me if I knew one Solomon Flamborough, in my part of
the country ; upon replying that he was my next door
neighbour ; 'If that be the case then,' returned he, 'I
'believe we shall deal. You shall have a draught upon
'him, payable at sight ; and let me tell you he is as warm
'a man as any within five miles round him. Honest
'Solomon and I have been acquainted for many years
'together. I remember I always beat him at three
'jumps ; but he could hop upon one leg farther than I.'
A draught upon my neighbour was to me the same as
money ; for I was sufficiently convinced of his ability.
The draught was signed, and put into my hands, and
Mr. Jenkinson, the old gentleman, his man Abraham, and
my horse, old Blackberry, trotted off very well pleased
with each other.

After a short interval, being left to reflection, I began to
recollect that I had done wrong in taking a draught from
a stranger, and so prudently resolved upon following the
purchaser, and having back my horse. But this was
now too late : I therefore made directly homewards,
resolving to get the draught changed into money at my
friend's as fast as possible. I found my honest neighbour smoking his pipe at his own door, and informing
him that I had a small bill upon him, he read it twice

over. 'You can read the name, I suppose,' cried I,
'Ephraim Jenkinson.' 'Yes,' returned he, 'the name
'is written plain enough, and I know the gentleman too,
'the greatest rascal under the canopy of heaven. This is
'the very same rogue who sold us the spectacles. Was
'he not a venerable looking man, with grey hair, and no
'flaps to his pocket-holes ? And did he not talk a long
'string of learning about Greek and cosmogony, and the
'world ? ' To this I replied with a groan. 'Ay,' continued he, 'he has but that one piece of learning in the
'world, and he always talks it away whenever he finds a
'scholar in company ; but I know the rogue, and will
'catch him yet.'

Though I was already sufficiently mortified, my
greatest struggle was to come, in facing my wife and
daughters. No truant was ever more afraid of returning
to school, there to behold the master's visage, than I was
of going home. I was determined, however, to anticipate
their fury, by first falling into a passion myself.

But, alas ! upon entering, I found the family no way
disposed for battle. My wife and girls were all in tears,
Mr. Thornhill having been there that day to inform them,
that their journey to town was entirely over. The two
ladies having heard reports of us from some malicious
person about us, were that day set out for London. He
could neither discover the tendency, nor the author of
these : but whatever they might be, or whoever might
have broached them, he continued to assure our family
of his friendship and protection. I found, therefore, that
they bore my disappointment with great resignation,
as it was eclipsed in the greatness of their own. But what
perplexed us most was to think who could be so base as
to asperse the character of a family so harmless as ours,
too humble to excite envy, and too inoffensive to create
disgust.

—— 'Yes, she is gone off with two gentlemen in a post-chaise, and one of them
kissed her, and said he would die for her.'—PAGE 289.

CHAPTER XV

All Mr. Burchell's villainy at once detected.   The folly of being
over-wise.

THAT evening and a part of the following day was employed in fruitless attempts to discover our enemies :
scarcely a family in the neighbourhood but incurred our
suspicions, and each of us had reasons for our opinion
best known to ourselves.   As we were in this perplexity,
one of our little boys, who had been playing abroad,

brought in a letter-case, which he found on the Green. It was quickly known to belong to Mr. Burchell, with whom it had been seen, and, upon examination, contained some hints upon different subjects ; but what particularly engaged our attention was a sealed note, superscribed, *the copy of a letter to be sent to the ladies at Thornhill-castle.* It instantly occurred that he was the base informer, and we deliberated whether the note should not be broke open. I was against it ; but Sophia, who said she was sure that of all men he would be the last to be guilty of so much baseness, insisted upon its being read. In this she was seconded by the rest of the family, and at their joint solicitation, I read as follows :

' LADIES,

' The bearer will sufficiently satisfy you as to the
' person from whom this comes : one at least the friend
' of innocence, and ready to prevent its being seduced.
' I am informed for a truth, that you have some intention
' of bringing two young ladies to town whom I have some
' knowledge of, under the character of companions. As
' I would neither have simplicity imposed upon, nor virtue
' contaminated, I must offer it as my opinion, that the
' impropriety of such a step will be attended with dan-
' gerous consequences. It has never been my way to
' treat the infamous or the lewd with severity ; nor
' should I now have taken this method of explaining
' myself, or reproving folly, did it not aim at guilt. Take
' therefore the admonition of a friend, and seriously reflect
' on the consequences of introducing infamy and vice
' into retreats where peace and innocence have hitherto
' resided.'

Our doubts were now at an end. There seemed indeed something applicable to both sides in this letter, and its censures might as well be referred to those to whom it was written, as to us; but the malicious meaning was obvious, and we went no farther. My wife had scarce patience to hear me to the end, but railed at the writer with unrestrained resentment. Olivia was equally severe, and Sophia seemed perfectly amazed at his baseness. As for my part, it appeared to me one of the vilest instances of unprovoked ingratitude I had met with. Nor could I account for it in any other manner than by imputing it to his desire of detaining my youngest daughter in the country, to have the more frequent opportunities of an interview. In this manner we all sate ruminating upon schemes of vengeance, when our other little boy came running in to tell us that Mr. Burchell was approaching at the other end of the field. It is easier to conceive than describe the complicated sensations which are felt from the pain of a recent injury, and the pleasure of approaching vengeance. Though our intentions were only to upbraid him with his ingratitude, yet it was resolved to do it in a manner that would be perfectly cutting. For this purpose we agreed to meet him with our usual smiles, to chat in the beginning with more than ordinary kindness, to amuse him a little; and then in the midst of the flattering calm to burst upon him like an earthquake, and overwhelm him with the sense of his own baseness. This being resolved upon, my wife undertook to manage the business herself, as she really had some talents for such an undertaking. We saw him approach, he entered, drew a chair, and sate down.——' A fine day, Mr. Burchell.'—' A very fine day, ' Doctor; though I fancy we shall have some rain by the ' shooting of my corns.'——' The shooting of your horns,' cried my wife in a loud fit of laughter, and then asked pardon for being fond of a joke.——' Dear madam,' replied he, ' I pardon you with all my heart, for I protest ' I should not have thought it a joke had you not told

' me.'—' Perhaps not, Sir,' cried my wife, winking at us,
' and yet I dare say you can tell us how many jokes go
' to an ounce.'——' I fancy, madam,' returned Burchell,
' you have been reading a jest book this morning, that
' ounce of jokes is so very good a conceit ; and yet,
' madam, I had rather see half an ounce of understanding.'
' I believe you might,' cried my wife, still smiling at us,
though the laugh was against her ; ' and yet I have seen
' some men pretend to understanding that have very
' little.' ' And no doubt,' replied her antagonist, ' you
' have known ladies set up for wit that had none.'—I
quickly began to find that my wife was likely to gain but
little at this business ; so I resolved to treat him in a style
of more severity myself. ' Both wit and understanding,'
cried I, ' are trifles without integrity ; it is that which
' gives value to every character. The ignorant peasant
' without fault, is greater than the philosopher with
' many ; for what is genius or courage without an heart ?
' *An honest man is the noblest work of God.*'

' I always held that hackney'd maxim of Pope,' returned Mr. Burchell, ' as very unworthy a man of genius,
' and a base desertion of his own superiority. As the
' reputation of books is raised not by their freedom from
' defect, but the greatness of their beauties ; so should
' that of men be prized, not for their exemption from
' fault, but the size of those virtues they are possessed of.
' The scholar may want prudence, the statesman may
' have pride, and the champion ferocity ; but shall we
' prefer to these the low mechanic, who laboriously plods
' through life without censure or applause ? We might
' as well prefer the tame correct paintings of the Flemish
' school to the erroneous, but sublime animations of the
' Roman pencil.'

' Sir,' replied I, ' your present observation is just,
' when there are shining virtues and minute defects ; but

' when it appears that great vices are opposed in the
' same mind to as extraordinary virtues, such a character
' deserves contempt.'

' Perhaps,' cried he, ' there may be some such monsters
' as you describe, of great vices joined to great virtues ;
' yet in my progress through life, I never yet found one
' instance of their existence : on the contrary, I have
' ever perceived, that where the mind was capacious, the
' affections were good. And indeed Providence seems
' kindly our friend in this particular, thus to debilitate
' the understanding where the heart is corrupt, and
' diminish the power, where there is the will to do mis-
' chief. This rule seems to extend even to other animals :
' the little vermin race are ever treacherous, cruel, and
' cowardly, whilst those endowed with strength and power
' are generous, brave, and gentle.'

' These observations sound well,' returned I, ' and yet
' it would be easy this moment to point out a man,' and
I fixed my eye stedfastly upon him, ' whose head and
' heart form a most detestable contrast. Ay, Sir,' continued I, raising my voice, ' and I am glad to have this
' opportunity of detecting him in the midst of his fancied
' security. Do you know this, Sir, this pocket-book ? '
——' Yes, Sir,' returned he, with a face of impenetrable
assurance, ' that pocket-book is mine, and I am glad you
' have found it.'——' And do you know,' cried I, ' this
' letter ? Nay, never falter, man ; but look me full in
' the face : I say, do you know this letter ? '——' That
' letter,'—returned he, ' yes, it was I that wrote that
' letter.'—' And how could you,' said I, 'so basely, so
' ungratefully presume to write this letter ? '—' And
' how came you,' replied he, with looks of unparalleled
effrontery, ' so basely to presume to break open this
' letter ? Don't you know, now, I could hang you all
' for this ? All that I have to do is to swear at the

' next justice's, that you have been guilty of breaking
' open the lock of my pocket-book, and so hang you all
' up at his door.' This piece of unexpected insolence
raised me to such a pitch, that I could scarcely govern
my passion. ' Ungrateful wretch, begone, and no longer
' pollute my dwelling with thy baseness : begone, and
' never let me see thee again : go from my door, and
' the only punishment I wish thee is an alarmed con-
' science, which will be a sufficient tormentor!' So saying,
I threw him his pocket book, which he took up with
a smile, and shutting the clasps with the utmost composure, left us, quite astonished at the serenity of his
assurance. My wife was particularly enraged that
nothing could make him angry, or make him seem
ashamed of his villanies. ' My dear,' cried I, willing to
calm those passions that had been raised too high among
us, ' we are not to be surprised that bad men want
' shame ; they only blush at being detected in doing
' good, but glory in their vices.

' Guilt and shame, says the allegory, were at first com-
' panions, and in the beginning of their journey insepar-
' ably kept together. But their union was soon found
' to be disagreeable and inconvenient to both ; guilt gave
' shame frequent uneasiness, and shame often betrayed
' the secret conspiracies of guilt. After long disagree-
' ment, therefore, they at length consented to part for
' ever. Guilt boldly walked forward alone, to overtake
' fate, that went before in the shape of an executioner :
' but shame being naturally timorous, returned back to
' keep company with virtue, which, in the beginning of
' their journey, they had left behind. Thus my children,
' after men have travelled through a few stages in vice,
' shame forsakes them, and returns back to wait upon
' the few virtues they have still remaining.'

—— I was struck dumb with the apprehensions of my own absurdity, when whom should I next see enter the room but my dear Miss Arabella Wilmot.— PAGE 304.

CHAPTER XVI

The family use art, which is opposed with still greater.

WHATEVER might have been Sophia's sensations, the rest of the family was easily consoled for Mr. Burchell's absence by the company of our landlord, whose visits now became more frequent and longer. Though he had been disappointed in procuring my daughters the amusements of the town as he designed, he took every opportunity of supplying them with those little recreations which our retirement would admit of. He usually came in the morning, and while my son and I followed our occupations abroad, he sat with the family at home, and amused them by describing the town, with every part of which he was particularly acquainted. He could repeat all the observations that were retailed in the atmosphere of the play-houses, and had all the good things of the high wits by rote long before they made way into the jest-books. The intervals between conversation were employed in teaching my daughters piquet, or sometimes in setting my two little ones to box to make them *sharp*, as he called it : but the hopes of having him for a son-in-law, in some measure blinded us to all his imperfections. It must be owned that my wife laid a thousand schemes to entrap him ; or, to speak it more tenderly, used every art to magnify the merit of her daughter. If the cakes at tea eat short and crisp, they were made by Olivia ; if the gooseberry wine was well knit, the gooseberries were of her gathering ; it was her fingers which gave the pickles their peculiar green ; and in the composition of a pudding, it was her judgment that mixed the ingredients. Then the poor woman would sometimes tell the 'Squire, that she thought him and Olivia extremely of a size, and would bid both stand up to see which was tallest. These instances of cunning, which she thought impenetrable, yet which every body saw through, were very pleasing to our benefactor, who gave every day some new proofs of his passion, which, though they had not arisen to proposals of marriage, yet we thought fell but little short of it ; and his slowness was attributed sometimes to native bashfulness, and sometimes to his fear of offending his uncle. An occurrence, however, which happened soon after, put it beyond a doubt that he designed to become one of our family ; my wife even regarded it as an absolute promise.

My wife and daughters happening to return a visit to neighbour Flamborough's, found that family had lately got their pictures drawn by a limner, who travelled the country, and took likenesses for fifteen shillings a head. As this family and ours had long a sort of rivalry in point of taste, our spirit took the alarm at this stolen march upon us, and notwithstanding all I could say, and I said much, it was resolved that we should have our pictures done too. Having, therefore, engaged the limner, for what could I do ? our next deliberation was to shew the superiority of our taste in the attitudes. As for our neighbour's family, there were seven of them, and they were drawn with seven oranges, a thing quite out of taste, no variety in life, no composition in the world. We desired to have something in a brighter style, and, after many debates, at length came to an unanimous resolution of being drawn together in one large historical family piece. This would be cheaper, since one frame would serve for all, and it would be infinitely more genteel ; for all families of any taste were now drawn in the same manner. As we did not immediately recollect an historical subject to hit us, we were contented each with being drawn as independent historical figures. My wife desired to be represented as Venus, and the painter was desired not to be too frugal of his diamonds in her stomacher and hair. Her two little ones were to be as Cupids by her side, while I, in my gown and band, was to present her with my books on the Whistonian controversy. Olivia would be drawn as an Amazon, sitting upon a bank of flowers, drest in a green joseph, richly laced with gold, and a whip in her hand ; Sophia was to be a shepherdess, with as many sheep as the painter could put in for nothing ; and Moses was to be drest out with an hat and white feather. Our taste so much pleased the 'Squire, that he insisted on being put in as one of the family in the character of Alexander the Great, at Olivia's feet. This was considered by us all as an indication of his desire to be introduced into the family, nor could we refuse his request. The painter was therefore set to work, and as he wrought with assiduity and expedition, in less than four days the whole was compleated. The piece was large, and it must be owned he did not spare his colours ; for which my wife gave him great encomiums. We were all perfectly satisfied with his performance ; but an unfortunate circumstance had not occurred till the picture was finished, which now struck us with dismay. It was so very large that we had no place in the house to fix it. How we all came to disregard so material a point is inconceivable ; but certain it is, we had been all greatly overseen. The picture, therefore, instead of gratifying our vanity, as we hoped, leaned, in a most mortifying manner, against the kitchen wall, where the canvas was stretched and painted, much too large to be got through any of the doors, and the jest of all our neighbours. One compared it to Robinson Crusoe's long-boat, too large to be removed ; another thought it more resembled a reel in a bottle ; some wondered how it could be got out, but still more were amazed how it ever got in.

But though it excited the ridicule of some, it effectually raised more malicious suggestions in many. The 'Squire's portrait being found united with ours, was an honour too great to escape envy. Scandalous whispers began to circulate at our expence, and our tranquillity was continually disturbed by persons who came as friends to tell us what was said of us by enemies. These reports we always resented with becoming spirit ; but scandal ever improves by opposition.

We once again therefore entered into a consultation upon obviating the malice of our enemies, and at last came to a resolution which had too much cunning to give me entire satisfaction. It was this : as our principal object was to discover the honour of Mr. Thornhill's

addresses, my wife undertook to sound him, by pretending to ask his advice in the choice of a husband
for her eldest daughter. If this was not found sufficient
to induce him to a declaration, it was then resolved to
terrify him with a rival. To this last step, however,
I would by no means give my consent, till Olivia gave
me the most solemn assurances that she would marry
the person provided to rival him upon this occasion, if
he did not prevent it, by taking her himself. Such was
the scheme laid, which, though I did not strenuously
oppose, I did not entirely approve.

The next time, therefore, that Mr. Thornhill came to
see us, my girls took care to be out of the way, in order
to give their mamma an opportunity of putting her
scheme in execution ; but they only retired to the next
room, from whence they could overhear the whole conversation : my wife artfully introduced it, by observing,
that one of the Miss Flamboroughs was like to have
a very good match of it in Mr. Spanker. To this the
'Squire assenting, she proceeded to remark, that they
who had warm fortunes were always sure of getting good
husbands : ' But heaven help,' continued she, ' the girls
' that have none. What signifies beauty, Mr. Thornhill ?
' or what signifies all the virtue, and all the qualifications
' in the world, in this age of self-interest ? It is not,
' what is she ? but what has she ? is all the cry.'

' Madam,' returned he, ' I highly approve the justice,
' as well as the novelty of your remarks, and if I were
' a king, it should be otherwise. It should then, indeed,
' be fine times with the girls without fortunes : our two
' young ladies should be the first for whom I would
' provide.'

' Ah, Sir,' returned my wife, ' you are pleased to be
' facetious : but I wish I were a queen, and then I know
' where my eldest daughter should look for an husband.

' But now, that you have put it into my head, seriously,
' Mr. Thornhill, can't you recommend me a proper hus-
' band for her ? she is now nineteen years old, well
' grown and well educated, and in my humble opinion,
' does not want for parts.'

    ' Madam,' replied he, ' if I were to choose, I would
' find out a person possessed of every accomplishment
' that can make an angel happy. One with prudence,
' fortune, taste, and sincerity ; such, madam, would be,
' in my opinion, the proper husband.' ' Ay, Sir,' said
she, ' but do you know of any such person ? '—' No,
' madam,' returned he, ' it is impossible to know any
' person that deserves to be her husband : she 's too
' great a treasure for one man's possession : she 's a god-
' dess. Upon my soul, I speak what I think, she 's an
' angel.'——' Ah, Mr. Thornhill, you only flatter my
' poor girl : but we have been thinking of marrying her
' to one of your tenants, whose mother is lately dead,
' and who wants a manager : you know whom I mean,
' farmer Williams ; a warm man, Mr. Thornhill, able to
' give her good bread ; and who has several times made
' her proposals :' (which was actually the case) 'but, Sir,'
concluded she, ' I should be glad to have your approba-
' tion of our choice.'——' How, Madam,' replied he, ' my
' approbation ! My approbation of such a choice ! Never.
' What ! Sacrifice so much beauty, and sense, and good-
' ness, to a creature insensible of the blessing ! Excuse
' me, I can never approve of such a piece of injustice !
' And I have my reasons ! '——' Indeed, Sir,' cried
Deborah, ' if you have your reasons, that 's another
' affair ; but I should be glad to know those reasons.'—
' Excuse me, Madam,' returned he, ' they lie too deep
' for discovery :' (laying his hand upon his bosom) 'they
' remain buried, riveted here.'

    After he was gone, upon general consultation, we could

not tell what to make of these fine sentiments. Olivia considered them as instances of the most exalted passion ; but I was not quite so sanguine : it seemed to me pretty plain, that they had more of love than matrimony in them : yet whatever they might portend, it was resolved to prosecute the scheme of farmer Williams, who, from my daughter's first appearance in the country, had paid her his addresses.

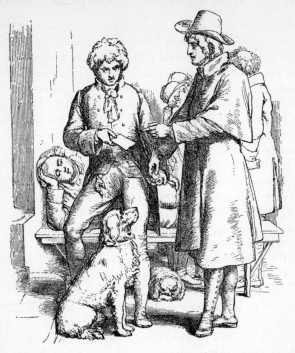

—— 'However, after bribing the servants with half my worldly fortune, I was at last shown into a spacious apartment, my letter being previously sent up for his lordship's inspection.'—Page 315.

CHAPTER XVII

Scarcely any virtue found to resist the power of long and pleasing temptation.

AS I only studied my child's real happiness, the assiduity of Mr. Williams pleased me, as he was in easy circumstances, prudent, and sincere. It required but very little encouragement to revive his former passion; so that in an evening or two he and Mr. Thornhill met at our house, and surveyed each other for some time with looks of anger, but Williams owed his landlord no rent, and little regarded his indignation. Olivia, on her side, acted the coquet to perfection, if that might be called acting which was her real character, pretending to lavish all her tenderness on her new lover. Mr. Thornhill appeared quite dejected at this preference, and with a pensive air took leave, though I own it puzzled me to find him so much in pain as he appeared to be, when he had it in his power so easily to remove the cause, by declaring an honourable passion. But whatever uneasiness he seemed to endure, it could easily be perceived that Olivia's anguish was still greater. After any of these interviews between her lovers, of which there were several, she usually retired to solitude, and there indulged her grief. It was in such a situation I found her one evening, after she had been for some time supporting a fictitious gaiety.—' You now see, my child,' said I, ' that your confidence in Mr. Thornhill's passion ' was all a dream : he permits the rivalry of another, ' every way his inferior, though he knows it lies in his ' power to secure you to himself by a candid declara- ' tion.'——' Yes, papa,' returned she, ' but he has his ' reasons for this delay : I know he has. The sincerity ' of his looks and words convinces me of his real esteem. ' A short time, I hope, will discover the generosity of ' his sentiments, and convince you that my opinion of ' him has been more just than yours.'—' Olivia, my ' darling,' returned I, ' every scheme that has been ' hitherto pursued to compel him to a declaration, has ' been proposed and planned by yourself, nor can you ' in the least say that I have constrained you. But you ' must not suppose, my dear, that I will ever be instru- ' mental in suffering his honest rival to be the dupe of ' your ill-placed passion. Whatever time you require to ' bring your fancied admirer to an explanation shall be ' granted ; but at the expiration of that term, if he is ' still regardless, I must absolutely insist that honest

' Mr. Williams shall be rewarded for his fidelity. The
' character which I have hitherto supported in life
' demands this from me, and my tenderness, as a parent,
' shall never influence my integrity as a man. Name
' then your day, let it be as distant as you think proper,
' and in the mean time take care to let Mr. Thornhill
' know the exact time on which I design delivering you
' up to another. If he really loves you, his own good
' sense will readily suggest that there is but one method
' alone to prevent his losing you for ever.'—This proposal, which she could not avoid considering as perfectly
just, was readily agreed to. She again renewed her most
positive promise of marrying Mr. Williams, in case of
the other's insensibility ; and at the next opportunity,
in Mr. Thornhill's presence, that day month was fixed
upon for her nuptials with his rival.

Such vigorous proceedings seemed to redouble Mr.
Thornhill's anxiety : but what Olivia really felt gave
me some uneasiness. In this struggle between prudence
and passion, her vivacity quite forsook her, and every
opportunity of solitude was sought, and spent in tears.
One week passed away ; but Mr. Thornhill made no
efforts to restrain her nuptials. The succeeding week he
was still assiduous ; but not more open. On the third
he discontinued his visits entirely, and instead of my
daughter testifying any impatience, as I expected, she
seemed to retain a pensive tranquillity, which I looked
upon as resignation. For my own part, I was now
sincerely pleased with thinking that my child was going
to be secured in a continuance of competence and peace,
and frequently applauded her resolution, in preferring
happiness to ostentation.

It was within about four days of her intended nuptials, that my little family at night were gathered round
a charming fire, telling stories of the past, and laying

schemes for the future. Busied in forming a thousand projects, and laughing at whatever folly came uppermost, ' Well, Moses,' cried I, ' we shall soon, my boy, ' have a wedding in the family ; what is your opinion of ' matters and things in general ? '—' My opinion, father, ' is, that all things go on very well ; and I was just now ' thinking, that when sister Livy is married to farmer ' Williams, we shall then have the loan of his cyder-press ' and brewing-tubs for nothing.'—' That we shall, Moses,' cried I, ' and he will sing us Death and the Lady, to ' raise our spirits, into the bargain.'—' He has taught ' that song to our Dick,' cried Moses, ' and I think he ' goes through it very prettily.' ' Does he so ? ' cried I, ' then let us have it : where's little Dick ? let him ' up with it boldly.'—' My brother Dick,' cried Bill my youngest, ' is just gone out with sister Livy : but ' Mr. Williams has taught me two songs, and I'll sing ' them for you, papa. Which song do you choose, *the* ' *Dying Swan*, or *the Elegy on the Death of a Mad Dog* ? ' ' The elegy, child, by all means,' said I ; ' I never heard ' that yet ; and Deborah, my love, grief you know is ' dry, let us have a bottle of the best gooseberry-wine, ' to keep up our spirits. I have wept so much at all ' sorts of elegies of late, that without an enlivening glass, ' I am sure this will overcome me ; and Sophy, love, ' take your guitar, and thrum in with the boy a little.'

An Elegy on the Death of a Mad Dog

> Good people all, of every sort,
>   Give ear unto my song ;
> And if you find it wond'rous short,
>   It cannot hold you long.
>
> In Islington there was a man,
>   Of whom the world might say,
> That still a godly race he ran,
>   Whene'er he went to pray.

A kind and gentle heart he had,
  To comfort friends and foes ;
The naked every day he clad,
  When he put on his cloaths.

And in that town a dog was found,
  As many dogs there be,
Both mungrel, puppy, whelp, and hound,
  And curs of low degree.

This dog and man at first were friends ;
  But when a pique began,
The dog, to gain some private ends,
  Went mad and bit the man.

Around from all the neighbouring streets,
  The wondering neighbours ran,
And swore the dog had lost his wits,
  To bite so good a man.

The wound it seem'd both sore and sad,
  To every christian eye ;
And while they swore the dog was mad,
  They swore the man would die.

But soon a wonder came to light,
  That shew'd the rogues they lied,
The man recover'd of the bite,
  The dog it was that died.[1]

' A very good boy, Bill, upon my word, and an elegy
' that may truly be called tragical. Come, my children,
' here 's Bill's health, and may he one day be a bishop.'
  ' With all my heart,' cried my wife ; ' and if he but
' preaches as well as he sings, I make no doubt of him.
' The most of his family, by the mother's side, could sing
' a good song : it was a common saying in our country,
' that the family of the Blenkinsops could never look

---

[1] Goldsmith had already inserted this *Elegy* in *The Bee*.

'straight before them, nor the Hugginsons blow out a
'candle; that there were none of the Grograms but
'could sing a song, or of the Marjorams but could tell
'a story.'——'However that be,' cried I, 'the most
'vulgar ballad of them all generally pleases me better
'than the fine modern odes, and things that petrify us
'in a single stanza; productions that we at once detest
'and praise. Put the glass to your brother, Moses. The
'great fault of these elegiasts is, that they are in despair
'for griefs that give the sensible part of mankind very little
'pain. A lady loses her muff, her fan, or her lap-dog, and
'so the silly poet runs home to versify the disaster.'

'That may be the mode,' cried Moses, 'in sublimer
'compositions; but the Ranelagh songs that come down
'to us are perfectly familiar, and all cast in the same
'mould: Colin meets Dolly, and they hold a dialogue
'together; he gives her a fairing to put in her hair, and she
'presents him with a nosegay; and then they go together
'to church, where they give good advice to young
'nymphs and swains to get married as fast as they can.'

'And very good advice too,' cried I, 'and I am told
'there is not a place in the world where advice can be
'given with so much propriety as there; for as it per-
'suades us to marry, it also furnishes us with a wife;
'and surely that must be an excellent market, my boy,
'where we are told what we want, and supplied with it
'when wanting.'

'Yes, Sir,' returned Moses, 'and I know but of two such
'markets for wives in Europe, Ranelagh in England, and
'Fontarabia in Spain. The Spanish market is open once
'a year. But our English wives are saleable every night.'

'You are right, my boy,' cried his mother, 'Old Eng-
'land is the only place in the world for husbands to get
'wives.'——'And for wives to manage their husbands,'
interrupted I. 'It is a proverb abroad, that if a bridge

'were built across the sea, all the ladies of the continent
'would come over to take pattern from ours ; for there
'are no such wives in Europe as our own. But let us
'have one bottle more, Deborah, my life, and Moses give
'us a good song. What thanks do we not owe to heaven
'for thus bestowing tranquillity, health and competence ?
'I think myself happier now than the greatest monarch
'upon earth. He has no such fire-side, nor such pleasant
'faces about it. Yes, Deborah, we are now growing old ;
'but the evening of our life is likely to be happy. We
'are descended from ancestors that knew no stain, and
'we shall leave a good and virtuous race of children
'behind us. While we live they will be our support and
'our pleasure here, and when we die they will transmit our
'honour untainted to posterity. Come, my son, we wait
'for a song : let us have a chorus. But where is my
'darling Olivia ? That little cherub's voice is always
'sweetest in the concert.'——Just as I spoke Dick came
running in, ' O pappa, pappa, she is gone from us, she is
'gone from us, my sister Livy is gone from us for ever.'—
'Gone, child ! ' ' Yes, she is gone off with two gentlemen
'in a post chaise, and one of them kissed her, and said he
'would die for her : and she cried very much, and was for
'coming back ; but he persuaded her again, and she
'went into the chaise, and said, "O what will my poor
'papa do when he knows I am undone !" '——'Now then,'
cried I, ' my children, go and be miserable ; for we shall
'never enjoy one hour more. And O may heaven's
'everlasting fury light upon him and his ! Thus to rob
'me of my child ! And sure it will, for taking back my
'sweet innocent that I was leading up to heaven. Such
'sincerity as my child was possessed of ! But all our
'earthly happiness is now over ! Go, my children, go and
'be miserable and infamous ; for my heart is broken
'within me ! '——' Father,' cried my son, ' is this your

fortitude ?' 'Fortitude, child ! Yes, he shall see I have
'fortitude ! Bring me my pistols. I'll pursue the
'traitor. While he is on earth I'll pursue him. Old as
'I am, he shall find I can sting him yet. The villain !
'The perfidious villain !' I had by this time reached
down my pistols, when my poor wife, whose passions
were not so strong as mine, caught me in her arms. 'My
'dearest, dearest husband,' cried she, 'the Bible is the
'only weapon that is fit for your old hands now. Open
'that, my love, and read our anguish into patience, for
'she has vilely deceived us.' 'Indeed, Sir,' resumed my
son, after a pause, 'your rage is too violent and unbe-
'coming. You should be my mother's comforter, and
'you encrease her pain. It ill suited you and your
'reverend character, thus to curse your greatest enemy :
'you should not have curst him, villain as he is.'——'I
'did not curse him, child, did I ?'——'Indeed, Sir, you
'did ; you curst him twice.'——'Then may heaven for-
'give me and him if I did. And now, my son, I see it
'was more than human benevolence that first taught us
'to bless our enemies ! Blest be his holy name for all the
'good he hath given, and for all that he hath taken
'away. But it is not, it is not, a small distress that can
'wring tears from these old eyes, that have not wept for
'so many years. My Child !—To undo my darling !
'May confusion seize !——Heaven forgive me, what am
'I about to say ! You may remember, my love, how
'good she was, and how charming ; till this vile moment
'all her care was to make us happy. Had she but died !
'But she is gone, the honour of our family contaminated,
'and I must look out for happiness in other worlds than
'here. But my child, you saw them go off : perhaps he
'forced her away ? If he forced her, she may yet be
'innocent.'—'Ah, no, Sir !' cried the child ; 'he only
'kissed her, and called her his angel, and she wept very

'much, and leaned upon his arm, and they drove off very
'fast.'——'She's an ungrateful creature,' cried my wife,
who could scarce speak for weeping, 'to use us thus.
'She never had the least constraint put upon her affec-
'tions. The vile strumpet has basely deserted her parents
'without any provocation, thus to bring your grey hairs
'to the grave, and I must shortly follow.'

In this manner that night, the first of our real misfortunes, was spent in the bitterness of complaint, and ill-
supported sallies of enthusiasm. I determined, however,
to find out our betrayer, wherever he was, and reproach
his baseness. The next morning we missed our wretched
child at breakfast, where she used to give life and chearfulness to us all. My wife, as before, attempted to ease
her heart by reproaches. 'Never,' cried she, 'shall that
'vilest stain of our family again darken these harmless
'doors. I will never call her daughter more. No, let
'the strumpet live with her vile seducer : she may bring
'us to shame, but she shall never more deceive us.'

'Wife,' said I, 'do not talk thus hardly : my detesta-
'tion of her guilt is as great as yours ; but ever shall this
'house and this heart be open to a poor returning repent-
'ant sinner. The sooner she returns from her transgres-
'sion, the more welcome shall she be to me. For the first
'time the very best may err ; art may persuade, and
'novelty spread out its charm. The first fault is the
'child of simplicity ; but every other the offspring of
'guilt. Yes, the wretched creature shall be welcome to
'this heart and this house, though stained with ten
'thousand vices. I will again hearken to the music of
'her voice, again will I hang fondly on her bosom, if
'I find but repentance there. My son, bring hither my
'Bible and my staff; I will pursue her, wherever she is,
'and though I cannot save her from shame, I may prevent
'the continuance of iniquity.'

—— ' Here I found a number of poor creatures, all in circumstances like myself,
expecting the arrival of Mr. Crispe, presenting a true epitome of English
impatience.'—PAGE 317.

CHAPTER XVIII

The pursuit of a father to reclaim a lost child to virtue.

THOUGH the child could not describe the gentleman's
person who handed his sister into the post-chaise,
yet my suspicions fell entirely upon our young landlord,
whose character for such intrigues was but too well
known. I therefore directed my steps towards Thornhill-
castle, resolving to upbraid him, and, if possible, to bring
back my daughter : but before I had reached his seat,
I was met by one of my parishioners, who said he saw a
young lady resembling my daughter, in a post-chaise with
a gentleman whom, by the description, I could only guess
to be Mr. Burchell, and that they drove very fast. This

information, however, did by no means satisfy me. I therefore went to the young 'Squire's, and though it was yet early, insisted upon seeing him immediately ; he soon appeared with the most open familiar air, and seemed perfectly amazed at my daughter's elopement, protesting upon his honour that he was quite a stranger to it. I now therefore condemned my former suspicions, and could turn them only on Mr. Burchell, who I recollected had of late several private conferences with her : but the appearance of another witness left me no room to doubt his villainy, who averred, that he and my daughter were actually gone towards the Wells, about thirty miles off, where there was a great deal of company. Being driven to that state of mind in which we are more ready to act precipitately than to reason right, I never debated with myself, whether these accounts might not have been given by persons purposely placed in my way to mislead me, but resolved to pursue my daughter and her fancied deluder thither. I walked along with earnestness, and inquired of several by the way ; but received no accounts, till entering the town, I was met by a person on horseback, whom I remembered to have seen at the 'Squire's, and he assured me, that if I followed them to the races, which were but thirty miles farther, I might depend upon over-taking them ; for he had seen them dance there the night before, and the whole assembly seemed charmed with my daughter's performance. Early the next day I walked forward to the races, and about four in the afternoon I came upon the course. The company made a very brilliant appearance, all earnestly employed in one pursuit, that of pleasure ; how different from mine, that of reclaiming a lost child to virtue ! I thought I perceived Mr. Burchell at some distance from me ; but, as if he dreaded an interview, upon my approaching him, he mixed among a crowd, and I saw him no more. I now reflected that it would be to no purpose to continue my pursuit farther, and resolved to return home to an innocent family, who wanted my assistance. But the agitations of my mind, and the fatigues I had undergone, threw me into a fever, the symptoms of which I perceived before I came off the course. This was another unexpected stroke, as I was more than seventy miles distant from home : however, I retired to a little ale-house by the roadside, and in this place, the usual retreat of indigence and frugality, I laid me down patiently to wait the issue of my disorder. I languished here for near three weeks ; but at last my constitution prevailed, though I was unprovided with money to defray the expences of my entertainment. It is possible the anxiety from this last circumstance alone might have brought on a relapse, had I not been supplied by a traveller, who stopt to take a cursory refreshment. This person was no other than the philanthropic bookseller in St. Paul's church-yard, who has written so many little books for children : he called himself their friend ; but he was the friend of all mankind. He was no sooner alighted, but he was in haste to be gone ; for he was ever on business of the utmost importance, and was at that time actually compiling materials for the history of one Mr. Thomas Trip. I immediately recollected this good-natured man's red pimpled face ; for he had published for me against the Deuterogamists of the age, and from him I had borrowed a few pieces, to be paid at my return. Leaving the inn, therefore, as I was yet but weak, I resolved to return home by easy journies of ten miles a day. My health and usual tranquillity were almost restored, and I now condemned that pride which had made me refractory to the hand of correction. Man little knows what calamities are beyond his patience to bear till he tries them ; as in ascending the heights of ambition, which look bright

from below, every step we rise shews us some new and
gloomy prospect of hidden disappointment ; so in our
descent from the summits of pleasure, though the vale
of misery below may appear at first dark and gloomy, yet
the busy mind, still attentive to its own amusement, finds
as we descend something to flatter and to please. Still,
as we approach, the darkest objects appear to brighten,
and the mental eye becomes adapted to its gloomy
situation.

I now proceeded forwards, and had walked about two
hours, when I perceived what appeared at a distance like
a waggon, which I was resolved to overtake ; but when
I came up with it, found it to be a strolling company's
cart, that was carrying their scenes and other theatrical
furniture to the next village, where they were to exhibit.
The cart was attended only by the person who drove it,
and one of the company, as the rest of the players were
to follow the ensuing day. Good company upon the
road, says the proverb, is the shortest cut, I therefore
entered into conversation with the poor player ; and as
I once had some theatrical powers myself, I disserted on
such topics with my usual freedom : but as I was pretty
much unacquainted with the present state of the stage,
I demanded who were the present theatrical writers in
vogue, who the Drydens and Otways of the day.——
' I fancy, Sir,' cried the player, ' few of our modern
' dramatists would think themselves much honoured by
' being compared to the writers you mention. Dryden
' and Rowe's manner, Sir, are quite out of fashion ; our
' taste has gone back a whole century ; Fletcher, Ben
' Jonson, and all the plays of Shakspear are the only
' things that go down.'——' How,' cried I, ' is it possible
' the present age can be pleased with that antiquated
' dialect, that obsolete humour, those over-charged
' characters, which abound in the works you mention ? '—

' Sir,' returned my companion, ' the public think nothing
' about dialect, or humour, or character : for that is
' none of their business, they only go to be amused, and
' find themselves happy when they can enjoy a panto-
' mime, under the sanction of Jonson's or Shakspear's
' name.'——' So then, I suppose,' cried I, ' that our
' modern dramatists are rather imitators of Shakspear
' than of nature.'——' To say the truth,' returned my
companion, ' I don't know that they imitate any thing at
' all ; nor indeed does the public require it of them : it is
' not the composition of the piece, but the number of
' starts and attitudes, that may be introduced into it,
' that elicits applause. I have known a piece, with not
' one jest in the whole, shrugged into popularity, and
' another saved by the poet's throwing in a fit of the
' gripes. No, Sir, the works of Congreve and Farquhar
' have too much wit in them for the present taste ; our
' modern dialect is much more natural.'

By this time the equipage of the strolling company was
arrived at the village, which, it seems, had been apprized
of our approach, and was come out to gaze at us : for
my companion observed, that strollers always have more
spectators without doors than within. I did not consider the impropriety of my being in such company, till
I saw a mob gather about me. I therefore took shelter,
as fast as possible, in the first ale-house that offered, and
being shewn into the common room, was accosted by
a very well-drest gentleman, who demanded whether
I was the real chaplain of the company, or whether it was
only to be my masquerade character in the play. Upon
informing him of the truth, and that I did not
belong in any sort to the company, he was condescending
enough to desire me and the player to partake in a bowl of
punch, over which he discussed modern politics with great
earnestness and interest. I set him down in my own mind

for nothing less than a parliament-man at least ; but was almost confirmed in my conjectures, when upon asking what there was in the house for supper, he insisted that the player and I should sup with him at his house, with which request, after some entreaties, we were prevailed on to comply.

—— 'I had some knowledge of music, with a tolerable voice, and now turned what was once my amusement into a present means of subsistence.'—PAGE 319.

CHAPTER XIX

The description of a person discontented with the present government, and apprehensive of the loss of our liberties.

THE house where we were to be entertained lying at a small distance from the village, our inviter observed, that as the coach was not ready, he would conduct us on foot, and we soon arrived at one of the most magnificent mansions I had seen in that part of the country. The apartment into which we were shewn was perfectly elegant and modern; he went to give orders for supper, while the player, with a wink, observed that we were perfectly in luck. Our entertainer soon returned, an elegant supper was brought in, two or three ladies, in an easy dishabille, were introduced, and the conversation began with some sprightliness. Politics, however, were the subject on which our entertainer chiefly expatiated : for he asserted that liberty was at once his boast and his terror. After the cloth was removed, he asked me if I had seen the last Monitor, to which replying in the negative, ' What, nor the Auditor, I suppose ? ' cried he. ' Neither, ' Sir,' returned I. ' That's strange, very strange,' replied my entertainer. ' Now I read all the politics ' that come out. The Daily, the Public Ledger, the ' Chronicle, the London Evening, the Whitehall Evening ' Post, the seventeen magazines and the two reviews ; and ' though they hate each other, I love them all. Liberty, ' Sir, liberty is the Briton's boast, and by all my coal ' mines in Cornwall, I reverence its guardians.' ' Then it ' is to be hoped,' cried I, ' you reverence the king.' ' Yes,' returned my entertainer, ' when he does what we ' would have him ; but if he goes on as he has done of ' late, I'll never trouble myself more with his matters. ' I say nothing. I think only. I could have directed ' some things better. I don't think there has been a ' sufficient number of advisers : he should advise with ' every person willing to give him advice, and then we ' should have things done in anotherguess manner.'

' I wish,' cried I, ' that such intruding advisers were ' fixed in the pillory. It should be the duty of honest ' men to assist the weaker side of our Constitution, that ' sacred power that has for some years been every day ' declining, and losing its due share of influence in the ' State. But these ignorants still continue the cry of ' liberty, and if they have any weight, basely throw it ' into the subsiding scale.'

' How,' cried one of the ladies ; 'do I live to see one
' so base, so sordid, as to be an enemy to liberty, and
' a defender of tyrants ? Liberty, that sacred gift of
' heaven, that glorious privilege of Britons ! '

' Can it be possible,' cried our entertainer, ' that there
' should be any found at present advocates for slavery ?
' Any who are for meanly giving up the privileges of
' Britons ? Can any, Sir, be so abject ? '

' No, Sir,' replied I, ' I am for liberty, that attribute of
' Gods ! Glorious liberty ! that theme of modern decla-
' mation. I would have all men kings. I would be a
' king myself. We have all naturally an equal right to
' the throne : we are all originally equal. This is my
' opinion, and was once the opinion of a set of honest men
' who were called Levellers. They tried to erect them-
' selves into a community, where all should be equally
' free. But, alas ! it would never answer ; for there were
' some among them stronger, and some more cunning than
' others, and these became masters of the rest ; for as sure
' as your groom rides your horses, because he is a cunninger
' animal than they, so surely will the animal that is
' cunninger or stronger than he, sit upon his shoulders in
' turn. Since then it is entailed upon humanity to sub-
' mit, and some are born to command, and others to obey,
' the question is, as there must be tyrants, whether it is
' better to have them in the same house with us, or in the
' same village, or still farther off, in the metropolis. Now,
' Sir, for my own part, as I naturally hate the face of a
' tyrant, the farther off he is removed from me, the better
' pleased am I. The generality of mankind also are of
' my way of thinking, and have unanimously created one
' king, whose election at once diminishes the number of
' tyrants, and puts tyranny at the greatest distance from
' the greatest number of people. Now the great who were
' tyrants themselves before the election of one tyrant,

' are naturally averse to a power raised over them, and
' whose weight must ever lean heaviest on the subordinate
' orders. It is the interest of the great, therefore, to
' diminish kingly power as much as possible ; because
' whatever they take from that is naturally restored to
' themselves ; and all they have to do in the state is to
' undermine the single tyrant, by which they resume
' their primaeval authority. Now the state may be so
' circumstanced, or its laws may be so disposed, or its
' men of opulence so minded, as all to conspire in carrying
' on this business of undermining monarchy. For, in the
' first place, if the circumstances of our state be such, as
' to favour the accumulation of wealth, and make the
' opulent still more rich, this will increase their ambition.
' An accumulation of wealth, however, must necessarily
' be the consequence, when, as at present, more riches
' flow in from external commerce than arise from internal
' industry ; for external commerce can only be managed
' to advantage by the rich, and they have also at the same
' time all the emoluments arising from internal industry ;
' so that the rich, with us, have two sources of wealth,
' whereas the poor have but one. For this reason, wealth,
' in all commercial states, is found to accumulate, and all
' such have hitherto in time become aristocratical.
' Again, the very laws also of this country may contribute
' to the accumulation of wealth ; as when by their means
' the natural ties that bind the rich and poor together
' are broken, and it is ordained, that the rich shall only
' marry with the rich ; or when the learned are held un-
' qualified to serve their country as counsellors merely
' from a defect of opulence, and wealth is thus made the
' object of a wise man's ambition ; by these means, I say,
' and such means as these, riches will accumulate. Now
' the possessor of accumulated wealth, when furnished
' with the necessaries and pleasures of life, has no other

‘ method to employ the superfluity of his fortune but in
‘ purchasing power. That is, differently speaking, in
‘ making dependants, by purchasing the liberty of the
‘ needy or the venal, of men who are willing to bear the
‘ mortification of contiguous tyranny for bread. Thus
‘ each very opulent man generally gathers round him a
‘ circle of the poorest of the people ; and the polity
‘ abounding in accumulated wealth, may be compared to
‘ a Cartesian system, each orb with a vortex of its own.
‘ Those, however, who are willing to move in a great man's
‘ vortex are only such as must be slaves, the rabble of
‘ mankind, whose souls and whose education are adapted
‘ to servitude, and who know nothing of liberty except
‘ the name.　But there must still be a large number of the
‘ people without the sphere of the opulent man's influence,
‘ namely, that order of men which subsists between the
‘ very rich and the very rabble ; those men who are
‘ possest of too large fortunes to submit to the neigh-
‘ bouring man in power, and yet are too poor to set up
‘ for tyranny themselves. In this middle order of man-
‘ kind are generally to be found all the arts, wisdom, and
‘ virtues of society. This order alone is known to be
‘ the true preserver of freedom, and may be called the
‘ People.　Now it may happen that this middle order of
‘ mankind may lose all its influence in a state, and its
‘ voice be in a manner drowned in that of the rabble : for
‘ if the fortune sufficient for qualifying a person at present
‘ to give his voice in state affairs be ten times less than
‘ was judged sufficient upon forming the constitution, it
‘ is evident that great numbers of the rabble will thus
‘ be introduced into the political system, and they, ever
‘ moving in the vortex of the great, will follow where
‘ greatness shall direct. In such a state, therefore, all
‘ that the middle order has left, is to preserve the prero-
‘ gative and privileges of the one principal governor with

'the most sacred circumspection. For he divides the
'power of the rich, and calls off the great from falling
'with tenfold weight on the middle order placed beneath
'them. The middle order may be compared to a town
'of which the opulent are forming the siege, and which
'the governor from without is hastening the relief.
'While the besiegers are in dread of an enemy over them,
'it is but natural to offer the townsmen the most specious
'terms ; to flatter them with sounds, and amuse them
'with privileges ; but if they once defeat the governor
'from behind, the walls of the town will be but a small
'defence to its inhabitants. What they may then expect,
'may be seen by turning our eyes to Holland, Genoa, or
'Venice, where the laws govern the poor, and the rich
'govern the law. I am then for, and would die for,
'monarchy, sacred monarchy ; for if there be any thing
'sacred amongst men, it must be the anointed Sovereign
'of his people, and every diminution of his power in war,
'or in peace, is an infringement upon the real liberties of
'the subject. The sounds of liberty, patriotism, and
'Britons have already done *much*, it is to be hoped that
'the true sons of freedom will prevent their ever doing
'*more*. I have known many of those pretended cham-
'pions for liberty in my time, yet do I not remember
'one that was not in his heart and in his family a
'tyrant.'

My warmth I found had lengthened this harangue
beyond the rules of good breeding : but the impatience
of my entertainer, who often strove to interrupt it, could
be restrained no longer. ' What,' cried he, ' then I have
' been all this while entertaining a Jesuit in parson's
' cloaths ; but by all the coal mines of Cornwall, out he
' shall pack, if my name be Wilkinson.' I now found I
' had gone too far, and asked pardon for the warmth with
which I had spoken. ' Pardon,' returned he in a fury :

'I think such principles demand ten thousand pardons.
'What, give up liberty, property, and, as the Gazetteer
'says, lie down to be saddled with wooden shoes! Sir,
'I insist upon your marching out of this house imme-
'diately, to prevent worse consequences; Sir, I insist
'upon it.' I was going to repeat my remonstrances; but
just then we heard a footman's rap at the door, and the
two ladies cried out, 'As sure as death there is our master
'and mistress come home.' It seems my entertainer was
all this while only the butler, who in his master's absence,
had a mind to cut a figure, and be for a while the gentleman himself; and, to say the truth, he talked politics as
well as most country gentlemen do. But nothing could
now exceed my confusion upon seeing the gentleman and
his lady enter, nor was their surprise at finding such company and good chear, less than ours. 'Gentlemen,' cried
the real master of the house to me and my companion,
'my wife and I are your most humble servants; but
'I protest this is so unexpected a favour, that we almost
'sink under the obligation.' However unexpected our
company might be to them, theirs, I am sure, was still
more so to us, and I was struck dumb with the apprehensions of my own absurdity, when whom should I next see
enter the room but my dear Miss Arabella Wilmot, who
was formerly designed to be married to my son George;
but whose match was broken off as already related. As
soon as she saw me, she flew to my arms with the utmost
joy.——'My dear sir,' cried she, 'to what happy accident
'is it that we owe so unexpected a visit? I am sure my
'uncle and aunt will be in raptures when they find they
'have the good Dr. Primrose for their guest.' Upon
hearing my name, the old gentleman and lady very
politely stept up, and welcomed me with most cordial
hospitality. Nor could they forbear smiling upon being
informed of the nature of my present visit: but the

unfortunate butler, whom they at first seemed disposed
to turn away, was at my intercession forgiven.

Mr. Arnold and his lady, to whom the house belonged,
now insisted upon having the pleasure of my stay for
some days, and as their niece, my charming pupil, whose
mind, in some measure, had been formed under my own
instructions, joined in their entreaties, I complied. That
night I was shewn to a magnificent chamber, and the
next morning early Miss Wilmot desired to walk with
me in the garden, which was decorated in the modern
manner. After some time spent in pointing out the
beauties of the place, she enquired with seeming uncon-
cern, when last I had heard from my son George. ' Alas !
' Madam,' cried I, ' he has now been near three years
' absent, without ever writing to his friends or me.
' Where he is I know not ; perhaps I shall never see
' him or happiness more. No, my dear Madam, we shall
' never more see such pleasing hours as were once spent
' by our fire-side at Wakefield. My little family are now
' dispersing very fast, and poverty has brought not only
' want, but infamy upon us.' The good-natured girl let
fall a tear at this account ; but as I saw her possessed
of too much sensibility, I forebore a more minute detail
of our sufferings. It was, however, some consolation to
me to find that time had made no alteration in her
affections, and that she had rejected several matches that
had been made her since our leaving her part of the
country. She led me round all the extensive improvements of the place, pointing to the several walks and
arbours, and at the same time catching from every
object a hint for some new question relative to my son.

In this manner we spent the forenoon, till the bell
summoned us in to dinner, where we found the manager of
the strolling company that I mentioned before, who was
come to dispose of tickets for the *Fair Penitent*, which

was to be acted that evening, the part of Horatio by
a young gentleman who had never appeared on any
stage. He seemed to be very warm in the praises of
the new performer, and averred that he never saw any
who bid so fair for excellence. Acting, he observed, was
not learned in a day ; ' But this gentleman,' continued
he, ' seems born to tread the stage. His voice, his
' figure, and attitudes are all admirable. We caught him
' up accidentally in our journey down.' This account,
in some measure, excited our curiosity, and, at the
entreaty of the ladies, I was prevailed upon to accompany them to the play-house, which was no other than
a barn. As the company with which I went was incontestably the chief of the place, we were received with
the greatest respect, and placed in the front seat of the
theatre ; where we sate for some time with no small
impatience to see Horatio make his appearance. The
new performer advanced at last, and let parents think
of my sensations by their own, when I found it was my
unfortunate son. He was going to begin, when turning
his eyes upon the audience, he perceived Miss Wilmot
and me, and stood at once speechless and immoveable.
The actors behind the scene, who ascribed this pause to
his natural timidity, attempted to encourage him ; but
instead of going on, he burst into a flood of tears, and
retired off the stage. I don't know what were my
feelings on this occasion ; for they succeeded with too
much rapidity for description : but I was soon awaked
from this disagreeable reverie by Miss Wilmot, who pale
and with a trembling voice desired me to conduct her
back to her uncle's. When got home, Mr. Arnold, who
was as yet a stranger to our extraordinary behaviour,
being informed that the new performer was my son,
sent his coach, and an invitation, for him ; and as he
persisted in his refusal to appear again upon the stage,

the players put another in his place, and we soon had him with us. Mr. Arnold gave him the kindest reception, and I received him with my usual transport ; for I could never counterfeit false resentment. Miss Wilmot's reception was mixed with seeming neglect, and yet I could perceive she acted a studied part. The tumult in her mind seemed not yet abated : she said twenty giddy things that looked like joy, and then laughed loud at her own want of meaning. At intervals she would take a sly peep at the glass, as if happy in the consciousness of unresisted beauty, and often would ask questions without giving any manner of attention to the answers.

—— 'Thus each day I grew more pensive, and he more insolent, till at last the monster had the assurance to offer me to a young baronet of his acquaintance.'—— Page 332.

CHAPTER XX

The history of a philosophic vagabond, pursuing novelty, but losing content.

AFTER we had supped, Mrs. Arnold politely offered to send a couple of her footmen for my son's baggage, which he at first seemed to decline; but upon her pressing the request, he was obliged to inform her, that a stick and a wallet were all the moveable things upon this earth that he could boast of. 'Why, ay my 'son,' cried I, 'you left me but poor, and poor I find 'you are come back; and yet I make no doubt you 'have seen a great deal of the world.'——'Yes, Sir,' replied my son, 'but travelling after fortune is not the 'way to secure her; and indeed, of late I have desisted from the pursuit.'—'I fancy, Sir,' cried Mrs. Arnold,

' that the account of your adventures would be amusing :
' the first part of them I have often heard from my
' niece ; but could the company prevail for the rest, it
' would be an additional obligation.'——' Madam,' replied my son, ' I promise you the pleasure you have in
' hearing, will not be half so great as my vanity in
' repeating them ; and yet in the whole narrative I can
' scarce promise you one adventure, as my account is
' rather of what I saw than what I did. The first mis-
' fortune of my life, which you all know, was great ; but
' though it distressed, it could not sink me. No person
' ever had a better knack at hoping than I. The less
' kind I found fortune at one time, the more I expected
' from her another, and being now at the bottom of her
' wheel, every new revolution might lift, but could not
' depress me. I proceeded, therefore, towards London
' in a fine morning, no way uneasy about to-morrow,
' but chearful as the birds that carolled by the road, and
' comforted myself with reflecting, that London was the
' mart where abilities of every kind were sure of meeting
' distinction and reward.

' Upon my arrival in town, Sir, my first care was to
' deliver your letter of recommendation to our cousin,
' who was himself in little better circumstances than I.
' My first scheme, you know, Sir, was to be usher at an
' academy, and I asked his advice on the affair. Our
' cousin received the proposal with a true Sardonic grin.
' Ay, cried he, this is indeed a very pretty career, that
' has been chalked out for you. I have been an usher at
' a boarding school myself; and may I die by an anodyne
' necklace, but I had rather be an under-turnkey in
' Newgate. I was up early and late : I was browbeat
' by the master, hated for my ugly face by the mistress,
' worried by the boys within, and never permitted to stir
' out to meet civility abroad. But are you sure you are

'fit for a school ? Let me examine you a little. Have
'you been bred apprentice to the business ? No. Then
'you won't do for a school. Can you dress the boys'
'hair ? No. Then you won't do for a school. Have
'you had the small-pox ? No. Then you won't do for
'a school. Can you lie three in a bed ? No. Then you
'will never do for a school. Have you got a good
'stomach ? Yes. Then you will by no means do for
'a school. No, Sir, if you are for a genteel, easy pro-
'fession, bind yourself seven years as an apprentice
'to turn a cutler's wheel ; but avoid a school by any
'means. Yet come, continued he, I see you are a lad
'of spirit and some learning, what do you think of com-
'mencing author, like me ? You have read in books,
'no doubt, of men of genius starving at the trade : At
'present I'll shew you forty very dull fellows about town
'that live by it in opulence. All honest jogg-trot men,
'who go on smoothly and dully, and write history and
'politics, and are praised : men, Sir, who, had they been
'bred cobblers, would all their lives have only mended
'shoes, but never made them.

  'Finding that there was no great degree of gentility
'affixed to the character of an usher, I resolved to accept
'his proposal ; and having the highest respect for litera-
'ture, hailed the *antiqua Mater* of Grub-street with
'reverence. I thought it my glory to pursue a track
'which Dryden and Otway trod before me. I considered
'the goddess of this region as the parent of excellence ;
'and however an intercourse with the world might give
'us good sense, the poverty she granted I supposed to
'be the nurse of genius ! Big with these reflections, I sate
'down, and finding that the best things remained to be
'said on the wrong side, I resolved to write a book that
'should be wholly new. I therefore drest up some
'paradoxes with ingenuity. They were false, indeed,

'but they were new. The jewels of truth have been so
'often imported by others, that nothing was left for me
'to import but some splendid things that, at a distance,
'looked every bit as well. Witness, you powers, what
'fancied importance sate perched upon my quill while
'I was writing. The whole learned world, I made no
'doubt, would rise to oppose my systems ; but then
'I was prepared to oppose the whole learned world.
'Like the porcupine I sate self-collected, with a quill
'pointed against every opposer.'

'Well said, my boy,' cried I, 'and what subject did
'you treat upon ? I hope you did not pass over the
'importance of monogamy. But I interrupt, go on ;
'you published your paradoxes ; well, and what did the
'learned world say to your paradoxes ? '

'Sir,' replied my son, 'the learned world said nothing
'to my paradoxes ; nothing at all, Sir. Every man of
'them was employed in praising his friends and himself,
'or condemning his enemies ; and unfortunately, as I
'had neither, I suffered the cruellest mortification,
'neglect.

'As I was meditating one day in a coffee-house on the
'fate of my paradoxes, a little man happening to enter
'the room, placed himself in the box before me, and after
'some preliminary discourse, finding me to be a scholar,
'drew out a bundle of proposals, begging me to subscribe
'to a new edition he was going to give to the world of
'Propertius, with notes. This demand necessarily pro-
'duced a reply that I had no money ; and that concession
'led him to inquire into the nature of my expectations.
'Finding that my expectations were just as great as my
'purse, I see, cried he, you are unacquainted with the
'town, I'll teach you a part of it. Look at these pro-
'posals ; upon these very proposals I have subsisted
'very comfortably for twelve years. The moment a

' nobleman returns from his travels, a Creolian arrives
' from Jamaica, or dowager from her country seat,
' I strike for a subscription. I first besiege their hearts
' with flattery, and then pour in my proposals at the
' breach. If they subscribe readily the first time, I renew
' my request to beg a dedication fee. If they let me
' have that, I smite them once more for engraving their
' coat of arms at the top. Thus, continued he, I live by
' vanity, and laugh at it. But between ourselves, I am
' now too well known. I should be glad to borrow your
' face a bit : a nobleman of distinction has just returned
' from Italy ; my face is familiar to his porter ; but if
' you bring this copy of verses, my life for it you succeed,
' and we divide the spoil.'

' Bless us, George,' cried I, ' and is this the employ-
' ment of poets now ! Do men of their exalted talents
' thus stoop to beggary ? Can they so far disgrace their
' calling, as to make a vile traffic of praise for bread ? '

' O no, Sir,' returned he, ' a true poet can never be so
' base ; for wherever there is genius there is pride. The
' creatures I now describe are only beggars in rhyme.
' The real poet, as he braves every hardship for fame, so
' he is equally a coward to contempt, and none but those
' who are unworthy protection condescend to solicit it.

' Having a mind too proud to stoop to such indig-
' nities, and yet a fortune too humble to hazard a second
' attempt for fame, I was now obliged to take a middle
' course, and write for bread. But I was unqualified for
' a profession where mere industry alone was to ensure
' success. I could not suppress my lurking passion for
' applause ; but usually consumed that time in efforts
' after excellence which takes up but little room, when
' it should have been more advantageously employed in
' the diffusive productions of fruitful mediocrity. My
' little piece would therefore come forth in the midst of

' periodical publications, unnoticed and unknown. The
' public were more importantly employed, than to observe
' the easy simplicity of my style, or the harmony of my
' periods. Sheet after sheet was thrown off to oblivion.
' My essays were buried among the essays upon liberty,
' eastern tales, and cures for the bite of a mad dog ;
' while Philautos, Philalethes, Philelutheros, and Philan-
' thropos all wrote better, because they wrote faster, than I.

' Now, therefore, I began to associate with none but
' disappointed authors, like myself, who praised, deplored,
' and despised each other. The satisfaction we found in
' every celebrated writer's attempts, was inversely as
' their merits. I found that no genius in another could
' please me. My unfortunate paradoxes had entirely
' dried up that source of comfort. I could neither read
' nor write with satisfaction ; for excellence in another
' was my aversion, and writing was my trade.

' In the midst of these gloomy reflections, as I was one
' day sitting on a bench in St. James's park, a young
' gentleman of distinction, who had been my intimate
' acquaintance at the university, approached me. We
' saluted each other with some hesitation, he almost
' ashamed of being known to one who made so shabby
' an appearance, and I afraid of a repulse. But my
' suspicions soon vanished ; for Ned Thornhill was at
' the bottom a very good-natured fellow.'

' What did you say, George ? ' interrupted I.—' Thorn-
' hill, was not that his name ? It can certainly be no
' other than my landlord.'——' Bless me,' cried Mrs.
Arnold, ' is Mr. Thornhill so near a neighbour of yours ?
' He has long been a friend in our family, and we expect
' a visit from him shortly.'

' My friend's first care,' continued my son, ' was to
' alter my appearance by a very fine suit of his own
' clothes, and then I was admitted to his table, upon

' the footing of half-friend, half-underling. My business
' was to attend him at auctions, to put him in spirits
' when he sate for his picture, to take the left hand in
' his chariot when not filled by another, and to assist at
' tattering a kip, as the phrase was, when we had a mind
' for a frolic. Besides this, I had twenty other little
' employments in the family. I was to do many small
' things without bidding ; to carry the cork-screw ; to
' stand god-father to all the butler's children ; to sing
' when I was bid ; to be never out of humour ; always
' to be humble, and, if I could, to be very happy.

' In this honourable post, however, I was not without
' a rival. A captain of marines, who was formed for the
' place by nature, opposed me in my patron's affections.
' His mother had been laundress to a man of quality, and
' thus he early acquired a taste for pimping and pedigree.
' As this gentleman made it the study of his life to be
' acquainted with lords, though he was dismissed from
' several for his stupidity ; yet he found many of them
' who were as dull as himself, that permitted his assi-
' duities. As flattery was his trade, he practised it with
' the easiest address imaginable : but it came aukward
' and stiff from me ; and as every day my patron's
' desire of flattery encreased, so every hour being better
' acquainted with his defects, I became more unwilling
' to give it. Thus I was once more fairly going to give
' up the field to the captain, when my friend found
' occasion for my assistance. This was nothing less than
' to fight a duel for him, with a gentleman whose sister
' it was pretended he had used ill. I readily complied
' with his request, and though I see you are displeased
' at my conduct, yet as it was a debt indispensably due
' to friendship, I could not refuse. I undertook the
' affair, disarmed my antagonist, and soon after had the
' pleasure of finding that the lady was only a woman of

'the town, and the fellow her bully and a sharper. This
' piece of service was repaid with the warmest professions
' of gratitude ; but as my friend was to leave town in
' a few days he knew no other method of serving me,
' but by recommending me to his uncle Sir William
' Thornhill, and another nobleman of great distinction
' who enjoyed a post under the government. When he
' was gone, my first care was to carry his recommendatory
' letter to his uncle, a man whose character for every
' virtue was universal, yet just. I was received by his
' servants with the most hospitable smiles ; for the looks
' of the domestics ever transmit their master's benevo-
' lence. Being shewn into a grand apartment, where
' Sir William soon came to me, I delivered my message
' and letter, which he read, and after pausing some
' minutes, Pray, Sir, cried he, inform me what you have
' done for my kinsman to deserve this warm recom-
' mendation ? But I suppose, Sir, I guess your merits,
' you have fought for him ; and so you would expect
' a reward from me for being the instrument of his vices.
' I wish, sincerely wish, that my present refusal may be
' some punishment for your guilt; but still more, that it
' may be some inducement to your repentance.——The
' severity of this rebuke I bore patiently, because I knew
' it was just. My whole expectations now, therefore, lay
' in my letter to the great man. As the doors of the
' nobility are almost ever beset with beggars, all ready
' to thrust in some sly petition, I found it no easy matter
' to gain admittance. However, after bribing the ser-
' vants with half my worldly fortune, I was at last shewn
' into a spacious apartment, my letter being previously
' sent up for his lordship's inspection. During this
' anxious interval I had full time to look round me.
' Every thing was grand, and of happy contrivance : the
' paintings, the furniture, the gildings petrified me with

' awe, and raised my idea of the owner. Ah, thought
' I to myself, how very great must the possessor of all
' these things be, who carries in his head the business of
' the state, and whose house displays half the wealth of
' a kingdom : sure his genius must be unfathomable !
' During these awful reflections, I heard a step come
' heavily forward. Ah, this is the great man himself !
' No, it was only a chambermaid. Another foot was
' heard soon after. This must be He ! No, it was only
' the great man's valet de chambre. At last his lordship
' actually made his appearance. Are you, cried he, the
' bearer of this here letter ? I answered with a bow.
' I learn by this, continued he, as how that—But just at
' that instant a servant delivered him a card, and without
' taking farther notice, he went out of the room, and left
' me to digest my own happiness at leisure. I saw no
' more of him, till told by a footman that his lordship
' was going to his coach at the door. Down I immediately
' followed, and joined my voice to that of three or four
' more, who came like me, to petition for favours. His
' lordship, however, went too fast for us, and was gaining
' his chariot door with large strides, when I hallooed out
' to know if I was to have any reply. He was by this
' time got in, and muttered an answer, half of which I
' only heard, the other half was lost in the rattling of his
' chariot wheels. I stood for some time with my neck
' stretched out, in the posture of one that was listening
' to catch the glorious sounds, till looking round me,
' I found myself alone at his lordship's gate.

' My patience,' continued my son, ' was now quite ex-
' hausted : stung with the thousand indignities I had met
' with, I was willing to cast myself away, and only wanted
' the gulph to receive me. I regarded myself as one of
' those vile beings that nature designed should be thrown
' by into her lumber room, there to perish in obscurity.

' I had still however half a guinea left, and of that I
' thought nature herself should not deprive me ; but in
' order to be sure of this, I was resolved to go instantly
' and spend it while I had it, and then trust to occur-
' rences for the rest. As I was going along with this
' resolution, it happened that Mr. Crispe's office seemed
' invitingly open to give me a welcome reception. In this
' office Mr. Crispe kindly offers all his majesty's subjects
' a generous promise of £30 a year, for which promise all
' they give in return is their liberty for life, and permission
' to let him transport them to America as slaves. I was
' happy at finding a place where I could lose my fears in
' desperation, and entered this cell, for it had the appear-
' ance of one, with the devotion of a monastic. Here
' I found a number of poor creatures, all in circumstances
' like myself, expecting the arrival of Mr. Crispe, presenting
' a true epitome of English impatience. Each untract-
' able soul at variance with fortune, wreaked her injuries
' on their own hearts : but Mr. Crispe at last came down
' and all our murmurs were hushed. He deigned to regard
' me with an air of peculiar approbation, and indeed he
' was the first man who for a month past talked to
' me with smiles. After a few questions, he found I was
' fit for every thing in the world. He paused a while upon
' the properest means of providing for me, and slapping
' his forehead as if he had found it, assured me, that
' there was at that time an embassy talked of from the
' synod of Pennsylvania to the Chickasaw Indians, and
' that he would use his interest to get me made secretary.
' I knew in my own heart that the fellow lied, and yet his
' promise gave me pleasure, there was something so magni-
' ficent in the sound. I fairly therefore divided my half
' guinea, one half of which went to be added to his thirty
' thousand pound, and with the other half I resolved to
' go to the next tavern to be there more happy than he.

' As I was going out with that resolution I was met
' at the door by the captain of a ship, with whom I had
' formerly some little acquaintance, and he agreed to be
' my companion over a bowl of punch. As I never chose
' to make a secret of my circumstances, he assured me
' that I was upon the very point of ruin, in listening to
' the office-keeper's promises ; for that he only designed
' to sell me to the plantations. But, continued he, I fancy
' you might, by a much shorter voyage, be very easily put
' into a genteel way of bread. Take my advice. My ship
' sails to-morrow for Amsterdam. What if you go in her
' as a passenger ? The moment you land all you have to
' do is to teach the Dutchmen English, and I'll warrant
' you'll get pupils and money enough. I suppose you
' understand English, added he, by this time, or the deuce
' is in it. I confidently assured him of that ; but ex-
' pressed a doubt whether the Dutch would be willing to
' learn English. He affirmed with an oath that they were
' fond of it to distraction ; and upon that affirmation I
' agreed with his proposal, and embarked the next day to
' teach the Dutch English in Holland. The wind was fair,
' our voyage short, and after having paid my passage with
' half my moveables, I found myself fallen as from the
' skies a stranger in one of the principal streets of
' Amsterdam. In this situation I was unwilling to let
' any time pass unemployed in teaching. I addressed
' myself therefore to two or three of those I met, whose
' appearance seemed most promising ; but it was impos-
' sible to make ourselves mutually understood. It was
' not till this very moment I recollected, that in order
' to teach Dutchmen English, it was necessary that
' they should first teach me Dutch. How I came to
' overlook so obvious an objection is to me amazing ;
' but certain it is I overlooked it.

' This scheme thus blown up, I had some thoughts

' of fairly shipping back to England again ; but falling
' into company with an Irish student who was returning
' from Louvain, our conversation turning upon topics of
' literature, (for by the way it may be observed that I
' always forgot the meanness of my circumstances when
' I could converse upon such subjects) from him I learned
' that there were not two men in his whole university
' who understood Greek. This amazed me. I instantly
' resolved to travel to Louvain, and there live by teaching
' Greek ; and in this design I was heartened by my
' brother student, who threw out some hints that a fortune
' might be got by it.

' I set boldly forward the next morning. Every day
' lessened the burthen of my moveables, like Aesop and
' his basket of bread ; for I paid them for my lodgings to
' the Dutch as I travelled on. When I came to Louvain,
' I was resolved not to go sneaking to the lower professors,
' but openly tendered my talents to the principal himself.
' I went, had admittance, and offered him my service as
' a master of the Greek language, which I had been told
' was a desideratum in this university. The principal
' seemed at first to doubt of my abilities ; but of these
' I offered to convince him by turning a part of any
' Greek author he should fix upon into Latin. Finding
' me perfectly earnest in my proposal, he addressed me
' thus : You see me, young man, continued he, I never
' learned Greek, and I don't find that I have ever missed
' it. I have had a doctor's cap and gown without Greek ;
' I have ten thousand florins a year without Greek; I eat
' heartily without Greek, and in short, continued he, as
' I don't know Greek, I do not believe there is any
' good in it.

' I was now too far from home to think of returning ;
' so I resolved to go forward. I had some knowledge of
' music, with a tolerable voice ; now turned what was

' once my amusement into a present means of subsistence.
' I passed among the harmless peasants of Flanders, and
' among such of the French as were poor enough to be
' very merry ; for I ever found them sprightly in pro-
' portion to their wants. Whenever I approached a
' peasant's house towards night-fall, I played one of my
' most merry tunes, and that procured me not only a
' lodging, but subsistence for the next day. I once or
' twice attempted to play for people of fashion ; but
' they always thought my performance odious, and never
' rewarded me even with a trifle. This was to me the
' more extraordinary, as whenever I used in better days
' to play for company, when playing was my amuse-
' ment, my music never failed to throw them into rap-
' tures, and the ladies especially ; but as it was now my
' only means, it was received with contempt ; a proof
' how ready the world is to underrate those talents by
' which a man is supported.

' In this manner I proceeded to Paris, with no design
' but just to look about me, and then to go forward. The
' people of Paris are much fonder of strangers that have
' money than of those that have wit. As I could not
' boast much of either, I was no great favourite. After
' walking about the town four or five days, and seeing
' the outsides of the best houses, I was preparing to leave
' this retreat of venal hospitality, when passing through
' one of the principal streets, whom should I meet but
' our cousin to whom you first recommended me. This
' meeting was very agreeable to me, and I believe not
' displeasing to him. He inquired into the nature of my
' journey to Paris, and informed me of his own business
' there, which was to collect pictures, medals, intaglios,
' and antiques of all kinds for a gentleman in London,
' who had just stept into taste and a large fortune. I was
' the more surprised at seeing our cousin pitched upon

'for this office, as he himself had often assured me he
'knew nothing of the matter. Upon asking how he had
'been taught the art of a cognoscento so very suddenly,
'he assured me that nothing was more easy. The whole
'secret consisted in a strict adherence to two rules : the
'one always to observe that the picture might have been
'better if the painter had taken more pains ; and the
'other, to praise the works of Pietro Perugino. But,
'says he, as I once taught you how to be an author in
'London, I'll now undertake to instruct you in the art
'of picture buying at Paris.

'With this proposal I very readily closed, as it was
'living, and now all my ambition was to live. I went
'therefore to his lodgings, improved my dress by his
'assistance, and after some time accompanied him to
'auctions of pictures, where the English gentry were
'expected to be purchasers. I was not a little surprised
'at his intimacy with people of the best fashion, who
'referred themselves to his judgment upon every picture
'or medal, as an unerring standard of taste. He
'made very good use of my assistance upon these occa-
'sions ; for when asked his opinion, he would gravely
'take me aside and ask mine, shrug, look wise, return,
'and assure the company that he could give no opinion
'upon an affair of so much importance. Yet there was
'sometimes an occasion for a more supported assurance.
'I remember to have seen him, after giving his opinion
'that the colouring of a picture was not mellow enough,
'very deliberately take a brush with brown varnish, that
'was accidentally lying by, and rub it over the piece with
'great composure before all the company, and then ask
'if he had not improved the tints.

'When he had finished his commission in Paris, he left
'me strongly recommended to several men of distinction,
'as a person very proper for a travelling tutor ; and after

' some time I was employed in that capacity by a gentle-
' man who brought his ward to Paris, in order to set him
' forward on his tour through Europe. I was to be the
' young gentleman's governor, but with a proviso that
' he should always be permitted to govern himself. My
' pupil in fact understood the art of guiding in money
' concerns much better than I. He was heir to a fortune
' of about two hundred thousand pounds, left him by an
' uncle in the West Indies ; and his guardians, to qualify
' him for the management of it, had bound him appren-
' tice to an attorney. Thus avarice was his prevailing
' passion : all his questions on the road were how money
' might be saved ; which was the least expensive course of
' travel ; whether any thing could be bought that would
' turn to account when disposed of again in London.
' Such curiosities on the way as could be seen for nothing
' he was ready enough to look at ; but if the sight of
' them was to be paid for, he usually asserted that he had
' been told they were not worth seeing. He never paid
' a bill that he would not observe how amazingly expen-
' sive travelling was ; and all this though he was not yet
' twenty-one. When arrived at Leghorn, as we took a
' walk to look at the port and shipping, he inquired the
' expence of the passage by sea home to England. This
' he was informed was but a trifle compared to his
' returning by land ; he was therefore unable to withstand
' the temptation ; so paying me the small part of my
' salary that was due, he took leave, and embarked with
' only one attendant for London.
  ' I now therefore was left once more upon the world at
' large ; but then it was a thing I was used to. However,
' my skill in music could avail me nothing in a country
' where every peasant was a better musician than I ; but
' by this time I had acquired another talent, which
' answered my purpose as well, and this was a skill in dis-

'putation. In all the foreign universities and convents,
' there are upon certain days philosophical theses main-
' tained against every adventitious disputant ; for which,
' if the champion opposes with any dexterity, he can
' claim a gratuity in money, a dinner, and a bed for one
' night. In this manner therefore I fought my way
' towards England, walked along from city to city,
' examined mankind more nearly, and, if I may so express
' it, saw both sides of the picture. My remarks, however,
' are but few : I found that monarchy was the best
' government for the poor to live in, and commonwealths
' for the rich. I found that riches in general were in every
' country another name for freedom ; and that no man is
' so fond of liberty himself as not to be desirous of sub-
' jecting the will of some individuals in society to his own.

' Upon my arrival in England I resolved to pay my
' respects first to you, and then to enlist as a volunteer in
' the first expedition that was going forward ; but on my
' journey down my resolutions were changed, by meeting
' an old acquaintance, who I found belonged to a company
' of comedians that were going to make a summer cam-
' paign in the country. The company seemed not much
' to disapprove of me for an associate. They all however
' apprized me of the importance of the task at which I
' aimed ; that the public was a many-headed monster,
' and that only such as had very good heads could please
' it : that acting was not to be learnt in a day, and that
' without some traditional shrugs which had been on
' the stage, and only on the stage, these hundred years,
' I could never pretend to please. The next difficulty
' was in fitting me with parts, as almost every character
' was in keeping. I was driven for some time from one
' character to another, till at last Horatio was fixed upon,
' which the presence of the present company has happily
' hindered me from acting.'

—— 'Now, cried I, holding up my children, 'now let the flames burn on, and all my possessions perish.'—Page 336.

CHAPTER XXI

The short continuance of friendship amongst the vicious, which is coeval only with mutual satisfaction.

MY son's account was too long to be delivered at once, the first part of it was begun that night, and he was concluding the rest after dinner the next day, when the appearance of Mr. Thornhill's equipage at the door seemed to make a pause in the general satisfaction. The butler who was now become my friend in the family, informed me with a whisper that the 'Squire had already made some overtures to Miss Wilmot, and that her aunt and uncle seemed highly to approve the match. Upon Mr. Thornhill's entering, he seemed at seeing my son and me to start back ; but I readily imputed that to surprise and not displeasure. However, upon our advancing to salute him, he returned our greeting with the most apparent candour ; and after a short time his presence served only to increase the general good humour.

After tea he called me aside to enquire after my daughter ; but upon my informing him that my enquiry was unsuccessful, he seemed greatly surprised ; adding, that he had been since frequently at my house in order to comfort the rest of my family, whom he left perfectly well. He then asked if I had communicated her misfortune to Miss Wilmot or my son ; and upon my replying that I had not told them as yet, he greatly approved my prudence and precaution, desiring me by all means to keep it a secret : ' For at best,' cried he, ' it is but ' divulging one's own infamy ; and perhaps Miss Livy ' may not be so guilty as we all imagine.' We were here interrupted by a servant who came to ask the 'Squire in to stand up at country dances ; so that he left me quite pleased with the interest he seemed to take in my concerns. His addresses, however, to Miss Wilmot were too obvious to be mistaken : and yet she seemed not perfectly pleased, but bore them rather in compliance to the will of her aunt than from real inclination. I had even the satisfaction to see her lavish some kind looks upon my unfortunate son, which the other could neither extort by his fortune nor assiduity. Mr. Thornhill's seeming composure however not a little surprised me : we had now continued here a week at the pressing instances of Mr. Arnold ; but each day the more tender-

ness Miss Wilmot shewed my son, Mr. Thornhill's friendship seemed proportionably to encrease for him.

He had formerly made us the most kind assurances of
using his interest to serve the family ; but now his
generosity was not confined to promises alone : the morning I designed for my departure, Mr. Thornhill came to
me with looks of real pleasure to inform me of a piece of
service he had done for his friend George. This was
nothing less than his having procured him an ensign's
commission in one of the regiments that were going to the
West Indies, for which he had promised but one hundred
pounds, his interest having been sufficient to get an abate-
ment of the other two. ' As for this trifling piece of
' service,' continued the young gentleman, ' I desire no
' other reward but the pleasure of having served my
' friend ; and as for the hundred pounds to be paid, if you
' are unable to raise it yourselves, I will advance it, and
' you shall repay me at your leisure.' This was a favour
we wanted words to express our sense of ; I readily therefore gave my bond for the money, and testified as much
gratitude as if I never intended to pay.

George was to depart for town the next day to secure
his commission, in pursuance of his generous patron's
directions, who judged it highly expedient to use despatch, lest in the mean time another should step in with
more advantageous proposals. The next morning therefore our young soldier was early prepared for his departure, and seemed the only person among us that was not
affected by it. Neither the fatigues and dangers he was
going to encounter, nor the friends and mistress, for Miss
Wilmot actually loved him, he was leaving behind, any
way damped his spirits. After he had taken leave of the
rest of the company, I gave him all I had, my blessing.
' And now, my boy,' cried I, ' thou art going to fight for
' thy country, remember how thy brave grandfather

'fought for his sacred King, when loyalty among Britons
'was a virtue. Go, my boy, and imitate him in all but
'his misfortunes, if it was a misfortune to die with Lord
'Falkland. Go, my boy, and if you fall, though distant,
'exposed, and unwept by those that love you, the most
'precious tears are those with which heaven bedews the
'unburied head of a soldier.'

The next morning I took leave of the good family
that had been kind enough to entertain me so long, not
without several expressions of gratitude to Mr. Thornhill
for his late bounty. I left them in the enjoyment of all
that happiness which affluence and good breeding procure, and returned towards home, despairing of ever
finding my daughter more, but sending a sigh to heaven
to spare and forgive her. I was now come within
about twenty miles of home, having hired an horse to
carry me, as I was yet but weak, and comforted myself
with the hopes of soon seeing all I held dearest upon earth.
But the night coming on, I put up at a little public-house
by the road-side, and asked for the landlord's company
over a pint of wine. We sate beside his kitchen fire,
which was the best room in the house, and chatted on
politics and the news of the country. We happened,
among other topics, to talk of young 'Squire Thornhill,
who the host assured me was hated as much as his uncle
Sir William, who sometimes came down to the country,
was loved. He went on to observe, that he made it his
whole study to betray the daughters of such as received
him to their houses, and after a fortnight or three weeks
possession, turned them out unrewarded and abandoned
to the world. As we continued our discourse in this
manner, his wife, who had been out to get change,
returned, and perceiving that her husband was enjoying
a pleasure in which she was not a sharer, she asked him
in an angry tone, what he did there, to which he only

replied in an ironical way, by drinking her health. ' Mr.
' Symmonds,' cried she, 'you use me very ill, and I'll bear
' it no longer.   Here three parts of the business is left for
' me to do, and the fourth left unfinished : while you do
' nothing but soak with the guests all day long, whereas
' if a spoonful of liquor were to cure me of a fever I never
' touch a drop.'   I now found what she would be at, and
immediately poured her out a glass, which she received
with a curtsey, and drinking towards my good health,
' Sir,' resumed she, ' it is not so much for the value of the
' liquor I am angry, but one cannot help it when the house
' is going out of the windows.   If the customers or guests
' are to be dunned, all the burthen lies upon my back,
' he'd as lief eat that glass as budge after them himself.
' There now above stairs, we have a young woman who
' has come to take up her lodgings here, and I don't
' believe she has got any money by her over-civility.
' I am certain she is very slow of payment, and I wish she
' were put in mind of it.'——' What signifies minding her,'
cried the host ? ' if she be slow she is sure.'—' I don't
' know that,' replied the wife ; ' but I know that I am
' sure she has been here a fortnight and we have not yet
' seen the cross of her money.'——' I suppose, my dear,'
cried he, ' we shall have it all in a lump.'—' In a lump ! '
cried the other, ' I hope we may get it any way ; and that
' I am resolved we will this very night, or out she tramps,
' bag and baggage.'—' Consider, my dear,' cried the
husband, ' she is a gentlewoman, and deserves more
' respect.'—' As for the matter of that,' returned the
hostess, ' gentle or simple, out she shall pack with a
' sussarara.   Gentry may be good things where they
' take ; but for my part I never saw much good of them
' at the sign of the Harrow.'——Thus saying, she ran up
a narrow flight of stairs that went from the kitchen to
a room over head, and I soon perceived by the loud-

ness of her voice, and the bitterness of her reproaches,
that no money was to be had from her lodger. I could
hear her remonstrances very distinctly : ' Out I say, pack
' out this moment, tramp thou infamous strumpet, or
' I'll give thee a mark thou won't be the better for these
' three months. What ! you trumpery, to come and
' take up an honest house without cross or coin to bless
' yourself with ; come along I say.'——' O dear madam,'
cried the stranger, ' pity me, pity a poor abandoned
' creature for one night, and death will soon do the rest.'
——I instantly knew the voice of my poor ruin'd child
Olivia. I flew to her rescue, while the woman was
dragging her along by her hair, and I caught the dear
forlorn wretch in my arms.——' Welcome, any way
' welcome, my dearest lost one, my treasure, to your
' poor old father's bosom. Though the vicious forsake
' thee, there is yet one in the world that will never for-
' sake thee ; though thou hadst ten thousand crimes to
' answer for, he will forget them all.'——' O my own dear,'
—for minutes she could no more——' my own dearest
' good papa ! Could angels be kinder ! How do I deserve
' so much ! The villain, I hate him and myself, to be a
' reproach to such goodness. You can't forgive me, I
' know you cannot.'——' Yes, my child, from my heart
' I do forgive thee ! Only repent, and we both shall yet
' be happy. We shall see many pleasant days yet, my
' Olivia ! '—' Ah ! never, Sir, never. The rest of my
' wretched life must be infamy abroad and shame at
' home. But, alas ! papa, you look much paler than you
' used to do. Could such a thing as I am, give you so
' much uneasiness ? Surely you have too much wisdom
' to take the miseries of my guilt upon yourself.'——' Our
' wisdom, young woman,' replied I—' Ah, why so cold
' a name, papa ? ' cried she. ' This is the first time you
' ever called me by so cold a name.'—' I ask pardon, my

'darling,' returned I; 'but I was going to observe, that 'wisdom makes but a slow defence against trouble, 'though at last a sure one.' The landlady now returned to know if we did not choose a more genteel apartment, to which assenting, we were shewn a room where we could converse more freely. After we had talked our- selves into some degree of tranquillity, I could not avoid desiring some account of the gradations that led to her present wretched situation. 'That villain, Sir,' said she, 'from the first day of our meeting made me honourable 'though private proposals.'

'Villain, indeed,' cried I; 'and yet it in some measure 'surprises me, how a person of Mr. Burchell's good sense 'and seeming honour could be guilty of such deliberate 'baseness, and thus step into a family to undo it.'

'My dear papa,' returned my daughter, 'you labour 'under a strange mistake, Mr. Burchell never attempted 'to deceive me; instead of that he took every oppor- 'tunity of privately admonishing me against the artifices 'of Mr. Thornhill, who I now find was even worse than 'he represented him.'—'Mr. Thornhill,' interrupted I, 'can it be?' 'Yes, Sir,' returned she, 'it was Mr. Thorn- 'hill who seduced me, who employed the two ladies as 'he called them, but who in fact were abandoned women 'of the town, without breeding or pity, to decoy us up 'to London. Their artifices, you may remember, would 'have certainly succeeded, but for Mr. Burchell's letter, 'who directed those reproaches at them, which we all 'applied to ourselves. How he came to have so much 'influence as to defeat their intentions still remains a 'secret to me; but I am convinced he was ever our 'warmest sincerest friend.'

'You amaze me, my dear,' cried I; 'but now I find 'my first suspicions of Mr. Thornhill's baseness were too 'well grounded: but he can triumph in security; for he

DISCOVERY OF OLIVIA

' is rich and we are poor. But tell me, my child, sure it
' was no small temptation that could thus obliterate all
' the impressions of such an education, and so virtuous
' a disposition as thine ? '

' Indeed, Sir,' replied she, ' he owes all his triumph to
' the desire I had of making him, and not myself, happy.
' I knew that the ceremony of our marriage, which was
' privately performed by a popish priest, was no way
' binding, and that I had nothing to trust to but his
' honour.' ' What,' interrupted I, ' and were you indeed
' married by a priest, and in orders ? '——' Indeed, Sir,
' we were,' replied she, ' though we were both sworn to
' conceal his name.'—' Why, then, my child, come to
' my arms again, and now you are a thousand times more
' welcome than before ; for you are now his wife to all
' intents and purposes ; nor can all the laws of man,
' though written upon tables of adamant, lessen the force
' of that sacred connection.'

' Alas, papa,' replied she, ' you are but little acquainted
' with his villainies ; he has been married already by the
' same priest to six or eight wives more, whom, like me,
' he has deceived and abandoned.'

' Has he so ? ' cried I, ' then we must hang the priest,
' and you shall inform against him to-morrow.'—' But,
' Sir,' returned she, ' will that be right, when I am sworn
' to secrecy ? '——' My dear,' I replied, ' if you have
' made such a promise, I cannot, nor will I tempt you to
' break it. Even though it may benefit the public, you
' must not inform against him. In all human institutions
' a smaller evil is allowed to procure a greater good ; as
' in politics, a province may be given away to secure a
' kingdom ; in medicine, a limb may be lopt off to pre-
' serve the body. But in religion the law is written, and
' inflexible, *never* to do evil. And this law, my child, is
' right : for otherwise, if we commit a smaller evil to

'procure a greater good, certain guilt would be thus in-
'curred, in expectation of contingent advantage. And
'though the advantage should certainly follow, yet the
'interval between commission and advantage, which is
'allowed to be guilty, may be that in which we are called
'away to answer for the things we have done, and the
'volume of human actions is closed for ever. But I
'interrupt you, my dear ; go on.'

'The very next morning,' continued she, 'I found what
'little expectations I was to have from his sincerity.
'That very morning he introduced me to two unhappy
'women more, whom, like me, he had deceived, but who
'lived in contented prostitution. I loved him too ten-
'derly to bear such rivals in his affections, and strove
'to forget my infamy in a tumult of pleasures. With
'this view I danced, dressed, and talked ; but still was
'unhappy. The gentlemen who visited there told me
'every moment of the power of my charms, and this only
'contributed to encrease my melancholy, as I had thrown
'all their power quite away. Thus each day I grew more
'pensive, and he more insolent, till at last the monster
'had the assurance to offer me to a young Baronet of his
'acquaintance. Need I describe, Sir, how his ingratitude
'stung me. My answer to this proposal was almost
'madness. I desired to part. As I was going, he offered
'me a purse ; but I flung it at him with indignation, and
'burst from him in a rage, that for a while kept me in-
'sensible of the miseries of my situation. But I soon
'looked round me, and saw myself a vile, abject, guilty
'thing, without one friend in the world to apply to.

'Just in that interval a stage-coach happening to pass
'by, I took a place, it being my only aim to be driven at
'a distance from a wretch I despised and detested. I was
'set down here, where, since my arrival, my own anxiety
'and this woman's unkindness have been my only com-

' panions.   The hours of pleasure that I have passed with
' my mamma and sister now grow painful to me.   Their
' sorrows are much ; but mine is greater than theirs ; for
' mine are mixed with guilt and infamy.'

 ' Have patience, my child,' cried I, ' and I hope things
' will yet be better.   Take some repose to-night, and to-
' morrow I'll carry you home to your mother and the
' rest of the family, from whom you will receive a kind
' reception.   Poor woman, this has gone to her heart : but
' she loves you still, Olivia, and will forget it.'

—— My compassion for my poor daughter, overpowered by this new disaster,
interrupted what I had farther to observe. I bade her mother support her, and
after a short time she recovered.—Page 343.

CHAPTER XXII

Offences are easily pardoned where there is love at bottom.

THE next morning I took my daughter behind me, and
set out on my return home. As we travelled along, I
strove, by every persuasion, to calm her sorrows and fears,
and to arm her with resolution to bear the presence of her
offended mother. I took every opportunity, from the
prospect of a fine country through which we passed, to
observe how much kinder heaven was to us than we to
each other, and that the misfortunes of nature's making
were very few. I assured her that she should never
perceive any change in my affections, and that during my
life, which yet might be long, she might depend upon a
guardian and an instructor. I armed her against the
censure of the world, shewed her that books were sweet

unreproaching companions to the miserable, and that if they could not bring us to enjoy life, they would at least teach us to endure it.

The hired horse that we rode was to be put up that night at an inn by the way, within about five miles from my house ; and as I was willing to prepare my family for my daughter's reception, I determined to leave her that night at the inn, and to return for her, accompanied by my daughter Sophia, early the next morning. It was night before we reached our appointed stage : however, after seeing her provided with a decent apartment, and having ordered the hostess to prepare proper refreshments, I kissed her, and proceeded towards home. And now my heart caught new sensations of pleasure the nearer I approached that peaceful mansion. As a bird that had been frighted from its nest, my affections outwent my haste, and hovered round my little fireside with all the rapture of expectation. I called up the many fond things I had to say, and anticipated the welcome I was to receive. I already felt my wife's tender embrace, and smiled at the joy of my little ones. As I walked but slowly, the night waned apace. The labourers of the day were all retired to rest ; the lights were out in every cottage ; no sounds were heard but of the shrilling cock, and the deep-mouthed watch-dog at hollow distance. I approached my abode of pleasure, and before I was within a furlong of the place, our honest mastiff came running to welcome me.

It was now near midnight that I came to knock at my door : all was still and silent : my heart dilated with unutterable happiness, when, to my amazement, I saw the house bursting out in a blaze of fire, and every aperture red with conflagration ! I gave a loud convulsive outcry, and fell upon the pavement insensible. This alarmed my son, who had till this been asleep, and he, perceiving the flames, instantly waked my wife and daughter, and all running out naked and wild with apprehension, recalled me to life with their anguish. But it was only to objects of new terror; for the flames had by this time caught the roof of our dwelling, part after part continuing to fall in, while the family stood with silent agony looking on as if they enjoyed the blaze. I gazed upon them and upon it by turns, and then looked round me for my two little ones; but they were not to be seen. O misery! 'Where,' cried I, 'where are my 'little ones?'——'They are burnt to death in the flames,' says my wife calmly, 'and I will die with them.'—That moment I heard the cry of the babes within, who were just awaked by the fire, and nothing could have stopped me. 'Where, where, are my children?' cried I, rushing through the flames, and bursting the door of the chamber in which they were confined; 'Where are my little ones?'——'Here, dear papa, here we are,' cried they together, while the flames were just catching the bed where they lay. I caught them both in my arms, and snatching them through the fire as fast as possible, while just as I was got out, the roof sank in. 'Now,' cried I, holding up my children, 'now let the flames burn on, 'and all my possessions perish. Here they are, I have 'saved my treasures. Here, my dearest, here are our 'treasures, and we shall yet be happy.' We kissed our little darlings a thousand times; they clasped us round the neck, and seemed to share our transports, while their mother laughed and wept by turns.

I now stood a calm spectator of the flames, and after some time began to perceive that my arm to the shoulder was scorched in a terrible manner. It was therefore out of my power to give my son any assistance, either in attempting to save our goods, or preventing the flames spreading to our corn. By this time the neighbours were

alarmed, and came running to our assistance ; but all
they could do was to stand, like us, spectators of the
calamity. My goods, among which were the notes I had
reserved for my daughters' fortunes, were entirely consumed, except a box with some papers that stood in
the kitchen, and two or three things more of little consequence, which my son brought away in the beginning.
The neighbours contributed, however, what they could
to lighten our distress. They brought us clothes, and
furnished one of our out-houses with kitchen utensils ;
so that by daylight we had another, though a wretched
dwelling, to retire to. My honest next neighbour and
his children were not the least assiduous in providing
us with every thing necessary, and offering whatever
consolation untutored benevolence could suggest.

When the fears of my family had subsided, curiosity
to know the cause of my long stay began to take place ;
having therefore informed them of every particular, I
proceeded to prepare them for the reception of our lost
one, and though we had nothing but wretchedness now
to impart, I was willing to procure her a welcome to
what we had. This task would have been more difficult
but for our recent calamity, which had humbled my
wife's pride and blunted it by more poignant afflictions.
Being unable to go for my poor child myself, as my arm
grew very painful, I sent my son and daughter, who
soon returned, supporting the wretched delinquent, who
had not the courage to look up at her mother, whom no
instructions of mine could persuade to a perfect recon-
ciliation ; for women have a much stronger sense of
female error than men. ' Ah Madam,' cried her mother,
' this is but a poor place you are come to after so much
' finery. My daughter Sophy and I can afford but little
' entertainment to persons who have kept company only
' with people of distinction. Yes, Miss Livy, your poor

' father and I have suffered very much of late ; but
' I hope heaven will forgive you.'——During this reception the unhappy victim stood pale and trembling, unable
to weep or to reply ; but I could not continue a silent
spectator of her distress, wherefore assuming a degree
of severity in my voice and manner, which was ever
followed with instant submission, ' I entreat, woman,
' that my words may be now marked once for all : I have
' here brought you back a poor deluded wanderer ; her
' return to duty demands the revival of our tenderness.
' The real hardships of life are now coming fast upon
' us ; let us not therefore encrease them by dissension
' among each other. If we live harmoniously together,
' we may yet be contented, as there are enough of us to
' shut out the censuring world, and keep each other in
' countenance. The kindness of heaven is promised to
' the penitent, and let ours be directed by the example.
' Heaven, we are assured, is much more pleased to view
' a repentant sinner than ninety-nine persons who have
' supported a course of undeviating rectitude. And this
' is right ; for that single effort by which we stop short
' in the down-hill path to perdition, is itself a greater
' exertion of virtue than an hundred acts of justice.'

—— The consequence of my incapacity was his driving my cattle that evening, and their being appraised and sold the next day for less than half their value.—— PAGE 349.

CHAPTER XXIII

None but the guilty can be long and completely miserable.

SOME assiduity was now required to make our present abode as convenient as possible, and we were soon again qualified to enjoy our former serenity. Being disabled myself from assisting my son in our usual occupations, I read to my family from the few books that were saved, and particularly from such as by amusing the imagination contributed to ease the heart. Our good neighbours, too, came every day with the kindest condolence, and fixed a time in which they were all to assist at repairing my former dwelling. Honest

farmer Williams was not last among these visitors ; but
heartily offered his friendship. He would even have
renewed his addresses to my daughter ; but she rejected
him in such a manner as totally represt his future
solicitations.—Her grief seemed formed for continuing,
and she was the only person of our little society that
a week did not restore to chearfulness. She now lost
that unblushing innocence which had once taught her to
respect herself, and to seek pleasure by pleasing. Anxiety
now had taken strong possession of her mind, her beauty
began to be impaired with her constitution, and neglect
still more contributed to diminish it. Every tender
epithet bestowed on her sister brought a pang to her
heart and a tear to her eye ; and as one vice, though
cured, ever plants others where it has been, so her former
guilt, though driven out by repentance, left jealousy and
envy behind. I strove a thousand ways to lessen her
care, and even forgot my own pain in a concern for hers,
collecting such amusing passages of history as a strong
memory and some reading could suggest.—' Our happi-
' ness, my dear,' I would say, ' is in the power of One
' who can bring it about a thousand unforeseen ways
' that mock our foresight. If example be necessary to
' prove this, I'll give you a story, my child, told us by
' a grave, though sometimes a romancing, historian.

' Matilda was married very young to a Neapolitan
' nobleman of the first quality, and found herself a widow
' and a mother at the age of fifteen. As she stood one
' day caressing her infant son in the open window of an
' apartment which hung over the river Volturna, the
' child with a sudden spring leaped from her arms into
' the flood below, and disappeared in a moment. The
' mother, struck with instant surprise, and making an
' effort to save him, plunged in after ; but far from being
' able to assist the infant, she herself with great difficulty

' escaped to the opposite shore, just when some French
' soldiers were plundering the country on that side, who
' immediately made her their prisoner.

' As the war was then carried on between the French
' and Italians with the utmost inhumanity, they were
' going at once to perpetrate those two extremes sug-
' gested by appetite and cruelty. This base resolution,
' however, was opposed by a young officer, who, though
' their retreat required the utmost expedition, placed her
' behind him, and brought her in safety to his native city.
' Her beauty at first caught his eye, her merit soon after
' his heart. They were married : he rose to the highest
' posts ; they lived long together, and were happy. But
' the felicity of a soldier can never be called permanent :
' after an interval of several years, the troops which he
' commanded having met with a repulse, he was obliged
' to take shelter in the city where he had lived with his
' wife. Here they suffered a siege, and the city at length
' was taken. Few histories can produce more various
' instances of cruelty, than those which the French and
' Italians at that time exercised upon each other. It
' was resolved by the victors upon this occasion, to put
' all the French prisoners to death ; but particularly
' the husband of the unfortunate Matilda, as he was
' principally instrumental in protracting the siege. Their
' determinations were in general executed almost as soon
' as resolved upon. The captive soldier was led forth,
' and the executioner with his sword stood ready, while
' the spectators in gloomy silence awaited the fatal blow,
' which was only suspended till the general, who pre-
' sided as judge, should give the signal. It was in this
' interval of anguish and expectation, that Matilda came
' to take her last farewell of her husband and deliverer,
' deploring her wretched situation, and the cruelty of
' fate, that had saved her from perishing by a premature

' death in the river Volturna, to be the spectator of still
' greater calamities. The general, who was a young man,
' was struck with surprise at her beauty, and pity at
' her distress ; but with still stronger emotions, when he
' heard her mention her former dangers. He was her
' son, the infant for whom she had encountered so much
' danger. He acknowledged her at once as his mother,
' and fell at her feet. The rest may be easily supposed ;
' the captive was set free, and all the happiness that love,
' friendship, and duty could confer on each, were united.'

In this manner I would attempt to amuse my daughter ;
but she listened with divided attention ; for her own
misfortunes engrossed all the pity she once had for those
of another, and nothing gave her ease. In company
she dreaded contempt ; and in solitude she only found
anxiety. Such was the colour of her wretchedness, when
we received certain information, that Mr. Thornhill was
going to be married to Miss Wilmot, for whom I always
suspected he had a real passion, though he took every
opportunity before me to express his contempt both of
her person and fortune. This news only served to
increase poor Olivia's affliction ; such a flagrant breach
of fidelity was more than her courage could support.
I was resolved, however, to get more certain information, and to defeat, if possible, the completion of his
designs, by sending my son to old Mr. Wilmot's with
instructions to know the truth of the report, and to
deliver Miss Wilmot a letter intimating Mr. Thornhill's
conduct in my family. My son went, in pursuance of
my directions, and in three days returned, assuring us
of the truth of the account ; but that he had found it
impossible to deliver the letter, which he was therefore
obliged to leave, as Mr. Thornhill and Miss Wilmot were
visiting round the country. They were to be married, he
said, in a few days, having appeared together at church

the Sunday before he was there, in great splendour, the
bride attended by six young ladies, and he by as many
gentlemen. Their approaching nuptials filled the whole
country with rejoicing, and they usually rode out together
in the grandest equipage that had been seen in the
country for many years. All the friends of both families,
he said, were there, particularly the 'Squire's uncle, Sir
William Thornhill, who bore so good a character. He
added, that nothing but mirth and feasting were going
forward ; that all the country praised the young bride's
beauty, and the bridegroom's fine person, and that they
were immensely fond of each other ; concluding that he
could not help thinking Mr. Thornhill one of the most
happy men in the world.

'Why let him if he can,' returned I : ' but, my son,
' observe this bed of straw and unsheltering roof ; those
' mouldering walls and humid floor ; my wretched body
' thus disabled by fire, and my children weeping round
' me for bread ; you have come home, my child, to all
' this, yet here, even here, you see a man that would
' not for a thousand worlds exchange situations. O, my
' children, if you could but learn to commune with your
' own hearts, and know what noble company you can
' make them, you would little regard the elegance and
' splendour of the worthless. Almost all men have
' been taught to call life a passage, and themselves the
' travellers. The similitude still may be improved when
' we observe that the good are joyful and serene, like
' travellers that are going towards home ; the wicked
' but by intervals happy, like travellers that are going
' into exile.'

My compassion for my poor daughter, overpowered
by this new disaster, interrupted what I had farther to
observe. I bade her mother support her, and after a
short time she recovered. She appeared from that time

more calm, and I imagined had gained a new degree of resolution : but appearances deceived me; for her tranquillity was the languor of over-wrought resentment. A supply of provisions, charitably sent us by my kind parishioners, seemed to diffuse new chearfulness amongst the rest of the family, nor was I displeased at seeing them once more sprightly and at ease. It would have been unjust to damp their satisfactions, merely to condole with resolute melancholy, or to burthen them with a sadness they did not feel. Thus once more the tale went round, and the song was demanded, and chearfulness condescended to hover round our little habitation.

— The consequences might have been fatal, had I not immediately interposed, and with some difficulty rescued the officers from the hands of the enraged multitude.—PAGE 352.

CHAPTER XXIV

Fresh calamities.

THE next morning the sun arose with peculiar warmth for the season; so that we agreed to breakfast together on the honey-suckle bank: where while we sat, my youngest daughter at my request joined her voice to the concert on the trees about us. It was in this place my poor Olivia first met her seducer, and every object served to recall her sadness. But that melancholy which is excited by objects of pleasure, or inspired by sounds of harmony, soothes the heart instead of corroding it. Her mother too, upon this occasion, felt a pleasing distress, and wept, and loved her daughter as before. ' Do, my ' pretty Olivia,' cried she, ' let us have that little melan- ' choly air your pappa was so fond of ; your sister Sophy ' has already obliged us. Do child, it will please your ' old father.' She complied in a manner so exquisitely pathetic as moved me.

> When lovely woman stoops to folly
>   And finds too late that men betray,
> What charm can soothe her melancholy,
>   What art can wash her guilt away ?
>
> The only art her guilt to cover,
>   To hide her shame from every eye,
> To give repentance to her lover,
>   And wring his bosom—is to die.

As she was concluding the last stanza, to which an in- terruption in her voice from sorrow gave peculiar softness, the appearance of Mr. Thornhill's equipage at a distance alarmed us all, but particularly encreased the uneasiness of my eldest daughter, who, desirous of shunning her betrayer, returned to the house with her sister. In a few minutes he was alighted from his chariot, and making up to the place where I was still sitting, inquired after my health with his usual air of familiarity. ' Sir,' replied I, 'your present assurance only serves to aggravate the ' baseness of your character ; and there was a time when ' I would have chastised your insolence for presuming ' thus to appear before me. But now you are safe ; for ' age has cooled my passions, and my calling restrains ' them.'

' I vow, my dear sir,' returned he, ' I am amazed at all ' this ; nor can I understand what it means ! I hope you

' don't think your daughter's late excursion with me had
' any thing criminal in it.'

    ' Go,' cried I, ' thou art a wretch, a poor pitiful wretch,
' and every way a liar : but your meanness secures you
' from my anger ! Yet, Sir, I am descended from a family
' that would not have borne this ! And so, thou vile thing,
' to gratify a momentary passion, thou hast made one
' poor creature wretched for life, and polluted a family
' that had nothing but honour for their portion.'

    ' If she or you,' returned he, ' are resolved to be miser-
' able, I cannot help it. But you may still be happy : and
' whatever opinion you may have formed of me, you shall
' ever find me ready to contribute to it. We can marry
' her to another in a short time, and what is more, she
' may keep her lover beside ; for I protest I shall ever
' continue to have a true regard for her.'

    I found all my passions alarmed at this new degrading
proposal ; for though the mind may often be calm under
great injuries, little villainy can at any time get within
the soul and sting it into rage.——' Avoid my sight, thou
' reptile,' cried I, ' nor continue to insult me with thy
' presence. Were my brave son at home he would not
' suffer this ; but I am old and disabled, and every way
' undone.'

    ' I find,' cried he, ' you are bent upon obliging me to
' talk in a harsher manner than I intended. But as I
' have shewn you what may be hoped from my friendship,
' it may not be improper to represent what may be the
' consequences of my resentment. My attorney, to whom
' your late bond has been transferred, threatens hard, nor
' do I know how to prevent the course of justice, except by
' paying the money myself, which, as I have been at some
' expences lately, previous to my intended marriage, is
' not so easy to be done. And then my steward talks of
' driving for the rent : it is certain he knows his duty ;

' for I never trouble myself with affairs of that nature.
' Yet still I could wish to serve you, and even to have you
' and your daughter present at my marriage, which is
' shortly to be solemnized with Miss Wilmot ; it is even
' the request of my charming Arabella herself, whom I
' hope you will not refuse.'

' Mr. Thornhill,' replied I, ' hear me once for all : as
' to your marriage with any but my daughter, that I
' never will consent to ; and though your friendship
' could raise me to a throne, or your resentment sink me
' to the grave, yet would I despise both. Thou hast
' once wofully, irreparably deceived me. I reposed my
' heart upon thine honour, and have found its baseness.
' Never more therefore expect friendship from me. Go,
' and possess what fortune has given thee, beauty, riches,
' health, and pleasure. Go, and leave me to want,
' infamy, disease, and sorrow. Yet humbled as I am,
' shall my heart still vindicate its dignity, and though
' thou hast my forgiveness, thou shalt ever have my
' contempt.'

' If so,' returned he, ' depend upon it you shall feel
' the effects of this insolence, and we shall shortly see
' which is the fittest object of scorn, you or me.'—Upon
which he departed abruptly.

My wife and son, who were present at this interview,
seemed terrified with the apprehension. My daughters
also, finding that he was gone, came out to be informed
of the result of our conference, which, when known,
alarmed them not less than the rest. But as to myself
I disregarded the utmost stretch of his malevolence : he
had already struck the blow, and now I stood prepared
to repel every new effort. Like one of those instruments
used in the art of war, which however thrown still presents
a point to receive the enemy.

We soon however found that he had not threatened in

vain ; for the very next morning his steward came to demand my annual rent, which, by the train of accidents already related, I was unable to pay. The consequence of my incapacity was his driving my cattle that evening, and their being appraised and sold the next day for less than half their value. My wife and children now therefore entreated me to comply upon any terms, rather than incur certain destruction. They even begged of me to admit his visits once more, and used all their little eloquence to paint the calamities I was going to endure : the terrors of a prison, in so rigorous a season as the present, with the danger that threatened my health from the late accident that happened by the fire. But I continued inflexible.

' Why, my treasures,' cried I, ' why will you thus ' attempt to persuade me to the thing that is not right ? ' My duty has taught me to forgive him ; but my ' conscience will not permit me to approve. Would you ' have me applaud to the world what my heart must ' internally condemn ? Would you have me tamely sit ' down and flatter our infamous betrayer ; and to avoid ' a prison continually suffer the more galling bonds of ' mental confinement ? No, never. If we are to be taken ' from this abode, only let us hold to the right, and where- ' ever we are thrown we can still retire to a charming ' apartment, when we can look round our own hearts ' with intrepidity and with pleasure ! '

In this manner we spent that evening. Early the next morning, as the snow had fallen in great abundance in the night, my son was employed in clearing it away, and opening a passage before the door. He had not been thus engaged long when he came running in, with looks all pale, to tell us that two strangers, whom he knew, to be officers of justice, were making towards the house.

Just as he spoke they came in, and approaching the

bed where I lay, after previously informing me of their employment and business, made me their prisoner, bidding me prepare to go with them to the county gaol, which was eleven miles off.

'My friends,' said I, 'this is severe weather in which 'you have come to take me to a prison ; and it is particu-'larly unfortunate at this time, as one of my arms has 'lately been burnt in a terrible manner, and it has thrown 'me into a slight fever, and I want clothes to cover me, 'and I am now too weak and old to walk far in such 'deep snow : but if it must be so——'

I then turned to my wife and children, and directed them to get together what few things were left us, and to prepare immediately for leaving this place. I entreated them to be expeditious, and desired my son to assist his eldest sister, who, from a consciousness that she was the cause of all our calamities, was fallen, and had lost anguish in insensibility. I encouraged my wife, who, pale and trembling, clasped our affrighted little ones in her arms, that clung to her bosom in silence, dreading to look round at the strangers. In the mean time my youngest daughter prepared for our departure, and as she received several hints to use dispatch, in about an hour we were ready to depart.

—— I was apprised of the usual perquisite required upon these occasions, and immediately complied with the demand, though the little money I had was very near being all exhausted.—Page 353.

CHAPTER XXV

No situation, however wretched it seems, but has some sort of comfort attending it.

WE set forward from this peaceful neighbourhood and walked on slowly. My eldest daughter being enfeebled by a slow fever, which had begun for some days to undermine her constitution, one of the officers, who had an horse, kindly took her behind him ; for even these men cannot entirely divest themselves of humanity. My son led one of the little ones by the hand, and my wife the other, while I leaned upon my youngest girl, whose tears fell not for her own but my distresses.

We were now got from my late dwelling about two miles, when we saw a crowd running and shouting behind us consisting of about fifty of my poorest parishioners. These, with dreadful imprecations, soon seized upon the two officers of justice, and swearing they would never see their minister go to a gaol while they had a drop of blood to shed in his defence, were going to use them with great severity. The consequence might have been fatal, had I not immediately interposed, and with some difficulty rescued the officers from the hands of the enraged multitude. My children, who looked upon my delivery now as certain, appeared transported with joy, and were incapable of containing their raptures. But they were soon undeceived, upon hearing me address the poor deluded people who came, as they imagined, to do me service.

' What ! my friends,' cried I, ' and is this the way you ' love me ! Is this the manner you obey the instructions ' I have given you from the pulpit ! Thus to fly in the ' face of justice, and bring down ruin on yourselves and ' me ! Which is your ringleader ? Shew me the man that ' has thus seduced you. As sure as he lives he shall feel my ' resentment. Alas ! my dear deluded flock, return back to ' the duty you owe to God, to your country, and to me. ' I shall yet perhaps one day see you in greater felicity ' here, and contribute to make your lives more happy. ' But let it at least be my comfort when I pen my fold for ' immortality, that not one here shall be wanting.'

They now seemed all repentance, and melting into tears came one after the other to bid me farewell. I shook each tenderly by the hand, and leaving them my blessing, proceeded forward without meeting any farther interruption. Some hours before night we reached the town or rather village ; for it consisted but of a few mean houses, having lost all its former opulence, and retaining no marks of its ancient superiority but the gaol.

Upon entering, we put up at an inn, where we had such refreshments as could most readily be procured, and I supped with my family with my usual chearfulness. After seeing them properly accommodated for that night, I next attended the sheriff's officers to the prison, which had formerly been built for the purposes of war, and consisted of one large apartment, strongly grated and paved with stone, common to both felons and debtors at certain hours in the four and twenty. Besides this, every prisoner had a separate cell where he was locked in for the night·

I expected upon my entrance to find nothing but lamentations and various sounds of misery ; but it was very different. The prisoners seemed all employed in one common design, that of forgetting thought in merriment or clamour. I was apprized of the usual perquisite required upon these occasions, and immediately complied with the demand, though the little money I had was very near being all exhausted. This was immediately sent away for liquor, and the whole prison soon was filled with riot, laughter and prophaneness.

' How,' cried I to myself, ' shall men so very wicked ' be chearful, and shall I be melancholy ! I feel only the ' same confinement with them, and I think I have more ' reason to be happy.'

With such reflections I laboured to become chearful ; but chearfulness was never yet produced by effort, which is itself painful. As I was sitting therefore in a corner of the gaol, in a pensive posture, one of my fellow-prisoners came up, and sitting by me, entered into conversation. It was my constant rule in life never to avoid the con-

versation of any man who seemed to desire it : for if good
I might profit by his instruction ; if bad he might be
assisted by mine.   I found this to be a knowing man of
strong unlettered sense ; but a thorough knowledge of
the world as it is called, or, more properly speaking, of
human nature on the wrong side.   He asked me if I had
taken care to provide myself with a bed, which was
a circumstance I had never once attended to.

' That 's unfortunate,' cried he, ' as you are allowed
' here nothing but straw, and your apartment is very
' large and cold.   However you seem to be something of
' a gentleman, and as I have been one myself in my time,
' part of my bed-clothes are heartily at your service.

I thanked him, professing my surprise at finding such
humanity in a gaol in misfortunes ; adding, to let him see
that I was a scholar, ' That the sage ancient seemed to
' understand the value of company in affliction when he
' said, Ton kosmon aire, ei dos ton etairon ; and in fact,'
continued I, ' what is the World if it affords only soli-
' tude ? '

' You talk of the World, Sir,' returned my fellow-
prisoner ; ' *the world is in its dotage, and yet the cosmogony*
' *or creation of the world has puzzled the philosophers of*
' *every age.   What a medley of opinions have they not*
' *broached upon the creation of the world.   Sanconiathon,*
' *Manetho, Berosus, and Ocellus Lucanus have all attempted*
' *it in vain.   The latter has these words, Anarchon ara*
' *kai atelutaion to pan, which implies* '——' I ask pardon,
' Sir,' cried I, ' for interrupting so much learning ; but
' I think I have heard all this before.   Have I not had
' the pleasure of once seeing you at Welbridge fair,
' and is not your name Ephraim Jenkinson ? '   At this
demand he only sighed.   ' I suppose you must recollect,'
resumed I, ' one Doctor Primrose, from whom you bought
' a horse.'

PICKERING

He now at once recollected me ; for the gloominess of the place and the approaching night had prevented his distinguishing my features before.——' Yes, Sir,' returned Mr. Jenkinson, ' I remember you perfectly well ; ' I bought a horse but forgot to pay for him. Your ' neighbour Flamborough is the only prosecutor I am any ' way afraid of at the next assizes : for he intends to ' swear positively against me as a coiner. I am heartily ' sorry, Sir, I ever deceived you, or indeed any man ; for ' you see,' continued he, shewing his shackles, ' what my ' tricks have brought me to.'

' Well, Sir,' replied I, ' your kindness in offering me ' assistance when you could expect no return, shall be ' repaid with my endeavours to soften or totally suppress ' Mr. Flamborough's evidence, and I will send my son ' to him for that purpose the first opportunity ; nor do ' I in the least doubt but he will comply with my request, ' and as to my own evidence you need be under no ' uneasiness about that.'

' Well, Sir,' cried he, ' all the return I can make shall ' be yours. You shall have more than half my bed- ' clothes to-night, and I'll take care to stand your friend ' in the prison, where I think I have some influence.'

I thanked him, and could not avoid being surprised at the present youthful change in his aspect ; for at the time I had seen him before he appeared at least sixty.—' Sir,' answered he, ' you are little acquainted with the world; ' I had at that time false hair, and have learnt the art of ' counterfeiting every age from seventeen to seventy. ' Ah, Sir, had I but bestowed half the pains in learning ' a trade that I have in learning to be a scoundrel, I might ' have been a rich man at this day. But rogue as I am, ' still I may be your friend, and that perhaps when you ' least expect it.'

We were now prevented from further conversation by

the arrival of the gaoler's servants, who came to call over
the prisoners' names, and lock up for the night.   A fellow
also, with a bundle of straw for my bed, attended, who
led me along a dark narrow passage into a room paved
like the common prison, and in one corner of this I spread
my bed and the clothes given me by my fellow-prisoner ;
which done, my conductor, who was civil enough, bade
me a good night.   After my usual meditations, and
having praised my heavenly corrector, I laid myself down
and slept with the utmost tranquillity till morning.

—— I therefore read them a portion of the service with a loud unaffected voice, and found my audience perfectly merry upon the occasion.—PAGE 359.

CHAPTER XXVI

A reformation in the gaol. To make laws compleat they should reward as well as punish.

THE next morning early I was awakened by my family, whom I found in tears at my bed-side. The gloomy strength of everything about us, it seems, had daunted them. I gently rebuked their sorrow, assuring them I had never slept with greater tranquillity, and next enquired after my eldest daughter, who was not among them. They informed me that yesterday's uneasiness and fatigue had encreased her fever, and it was judged proper to leave her behind. My next care was to send my son to procure a room or two to lodge the family in, as near the prison as conveniently could be found.   He obeyed ; but could only find one apartment, which was hired at a small expence for his mother and sisters, the gaoler with humanity consenting to let him and his two little brothers lie in the prison with me.   A bed was therefore prepared for them in a corner of the room, which I thought answered very conveniently.   I was willing, however, previously to know whether my little children chose to lie in a place which seemed to fright them upon entrance.

'Well,' cried I, 'my good boys, how do you like your 'bed ?   I hope you are not afraid to lie in this room, dark 'as it appears.'

'No, papa,' says Dick, 'I am not afraid to lie anywhere 'where you are.'

'And I,' says Bill, who was yet but four years old, 'love every place best that my papa is in.'

After this I allotted to each of the family what they were to do.   My daughter was particularly directed to watch her declining sister's health ;   my wife was to attend me ;   my little boys were to read to me :   'And as 'for you my son,' continued I, 'it is by the labour of 'your hands we must all hope to be supported.   Your 'wages, as a day-labourer, will be fully sufficient with 'proper frugality to maintain us all, and comfortably too. 'Thou art now sixteen years old, and hast strength, and 'it was given thee, my son, for very useful purposes ;   for 'it must save from famine your helpless parents and 'family.   Prepare then this evening to look out for work 'against to-morrow, and bring home every night what 'money you earn, for our support.'

Having thus instructed him, and settled the rest, I walked down to the common prison, where I could enjoy more air and room.   But I was not long there when the execrations, lewdness, and brutality that invaded me on every side drove me back to my apartment again. Here I sate for some time pondering upon the strange infatuation of wretches who, finding all mankind in open arms against them, were labouring to make themselves a future and a tremendous enemy.

Their insensibility excited my highest compassion, and blotted my own uneasiness from my mind. It even appeared a duty incumbent upon me to attempt to reclaim them. I resolved therefore once more to return, and in spite of their contempt to give them my advice, and conquer them by perseverance. Going therefore among them again, I informed Mr. Jenkinson of my design, at which he laughed heartily, but communicated it to the rest. The proposal was received with the greatest good-humour, as it promised to afford a new fund of entertainment to persons who had now no other resource for mirth, but what could be derived from ridicule or debauchery.

I therefore read them a portion of the service with a loud unaffected voice, and found my audience perfectly merry upon the occasion. Lewd whispers, groans of contrition burlesqued, winking and coughing alternately excited laughter. However, I continued with my natural solemnity to read on, sensible that what I did might mend some, but could itself receive no contamination from any.

After reading, I entered upon my exhortation, which was rather calculated at first to amuse them than to reprove. I previously observed, that no other motive but their welfare could induce me to this ; that I was their fellow prisoner, and now got nothing by preaching. I was sorry, I said, to hear them so very profane ; because they got nothing by it, but might lose a great deal: 'For ' be assured, my friends,' cried I, 'for you are my friends, ' however the world may disclaim your friendship, though

' you swore twelve thousand oaths in a day, it would not
' put one penny in your purse. Then what signifies calling
' every moment upon the devil, and courting his friend-
' ship, since you find how scurvily he uses you. He has
' given you nothing here, you find, but a mouthful of oaths
' and an empty belly ; and by the best accounts I have
' of him, he will give you nothing that 's good hereafter.

' If used ill in our dealings with one man we naturally
' go elsewhere. Were it not worth your while then just
' to try how you may like the usage of another master,
' who gives you fair promises at least to come to him ?
' Surely, my friends, of all stupidity in the world, his
' must be the greatest, who after robbing a house runs to
' the thieftakers for protection. And yet how are you
' more wise ? You are all seeking comfort from one that
' has already betrayed you, applying to a more malicious
' being than any thieftaker of them all ; for they only
' decoy and then hang you ; but he decoys and hangs,
' and what is worst of all, will not let you loose after the
' hangman has done.'

When I had concluded, I received the compliments of
my audience, some of whom came and shook me by the
hand, swearing that I was a very honest fellow, and that
they desired my further acquaintance. I therefore
promised to repeat my lecture next day, and actually
conceived some hopes of making a reformation here ;
for it had ever been my opinion that no man was past the
hour of amendment, every heart lying open to the shafts
of reproof if the archer could but take a proper aim.
When I had thus satisfied my mind, I went back to my
apartment, where my wife prepared a frugal meal, while
Mr. Jenkinson begged leave to add his dinner to ours and
partake of the pleasure, as he was kind enough to express
it, of my conversation. He had not yet seen my family,
for as they came to my apartment by a door in the narrow

passage already described, by this means they avoided the common prison. Jenkinson at the first interview therefore seemed not a little struck with the beauty of my youngest daughter, which her pensive air contributed to heighten, and my little ones did not pass unnoticed.

' Alas, Doctor,' cried he, ' these children are too hand-
' some and too good for such a place as this ! '

' Why, Mr. Jenkinson,' replied I, ' thank heaven my
' children are pretty tolerable in morals, and if they be
' good, it matters little for the rest.'

' I fancy, Sir,' returned my fellow-prisoner, ' that it
' must give you great comfort to have this little family
' about you.'

' A comfort, Mr. Jenkinson,' replied I ; ' yes it is indeed
' a comfort, and I would not be without them for all the
' world ; for they can make a dungeon seem a palace.
' There is but one way in this life of wounding my happi-
' ness, and that is by injuring them.'

' I am afraid then, Sir,' cried he, ' that I am in some
' measure culpable ; for I think I see here ' (looking at
my son Moses) ' one that I have injured, and by whom
' I wish to be forgiven.'

My son immediately recollected his voice and features, though he had before seen him in disguise, and taking him by the hand, with a smile forgave him. ' Yet,' continued he, ' I can't help wondering at what you could
' see in my face to think me a proper mark for deception.'

' My dear Sir,' returned the other, ' it was not your
' face, but your white stockings and the black ribband
' in your hair that allured me. But no disparagement
' to your parts, I have deceived wiser men than you in
' my time ; and yet with all my tricks, the blockheads
' have been too many for me at last.'

' I suppose,' cried my son, ' that the narrative of such a
' life as yours must be extremely instructive and amusing.'

' Not much of either,' returned Mr. Jenkinson. ' Those
' relations which describe the tricks and vices only of
' mankind, by increasing our suspicion in life, retard our
' success. The traveller that distrusts every person he
' meets, and turns back upon the appearance of every
' man that looks like a robber, seldom arrives in time at
' his journey's end.

' Indeed I think from my own experience, that the
' knowing one is the silliest fellow under the sun. I was
' thought cunning from my very childhood ; when but
' seven years old the ladies would say that I was a perfect
' little man ; at fourteen I knew the world, cocked my
' hat, and loved the ladies ; at twenty, though I was
' perfectly honest, yet every one thought me so cunning
' that not one would trust me. Thus I was at last obliged
' to turn sharper in my own defence, and have lived ever
' since, my head throbbing with schemes to deceive, and
' my heart palpitating with fears of detection. I used
' often to laugh at your honest simple neighbour Flam-
' borough, and one way or another generally cheated him
' once a year. Yet still the honest man went forward
' without suspicion, and grew rich while I still continued
' tricksy and cunning, and was poor, without the con-
' solation of being honest. However,' continued he,
' let me know your case, and what has brought you
' here ; perhaps, though I have not skill to avoid a gaol
' myself, I may extricate my friends.'

In compliance with this curiosity, I informed him of
the whole train of accidents and follies that had plunged
me into my present troubles, and my utter inability to
get free.

After hearing my story, and pausing some minutes,
he slapt his forehead as if he had hit upon something
material, and took his leave, saying he would try what
could be done.

—— My design succeeded, and in less than six days some were penitent, and all attentive.—Page 364.

CHAPTER XXVII

The same subject continued.

THE next morning I communicated to my wife and children the scheme I had planned of reforming the prisoners, which they received with universal disapprobation, alleging the impossibility and impropriety of it; adding, that my endeavours would no way contribute to their amendment, but might probably disgrace my calling.

'Excuse me,' returned I, 'these people, however fallen, 'are still men, and that is a very good title to my affec-'tions.   Good counsel rejected returns to enrich the

' giver's bosom ; and though the instruction I communi-
' cate may not mend them, yet it will assuredly mend
' myself. If these wretches, my children, were princes,
' there would be thousands ready to offer their ministry ;
' but in my opinion, the heart that is buried in a dungeon
' is as precious as that seated upon a throne. Yes, my
' treasures, if I can mend them I will ; perhaps they will
' not all despise me. Perhaps I may catch up even one
' from the gulph, and that will be great gain ; for is there
' upon earth a gem so precious as the human soul ? '

Thus saying I left them, and descended to the common
prison, where I found the prisoners very merry, expecting
my arrival ; and each prepared with some gaol trick to
play upon the doctor. Thus, as I was going to begin,
one turned my wig awry, as if by accident, and then
asked my pardon. A second, who stood at some distance, had a knack of spitting through his teeth, which
fell in showers upon my book. A third would cry Amen
in such an affected tone as gave the rest great delight.
A fourth had slily picked my pocket of my spectacles.
But there was one whose trick gave more universal
pleasure than all the rest ; for observing the manner in
which I had disposed my books on the table before me,
he very dextrously displaced one of them, and put an
obscene jest-book of his own in the place. However,
I took no notice of all that this mischievous group of
little beings could do ; but went on, perfectly sensible
that what was ridiculous in my attempt would excite
mirth only the first or second time, while what was
serious would be permanent. My design succeeded, and
in less than six days some were penitent, and all attentive.

It was now that I applauded my perseverance and
address, at thus giving sensibility to wretches divested
of every moral feeling, and now began to think of doing
them temporal services also, by rendering their situation

INTERIOR OF PICKERING CASTLE, YORKSHIRE

somewhat more comfortable. Their time had hitherto been divided between famine and excess, tumultuous riot and bitter repining. Their only employment was quarrelling among each other, playing at cribbage, and cutting tobacco stoppers. From this last mode of idle industry I took the hint of setting such as chose to work at cutting pegs for tobacconists and shoemakers, the proper wood being bought by a general subscription, and when manufactured, sold by my appointment ; so that each earned something every day : a trifle indeed, but sufficient to maintain him.

I did not stop here, but instituted fines for the punishment of immorality, and rewards for peculiar industry. Thus in less than a fortnight I had formed them into something social and humane, and had the pleasure of regarding myself as a legislator, who had brought men from their native ferocity into friendship and obedience.

And it were highly to be wished, that legislative power would thus direct the law rather to reformation than severity : that it would seem convinced that the work of eradicating crimes is not by making punishments familiar, but formidable. Then instead of our present prisons, which find or make men guilty, which enclose wretches for the commission of one crime, and return them, if returned alive, fitted for the perpetration of thousands ; we should see, as in other parts of Europe, places of penitence and solitude, where the accused might be attended by such as could give them repentance if guilty, or new motives to virtue, if innocent. And this, but not the increasing punishments, is the way to mend a state ; nor can I avoid even questioning the validity of that right which social combinations have assumed of capitally punishing offences of a slight nature. In cases of murder their right is obvious, as it is the duty of us all, from the law of self-defence, to cut off that man who has shewn a disregard for the life of another. Against such all nature rises in arms ; but it is not so against him who steals my property. Natural law gives me no right to take away his life, as by that the horse he steals is as much his property as mine. If then I have any right, it must be from a compact made between us, that he who deprives the other of his horse shall die. But this is a false compact ; because no man has a right to barter his life any more than to take it away, as it is not his own. And besides, the compact is inadequate, and would be set aside even in a court of modern equity, as there is a great penalty for a very trifling convenience, since it is far better that two men should live than that one man should ride. But a compact that is false between two men is equally so between an hundred, or an hundred thousand ; for as ten millions of circles can never make a square, so the united voice of myriads cannot lend the smallest foundation to falsehood. It is thus that reason speaks, and untutored nature says the same thing. Savages that are directed by natural law alone are very tender of the lives of each other ; they seldom shed blood but to retaliate former cruelty.

Our Saxon ancestors, fierce as they were in war, had but few executions in times of peace ; and in all commencing governments that have the print of nature still strong upon them, scarce any crime is held capital.

It is among the citizens of a refined community that penal laws, which are in the hands of the rich, are laid upon the poor. Government, while it grows older, seems to acquire the moroseness of age ; and as if our property were become dearer in proportion as it increased, as if the more enormous our wealth, the more extensive our fears, all our possessions are paled up with new edicts every day, and hung round with gibbets to scare every invader.

I cannot tell whether it is from the number of our

penal laws, or the licentiousness of our people, that this country should shew more convicts in a year than half the dominions of Europe united. Perhaps it is owing to both ; for they mutually produce each other. When by indiscriminate penal laws a nation beholds the same punishment affixed to dissimilar degrees of guilt, from perceiving no distinction in the penalty the people are led to lose all sense of distinction in the crime, and this distinction is the bulwark of all morality ; thus the multitude of laws produce new vices, and new vices call for fresh restraints.

It were to be wished then that power, instead of contriving new laws to punish vice, instead of drawing hard the cords of society till a convulsion come to burst them, instead of cutting away wretches as useless before we have tried their utility, instead of converting correction into vengeance, it were to be wished that we tried the restrictive arts of government, and made law the protector, but not the tyrant of the people. We should then find that creatures, whose souls are held as dross, only wanted the hand of a refiner ; we should then find that creatures, now stuck up for long tortures, lest luxury should feel a momentary pang, might, if properly treated, serve to sinew the state in times of danger ; that as their faces are like ours, their hearts are so too ; that few minds are so base as that perseverance cannot amend ; that a man may see his last crime without dying for it ; and that very little blood will serve to cement our security.

—— a post-chaise and pair drove up to them and instantly stopt. Upon which
a well-drest man, but not Mr. Thornhill, stepping out, clasped my daughter
round the waist, and forcing her in, bid the postillion drive on, so that they
were out of sight in a moment.—PAGE 374.

CHAPTER XXVIII

Happiness and misery rather the result of prudence than of
virtue in this life. Temporal evils or felicities being regarded by heaven as things merely in themselves trifling,
and unworthy its care in the distribution.

I HAD now been confined more than a fortnight, but
had not since my arrival been visited by my dear Olivia
and I greatly longed to see her. Having communicated
my wishes to my wife, the next morning the poor girl

entered my apartment leaning on her sister's arm. The
change which I saw in her countenance struck me. The
numberless graces that once resided there were now
fled, and the hand of death seemed to have molded every
feature to alarm me. Her temples were sunk, her forehead was tense, and a fatal paleness sate upon her cheek.

'I am glad to see thee, my dear,' cried I; 'but why
'this dejection, Livy? I hope, my love, you have too
'great a regard for me to permit disappointment thus
'to undermine a life which I prize as my own. Be
'chearful, child, and we yet may see happier days.'

'You have ever, Sir,' replied she, 'been kind to me,
'and it adds to my pain that I shall never have an
'opportunity of sharing that happiness you promise.
'Happiness, I fear, is no longer reserved for me here;
'and I long to be rid of a place where I have only found
'distress. Indeed, Sir, I wish you would make a proper
'submission to Mr. Thornhill; it may in some measure
'induce him to pity you, and it will give me relief in
'dying.'

'Never, child,' replied I, 'never will I be brought to
'acknowledge my daughter a prostitute; for though the
'world may look upon your offence with scorn, let it be
'mine to regard it as a mark of credulity, not of guilt.
'My dear, I am no way miserable in this place, however
'dismal it may seem; and be assured that while you
'continue to bless me by living, he shall never have my
'consent to make you more wretched by marrying
'another.'

After the departure of my daughter, my fellow-
prisoner, who was by at this interview, sensibly enough
expostulated upon my obstinacy in refusing a submission
which promised to give me freedom. He observed, that
the rest of my family was not to be sacrificed to the
peace of one child alone, and she the only one who had

offended me. ' Beside,' added he, ' I don't know if it
' be just thus to obstruct the union of man and wife,
' which you do at present by refusing to consent to
' a match you cannot hinder, but may render unhappy.'

' Sir,' replied I, ' you are unacquainted with the man
' that oppresses us. I am very sensible that no submis-
' sion I can make could procure me liberty even for an
' hour. I am told that even in this very room a debtor
' of his no later than last year died for want. But though
' my submission and approbation could transfer me from
' hence to the most beautiful apartment he is possessed
' of ; yet I would grant neither, as something whispers
' me that it would be giving a sanction to adultery.
' While my daughter lives, no other marriage of his shall
' ever be legal in my eye. Were she removed, indeed,
' I should be the basest of men, from any resentment
' of my own, to attempt putting asunder those who wish
' for an union. No, villain as he is, I should then wish
' him married to prevent the consequences of his future
' debaucheries. But now should I not be the most cruel
' of all fathers, to sign an instrument which must send
' my child to the grave, merely to avoid a prison myself :
' and thus to escape one pang break my child's heart
' with a thousand ? '

He acquiesced in the justice of this answer, but could
not avoid observing, that he feared my daughter's life
was already too much wasted to keep me long a prisoner.
' However,' continued he, ' though you refuse to submit
' to the nephew, I hope you have no objections to laying
' your case before the uncle, who has the first character
' in the kingdom for every thing that is just and good.
' I would advise you to send him a letter by the post,
' intimating all his nephew's ill usage, and my life for it,
' that in three days you shall have an answer.' I thanked
him for the hint, and instantly set about complying ;

but I wanted paper, and unluckily all our money had been laid out that morning in provisions : however, he supplied me.

For the three ensuing days I was in a state of anxiety to know what reception my letter might meet with ; but in the mean time was frequently solicited by my wife to submit to any conditions rather than remain here, and every hour received repeated accounts of the decline of my daughter's health. The third day and the fourth arrived, but I received no answer to my letter ; the complaints of a stranger against a favourite nephew were no way likely to succeed ; so that these hopes soon vanished like all my former. My mind, however, still supported itself, though confinement and bad air began to make a visible alteration in my health, and my arm that had suffered in the fire grew worse. My children however sate by me, and while I was stretched on my straw read to me by turns, or listened and wept at my instructions. But my daughter's health declined faster than mine ; every message from her contributed to encrease my apprehensions and pain. The fifth morning after I had written the letter which was sent to Sir William Thornhill, I was alarmed with an account that she was speechless. Now it was, that confinement was truly painful to me ; my soul was bursting from its prison to be near the pillow of my child, to comfort, to strengthen her, to receive her last wishes, and teach her soul the way to heaven ! Another account came. She was expiring, and yet I was debarred the small comfort of weeping by her. My fellow-prisoner some time after came with the last account. He bade me be patient. She was dead !——
The next morning he returned, and found me with my two little ones, now my only companions, who were using all their innocent efforts to comfort me. They entreated to read to me, and bade me not to cry, for

I was now too old to weep. 'And is not my sister an 'angel now, papa?' cried the eldest, 'and why then are 'you sorry for her? I wish I were an angel out of this 'frightful place, if my papa were with me.' 'Yes,' added my youngest darling, 'Heaven, where my sister 'is, is a finer place than this, and there are none but 'good people there, and the people here are very bad.'

Mr. Jenkinson interrupted their harmless prattle, by observing that now my daughter was no more, I should seriously think of the rest of my family, and attempt to save my own life, which was every day declining for want of necessaries and wholesome air. He added, that it was now incumbent on me to sacrifice any pride or resentment of my own, to the welfare of those who depended on me for support; and that I was now, both by reason and justice, obliged to try to reconcile my landlord.

'Heaven be praised,' replied I, 'there is no pride left 'me now, I should detest my own heart if I saw either 'pride or resentment lurking there. On the contrary, 'as my oppressor has been once my parishioner, I hope 'one day to present him up an unpolluted soul at the 'eternal tribunal. No, Sir, I have no resentment now, 'and though he has taken from me what I held dearer 'than all his treasures, though he has wrung my heart, 'for I am sick almost to fainting, very sick, my fellow 'prisoner, yet that shall never inspire me with vengeance. 'I am now willing to approve his marriage, and if this 'submission can do him any pleasure, let him know, 'that, if I have done him any injury, I am sorry for it.'

Mr. Jenkinson took pen and ink and wrote down my submission nearly as I have expressed it, to which I signed my name. My son was employed to carry the letter to Mr. Thornhill, who was then at his seat in the country. He went, and in about six hours returned with a verbal answer. He had some difficulty, he said, to get a sight of his landlord, as the servants were insolent and suspicious ; but he accidentally saw him as he was going out upon business, preparing for his marriage, which was to be in three days. He continued to inform us that he stept up in the humblest manner and delivered the letter, which, when Mr. Thornhill had read, he said that all submission was now too late and unnecessary ; that he had heard of our application to his uncle, which met with the contempt it deserved ; and as for the rest, that all future applications should be directed to his attorney, not to him. He observed, however, that as he had a very good opinion of the discretion of the two young ladies, they might have been the most agreeable intercessors.

' Well, Sir,' said I to my fellow prisoner, ' you now
' discover the temper of the man who oppresses me. He
' can at once be facetious and cruel ; but let him use me
' as he will, I shall soon be free, in spite of all his bolts
' to restrain me. I am now drawing towards an abode
' that looks brighter as I approach it ; this expectation
' chears my afflictions, and though I leave an helpless
' family of orphans behind me, yet they will not be
' utterly forsaken ; some friend perhaps will be found
' to assist them for the sake of their poor father, and
' some may charitably relieve them for the sake of their
' heavenly Father.'

Just as I spoke, my wife, whom I had not seen that day before, appeared with looks of terror, and making efforts, but unable to speak. ' Why, my love,' cried I, ' why will you thus encrease my afflictions by your
' own, what though no submissions can turn our severe
' master, though he has doomed me to die in this place
' of wretchedness, and though we have lost a darling
' child, yet still you will find comfort in your other

'children when I shall be no more.' 'We have indeed
'lost,' returned she, 'a darling child. My Sophia,
'my dearest is gone, snatched from us, carried off by
'ruffians!'

'How, madam,' cried my fellow-prisoner, 'Miss Sophia
'carried off by villains, sure it cannot be?'

She could only answer with a fixed look and a flood of
tears. But one of the prisoner's wives who was present,
and came in with her, gave us a more distinct account:
she informed us that as my wife, my daughter, and herself were taking a walk together on the great road a little
way out of the village, a post-chaise and pair drove up
to them and instantly stopt. Upon which a well-drest
man, but not Mr. Thornhill, stepping out, clasped my
daughter round the waist, and forcing her in, bid the
postillion drive on, so that they were out of sight in
a moment.

'Now,' cried I, 'the sum of my miseries is made up,
'nor is it in the power of any thing on earth to give me
'another pang. What! not one left! not to leave me
'one! the monster! the child that was next my heart!
'she had the beauty of an angel, and almost the wisdom
'of an angel. But support that woman, nor let her fall.
'Not to leave me one!'

'Alas! my husband,' said my wife, 'you seem to
'want comfort even more than I. Our distresses are
'great; but I could bear this and more, if I saw you
'but easy. They may take away my children, and all
'the world, if they leave me but you.'

My son, who was present, endeavoured to moderate
our grief; he bade us take comfort, for he hoped that
we might still have reason to be thankful.——'My child,'
cried I, 'look round the world, and see if there be any
'happiness left me now. Is not every ray of comfort
'shut out; while all our bright prospects only lie beyond

' the grave ! '——' My dear father,' returned he, ' I hope
' there is still something that will give you an interval
' of satisfaction ; for I have a letter from my brother
' George.'——' What of him, child,' interrupted I, ' does
' he know our misery ?   I hope my boy is exempt
' from any part of what his wretched family suffers ? '—
' Yes, Sir,' returned he, ' he is perfectly gay, chearful,
' and happy. His letter brings nothing but good news ;
' he is the favourite of his colonel, who promises to
' procure him the very next lieutenancy that becomes
' vacant ! '

 ' And are you sure of all this,' cried my wife, ' are
' you sure that nothing ill has befallen my boy ? '——
' Nothing indeed, Madam,' returned my son, ' you shall
' see the letter, which will give you the highest pleasure ;
' and if any thing can procure you comfort I am sure
' that will.' ' But are you sure,' still repeated she, ' that
' the letter is from himself, and that he is really so
' happy ? '——' Yes, Madam,' replied he, ' it is certainly
' his, and he will one day be the credit and the support
' of our family ! '——' Then I thank Providence,' cried
she, ' that my last letter to him has miscarried.—Yes,
' my dear,' continued she, turning to me, ' I will now
' confess, that though the hand of heaven is sore upon
' us in other instances, it has been favourable here. By
' the last letter I wrote my son, which was in the bitter-
' ness of anger, I desired him, upon his mother's blessing,
' and if he had the heart of a man, to see justice done
' his father and sister, and avenge our cause.   But thanks
' be to Him that directs all things, it has miscarried, and
' I am at rest.' 'Woman,' cried I, ' thou hast done very
' ill, and at another time my reproaches might have been
' more severe. Oh ! what a tremendous gulph hast thou
' escaped, that would have buried both thee and him in
' endless ruin. Providence indeed, has here been kinder

' to us than we to ourselves. It has reserved that son to
' be the father and protector of my children when I shall
' be away. How unjustly did I complain of being stript
' of every comfort, when still I hear that he is happy
' and insensible of our afflictions ; still kept in reserve
' to support his widowed mother, and to protect his
' brothers and sisters. But what sisters has he left ? he
' has no sisters now, they are all gone, robbed from me,
' and I am undone.'——' Father,' interrupted my son,
' I beg you will give me leave to read this letter, I know
' it will please you.' Upon which, with my permission,
he read as follows.

HONOURED SIR,

I have called off my imagination a few moments from
the pleasures that surround me, to fix it upon objects
that are still more pleasing, the dear little fire-side at
home. My fancy draws that harmless groupe as listening
to every line of this with great composure. I view those
faces with delight which never felt the deforming hand
of ambition or distress ! But whatever your happiness
may be at home, I am sure it will be some addition to
it to hear that I am perfectly pleased with my situation,
and every way happy here.

Our regiment is countermanded, and is not to leave
the kingdom ; the colonel, who professes himself my
friend, takes me with him to all companies where he is
acquainted, and after my first visit I generally find myself received with encreased respect upon repeating it.
I danced last night with Lady G——, and could I forget
you know whom, I might be perhaps successful. But it
is my fate still to remember others while I am myself
forgotten by most of my absent friends, and in this
number I fear, Sir, that I must consider you ; for I have
long expected the pleasure of a letter from home, to no

purpose. Olivia and Sophia too promised to write, but seem to have forgotten me. Tell them they are two arrant little baggages, and that I am this moment in a most violent passion with them : yet still I know not how ; though I want to bluster a little, my heart is respondent only to softer emotions. Then tell them, Sir, that after all, I love them affectionately, and be assured of my ever remaining

Your dutiful son.

'In all our miseries,' cried I, 'what thanks have we
'not to return, that one at least of our family is exempted
'from what we suffer. Heaven be his guard, and keep
'my boy thus happy to be the support of his widowed
'mother, and the father of these two babes, which is all
'the patrimony I can now bequeath him. May he keep
'their innocence from the temptations of want, and be
'their conductor in the paths of honour.' I had scarce
said these words when a noise, like that of a tumult,
seemed to proceed from the prison below ; it died away
soon after, and a clanking of fetters was heard along the
passage that led to my apartment. The keeper of the
prison entered, holding a man all bloody, wounded and
fettered with the heaviest irons. I looked with compassion on the wretch as he approached me, but with
horror when I found it was my own son.——'My George !
'My George ! and do I behold thee thus. Wounded !
'Fettered ! Is this thy happiness ? Is this the manner
'you return to me ? O that this sight could break my
'heart at once and let me die ! '

'Where, Sir, is your fortitude ? ' returned my son with
an intrepid voice. 'I must suffer, my life is forfeited,
'and let them take it.'

I tried to restrain my passions for a few minutes in
silence, but I thought I should have died with the effort.

———' O, my boy, my heart weeps to behold thee thus,
' and I cannot, cannot help it. In the moment that
' I thought thee blest, and prayed for thy safety, to
' behold thee thus again ! Chained, wounded ! And yet
' the death of the youthful is happy. But I am old,
' a very old man, and have lived to see this day. To
' see my children all untimely falling about me, while
' I continue a wretched survivor in the midst of ruin !
' May all the curses that ever sunk a soul fall heavy
' upon the murderer of my children. May he live, like
' me, to see———'

' Hold, Sir,' replied my son, ' or I shall blush for thee.
' How, Sir, forgetful of your age, your holy calling, thus
' to arrogate the justice of heaven, and fling those curses
' upward that must soon descend to crush thy own grey
' head with destruction ! No, Sir, let it be your care
' now to fit me for that vile death I must shortly suffer,
' to arm me with hope and resolution, to give me courage
' to drink of that bitterness which must shortly be my
' portion.'

' My child, you must not die : I am sure no offence of
' thine can deserve so vile a punishment. My George
' could never be guilty of any crime to make his ancestors
' ashamed of him.'

' Mine, Sir,' returned my son, ' is I fear an unpardon-
' able one. When I received my mother's letter from
' home, I immediately came down, determined to punish
' the betrayer of our honour, and sent him an order to
' meet me, which he answered not in person, but by
' his dispatching four of his domestics to seize me.
' I wounded one who first assaulted me, and I fear
' desperately ; but the rest made me their prisoner.
' The coward is determined to put the law in execution
' against me ; the proofs are undeniable ; I have sent
' a challenge, and as I am the first transgressor upon

' the statute, I see no hopes of pardon. But you have
' often charmed me with your lessons of fortitude, let
' me now, Sir, find them in your example.'

    ' And, my son, you shall find them. I am now raised
' above this world, and all the pleasures it can produce.
' From this moment I break from my heart all the ties
' that held it down to earth, and will prepare to fit us
' both for eternity. Yes, my son, I will point out the
' way, and my soul shall guide yours in the ascent, for
' we will take our flight together. I now see and am
' convinced you can expect no pardon here, and I can
' only exhort you to seek it at that greatest tribunal
' where we both shall shortly answer. But let us not
' be niggardly in our exhortation, but let all our fellow
' prisoners have a share : good gaoler, let them be per-
' mitted to stand here while I attempt to improve them.'
Thus saying, I made an effort to rise from my straw,
but wanted strength, and was able only to recline against
the wall. The prisoners assembled themselves according
to my directions, for they loved to hear my counsel ;
my son and his mother supported me on either side ;
I looked and saw that none were wanting, and then
addressed them with the following exhortation.

—— The prisoners assembled themselves according to my directions, for they loved to hear my counsel ; my son and his mother supported me on either side.——
PAGE 379.

CHAPTER XXIX

The equal dealings of Providence demonstrated with regard to the happy and the miserable here below. That from the nature of pleasure and pain, the wretched must be repaid the balance of their sufferings in the life hereafter.

MY friends, my children, and fellow sufferers, when I reflect on the distribution of good and evil here below, I find that much has been given man to enjoy, yet still more to suffer. Though we should examine the whole world, we shall not find one man so happy as to have nothing left to wish for ; but we daily see thousands who by suicide shew us they have nothing left to hope.

In this life then it appears that we cannot be entirely blest, but yet we may be completely miserable.

Why man should thus feel pain, why our wretchedness should be requisite in the formation of universal felicity ; why, when all other systems are made perfect by the perfection of their subordinate parts, the great system should require for its perfection parts that are not only subordinate to others, but imperfect in themselves ; these are questions that never can be explained, and might be useless if known. On this subject Providence has thought fit to elude our curiosity, satisfied with granting us motives to consolation.

In this situation, man has called in the friendly assistance of philosophy, and heaven, seeing the incapacity of that to console him, has given him the aid of religion. The consolations of philosophy are very amusing, but often fallacious. It tells us that life is filled with comforts, if we will but enjoy them ; and on the other hand, that though we unavoidably have miseries here, life is short, and they will soon be over. Thus do these consolations destroy each other ; for if life is a place of comfort, its shortness must be misery, and if it be long, our griefs are protracted. Thus philosophy is weak ; but religion comforts in an higher strain. Man is here, it tells us, fitting up his mind, and preparing it for another abode. When the good man leaves the body, and is all a glorious mind, he will find he has been making himself a heaven of happiness here ; while the wretch that has been maimed and contaminated by his vices, shrinks from his body with terror, and finds that he has anticipated the vengeance of heaven. To religion then we must hold in every circumstance of life for our truest comfort ; for if already we are happy, it is a pleasure to think that we can make that happiness unending ; and if we are miserable, it is very consoling to think that there is a place of rest. Thus to the fortunate religion holds out a continuance of bliss, to the wretched a change from pain.

But though religion is very kind to all men, it has promised peculiar rewards to the unhappy ; the sick, the naked, the houseless, the heavy-laden, and the prisoner, have ever most frequent promises in our sacred law. The Author of our religion everywhere professes himself the wretch's friend, and unlike the false ones of this world, bestows all his caresses upon the forlorn. The unthinking have censured this as partiality, as a preference without merit to deserve it. But they never reflect that it is not in the power even of Heaven itself to make the offer of unceasing felicity as great a gift to the happy as to the miserable. To the first eternity is but a single blessing, since at most it but encreases what they already possess. To the latter it is a double advantage; for it diminishes their pain here, and rewards them with heavenly bliss hereafter.

But Providence is in another respect kinder to the poor than the rich ; for as it thus makes the life after death more desirable, so it smoothes the passage there. The wretched have had a long familiarity with every face of terror. The man of sorrows lays himself quietly down, without possessions to regret, and but few ties to stop his departure : he feels only nature's pang in the final separation, and this is no way greater than he has often fainted under before ; for after a certain degree of pain, every new breach that death opens in the constitution, nature kindly covers with insensibility.

Thus Providence has given the wretched two advantages over the happy in this life, greater felicity in dying, and in heaven all that superiority of pleasure which arises from contrasted enjoyment. And this superiority, my friends, is no small advantage, and seems to be one of the pleasures of the poor man in the parable ; for though he was already in heaven, and felt all the raptures it could give, yet it was mentioned as an addition to his happiness, that he had once been wretched, and now was comforted ; that he had known what it was to be miserable, and now felt what it was to be happy.

Thus, my friends, you see religion does what philosophy could never do : it shews the equal dealings of heaven to the happy and the unhappy, and levels all human enjoyments to nearly the same standard. It gives to both rich and poor the same happiness hereafter, and equal hopes to aspire after it ; but if the rich have the advantage of enjoying pleasure here, the poor have the endless satisfaction of knowing what it was once to be miserable, when crowned with endless felicity hereafter ; and even though this should be called a small advantage, yet being an eternal one, it must make up by duration what the temporal happiness of the great may have exceeded by intenseness.

These are therefore the consolations which the wretched have peculiar to themselves, and in which they are above the rest of mankind ; in other respects they are below them. They who would know the miseries of the poor, must see life and endure it. To declaim on the temporal advantages they enjoy is only repeating what none either believe or practise. The men who have the necessaries of living are not poor, and they who want them must be miserable. Yes my friends, we must be miserable. No vain efforts of a refined imagination can soothe the wants of nature, can give elastic sweetness to the dank vapour of a dungeon, or ease the throbbings of a broken heart. Let the philosopher from his couch of softness tell us that we can resist all these. Alas ! the effort by which we resist them is still the greatest pain ! Death is slight, and any man may sustain it; but torments are dreadful, and these no man can endure.

To us then my friends the promises of happiness in heaven should be peculiarly dear ; for if our reward be in this life alone, we are then indeed of all men the most miserable. When I look round these gloomy walls, made to terrify as well as to confine us ; this light that only serves to show the horrors of the place, those shackles that tyranny has imposed or crime made necessary ; when I survey these emaciated looks, and hear those groans, O ! my friends, what a glorious exchange would heaven be for these. To fly through regions unconfined as air, to bask in the sunshine of eternal bliss, to carol over endless hymns of praise, to have no master to threaten or insult us, but the form of Goodness himself for ever in our eyes ; when I think of these things, death becomes the messenger of very glad tidings ; when I think of these things his sharpest arrow becomes the staff of my support; when I think of these things, what is there in life worth having ? when I think of these things what is there that should not be spurned away ? kings in their palaces should groan for such advantages ; but we, humbled as we are, should yearn for them.

And shall these things be ours ? Ours they will certainly be if we but try for them; and what is a comfort, we are shut out from many temptations that would retard our pursuit. Only let us try for them and they will certainly be ours, and what is still a comfort, shortly too ; for if we look back on a past life it appears but a very short span, and whatever we may think of the rest of life, it will yet be found of less duration; as we grow older the days seem to grow shorter, and our intimacy with time ever lessens the perception of his stay. Then let us take comfort now, for we shall soon be at our journey's end; we shall soon lay down the heavy burthen laid by heaven upon us ; and though death, the only friend of the wretched, for a little while mocks the weary traveller with the view, and, like his horizon still flies before him ; yet the time will certainly and shortly come when we shall cease from our toil ; when the luxuriant great ones of the world shall no more tread us to the earth ; when we shall think with pleasure on our sufferings below; when we shall be surrounded with all our friends, or such as deserved our friendship ; when our bliss shall be unutterable, and still to crown all, unending.

—— Just as he delivered this news my dearest girl entered, and with looks almost wild with pleasure ran to kiss me in a transport of affection.—PAGE 387.

CHAPTER XXX

Happier prospects begin to appear. Let us be inflexible, and fortune will at last change in our favour.

WHEN I had thus finished, and my audience was retired, the gaoler, who was one of the most humane of his profession, hoped I would not be displeased, as what he did was but his duty, observing that he must be obliged to remove my son into a stronger cell, but that he should be permitted to visit me every morning. I thanked him for his clemency, and grasping my boy's hand bade him farewell, and be mindful of the great duty that was before him.

I again therefore laid me down, and one of my little ones sate by my bed side reading, when Mr. Jenkinson entering, informed me that there was news of my daughter ; for that she was seen by a person about two hours before in a strange gentleman's company, and that they had stopt at a neighbouring village for refreshment, and seemed as if returning to town. He had scarcely delivered this news, when the gaoler came with looks of haste and pleasure to inform me that my daughter was found. Moses came running in a moment after, crying out that his sister Sophy was below, and coming up with our old friend Mr. Burchell.

Just as he delivered this news my dearest girl entered, and with looks almost wild with pleasure ran to kiss me in a transport of affection. Her mother's tears and silence also shewed her pleasure.—'Here, papa,' cried the charming girl, ' here is the brave man to whom ' I owe my delivery ; to this gentleman's intrepidity ' I am indebted for my happiness and safety——' A kiss from Mr. Burchell, whose pleasure seemed even greater than hers, interrupted what she was going to add.

' Ah, Mr. Burchell,' cried I, ' this is but a wretched ' habitation you now find us in ; and we are now very ' different from what you last saw us. You were ever ' our friend : we have long discovered our errors with ' regard to you, and repented of our ingratitude. After ' the vile usage you then received at my hands, I am ' almost ashamed to behold your face ; yet I hope you'll ' forgive me, as I was deceived by a base ungenerous ' wretch, who under the mask of friendship has un- ' done me.'

' It is impossible,' cried Mr. Burchell, ' that I should ' forgive you, as you never deserved my resentment. ' I partly saw your delusion then, and as it was out of ' my power to restrain, I could only pity it ! '

' It was ever my conjecture,' cried I, ' that your mind
' was noble, but now I find it so. But tell me, my dear
' child, how hast thou been relieved, or who the ruffians
' were who carried thee away.'

' Indeed, Sir,' replied she, ' as to the villain who carried
' me off, I am yet ignorant. For as my mamma and
' I were walking out, he came behind us, and almost
' before I could call for help, forced me into the post-
' chaise, and in an instant the horses drove away. I met
' several on the road to whom I cried out for assistance ;
' but they disregarded my entreaties. In the mean time
' the ruffian himself used every art to hinder me from
' crying out : he flattered and threatened by turns, and
' swore that if I continued but silent he intended no
' harm. In the mean time I had broken the canvas that
' he had drawn up, and whom should I perceive at some
' distance but your old friend Mr. Burchell, walking along
' with his usual swiftness, with the great stick for which
' we used so much to ridicule him. As soon as we came
' within hearing, I called out to him by name and
' entreated his help. I repeated my exclamation several
' times, upon which with a very loud voice he bid the
' postillion stop ; but the boy took no notice, but drove
' on with still greater speed. I now thought he could
' never overtake us, when in less than a minute I saw
' Mr. Burchell come running up by the side of the horses,
' and with one blow knock the postillion to the ground.
' The horses when he was fallen soon stopt of themselves,
' and the ruffian, stepping out, with oaths and menaces
' drew his sword, and ordered him at his peril to retire ;
' but Mr. Burchell running up shivered his sword to
' pieces, and then pursued him for near a quarter of
' a mile ; but he made his escape. I was at this time
' come out myself, willing to assist my deliverer ; but
' he soon returned to me in triumph. The postillion,

' who was recovered, was going to make his escape too ;
' but Mr. Burchell ordered him at his peril to mount
' again and drive back to town. Finding it impossible
' to resist, he reluctantly complied, though the wound
' he had received seemed, to me at least, to be dangerous.
' He continued to complain of the pain as we drove
' along, so that he at last excited Mr. Burchell's com-
' passion, who at my request exchanged him for another
' at an inn where we called on our return.'

' Welcome, then,' cried I, ' my child, and thou her
' gallant deliverer, a thousand welcomes. Though our
' chear is but wretched yet our hearts are ready to receive
' you. And now, Mr. Burchell, as you have delivered
' my girl, if you think her a recompence she is yours; if
' you can stoop to an alliance with a family so poor as
' mine, take her, obtain her consent, as I know you have
' her heart, and you have mine. And let me tell you,
' Sir, that I give you no small treasure ; she has been
' celebrated for beauty it is true, but that is not my
' meaning, I give you up a treasure in her mind.'

' But I suppose, Sir,' cried Mr. Burchell, ' that you
' are apprized of my circumstances, and of my incapacity
' to support her as she deserves ? '

' If your present objection,' replied I, ' be meant as an
' evasion of my offer, I desist : but I know no man so
' worthy to deserve her as you : and if I could give her
' thousands, and thousands sought her from me, yet
' my honest brave Burchell should be my dearest
' choice.'

To all this his silence alone seemed to give a mortifying refusal, and without the least reply to my offer,
he demanded if he could not be furnished with refreshments from the next inn, to which being answered in
the affirmative, he ordered them to send in the best
dinner that could be provided upon such short notice.

He bespoke also a dozen of their best wine, and some cordials for me, adding, with a smile, that he would stretch a little for once, and though in a prison asserted he was never better disposed to be merry. The waiter soon made his appearance with preparations for dinner ; a table was lent us by the gaoler, who seemed remarkably assiduous, the wine was disposed in order, and two very well-drest dishes were brought in.

My daughter had not yet heard of her poor brother's melancholy situation, and we all seemed unwilling to damp her chearfulness by the relation. But it was in vain that I attempted to appear chearful, the circumstances of my unfortunate son broke through all efforts to dissemble ; so that I was at last obliged to damp our mirth by relating his misfortunes, and wishing that he might be permitted to share with us in this little interval of satisfaction. After my guests were recovered from the consternation my account had produced, I requested also that Mr. Jenkinson, a fellow prisoner, might be admitted, and the gaoler granted my request with an air of unusual submission. The clanking of my son's irons was no sooner heard along the passage than his sister ran impatiently to meet him ; while Mr. Burchell in the mean time asked me if my son's name were George, to which replying in the affirmative he still continued silent. As soon as my boy entered the room, I could perceive he regarded Mr. Burchell with a look of astonishment and reverence. ' Come on,' cried I, ' my son, ' though we are fallen very low, yet Providence has been ' pleased to grant us some small relaxation from pain. ' Thy sister is restored to us, and there is her deliverer : ' to that brave man it is that I am indebted for yet ' having a daughter ; give him, my boy, the hand of ' friendship, he deserves our warmest gratitude.'

My son seemed all this while regardless of what I said,

and still continued fixed at a respectful distance.——'My 'dear brother,' cried his sister, 'why don't you thank my 'good deliverer? the brave should ever love each other.'

He still continued his silence and astonishment, till our guest at last perceived himself to be known, and assuming all his native dignity desired my son to come forward. Never before had I seen any thing so truly majestic as the air he assumed upon this occasion. The greatest object in the universe, says a certain philosopher, is a good man struggling with adversity; yet there is still a greater, which is the good man that comes to relieve it. After he had regarded my son for some time with a superior air, 'I again find,' said he, 'un-'thinking boy, that the same crime '—But here he was interrupted by one of the gaoler's servants, who came to inform us that a person of distinction, who had driven into town with a chariot and several attendants, sent his respects to the gentleman that was with us and begged to know when he should think proper to be waited upon.——'Bid the fellow wait,' cried our guest, 'till I shall have leisure to receive him;' and then turning to my son, 'I again find, Sir,' proceeded he, 'that you are guilty of the same offence, for which you 'once had my reproof, and for which the law is now 'preparing its justest punishments. You imagine, per-'haps, that a contempt for your own life gives you 'a right to take that of another : but where, Sir, is the 'difference between a duellist who hazards a life of no 'value, and the murderer who acts with greater security ? 'Is it any diminution of the gamester's fraud when he 'alleges that he has staked a counter ? '

'Alas, Sir,' cried I, 'whoever you are, pity the poor 'misguided creature; for what he has done was in 'obedience to a deluded mother, who in the bitterness 'of her resentment required him upon her blessing to

' avenge her quarrel. Here, Sir, is the letter which will
' serve to convince you of her imprudence and diminish
' his guilt.'

He took the letter and hastily read it over. ' This,'
says he, ' though not a perfect excuse, is such a palliation
' of his fault, as induces me to forgive him. And now,
' Sir,' continued he, kindly taking my son by the hand,
' I see you are surprised at finding me here ; but I have
' often visited prisons upon occasions less interesting.
' I am now come to see justice done a worthy man, for
' whom I have the most sincere esteem. I have long
' been a disguised spectator of thy father's benevolence.
' I have at his little dwelling enjoyed respect uncon-
' taminated by flattery, and have received that happi-
' ness that courts could not give, from the amusing
' simplicity round his fire-side. My nephew has been
' apprized of my intentions of coming here, and I find
' is arrived ; it would be wronging him and you to
' condemn him without examination : if there be injury
' there shall be redress ; and this I may say without
' boasting, that none have ever taxed the injustice of
' Sir William Thornhill.'

We now found the personage whom we had so long
entertained as an harmless amusing companion was no
other than the celebrated Sir William Thornhill, to whose
virtues and singularities scarce any were strangers.
The poor Mr. Burchell was in reality a man of large
fortune and great interest, to whom senates listened
with applause, and whom party heard with conviction ;
who was the friend of his country, but loyal to his king.
My poor wife recollecting her former familiarity seemed
to shrink with apprehension ; but Sophia, who a few
moments before thought him her own, now perceiving
the immense distance to which he was removed by
fortune, was unable to conceal her tears.

'Ah, Sir,' cried my wife with a piteous aspect, 'how
'is it possible that I can ever have your forgiveness? The
'slights you received from me the last time I had the
'honour of seeing you at our house, and the jokes which
'I audaciously threw out, these jokes, Sir, I fear can
'never be forgiven.'

'My dear good lady,' returned he with a smile, 'if
'you had your joke I had my answer : I'll leave it to
'all the company if mine were not as good as yours.
'To say the truth I know nobody whom I am disposed
'to be angry with at present but the fellow who so
'frighted my little girl here. I had not even time to
'examine the rascal's person so as to describe him in an
'advertisement. Can you tell me, Sophia, my dear,
'whether you should know him again ? '

'Indeed, Sir,' replied she, 'I can't be positive ; yet
'now I recollect he had a large mark over one of his
'eye-brows.' 'I ask pardon, Madam,' interrupted Jenkinson, who was by, 'but be so good as to inform me
'if the fellow wore his own red hair ? '—'Yes, I think
'so,' cried Sophia.—'And did your honour,' continued
he, turning to Sir William, 'observe the length of his
'legs ? '—'I can't be sure of their length,' cried the
Baronet, 'but I am convinced of their swiftness ; for
'he outran me, which is what I thought few men in
'the kingdom could have done.'—'Please your honour,'
cried Jenkinson, 'I know the man : it is certainly the
'same ; the best runner in England ; he has beaten
'Pinwire of Newcastle, Timothy Baxter is his name,
'I know him perfectly, and the very place of his retreat
'this moment. If your honour will bid Mr. Gaoler let
'two of his men go with me, I'll engage to produce him
'to you in an hour at farthest.' Upon this the gaoler
was called, who instantly appearing, Sir William demanded if he knew him. 'Yes, please your honour,'

replied the gaoler, ' I know Sir William Thornhill well,
' and everybody that knows any thing of him will desire to
' know more of him.'——' Well, then,' said the Baronet,
' my request is, that you will permit this man and two
' of your servants to go upon a message by my authority,
' and as I am in the Commission of the Peace, I undertake
' to secure you.'——' Your promise is sufficient,' replied
' the other, 'and you may at a minute's warning send
' them over England whenever your honour thinks fit.'

In pursuance of the gaoler's compliance, Jenkinson
was dispatched in search of Timothy Baxter, while we
were amused with the assiduity of our youngest boy Bill,
who had just come in and climbed up to Sir William's neck
in order to kiss him. His mother was immediately going
to chastise his familiarity, but the worthy man prevented
her ; and taking the child, all ragged as he was, upon
his knee, ' What, Bill, you chubby rogue,' cried he, ' do
' you remember your old friend Burchell ? and Dick too,
' my honest veteran, are you here ? you shall find I have
' not forgot you.'   So saying, he gave each a large piece of
gingerbread, which the poor fellows ate very heartily, as
they had got that morning but a very scanty breakfast.

We now sate down to dinner, which was almost cold ;
but previously, my arm still continuing painful, Sir William wrote a prescription, for he had made the study of
physic his amusement, and was more than moderately
skilled in the profession : this being sent to an apothecary
who lived in the place, my arm was dressed, and I found
almost instantaneous relief. We were waited upon at
dinner by the gaoler himself, who was willing to do our
guest all the honour in his power. But before we had
well dined, another message was brought from his nephew,
desiring permission to appear in order to vindicate his
innocence and honour, with which request the Baronet
complied, and desired Mr. Thornhill to be introduced.

—— 'And to convince you that I speak nothing but truth, here is the licence by which you were married together.'—PAGE 406.

CHAPTER XXXI

Former benevolence now repaid with unexpected interest.

MR. THORNHILL made his appearance with a smile, which he seldom wanted, and was going to embrace his uncle, which the other repulsed with an air of disdain. 'No fawning, Sir, at present,' cried the Baronet, with a look of severity, 'the only way to my 'heart is by the road of honour; but here I only see 'complicated instances of falsehood, cowardice, and 'oppression. How is it, Sir, that this poor man, for 'whom I know you professed a friendship, is used thus 'hardly? His daughter vilely seduced, as a recompence

' for his hospitality, and he himself thrown into a prison,
' perhaps but for resenting the insult ? His son too
' whom you feared to face as a man—— '

' Is it possible, Sir,' interrupted his nephew, ' that my
' uncle could object that as a crime, which his repeated
' instructions alone have persuaded me to avoid.'

' Your rebuke,' cried Sir William, ' is just : you have
' acted in this instance prudently and well, though not
' quite as your father would have done : my brother
' indeed was the soul of honour ; but thou—yes you
' have acted in this instance perfectly right, and it has
' my warmest approbation.'

' And I hope,' said his nephew, ' that the rest of my
' conduct will not be found to deserve censure. I ap-
' peared, Sir, with this gentleman's daughter at some
' places of public amusement : thus, what was levity,
' scandal called by a harsher name, and it was reported
' that I had debauched her. I waited on her father in
' person, willing to clear the thing to his satisfaction, and
' he received me only with insult and abuse. As for the
' rest, with regard to his being here, my attorney and
' steward can best inform you, as I commit the manage-
' ment of business entirely to them. If he has contracted
' debts and is unwilling or even unable to pay them, it
' is their business to proceed in this manner, and I see
' no hardship or injustice in pursuing the most legal
' means of redress.'

' If this,' cried Sir William, ' be as you have stated it,
' there is nothing unpardonable in your offence ; and
' though your conduct might have been more generous
' in not suffering this gentleman to be oppressed by
' subordinate tyranny, yet it has been at least equitable.'

' He cannot contradict a single particular,' replied the
'Squire ; ' I defy him to do so, and several of my servants
' are ready to attest what I say. Thus, Sir,' continued

he, finding that I was silent, for in fact I could not contradict him, ' thus, Sir, my own innocence is vindicated ;
' but though at your entreaty I am ready to forgive this
' gentleman every other offence, yet his attempts to
' lessen me in your esteem excite a resentment that
' I cannot govern. And this too at a time when his
' son was actually preparing to take away my life ; this
' I say was such guilt that I am determined to let the
' law take its course. I have here the challenge that
' was sent me, and two witnesses to prove it ; one of
' my servants has been wounded dangerously, and even
' though my uncle himself should dissuade me, which
' I know he will not, yet I will see public justice done,
' and he shall suffer for it.'

' Thou monster,' cried my wife, ' hast thou not had
' vengeance enough already, but must my poor boy feel
' thy cruelty ? I hope that good Sir William will protect
' us, for my son is as innocent as a child ; I am sure he
' is and never did harm to man.'

' Madam,' replied the good man, ' your wishes for his
' safety are not greater than mine ; but I am sorry to
' find his guilt too plain ; and if my nephew persists '——
But the appearance of Jenkinson and the gaoler's two
servants now called off our attention, who entered hauling
in a tall man very genteelly drest, and answering the
description already given of the ruffian who had carried
off my daughter——' Here,' cried Jenkinson, pulling him
in, ' here we have him ; and if ever there was a candi-
' date for Tyburn this is one.'

The moment Mr. Thornhill perceived the prisoner, and
Jenkinson who had him in custody, he seemed to shrink
back with terror. His face became pale with conscious
guilt, and he would have withdrawn ; but Jenkinson,
who perceived his design, stopt him.——' What, 'Squire,'
cried he, ' are you ashamed of your two old acquain-

'tances, Jenkinson and Baxter ? but this is the way
'that all great men forget their friends, though I am
'resolved we will not forget you. Our prisoner, please
'your honour,' continued he, turning to Sir William,
'has already confessed all. This is the gentleman re-
'ported to be so dangerously wounded ; he declares that
'it was Mr. Thornhill who first put him upon this affair,
'that he gave him the clothes he now wears to appear
'like a gentleman, and furnished him with the post-
'chaise. The plan was laid between them that he
'should carry off the young lady to a place of safety,
'and that there he should threaten and terrify her ;
'but Mr. Thornhill was to come in in the mean time, as
'if by accident, to her rescue, and that they should
'fight a while, and then he was to run off, by which
'Mr. Thornhill would have the better opportunity of
'gaining her affections himself under the character of
'her defender.'

Sir William remembered the coat to have been frequently worn by his nephew, and all the rest the prisoner
himself confirmed by a more circumstantial account ;
concluding, that Mr. Thornhill had often declared to him
that he was in love with both sisters at the same time.

'Heavens !' cried Sir William, 'what a viper have
'I been fostering in my bosom ! And so fond of public
'justice too as he seemed to be. But he shall have it ;
'secure him, Mr. Gaoler—yet hold, I fear there is not
'legal evidence to detain him.'

Upon this, Mr. Thornhill, with the utmost humility,
entreated that two such abandoned wretches might not
be admitted as evidences against him, but that his servants should be examined.——' Your servants !' replied
Sir William, 'wretch, call them yours no longer : but
'come, let us hear what those fellows have to say, let
'his butler be called.'

When the butler was introduced, he soon perceived by his former master's looks that all his power was now over. 'Tell me,' cried Sir William sternly, 'have you 'ever seen your master and that fellow drest up in his 'clothes in company together?' 'Yes, please your 'honour,' cried the butler, 'a thousand times: he was 'the man that always brought him his ladies.'—'How,' interrupted young Mr. Thornhill, 'this to my face!'—— 'Yes,' replied the butler, 'or to any man's face. To tell 'you a truth, Master Thornhill, I never either loved you 'or liked you, and I don't care if I tell you now a piece 'of my mind.'——'Now then,' cried Jenkinson, 'tell his 'honour whether you know any thing of me.'——'I can't 'say,' replied the butler, 'that I know much good of 'you. The night that gentleman's daughter was deluded 'to our house you were one of them.'——'So then,' cried Sir William, 'I find you have brought a very 'fine witness to prove your innocence: thou stain to 'humanity! to associate with such wretches!' (But continuing his examination) 'You tell me, Mr. Butler, 'that this was the person who brought him this old 'gentleman's daughter.'—'No, please your honour,' replied the butler, 'he did not bring her, for the 'Squire 'himself undertook that business; but he brought the 'priest that pretended to marry them.'—'It is but too 'true,' cried Jenkinson, 'I cannot deny it; that was 'the employment assigned me, and I confess it to my 'confusion.'

'Good heavens!' exclaimed the Baronet, 'how every 'new discovery of his villainy alarms me. All his guilt 'is now too plain, and I find his prosecution was dictated 'by tyranny, cowardice, and revenge; at my request, 'Mr. Gaoler, set this young officer, now your prisoner, 'free, and trust to me for the consequences. I'll make 'it my business to set the affair in a proper light to my

'friend the magistrate who has committed him. But
'where is the unfortunate young lady herself ? let her
'appear to confront this wretch ; I long to know by
'what arts he has seduced her. Entreat her to come in.
'Where is she ?'

'Ah, Sir,' said I, 'that question stings me to the
'heart : I was once indeed happy in a daughter, but
'her miseries——' Another interruption here prevented
me ; for who should make her appearance but Miss
Arabella Wilmot, who was next day to have been
married to Mr. Thornhill. Nothing could equal her
surprise at seeing Sir William and his nephew here before
her ; for her arrival was quite accidental. It happened
that she and the old gentleman her father were passing
through the town, on their way to her aunt's, who had
insisted that her nuptials with Mr. Thornhill should be
consummated at her house ; but stopping for refreshment, they put up at an inn at the other end of the
town. It was there from the window that the young
lady happened to observe one of my little boys playing
in the street, and instantly sending a footman to bring
the child to her, she learnt from him some account of
our misfortunes ; but was still kept ignorant of young
Mr. Thornhill's being the cause. Though her father
made several remonstrances on the impropriety of going
to a prison to visit us, yet they were ineffectual ; she
desired the child to conduct her, which he did, and it
was thus she surprised us at a juncture so unexpected.

Nor can I go on, without a reflection on those accidental
meetings, which, though they happen every day, seldom
excite our surprise but upon some extraordinary occasion.
To what a fortuitous occurrence do we not owe every
pleasure and convenience of our lives. How many
seeming accidents must unite before we can be clothed
or fed. The peasant must be disposed to labour, the

shower must fall, the wind fill the merchant's sail, or numbers must want the usual supply.

We all continued silent for some moments, while my charming pupil, which was the name I generally gave this young lady, united in her looks compassion and astonishment, which gave new finishings to her beauty. ' Indeed, my dear Mr. Thornhill,' cried she to the 'Squire, who she supposed was come here to succour and not to oppress us, ' I take it a little unkindly that you should ' come here without me, or never inform me of the ' situation of a family so dear to us both : you know ' I should take as much pleasure in contributing to the ' relief of my reverend old master here, whom I shall ' ever esteem, as you can. But I find that, like your ' uncle, you take pleasure in doing good in secret.'

' *He* find pleasure in doing good ! ' cried Sir William, interrupting her. ' No, my dear, his pleasures are as ' base as he is. You see in him, madam, as compleat ' a villain as ever disgraced humanity. A wretch, who ' after having deluded this poor man's daughter, after ' plotting against the innocence of her sister, has thrown ' the father into prison, and the eldest son into fetters, ' because he had courage to face his betrayer. And give ' me leave, madam, now to congratulate you upon an ' escape from the embraces of such a monster.'

' Oh goodness,' cried the lovely girl, ' how have I been ' deceived ! Mr. Thornhill informed me for certain that ' this gentleman's eldest son, Captain Primrose, was gone ' off to America with his new-married lady.'

' My sweetest miss,' cried my wife, ' he has told you ' nothing but falsehoods. My son George never left the ' kingdom, nor never was married.—Though you have ' forsaken him, he has always loved you too well to think ' of any body else ; and I have heard him say he would ' die a bachelor for your sake.' She then proceeded to expatiate upon the sincerity of her son's passion, she set his duel with Mr. Thornhill in a proper light, from thence she made a rapid digression to the 'Squire's debaucheries, his pretended marriages, and ended with a most insulting picture of his cowardice.

'Good heaven!' cried Miss Wilmot, 'how very near 'have I been to the brink of ruin! But how great is 'my pleasure to have escaped it! Ten thousand false- 'hoods has this gentleman told me! He had at last art 'enough to persuade me that my promise to the only 'man I esteemed was no longer binding, since he had 'been unfaithful. By his falsehoods I was taught to 'detest one equally brave and generous!'

But by this time my son was freed from the incum- brances of justice, as the person supposed to be wounded was detected to be an impostor. Mr. Jenkinson also, who had acted as his valet de chambre, had drest up his hair, and furnished him with whatever was necessary to make a genteel appearance. He now therefore entered, handsomely drest in his regimentals, and, without vanity (for I am above it), he appeared as handsome a fellow as ever wore a military dress. As he entered, he made Miss Wilmot a modest and distant bow, for he was not as yet acquainted with the change which the eloquence of his mother had wrought in his favour. But no decorums could restrain the impatience of his blushing mistress to be forgiven. Her tears, her looks, all contributed to discover the real sensations of her heart for having forgotten her former promise, and having suffered herself to be deluded by an impostor. My son appeared amazed at her condescension, and could scarce believe it real.—'Sure, madam,' cried he, 'this is 'but delusion! I can never have merited this! To be 'blessed thus is to be too happy.'——'No, Sir,' replied she, 'I have been deceived, basely deceived, else nothing

' could ever have made me unjust to my promise. You
' know my friendship, you have long known it ; but
' forget what I have done, and as you once had my
' warmest vows of constancy, you shall now have them
' repeated ; and be assured that if your Arabella cannot
' be yours she shall never be another's.'—' And no
' other's you shall be,' cried Sir William, ' if I have any
' influence with your father.'

This hint was sufficient for my son Moses, who immediately flew to the inn where the old gentleman was, to
inform him of every circumstance that had happened.
But in the mean time the 'Squire perceiving that he was
on every side undone, now finding that no hopes were
left from flattery or dissimulation, concluded that his
wisest way would be to turn and face his pursuers.
Thus laying aside all shame, he appeared the open hardy
villain. ' I find then,' cried he, ' that I am to expect
' no justice here ; but I am resolved it shall be done me.
' You shall know, Sir,' turning to Sir William, ' I am no
' longer a poor dependant upon your favours. I scorn
' them. Nothing can keep Miss Wilmot's fortune from
' me, which, I thank her father's assiduity, is pretty
' large. The articles, and a bond for her fortune, are
' signed, and safe in my possession. It was her fortune,
' not her person, that induced me to wish for this match ;
' and possesst of the one, let who will take the other.'

This was an alarming blow ; Sir William was sensible
of the justice of his claims, for he had been instrumental
in drawing up the marriage articles himself. Miss Wilmot, therefore, perceiving that her fortune was irre-
trievably lost, turning to my son, she asked if the loss
of fortune could lessen her value to him. ' Though
' fortune,' said she, ' is out of my power, at least I have
' my hand to give.'

' And that, madam,' cried her real lover, ' was indeed

' all that you ever had to give ; at least all that I ever
' thought worth the acceptance. And I now protest, my
' Arabella, by all that 's happy, your want of fortune
' this moment encreases my pleasure, as it serves to
' convince my sweet girl of my sincerity.'

Mr. Wilmot now entering, he seemed not a little pleased
at the danger his daughter had just escaped, and readily
consented to a dissolution of the match. But finding
that her fortune, which was secured to Mr. Thornhill by
bond, would not be given up, nothing could exceed his
disappointment. He now saw that his money must all
go to enrich one who had no fortune of his own. He
could bear his being a rascal, but to want an equivalent
to his daughter's fortune was wormwood. He sate therefore for some minutes employed in the most mortifying
speculations, till Sir William attempted to lessen his
anxiety.—' I must confess, Sir,' cried he, ' that your
' present disappointment does not entirely displease me.
' Your immoderate passion for wealth is now justly
' punished. But though the young lady cannot be rich,
' she has still a competence sufficient to give content.
' Here you see an honest young soldier, who is willing
' to take her without fortune ; they have long loved
' each other, and for the friendship I bear his father, my
' interest shall not be wanting in his promotion. Leave
' then that ambition which disappoints you, and for once
' admit that happiness which courts your acceptance.'

' Sir William,' replied the old gentleman, ' be assured
' I never yet forced her inclinations, nor will I now. If
' she still continues to love this young gentleman, let
' her have him with all my heart.—There is still, thank
' heaven, some fortune left, and your promise will make
' it something more. Only let my old friend here
' (meaning me) give me a promise of settling six thousand
' pounds upon my girl if ever he should come to his

'fortune, and I am ready this night to be the first to
'join them together.'

As it now remained with me to make the young couple
happy, I readily gave a promise of making the settlement
he required, which, to one who had such little expectations as I, was no great favour.—We had now therefore
the satisfaction of seeing them fly into each other's arms
in a transport.——'After all my misfortunes,' cried my
son George, 'to be thus rewarded ! Sure this is more
'than I could ever have presumed to hope for. To be
'possesst of all that's good, and after such an interval
'of pain ! My warmest wishes could never rise so high ! '

'Yes, my George,' returned his lovely bride, 'now let
'the wretch take my fortune ; since you are happy with-
'out it, so am I. Oh, what an exchange have I made,
'from the basest of men to the dearest, best !—Let
'him enjoy our fortune, I can now be happy even in
'indigence.'——'And I promise you,' cried the 'Squire,
with a malicious grin, 'that I shall be very happy with
'what you despise.' 'Hold, hold, Sir,' cried Jenkinson,
'there are two words to that bargain. As for that lady's
'fortune, Sir, you shall never touch a single stiver of it.
'Pray your honour,' continued he to Sir William, 'can
'the 'Squire have this lady's fortune if he be married
'to another ? '——'How can you make such a simple
'demand ? ' replied the Baronet ; 'undoubtedly he can-
'not.'—'I am sorry for that,' cried Jenkinson ; 'for as
'this gentleman and I have been old fellow-sporters,
'I have a friendship for him. But I must declare, well
'as I love him, that his contract is not worth a tobacco
'stopper, for he is married already.'——'You lie, like
'a rascal,' returned the 'Squire, who seemed roused by
this insult ; 'I never was legally married to any woman.'

'Indeed, begging your honour's pardon,' replied the
other, 'you were ; and I hope you will shew a proper

' return of friendship to your own honest Jenkinson, who
' brings you a wife, and if the company restrains their
' curiosity a few minutes, they shall see her.'——So
saying he went off with his usual celerity, and left us all
unable to form any probable conjecture as to his design.
——' Ay let him go,' cried the 'Squire ; ' whatever else
' I may have done I defy him there. I am too old now
' to be frightened with squibs.'

' I am surprised,' said the Baronet, ' what the fellow
' can intend by this. Some low piece of humour I sup-
' pose ! '——' Perhaps, Sir,' replied I, ' he may have a
' more serious meaning. For when we reflect on the
' various schemes this gentleman has laid to seduce inno-
' cence, perhaps some one more artful than the rest has
' been found able to deceive him. When we consider
' what numbers he has ruined, how many parents now
' feel with anguish the infamy and the contamination
' which he has brought into their families, it would not
' surprise me if some one of them—Amazement ! Do
' I see my lost daughter ? Do I hold her ? It is, it is
' my life, my happiness. I thought thee lost, my Olivia,
' yet still 1 hold thee—and still thou shalt live to bless
' me.' The warmest transports of the fondest lover were
not greater than mine when I saw him introduce my
child, and held my daughter in my arms, whose silence
only spoke her raptures.

' And art thou returned to me, my darling,' cried
I, ' to be my comfort in age ! '——' That she is,' cried
Jenkinson, ' and make much of her, for she is your own
' honourable child, and as honest a woman as any in the
' whole room, let the other be who she will. And as for
' you, 'Squire, as sure as you stand there, this young
' lady is your lawful wedded wife. And to convince you
' that I speak nothing but truth, here is the licence by
' which you were married together.'——So saying he

put the licence into the Baronet's hands, who read it and found it perfect in every respect. 'And now, gentle-'men,' continued he, 'I find you are surprised at all 'this ; but a few words will explain the difficulty. That 'there 'Squire of renown, for whom I have a great 'friendship, but that's between ourselves, has often 'employed me in doing odd little things for him. Among 'the rest, he commissioned me to procure him a false 'licence and a false priest, in order to deceive this young 'lady. But as I was very much his friend, what did 'I do but went and got a true licence and a true priest, 'and married them both as fast as the cloth could make 'them ? Perhaps you'll think it was generosity that 'made me do all this. But no. To my shame I con-'fess it, my only design was to keep the licence and let 'the 'Squire know that I could prove it upon him when-'ever I thought proper, and so make him come down 'whenever I wanted money.' A burst of pleasure now seemed to fill the whole apartment ; our joy reached even to the common room, where the prisoners them-selves sympathized,

And shook their chains
In transport and rude harmony.

Happiness was expanded upon every face, and even Olivia's cheek seemed flushed with pleasure. To be thus restored to reputation, to friends and fortune at once, was a rapture sufficient to stop the progress of decay and restore former health and vivacity. But perhaps among all there was not one who felt sincerer pleasure than I. Still holding the dear-loved child in my arms, I asked my heart if these transports were not delusion. 'How could you,' cried I, turning to Mr. Jenkinson, 'how could you add to my miseries by the story of her 'death ? But it matters not ; my pleasure at finding 'her again is more than a recompence for the pain.'

'As to your question,' replied Jenkinson, 'that is
'easily answered. I thought the only probable means
'of freeing you from prison, was by submitting to the
''Squire, and consenting to his marriage with the other
'young lady. But these you had vowed never to grant
'while your daughter was living ; there was therefore
'no other method to bring things to bear but by per-
'suading you that she was dead. I prevailed on your
'wife to join in the deceit, and we have not had a fit
'opportunity of undeceiving you till now.'

In the whole assembly now there only appeared two
faces that did not glow with transport. Mr. Thornhill's
assurance had entirely forsaken him : he now saw the
gulph of infamy and want before him, and trembled to
take the plunge. He therefore fell on his knees before
his uncle, and in a voice of piercing misery implored
compassion. Sir William was going to spurn him away,
but at my request he raised him, and after pausing
a few moments, 'Thy vices, crimes, and ingratitude,'
cried he, ' deserve no tenderness ; yet thou shalt not be
' entirely forsaken, a bare competence shall be supplied
'to support the wants of life, but not its follies. This
'young lady, thy wife, shall be put in possession of
'a third part of that fortune which once was thine, and
'from her tenderness alone thou art to expect any extra-
'ordinary supplies for the future.' He was going to
express his gratitude for such kindness in a set speech ;
but the Baronet prevented him by bidding him not
aggravate his meanness, which was already but too
apparent. He ordered him at the same time to be gone,
and from all his former domestics to chuse one such as
he should think proper, which was all that should be
granted to attend him.

As soon as he left us, Sir William very politely stept
up to his new niece with a smile and wished her joy.

His example was followed by Miss Wilmot and her
father ; my wife too kissed her daughter with much
affection, as, to use her own expression, she was now
made an honest woman of. Sophia and Moses followed
in turn, and even our benefactor Jenkinson desired to
be admitted to that honour. Our satisfaction seemed
scarce capable of encrease. Sir William, whose greatest
pleasure was in doing good, now looked round with
a countenance open as the sun, and saw nothing but
joy in the looks of all except that of my daughter Sophia,
who, for some reasons we could not comprehend, did
not seem perfectly satisfied. ' I think now,' cried he
with a smile, ' that all the company except one or two
' seem perfectly happy. There only remains an act of
' justice for me to do. You are sensible, Sir,' continued
he, turning to me, ' of the obligations we both owe
' Mr. Jenkinson. And it is but just we should both
' reward him for it. Miss Sophia will, I am sure, make
' him very happy, and he shall have from me five hundred
' pounds as her fortune, and upon this I am sure they
' can live very comfortably together. Come, Miss Sophia,
' what say you to this match of my making ? Will you
' have him ? '——My poor girl seemed almost sinking
into her mother's arms at the hideous proposal.—' Have
' him, Sir ! ' cried she faintly. ' No, Sir, never.'——
' What,' cried he again, ' not have Mr. Jenkinson, your
' benefactor, a handsome young fellow with five hundred
' pounds and good expectations ! '——' I beg, Sir,' returned she, scarce able to speak, ' that you'll desist,
and not make me so very wretched.'——' Was ever such
' obstinacy known,' cried he again, ' to refuse a man
' whom the family has such infinite obligations to, who
' has preserved your sister and who has five hundred
' pounds ! What, not have him ! '——' No, Sir, never,'
replied she angrily, ' I'd sooner die first.'——' If that be

'the case then,' cried he, 'if you will not have him—
'I think I must have you myself.' And so saying he
caught her to his breast with ardour. 'My loveliest,
'my most sensible of girls,' cried he, 'how could you
'ever think your own Burchell could deceive you, or
'that Sir William Thornhill could ever cease to admire
'a mistress that loved him for himself alone? I have
'for some years sought for a woman, who, a stranger
'to my fortune, could think that I had merit as a man.
'After having tried in vain, even amongst the pert and
'the ugly, how great at last must be my rapture to have
'made a conquest over such sense and such heavenly
'beauty.' Then turning to Jenkinson, 'As I cannot,
'Sir, part with this young lady myself, for she has taken
'a fancy to the cut of my face, all the recompence I can
'make is to give you her fortune, and you may call
'upon my steward to-morrow for five hundred pounds.'
Thus we had all our compliments to repeat, and Lady
Thornhill underwent the same round of ceremony that
her sister had done before. In the mean time Sir William's gentleman appeared to tell us that the equipages
were ready to carry us to the inn, where every thing
was prepared for our reception. My wife and I led the
van, and left those gloomy mansions of sorrow. The
generous Baronet ordered forty pounds to be distributed
among the prisoners, and Mr. Wilmot, induced by his
example, gave half that sum. We were received below
by the shouts of the villagers, and I saw and shook by
the hand two or three of my honest parishioners who
were among the number. They attended us to our inn,
where a sumptuous entertainment was provided, and
coarser provisions were distributed in great quantities
among the populace.

After supper, as my spirits were exhausted by the
alternation of pleasure and pain, which they had sus-

tained during the day, I asked permission to withdraw, and leaving the company in the midst of their mirth, as soon as I found myself alone I poured out my heart in gratitude to the Giver of joy as well as of sorrow, and then slept undisturbed till morning.

——But as I stood all this time with my book ready, I was at last quite tired of the contest, and shutting it, 'I perceive,' cried I, 'that none of you have a mind to be married.'—PAGE 413.

CHAPTER XXXII

The Conclusion.

THE next morning as soon as I awaked I found my eldest son sitting by my bedside, who came to encrease my joy with another turn of fortune in my favour. First having released me from the settlement that I had made the day before in his favour, he let me know that my merchant who had failed in town was arrested at Antwerp, and there had given up effects to a much greater amount than what was due to his creditors. My boy's generosity pleased me almost as much as this unlooked-for good fortune. But I had some doubts whether I ought in justice to accept his offer. While I was pondering upon this, Sir William entered the room, to whom I communicated my doubts. His opinion was, that as my son was already possessed of a very affluent fortune by his marriage, I might accept his offer without any hesitation. His business, however, was to inform me that as he had the night before sent for the licences, and expected them every hour, he hoped that I would not refuse my assistance in making all the company happy that morning. A footman entered while we were speaking, to tell us that the messenger was returned, and as I was by this time ready I went down, where I found the whole company as merry as affluence and innocence could make them. However as they were now preparing for a very solemn ceremony, their laughter entirely displeased me. I told them of the grave, becoming, and sublime deportment they should assume upon this mystical occasion, and read them two homilies and a thesis of my own composing in order to prepare them. Yet they still seemed perfectly refractory and ungovernable. Even as we were going along to church, to which I led the way, all gravity had quite forsaken them, and I was often tempted to turn back in indignation. In church a new dilemma arose, which promised no easy solution. This was, which couple should be married first ; my son's bride warmly insisted that Lady Thornhill (that was to be) should take the lead ; but this the other refused with equal ardour, protesting she would not be guilty of such rudeness for the world. The argument was supported for some time between both with equal obstinacy and good breeding. But as I stood all this time with my book ready, I was

at last quite tired of the contest, and shutting it, ' I per-
' ceive,' cried I, ' that none of you have a mind to be
' married, and I think we had as good go back again ;
' for I suppose there will be no business done here
' to-day.'——This at once reduced them to reason. The
Baronet and his lady were first married, and then my
son and his lovely partner.

I had previously that morning given orders that a
coach should be sent for my honest neighbour Flamborough and his family, by which means, upon our return
to the inn, we had the pleasure of finding the two Miss
Flamboroughs alighted before us. Mr. Jenkinson gave
his hand to the eldest, and my son Moses led up the
other ; (and I have since found that he has taken a real
liking to the girl, and my consent and bounty he shall
have, whenever he thinks proper to demand them.) We
were no sooner returned to the inn, but numbers of my
parishioners, hearing of my success, came to congratulate
me, but among the rest were those who rose to rescue
me, and whom I formerly rebuked with such sharpness.
I told the story to Sir William, my son-in-law, who went
out and reproved them with great severity ; but finding
them quite disheartened by his harsh reproof, he gave
them half a guinea a piece to drink his health and raise
their dejected spirits.

Soon after this we were called to a very genteel entertainment, which was drest by Mr. Thornhill's cook.
And it may not be improper to observe with respect to
that gentleman, that he now resides in quality of companion, at a relation's house, being very well liked and
seldom sitting at the side-table, except when there is no
room at the other ; for they make no stranger of him.
His time is pretty much taken up in keeping his relation,
who is a little melancholy, in spirits, and in learning to
blow the French horn. My eldest daughter, however,

THE VICAR AND HIS FAMILY

still remembers him with regret ; and she has even told me, though I make a great secret of it, that when he reforms she may be brought to relent.

But to return, for I am not apt to digress thus, when we were to sit down to dinner our ceremonies were going to be renewed. The question was whether my eldest daughter, as being a matron should not sit above the two young brides, but the debate was cut short by my son George, who proposed that the company should sit indiscriminately, every gentleman by his lady. This was received with great approbation by all, excepting my wife, who I could perceive was not perfectly satisfied, as she expected to have had the pleasure of sitting at the head of the table and carving all the meat for all the company. But notwithstanding this, it is impossible to describe our good humour. I can't say whether we had more wit amongst us now than usual, but I am certain we had more laughing, which answered the end as well. One jest I particularly remember ; old Mr. Wilmot drinking to Moses, whose head was turned another way, my son replied, ' Madam, I thank you.' Upon which the old gentleman, winking upon the rest of the company, observed that he was thinking of his mistress. At which jest I thought the two Miss Flamboroughs would have died with laughing. As soon as dinner was over, according to my old custom, I requested that the table might be taken away to have the pleasure of seeing all my family assembled once more by a chearful fire-side. My two little ones sat upon each knee, the rest of the company by their partners. I had nothing now on this side of the grave to wish for ; all my cares were over, my pleasure was unspeakable. It now only remained that my gratitude in good fortune should exceed my former submission in adversity.

FINIS.

GLOSSARIAL INDEX

A'. Dialect form of 'he', very widely distributed throughout England, except in the north. *She Stoops*, 103. See *Eng. Dialect Dict.*, s.v. A, *v.* 1, and He, *pron.*

ABENSBERG, COUNT, on Henry II's progress through Germany, presents his thirty-two children to their sovereign. *Vicar*, 189.

ACADEMY, 'a place of education, in contradistinction to the universities or publick schools' (Johnson). *Vicar*, 309. Cp. Lord Auchinleck's description of Johnson as 'a dominie, mon—an auld dominie; he keeped a schule, and cau'd it an acaadamy' (Birkbeck Hill's *Johnson*, i. 96 *n*).

ACTORS: their starts and attitudes. *Vicar*, 296, 323. Cp. *The Bee*, Oct. 13, 1759; *Citizen of the World*, Letter 21; and *The Present State of Polite Learning*, chap. xi.

Dr. Primrose's son among the. *Vicar*, 306. *See also* Strolling Company.

ADULATION, the dangers of. *Vicar*, 202.

ADVENTITIOUS, casual, coming unexpectedly. *Vicar*, 323.

Adventures of Catskin. See Catskin.

'AESOP' AND HIS BASKET OF BREAD. *Vicar*, 319. 'A new and beautiful edition of *Aesop's Fables*, with instructive morals, adorned with cuts' was published by Francis Newbery about 1779. The so-called 'Fables of Aesop' are now supposed to be all spurious.

AGE. 'I must not tell my age. They say women and music should never be dated.' *She Stoops*, 135.

AGITATORS. *See* Leveller, *and* Appendix, Note 22.

ALBEMARLE STREET CLUB. *See* Ladies' Club.

ALE. 'There is no business "for us that sell ale".' The quotation marks seem to show that Hardcastle was repeating a phrase understood at the time, perhaps with a political meaning. *She Stoops*, 110.

ALL BUT, nearly, almost. ' All but the whining end of a modern novel.' *She Stoops*, 167.

ALLEGORY OF GUILT AND SHAME. *Vicar*, 275.

ALLEMANDE, the name of a German dance. *Grumbler*, 176.

ALLY CAWN, i.e. Ali Khan, Subah of Bengal. *She Stoops*, 111. *Khan* = Lord or Prince. In Persia and Afghanistan a common affix to, or part of, the name of Hindustanis out of every rank ; properly, however, of those claiming a Pathān descent. Other forms are *Casunas Channa* = (*Khan of Khans*) *Gingi* ; *The Cawn of Chengie*, &c. (*Hobson-Jobson*.) The affairs of the Nawab Jaffier Ali Khan and his son-in-law Mir Cossin Khan, with the deposition of the one from the Subahship and the usurpation of the other, occupied a good deal of the attention of the Directors of the East India Company in 1760 and following years, as appears from various articles in the *Universal Museum* for 1764 (pp. 84–5, 135–9, 207–8).

Ally Croaker, a popular Irish song. *She Stoops*, 111.

ALMACK'S, a suite of assembly rooms in King Street, St. James, so called after the original proprietor. *Good-Natur'd Man*, 17.

AMAZONS : in Greek legend, a race in Asia Minor said to consist entirely of women, who excluded men from their territory, and waged war on their own behalf ; hence, a female warrior. *Vicar*, 278. The term is now usually applied to a bold, masculine woman ; a virago. Cp. Goldsmith's *Essay*, ' Female Warriors '.

AMBITION, THE HEIGHTS OF. ' The heights of ambition, and the vale of misery.' *Vicar*, 294.

AMES-ACE, the lowest possible throw at dice (from O. French through Latin = both aces), the double ace ; hence *fig.* bad luck, worthlessness, naught. ' *Marlow.* My old luck : I never nicked seven that I did not throw ames-ace three times following.' *She Stoops*, 137. Cp. *All's Well*, II. iii. 85, ' I had rather be in this choice than throw ames-ace for my life ' ; Fielding, *Lottery* (1755), ' If I can but nick this time, ames-ace, I defy thee.'

AMHERST. Jeffery, Baron Amherst (1717–97), commander of the troops in North America, and Field Marshal. *Good-Natur'd Man*, 41.

ANIMALS, contrasted with ' the vermin race '. *Vicar*, 274.

ANODYNE NECKLACE. *Vicar*, 309. This was a charm for children against convulsions, fits, &c., whilst teething. Cp.

Johnson's *Idler*, No. 40: ' The true pathos of advertisements must have sunk deep into the heart of every man that remembers the zeal shewn by the seller of the Anodyne Necklace, for the ease and safety of poor toothing infants ; and the affection with which he warned every mother, that she would never forgive herself if her infant should perish without a necklace.'

ANON, at your service, sir. *She Stoops*, 125. ' Like a call without Anon, sir, Or a question without an answer,' *Witts Recreations*. See 1 *Henry IV*, II. iv.

ANOTHER-GUESS, of another kind, a corruption of *another guise*. ' Another-guess lover,' *Good-Natur'd Man*, 24. ' Another-guess manner,' *Vicar*, 299.

ANTICHAMBER, Fr. *antichambre*, an outer chamber or waiting-room. ' It is generally written, improperly, *antichambre*' (Johnson). *Good-Natur'd Man*, 77.

ANTIQUA MATER of Grub Street. *Vicar*, 310.

APRIL, FIRST OF, exercise of wit on. *Vicar*, 206.

ARGUE DOWN, to overcome in argument. ' All I can say will never argue down a single button from his clothes.' *She Stoops*, 121. Cp. *downarg*, to contradict in an overbearing manner (*Eng. Dialect Dict.*).

Ariadne, an opera by Handel ; at the end of the overture occurs the well-known minuet. *She Stoops*, 99.

ASPIRING BEGGARY. *Vicar*, 198.

ASSYRIA, KINGS OF. *Vicar*, 267. *See* Berosus.

AUCTIONS. *Good-Natur'd Man*, 16 ; *Vicar*, 314, 321. Attending auction-sales was a fashionable method of killing time in Goldsmith's day.

Auditor, The, a short-lived paper edited by Arthur Murphy. *Vicar*, 299. This paper was established in opposition to the *North Briton*, in order to vindicate the administration of Lord Bute. The first number appeared on June 10, 1762, and was continued weekly until February 8, 1763, when it ceased to exist. The allusion to this paper seems to show that the *Vicar* must have been written in 1762.

AUTHORS, disappointed. *Vicar*, 313.

BACK. ' Back to back, my pretties, that Mr. Hastings may see you.' *She Stoops*, 122. Compare the similar incident in the

Vicar, 277 : 'She thought him [Thornhill] and Olivia extremely of a size, and would bid both stand up to see which was tallest.'

BACKGAMMON, 'a twopenny hit at.' *Vicar*, 194. *See* Hit (2).

BAG AND BAGGAGE, one's whole belongings. *Vicar*, 328. Cp. *As You Like It*, III. ii. 171, 'Though not with bag and baggage, yet with scrip and scrippage.'

BAGGAGES, young girls of but little character ; sometimes used, as here, in a tone of mock censure as a term of affection. *Vicar*, 377.

BAGNIO, 'a house for bathing and sweating' (Johnson) ; hence applied to houses of ill fame. *Vicar*, 217.

BAILIFFS. 'The scene of the bailiffs was retrenched in representation.' *Good-Natur'd Man*, Preface, 3. This scene (the opening of Act III, pp. 37 seq.) was omitted after the first performance, at the desire of the manager. It was restored in preparing the play for publication, and eventually took its legitimate place in the acting version (*see* Appendix, p. 490). Cp. the story of Steele and *his* bailiffs, Austin Dobson's *Richard Steele*, p. 222.

BALDERDASH, confused speech or writing, jargon. *Good-Natur'd Man*, 20.

BANDBOX, used derisively : ' Bandbox ! She's all a made-up thing, mun.' *She Stoops*, 125. Cp. ' Bandbox thing ' in O.E.D.

Barbara Allen, The Cruelty of, an old English ballad. The story tells how a young man died of love for Barbara, and how the maid afterwards died of remorse. Goldsmith wrote in *The Bee*, October 13, 1759, ' The music of the finest singer is dissonance to what I felt when our old dairymaid sung me into tears with " Johnny Armstrong's Last Good-night ", or the cruelty of " Barbara Allen ".' The latter ballad is printed in the *Oxford Book of English Verse*, No. 389.

BASKET (1), a wicker-work protection for the hand on a sword-stick, in the form of a small basket. *She Stoops*, 150.

BASKET (2), the overhanging back compartment on the outside of a stage coach. *She Stoops*, 91, 157.

BAYES, a character in Buckingham's *Rehearsal*, originally intended for Dryden, afterwards applied to poets generally. *She Stoops*, 170. Rowe was sometimes called ' Mr. Bayes the Younger ' ; see *Dryden*, ed. Scott and Saintsbury, i. 384 *n.*

Beaux' Stratagem, a comedy by George Farquhar, produced in 1707. Cherry in that play is an innkeeper's daughter. *She Stoops*, 133. *See* Farquhar.

BEDLAM, the hospital of St. Mary Bethlehem for lunatics in St. George's Fields ; hence applied to any great uproar, as here, ' Bedlam broke loose.' *She Stoops*, 151.

BED-TIME. ' Would it were bed-time and all were well.' *She Stoops*, 98. Falstaff's exclamation on the eve of the battle of Shrewsbury, 1 *Henry IV*, v. i. 125.

BEES, dialect form of the verb Be (see *Eng. Dialect Dict.*, Be, I. 1). *She Stoops*, 99.

BEGGARS, doors of the nobility beset with. *Vicar*, 315.

BELGRADE, battle of. This was fought in 1717, when Belgrade was retaken from the Turks by Prince Eugene. *She Stoops*, 111.

BENEVOLENCE : Human, *Vicar*, 290. Universal, *Good-Natur'd Man*, 8, 65 ; *Vicar*, 202 ; cp. *Citizen of the World*, Letters 23 and 27. Untutored, *Vicar*, 337.

BENSLEY, MR. *Good-Natur'd Man*, 4. Robert Bensley (1738–1817), who took the part of Leontine. His ponderous delivery of Johnson's lines is said to have dashed the spirits of the audience at the outset (Forster's *Life*, Book IV, chap. i).

BEROSUS. *Vicar*, 267. Berosus was a Babylonian priest who wrote a *History of Babylonia*, which is lost, though considerable fragments are preserved in Josephus, Eusebius, Syncellus, and the Christian Fathers. *See* Pattison's *Essays*, i. 644 seq., and notes on the *Eusebian Chronicle*.

BEST THINGS. ' The best things remained to be said on the wrong side.' *Vicar*, 310.

BIDDY BUCKSKIN, OLD MISS. *She Stoops*, 136. This hit was intended for Miss Rachael Lloyd, foundress of the Ladies' Club. See Walpole's *Letters*, viii. 263–4 (March 27, 1773) : ' Miss Loyd is in the new play by the name of Rachael Buckskin, though he [Goldsmith] has altered it in the printed copies. Somebody wrote for her a very sensible reproof to him. . . . However, the fool took it seriously, and wrote a most dull and scurrilous answer ; but, luckily for him, Mr. Beauclerk and Mr. Garrick intercepted it.'

BLADE, ' a brisk man either fierce or gay, so called in contempt ' (Johnson). *She Stoops*, 103, 171 and *passim*.

BLENKINSOP FAMILY. ' The Blenkinshop mouth to a T.'

She Stoops, 122. Prior records as a coincidence that there was an old family of this name living in Yorkshire, not far from the scene where the action of the *Vicar of Wakefield* was laid.

BLIND MAN'S BUFF, the game of. *Vicar*, 247.

BLOWN UP, destroyed, rendered void. *Vicar*, 318.

BLOWZED, disordered in dress or hair. *Vicar*, 244, 247.

BLUE BED TO THE BROWN. *See* Migrations.

BOBS, pendants, ear-rings. *She Stoops*, 128. Cp. *Citizen of the World*, Letter 52 : ' Resembling those Indians, who are found to wear all the gold they have in the world, in a bob at the nose.'

BODY, sensibility of the. *Vicar*, 202.

BOOKS, the reputation of, *Vicar*, 273 ; ' sweet unreproaching companions to the miserable,' ib. 335.

BOOKSELLER, the philanthropic. *Vicar*, 294. *See* Newbery, John.

BOROUGH, THE, a short name for the Borough of Southwark. *She Stoops*, 121.

BOTS, small worms in the entrails of horses. *Vicar*, 264. Cp. Shakespeare, 1 *Henry IV*, II. i. 9 : ' *Sec. Carrier*. Peas and beans are as dank here as a dog, and that is the next way to give poor jades the bots.' Commenting on this Mr. Madden writes : ' If carriers on the Kentish road were ignorant of the natural history of the bot (which we know to be the offspring of eggs, attached to certain leaves and swallowed by the horse), they erred in good company.' See further in Madden's *Diary of Master William Silence*, p. 267, ed. 1907.

BOX, to fight, spar. ' Setting the little ones to box, to make them sharp.' *Vicar*, 277.

BRASS, a person of brazen manners. *She Stoops*, 126. Cp. Bronze.

BREADSTITCH, properly ' brede-stitch ', ' applied by poets to things that show or suggest interweaving of colours, or embroidery ' (O.E.D., s.v. Brede, sb.[3] 4). *Vicar*, 251. Since the seventeenth century the variant *Brede* has been used poetically in the sense of *plait*, and by modern writers also in various vague senses.

BRONZE. ' O, there indeed I'm in bronze.' *Good-Natur'd Man*, 30. Le Bronze was Lofty's original stage name, afterwards withdrawn.

Buck of Beverland, story of. *Vicar*, 216.

Bugles, long slender glass beads, attached in ornamental manner to various articles of apparel. *Vicar*, 207. Steele, *Tatler*, No. 45, writes of ' Adam and Eve in Bugle-Work, curiously wrought '.

Bulkley, Mrs. (d. 1792), an actress, who took the part of Miss Richland in *The Good-Natur'd Man* (see p. 6), and that of Miss Hardcastle in *She Stoops to Conquer*. In both plays she spoke the Epilogue (pp. 82, 169). Indeed, in the latter play she threatened to throw up her part unless she were permitted to speak it (see Forster's *Life*, Book IV, chap. xv). The song, ' Ah me ! when shall I marry me ? ' (see *Poems*, 94) was written for the character of Miss Hardcastle in *She Stoops to Conquer*, but was eventually omitted, because Mrs. Bulkley, who performed the part, did not sing.

Bully, the protector of a prostitute. *Vicar*, 315.

Bully Dawson, a notorious London sharper of Whitefriars and a contemporary of Etherege ; he lived and died in the seventeenth century. *She Stoops*, 127. See *Spectator*, No. 2 : ' Sir Roger . . . kicked Bully Dawson in a public coffee-house for calling him youngster.'

Burchell, Mr. : his philosophical disputes with Dr. Primrose, *Vicar*, 201 ; his nickname, ib. 216. *See also* Thornhill, Sir William.

Burning Nuts on Michaelmas Eve. *Vicar*, 246. *See* Nut-burning.

By Jingo, used as a mild oath. *She Stoops*, 158.

By the Laws, used as a mild oath. *She Stoops*, 104, 132, 150. The *Dialect Dict.*, s.v. By, gives this phrase from Wexford only, quoting Kennedy, *Banks of Boro* (1867) 29 : ' Be the laws if you don't make haste we'll give you a cobbing.'

Canopy of Heaven, the overhanging firmament. *Vicar*, 269. Cp. *Hamlet*, ii. ii. 317–18, 'This most excellent canopy, the air, . . . this brave o'erhanging firmament, this majestical roof fretted with golden fire.' Sir Thomas Browne quotes from Lucan's *Pharsalia*, vii. 819 ' Caelo tegitur qui non habet urnam '.

Capital Punishment, Dr. Primrose on. *Vicar*, 365–6.

Caricatura, a satirical picture, now spelt ' caricature '. *She Stoops*, 145.

CARTESIAN SYSTEM, the system of philosophy taught by Descartes (1596–1650). *Vicar*, 302. Cp. *Present State of Polite Learning*, chap. v, where Goldsmith speaks of it as ' an exploded system '.

CAT AND FIDDLE. Used here as a term of contempt, perhaps with the nursery rime in mind. *She Stoops*, 93.

CAT-GUT, a coarse cloth formed of thick cord, woven widely, and used in the eighteenth century for lining and stiffening dress, particularly the skirts and sleeves. *Vicar*, 207, 242, 251. See ' ruffles of catgut ', *N. & Q.* 10th S. xi. January 2, 1909.

CATHERINE-WHEEL, a firework in the shape of a wheel, which revolves rapidly while burning. *She Stoops*, 131.

Catskin, The Adventures of. *Vicar*, 216. This was an old ballad, entitled *The Catskins' Garland, or the Wandering Young Gentlewoman.* The heroine is made a scullery-maid and reduced to dress in catskins. It is a form of the well-known fairy-tale of *Cinderella.* See *Century Encyc. of Names.*

CENTAURY, a popular name of a widely distributed plant, anciently said to have been discovered by Chiron the *Centaur.* Lat. *Centaurea.* *Vicar*, 211. See Chaucer, *Nonne Priestes Tale*, B. 4153, ' Of lauriol, centaure, and fumetore.'

CENTINEL, an old spelling of ' sentinel '. *Vicar*, 214. The derivation from *centenaria*, ' a centurion's post,' seems to be now generally accepted. See O.E.D.

CHAPMAN, one who buys and sells, a dealer. *Vicar*, 264.

Che Faro. ' And quits her Nancy Dawson, for Che Faro.' *She Stoops*, 170. *Che farò senza Euridice*, a beautiful lament from Gluck's *Orfeo ed Euridice*, was very popular in England at the time this Epilogue was spoken: the opera had been first produced in 1762, and printed in 1764 (see Grove's *Dictionary of Music*, ii. 184, ed. 1906).

CHICKASAW INDIANS, a tribe of the Apallachian nation, occupying the territory between the Ohio and Tennessee Rivers, now reduced to a few thousands, and settled in the Indian Territory. *Vicar*, 317. The Chickasaws were hostile in the early part of the eighteenth century (see *A Paladin of Philanthropy*, Gen. Oglethorpe, by Austin Dobson, p. 10); but afterwards grew more friendly. See the *Universal Museum* (1764), 43: ' American news. Charlestown, November 23 [1763]. The

Chickesaws, we hear, remain steady in their assurances of friendship, which this province in particular has had repeated
proofs of.'

CHIEF, the best, most select, of the first order. 'The company was incontestably the chief of the place.' *Vicar*, 306.
Cp. Miss Austen's Works.

CHIT, a child, infant; hence applied disrespectfully to a young
woman. *Vicar*, 250.

CHOICE SPIRIT (cp. *Julius Caesar*, III. i. 163, 'The choice and
master spirits of this age'): here used ironically, 'Dull as
a choice spirit.' *Good-Natur'd Man*, 47. See Goldsmith's
sketch of Tim Syllabub in Letter 20 of *The Citizen of the World*:
'He sometimes shines as a star of the first magnitude among
the choice spirits of the age: he is reckoned equally well at
a rebus, a riddle, a bawdy song, and an hymn for the Tabernacle.
You will know him by his shabby finery, his powdered wig,
dirty shirt, and broken silk stockings.' See also 'Description of
Various Clubs' in the *Essays*: 'The first club I entered upon
coming to town was that of the Choice Spirits.'

CHRISTMAS CAROLS, in Yorkshire. *Vicar*, 206.

Chronicle, The, i.e. *The London Chronicle*. *Vicar*, 299.

CIRCUMBENDIBUS, a circuit. *She Stoops*, 158. Cp. Dryden,
Spanish Friar, V. ii: 'Let him alone; I shall fetch him back with
a circumbendibus' (Dryden's *Works*, ed. Scott and Saintsbury,
vi. 515); Pope, *Art of Sinking*, 100, 'The Periphrasis, which the
moderns call the circumbendibus.'

COAL MINES IN CORNWALL are a figment of the Butler's
imagination. *Vicar*, 299, 303.

COCKATRICE, anything venomous or deadly; here used as an
exclamation of dislike. *Grumbler*, 179.

COFFEE-HOUSE. In the seventeenth and eighteenth centuries
coffee-houses were the resort of all classes for friendly intercourse
as well as refreshment. *Vicar*, 311. See Macaulay's *History*,
chap. iii, as to the importance of coffee-houses as a political
institution.

COGNOSCENTO, a connoisseur, an expert. *Vicar*, 321. *See*
Connoisseurship.

COINER, a maker of base money. *Vicar*, 355. The West
Riding of Yorkshire was a noted place for this criminal industry.

COLMAN, GEORGE (1732–1794), dramatist, and manager of Covent Garden Theatre from 1767 to 1774. *Good-Natur'd Man*, 3, 82 ; *She Stoops*, 87. See Appendix, pp. 488 seq., 499 seq.

COMEDY. French, *Good-Natur'd Man*, 3. Genteel, *Good-Natur'd Man*, 3. Low, *Good-Natur'd Man*, 3 ; cp. *She Stoops*, 99. Sentimental, *Good-Natur'd Man*, 3 ; *She Stoops*, 87, 88.

COMMENCING AUTHOR. *Vicar*, 310. The story told here and in the following pages is largely reminiscent of Goldsmith's own struggles as an author.

COMMERCE AND INDUSTRY, Dr. Primrose on. *Vicar*, 301. Cp. *Deserted Village*, ll. 309 seq.

COMMISSION, a warrant, conferring rank and authority upon an officer in the army. ' Procured him an ensign's commission . . . for which he had promised but one hundred pounds.' *Vicar*, 326. To purchase a commission, and to follow that up by purchasing successive steps in rank, was formerly the rule in the army. The custom was abolished by royal warrant on July 20, 1871; the Army Reform Bill of Mr. Edward Cardwell had sought to make the change, but the proposals were rejected by the House of Lords, on which the royal prerogative was invoked.

Compleat Housewife, The. She Stoops, 123.

CON, COUSIN. *She Stoops*, 147. It has been suggested by Mr. Austin Dobson that Goldsmith was thinking of his cousin, Jane Contarine, when he penned this description (*Life of Goldsmith*, p. 88, ed. 1888).

CONCATENATION, a series of links ; a succession of things in a series, dependent·on each other. ' If so be that a gentleman bees in a concatenation accordingly,' *She Stoops*, 99 ; ' The concatenation of self-existence, proceeding in a reciprocal duplicate ratio,' *Vicar*, 222.

CONCEALED, hidden, disguised. ' I have been now for some time a concealed spectator of his follies.' *Good-Natur'd Man*, 8. Cp. *Romeo and Juliet*, III. iii. 97–8 : ' What says My conceal'd lady to our cancelled [conceal'd, 1623] love ? ' Sir William Honeywood enacts here a similar part to that played by Sir Oliver Surface in Sheridan's *School for Scandal*.

CONGREVE, WILLIAM (1670–1729), poet and dramatist. His plays criticized by Dr. Primrose, *Vicar*, 296. His *Mourning Bride* quoted, *Vicar*, 407. The full passage (Act I, Sc. ii) reads :

MANUEL. By Heaven,
There's not a slave, a shackled slave of mine,
But should have smiled that hour, through all his care,
And shook his chains in transport and rude harmony.
Goldsmith considered that people were rarely so witty in their
dialogues as Congreve makes them (Prior's *Life of Goldsmith*,
ii. 160).

CONNOISSEURSHIP, how attained. *Vicar*, 321. Lord Byron,
according to Forster, delighted in the truth and wit of the two
rules which formed George Primrose's qualifications as a connoisseur, and often repeated them to Mr. Rogers in Italy (*Life
of Goldsmith*, Book IV, chap. xiv). Cp. *Citizen of the World*,
Letter 34. *See* Cognoscento.

CONSCIENCE, Dr. Primrose on. *Vicar*, 262.

CONSTITUTION, THE. Dr. Primrose on. *Vicar*, 299.

CONTRIVANCES in housekeeping. *Vicar*, 188.

CONTROVERSY. ' He [the Vicar] was too mild and too gentle
to contend for victory.' *Vicar*, 267. Contrast this mildness
with the vigour of Dr. Johnson, who owned that he often 'talked
for victory' (Boswell's *Life*, ii. 238, ed. Birkbeck Hill).

Between Robinson Crusoe and Friday. *Vicar*, 224. In
Religious Courtship, ib. The controversy between Robinson
Crusoe and Friday the savage is known, by name at least, to
everybody, and the controversy in *Religious Courtship* is among
Defoe's most characteristic works and affords a good deal of
amusement and instruction in his practised hands.

See also Disputation.

COQUET, to pretend to make love to ; to flirt. *She Stoops*, 120,
169.

COSMOGONY, Jenkinson's harangue on. *Vicar*, 266, 354.
For a little more information than is to be found in the frag-
mentary utterances of Ephraim Jenkinson, the reader may
consult Pattison's *Essays*, i. 164 seq. ; *The Eusebian Chronicle*,
i. 164 seq.; and the references to Sanchoniathon, Berosus, Ocellus
Lucanus, Manetho, Tiglath Pul Asser, &c., in Whiston's *Memoirs*,
with which Goldsmith must certainly have been acquainted.
See Whiston.

COUNTER, a false or counterfeit coin. *Vicar*, 391.

COUNTRY DANCES. *Vicar*, 237, 325.

COURANTE, ' a kind of dance formerly in vogue, characterized by a running or gliding step ' (O.E.D.). *Grumbler*, 178.

COURT REGISTER. *Good-Natur'd Man*, 51. Perhaps a fictitious name. Hugh Kelly edited *The Court Magazine* (1761–3), and there was also *The Court Miscellany, or Lady's New Magazine* (1765–8).

COURTSHIP. ' To go through all the terrors of a formal court-ship,' &c. *She Stoops*, 107–8. This passage is almost identical with one in the *Citizen of the World*, Letter 72.

COVENT GARDEN THEATRE, MANAGER OF. *See* Colman *and* Appendix, pp. 488 seq., 499 seq.

CRACK, a lie, exaggerated talk. *She Stoops*, 122. Cp. Burton, *Anat. Melancholy*, I. ii. III. xiv. 22, ' Out of this fountain [conceit] proceed all those cracks and brags ' (O.E.D.).

CRACK'D CHINA. ' I'm to be a mere article of family lumber; a piece of crack'd china to be stuck up in a corner.' *Good Natur'd Man*, 34. Cp. *The Deserted Village*, l. 235, ' Broken tea-cups, wisely kept for show.' Cracked china was much sought after by collectors. See Walpole's *Letters*, ii. 447 (May 19, 1750) : ' Turner, a great china-man, at the corner of the next street, had a jar cracked by the shock : he originally asked ten guineas for the pair : he now asks twenty, " because it is the only jar in Europe that has been cracked by an earthquake." '

CRADOCK, JOSEPH (1742–1826), of Gumley, Leicestershire. *She Stoops*, 171. He was the author of a tragedy called *Zobeide*, which Horace Walpole describes as ' very indifferent, though written by a country gentleman ' (*Letters*, viii. 117). For this tragedy Goldsmith supplied a Prologue : see *Poetical Works*, p. 72. The Epilogue written by Cradock for *She Stoops to Conquer* was rejected as too bad, but was printed with the play with the polite excuse that it came too late to be spoken. Cradock wrote his *Memoirs* in old age, in which he places on record many interesting anecdotes of Goldsmith. For Gold-smith's friendship with Cradock see Forster's *Life*, Book IV, chap xiii. See also an article by Mr. Austin Dobson, 'Mr. Cradock of Gumley,' in the *National Review* for July, 1909, pp. 774–87.

CRAMP, used for ' cramped ' ; of writing, close, crabbed, not written distinctly. *Good-Natur'd Man*, 58 ; *She Stoops*, 148, 149. Cp. Fielding, *Don Quixote in England* (1733), Introd.,

'They are written in such damned cramp hands you will never be able to read them.'

CREOLIAN, a Creole; a native of the West Indies or Spanish America, but not of native blood. *Vicar*, 312.

CRIBBAGE in prison. *Vicar*, 365. Compare similar occupations by prisoners in *Humours of the Fleet* (1749) 14:

> These are at Cribbage, those at Whist engag'd,
> And as they lose, by turns become enrag'd.

CRISPIN, a cobbler or shoemaker; from St. Crispin, who is said to have helped the poor by making shoes for them and became the patron saint of the craft. *Good-Natur'd Man*, 4.

CROAKER, MR., 'a raven that bodes nothing but mischief.' *Good-Natur'd Man*, 13 and *passim*. Goldsmith is said to have admitted that he borrowed the character of Croaker from Johnson's Suspirius in *The Rambler*, No. 59. See Dr. Birkbeck Hill's *Boswell*, i. 213. For further information and a transcript from *The Rambler* see Appendix, Note 5.

CROOKED-LANE, Cannon Street, City. *Good-Natur'd Man*, 9; *She Stoops*, 121.

CROSS, *sb.* (1) money; so called because the reverse side was stamped with a cross; (2) the side of a coin stamped with a cross. (1) 'To come and take up an honest house, without cross or coin to bless yourself with.' *Vicar*, 329. Cp. Heywood, *Wise Woman*, I. i (1638), 'I'le play the franck gamester. I will not leave myself one Crosse to blesse me' (O.E.D.). (2) 'We have not yet seen the cross of her money.' *Vicar*, 328. So Cowley, *Cutter of Colman Street* (1663), v, 'What, did you think I knew not Cross from Pile?'

CROSS, *v.* 'To cross a fortune-teller's hand with silver: to describe crossing lines on her hand with a silver coin given by the consulter: hence to give money to' (O.E.D.). 'My girls came running to me for a shilling apiece to cross her [a gipsy's] hand with silver.' *Vicar*, 242.

CROSS AND CHANGE, a term in needlework. *Vicar*, 251.

CUP, 'a name for various beverages, consisting of wine, sweetened and flavoured with various ingredients, and usually iced' (O.E.D., s.v. Cup, *sb.* 11). *She Stoops*, 110.

CURE, the benefice or employment of a curate or a clergyman.

Vicar, 198. An article in the *National Review* for May, 1883, by Mr. Edward Ford, has suggested Kirkby Moorside, in the North Riding, as the 'small Cure' to which Dr. Primrose removed. The sum offered, fifteen pounds a year, shows to some extent the condition of the inferior clergy at this time.

CUT, *sb.* In phrase 'the cut of one's face', the form or shape of one's features. *Vicar*, 410. Cp. 'cut of one's jib.' *See* O.E.D., s.v. Cut, *sb.*[1] III. 16.

CUT PAPER, to cut out in profile, as a silhouette. 'My eldest [daughter] can cut paper.' *Vicar*, 251. Cp. *Citizen of the World*, Letter 90, 'I shaped tobacco-stoppers, wrote verses, and cut paper.' See Austin Dobson's *Fielding*, 1889, p. 184, 'Hogarth, being unable to recall his dead friend's features, had recourse to a profile cut in paper by a lady, who possessed the happy talent which Pope ascribes to Lady Burlington.' See Appendix, Note 20.

'CUTENESS, sharpness, cleverness, acuteness. *Good-Natur'd Man*, 23.

DARBY AND JOAN, a married couple, proverbial types of contentment. *She Stoops*, 92. Darby and Joan are said to have lived in the eighteenth century in the West Riding of Yorkshire, and are noted traditionally for their long and happy married life. There is a ballad on the subject called 'The Happy Old Couple', supposed to have been written by Henry Woodfall, though it has been attributed to Prior. A poem entitled 'Dobson and Joan'; by Mr. B., is published with Prior's *Poems* (see *Century Cyclopaedia of Names*).

DAWSON, NANCY (d. 1767), a famous hornpipe dancer. *She Stoops*, 170. See note in *Poetical Works*, 221.

DEATH, the only friend of the wretched. *Vicar*, 382. On the whole of this passage cp. *The Traveller*, ll. 27–8.

Death and the Lady. Vicar, 286. This old ballad will be found in Bell's *Ballads of the Peasantry* (1857), p. 32.

DECLARE OFF, withdraw from anything. *Vicar*, 260. Cp. *Citizen of the World*, Letter 46, 'As lord Beetle says, I absolutely declare off.'

DEFOE, DANIEL (1661–1731). *Vicar*, 224. *See* Controversy.

DELICATE, refined, gentle, pleasing to the senses. 'Delicate creature!' *Good-Natur'd Man*, 49.

DENAIN, a town in France, where Prince Eugène, commanding the allied troops, was defeated by Marshal Villars in 1712.

DEPARTMENT, business assigned to a particular person (Johnson). ' *French Servant.* He be only giving four five instruction, read two tree memorial, call upon von ambassadeur. *Mrs. Croaker.* What an extensive department.' *Good-Natur'd Man,* 28. So Scott, *Quentin Durward,* 308, ' My head is somewhat of the dullest out of my own department.'

DEUCE ACE, ' two and one, i.e. a throw that turns up deuce with one die and ace with the other ' (O.E.D.). *Vicar,* 194. Cp. *Love's Labour's Lost,* I. ii. 49–51, ' *Moth.* You know how much the gross sum of deuce-ace amounts to. *Arm.* It doth amount to one more than two.'

DEUTEROGAMIST, one who makes or upholds a second marriage. *Vicar,* 294.

DEUTEROGAMY, a second marriage. *Vicar,* 266.

DIALOGICALLY, in the manner of a dialogue. *Vicar,* 221.

DING, to impress by force or reiteration. ' Not to keep dinging it, dinging it into one so.' *She Stoops,* 123.

DISPROPORTIONED FRIENDSHIPS. *Vicar,* 213.

DISPUTATION :

Between 'Squire Thornhill and Moses. *Vicar,* 221–2.

Between Thwackum and Square. Ib. 224. The disputes between Mr. Thwackum the divine and Mr. Square the philosopher are reported in Fielding's *Tom Jones,* Book III, chap. iii : ' This gentleman [Mr. Square] and Mr. Thwackum scarce ever met without a disputation ; for their tenets were indeed diametrically opposed to each other. Square held human nature to be the perfection of all virtue, and that vice was a deviation from our nature, in the same manner as deformity is. Thwackum, on the contrary, maintained that the human mind, since the fall, was nothing but a sink of iniquity, till purified and redeemed by grace. . . . The former measured all actions by the unalterable rule of right, and the eternal fitness of things ; the latter decided all matters by authority ; but in doing this, he always used the scriptures and their commentators, as the lawyer doth his Coke upon Littleton, where the comment is of equal authority with the text.' *See also under* Square *and* Thwackum.

The Philosophic Vagabond's skill in disputation. *Vicar,*

322–3. This is another trait of Goldsmith's. See Forster's *Life*, Book I, chap. v : ' He always boasted of himself as hero in the disputations to which his philosophic vagabond refers. . . . "Sir," said Boswell to Johnson, "he *disputed* his passage through Europe." '

Do, *v.*, ' to hoax, cheat, swindle, overreach ' (O.E.D., s.v. Do, 11 f.). ' If the man comes from the Cornish borough, you must do him ; you must do him I say,' *Good-Natur'd Man*, 29 ; ' Do me here, do you there : interest of both sides, few words, flat, done and done, and it 's over,' ib. 48.

DRAMA, state of the. *Vicar*, 295–6.

DREAMS, as portents. *Vicar*, 243.

DRIVING, ' an Irish term, descriptive of the mode which a landlord in Ireland takes to enforce payment from a tenant ' (Goldsmith's *Works*, i. 417, ed. Cunningham, 1854). ' My steward talks of driving for the rent,' *Vicar*, 347 ; ' The consequence of my incapacity was his driving my cattle that evening,' ib. 349. ' Cattle-driving ' is a term which has been very familiar during the last few years in connexion with grazing-land disputes in Ireland.

DRYDEN, JOHN (1631–1707), poet and dramatist. A favourite song of, *Vicar*, 212 ; out of fashion, ib. 295 ; as an exemplar, ib. 310.

DUCHESSES OF DRURY LANE, loose women of pleasure, passing themselves off as persons of rank and position. *She Stoops*, 108.

DUELLING. George Primrose's offence against the Statute, *Vicar*, 378. Dr. Primrose's censure, *Vicar*, 391. See Appendix, Note 26.

DULLISSIMO-MACCARONI, a series of satirical prints, caricaturing prominent persons as maccaronies. *She Stoops*, 145. See *Poetical Works*, Notes, p. 247.

EARTHQUAKE, THE LATE. *Good-Natur'd Man*, 15. This refers to the earthquake at Lisbon on November 1, 1755. Writing on November 25, 1755, Horace Walpole says, ' There is a most dreadful account of an earthquake at Lisbon, but several people will not believe it. There have been lately such earthquakes and waterquakes, and rocks rent, and other strange phenomena, that one would think the world exceedingly out of repair ' (*Letters*, iii. 373).

EASTERN TALES. 'My essays were buried among eastern tales,' &c. *Vicar*, 313. 'Asem, an Eastern Tale,' was one of Goldsmith's essays. Cp. *Citizen of the World*, Letter 33, 'The Eastern tales of magazines, &c. ridiculed.' On the history of Oriental tales see Appendix, Note 23.

ECOD, used as a mild oath. *She Stoops*, 122 and *passim*.

Edwin and Angelina, ballad of. *Vicar*, 227 seq. This poem, written in the old ballad style, had been privately printed previous to its publication in the novel in 1766. The earlier version differs considerably from that in the *Vicar*, and subsequent editions show further changes. It was probably an interpolation to make the novel a little longer. For a full account of the ballad see Mr. Austin Dobson's notes in *Poetical Works*, 206–12, ed. 1906.

EGGS. 'As sure as eggs is eggs.' *Good-Natur'd Man*, 55. A proverbial expression, indicating anything very sure.

ELEVENS. 'By the elevens.' A phrase of uncertain origin (O.E.D.). *Good-Natur'd Man*, 43 ; *She Stoops*, 106.

EMBROIDERY. 'You must shew me your embroidery. I embroider and draw patterns myself a little.' *She Stoops*, 137. Young Marlow is here imitative of Archer in *The Beaux' Stratagem* (Act IV, sc. i), where he says to Mrs. Sullen, 'I can't at this distance, Madam, distinguish the figures of the embroidery.' See Appendix, Note 15.

ENSIGN, 'the officer of foot who carries the flag' (Johnson). *Vicar*, 326. *See* Commission.

ENTHUSIASM, 'heat of imagination, violence of passion' (Johnson). 'That night . . . was spent in the bitterness of complaint, and ill-supported sallies of enthusiasm.' *Vicar*, 291.

EPILOGUES :

Good-Natur'd Man, 82. See notes to *Poetical Works*, 214.

She Stoops to Conquer, 169, 171. See notes to *Poetical Works*, 220, 246–9.

EPITAPHS :

On the Vicar's wife, placed over the mantelpiece. *Vicar*, 193.

On Whiston's wife, ib. See Appendix, Note 16, and cp. *Citizen of the World*, Letter 12, on Flattering Epitaphs.

EUGÈNE, PRINCE, stories of. *She Stoops*, 91, 111, 127. Francis Eugène, of Savoy (1663–1736), known as Prince Eugène, was a distinguished military commander, and participated with the Duke of Marlborough in the victories of Blenheim, Oudenarde, &c. He was very popular in England.

EVIL, a smaller, to produce a greater good. *Vicar*, 331.

'EXITS AND ENTRANCES.' *She Stoops*, 169. Quoted from *As You Like It*, II. vii. 141.

EXPRESS, 'a messenger sent on purpose' (Johnson). *Good-Natur'd Man*, 28.

FABLE. 'A feigned story intended to enforce some moral precept' (Johnson). The Giant and the Dwarf, *Vicar*, 259 ; Aesop and his basket of bread, ib. 319.

FAIR, Moses Primrose at the, *Vicar*, 256 ; Dr. Primrose at the, ib. 264 seq.

FAIRING, a present given or purchased at a fair. *Vicar*, 288. One of John Newbery's books for children was entitled 'The Fairing ; or Golden Toy for children, in which they can see all the Fun in the Fair, and at home be as happy as if they were there.'

Fair Penitent, by Nicholas Rowe. *Vicar*, 305.

Fair Rosamond's Bower, the story of. *Vicar*, 216. The heroine of this story was Rosamond Clifford, the concubine of Henry II, who was said to have been poisoned by Queen Eleanor about 1173. The historical facts are not well authenticated, and the more romantic incidents are wholly derived from a popular ballad written a long time after their supposed occurrence. The 'bower' was in the royal park at Woodstock (now known as Blenheim Park), where Fair Rosamond is said to have been kept by her royal lover in a labyrinth, and discovered by Queen Eleanor by means of a clue of thread. Rosamond was buried in the nunnery of Godstow, near Oxford. For all that is known of the historical facts, and for an account of the growth of the story, see the *Dictionary of National Biography*, vol. xi.

FALKLAND, LORD (1610-43), as an exemplar. *Vicar*, 327. Viscount Falkland was slain at Newbury in 1643. Goldsmith's dates are here grievously at fault, as elsewhere. George Primrose is told to emulate his grandfather, who fell in the same field with Falkland. As Prior points out, 'this, if taken literally, would make the Vicar more than a century old.' Clarendon's account of Falkland is generally recognized as one of the most eloquent passages in his or any other history.

FARMERS, simplicity of manners of. *Vicar*, 205. *See* Flamborough.

FARQUHAR, GEORGE (1678–1707), dramatist. His plays criticized by Dr. Primrose. *Vicar*, 296. *The Beaux' Stratagem* was written in six weeks, in the midst of disappointment and poverty. At the height of its success Farquhar died. The chief action of the play turns upon fortune-hunting in the marriage-market. On one occasion, when it was proposed to go down to Lichfield, and, in honour of Johnson and Garrick, act this play, Goldsmith expressed a wish to play the part of Scrub (see Forster's *Goldsmith*, Book IV, chap. xiv). Goldsmith is said to have considered Farquhar to possess the spirit of genuine comedy in a superior degree to any modern writer, though often coarse and licentious (Prior's *Goldsmith*, ii. 160). There is no doubt Goldsmith took Farquhar as his exemplar, and the *Beaux' Stratagem* is regarded by Dr. A. W. Ward as the prototype of *She Stoops to Conquer* : see Ward's *English Dramatic Literature*, iii. 485, ed. 1899.

FEEDER, lit. one who feeds up or fattens ; here used humorously : a crammer, tutor. *Vicar*, 220. See O.E.D., s.v. Feeder, *sb.* 5, which quotes from the *Gentleman's Magazine*, 1787, lvii. 869, ' A Feeder, by which is meant a person who . . . crams into the head of a candidate for a degree certain ideas which [&c.].' Cp. Dickens, *Dombey and Son*, chap. xi, ' Mr. Feeder, B.A., assistant in Dr. Blimber's boarding-school.'

FINERY. ' What a quantity of superfluous silk hast thou got about thee, girl ! ' *She Stoops*, 94. With this speech of Mr. Hardcastle's, compare the Vicar's remarks on the attachment of his family to finery, *Vicar*, 207–8.

FIRE at the Vicar's dwelling-house. *Vicar*, 335–7. The incidents here narrated bear a great resemblance to the fire which destroyed the Rev. Samuel Wesley's residence at Epworth in 1706. Here two children were in danger, one of those rescued being the famous John Wesley. See Southey's *Life of John Wesley*, i. 13–14, ed. 1846.

FIRE-SIDE, happiness of the Vicar's. *Vicar*, 215–6, 305, 376, 392, 415. Sir Walter Scott, in his *Lives of the Novelists*, declares this scene of domestic happiness to be without parallel, in all his novel-reading, as a fireside picture of perfect beauty. Cp. *The Traveller*, ll. 11–12.

FIRST SIGHT, nonce-use : that which is seen for the first time (O.E.D.). *She Stoops*, 127.

FLAMBOROUGH, FARMER. *Vicar*, 207. His ' rosy daughters ', ib. 237. Writing to the Rev. Thomas Contarine in 1754, Goldsmith says, ' Of all objects on this earth, an English farmer's daughter is most charming ' (Prior's *Life*, i. 162).

FLANDERS, the philosophic vagabond in. *Vicar*, 320. Cp. Forster's *Life*, Book I, chap. v.

FLATTERY : of the ambitious, *Vicar*, 202 ; of authors, ib. 266.

FLEET, THE, a prison for debtors, bankrupts, and persons charged with contempt of Court ; whole families were incarcerated. *Good-Natur'd Man*, 9, 41. For an account of life in the prison see *The Humours of the Fleet*, a humorous poetical description, ' written by a Gentleman of the College,' London, 1749.

FLETCHER, JOHN (1576–1625), dramatist. His plays criticized by Dr. Primrose. *Vicar*, 295.

FLORENTINE, ' a sort of bak'd Tart, or Pudding ' (Bailey). *She Stoops*, 113. See *Complete Housewife*, 1750, ' a Florentine of a kidney of veal.' A receipt for making a Florentine may be found in *A True Gentleman's Delight*, 1676, 98 (Nares). For different ways of making this dish see *Eng. Dialect Dict.*

FLOURISHING MANNER. To flourish = ' to use florid language ' (Johnson). *Good-Natur'd Man*, 35.

FONTARABIA, a town in the province of Guipuzcoa, Spain, at the mouth of the River Bidassoa. Marriage fair at. *Vicar*, 288. Of this fair nothing definite can be discovered. Cp. Scott, *Rob Roy*, chap. v : ' " Fontarabian echoes ! " . . . the Fontarabian Fair would have been more to the purpose.' This, however, as Mr. Austin Dobson points out, may have been merely a reminiscence of Goldsmith, with whose works Scott was familiar.

FOREST, an extensive tract of land covered with trees and undergrowth (O.E.D.). ' They have lost their way upo' the forest.' *She Stoops*, 100.

FORFEITS, game of. *Vicar*, 194. ' Something deposited, and to be redeemed by a jocular fine, whence the game of *forfeits* ;

one of our festive sports, not yet forgotten; and observed, especially in the country, about Christmas time' (Todd-Johnson).

FORTUNE-HUNTERS, character of. *Vicar*, 213-4.

FRANCE, the philosophic vagabond in. *Vicar*, 320-2.

FRENCH AMBASSADOR, his 'green and yellow dinners'. *She Stoops*, 113. See Appendix, Note 12.

FRENCH COMEDY. *Good-Natur'd Man*, 3.

FRENCH FRISEURS. *See* Friseur.

FRENCH HORN, a wind instrument of metal, twisted into several folds. *Vicar*, 414. Cp. Pope, *Dunciad*, iv. 378:

> The voice was drowned
> By the French horn or by the op'ning hound.

FRENCH TASTE, its effect on prices. *Good-Natur'd Man*, 41-2.

FRENCHIFIED COVER, the wrapper of a letter folded after a French manner; used contemptuously. *Good-Natur'd Man*, 26.

FRIDAY, THE SAVAGE, his inquiries on religion in *Robinson Crusoe*. *Vicar*, 224.

FRIENDSHIP, UNIVERSAL. *Good-Natur'd Man*, 44, 45.

FRIPPERY, tawdry finery. *She Stoops*, 94; *Vicar*, 208. Cp. Carey, *Hills of Hybla* (1767) 20, 'Behold her sailing in the pink of taste, Trump'd up with powder, frippery and paste.'

FRISEUR, a hairdresser. 'Your friseur is a Frenchman, I suppose?' *She Stoops*, 121. Cp. *Epilogue intended for She Stoops to Conquer*, l. 32, 'Of French friseurs, and nosegays, justly vain.'

FRIZZLE, MRS. *See* Wig.

FUDGE, 'stuff and nonsense! Bosh! Apparently first used by Goldsmith' (O.E.D.). *Vicar*, 249 and *passim*. The exclamation *Fudge!* at the end of the paragraphs on pp. 249 and 250 was added in the second edition—a notable improvement to the text. The interjection was probably derived from the name of a person. See *Webster's Dictionary*, Noted Names of Fiction. 'Fudge, Mr.: A contemptuous designation bestowed upon any absurd or lying writer or talker.' Webster adds the following quotation: 'There was, sir, in our time, one Captain *Fudge*, commander of a merchantman, who, upon his return from a voyage, how ill fraught so ever his voyage was, always brought home to his owners a good cargo of *lies*, insomuch that now aboard ship the sailors, when they hear a great lie told, cry out,

" You *fudge* it ".' *Remarks upon the Navy* (London, 1700). According to the O.E.D., in a dialogue of 1702, 'The present condition of the English Navy,' one of the interlocutors is called ' Young Fudg of the Admiralty '. The name has since been extensively used in English literature ; cp. *Virgil in London, or, Town Fudges*, 1814 ; *Fashionable Fudges in London* : a Poem by Benj. Flaccus, 1818 ; *The Fudge Family in Paris*, by Thomas Moore, 1818.

GALLED HACK. *Vicar*, 264. To ' gall ' is to fret or wear away the skin by rubbing. Cp. *Hamlet*, III. ii. 253, ' Let the galled jade wince, our withers are unwrung.'

GALLERY at Mr. Hardcastle's house. *She Stoops*, 134. *See* Inns.

GAMING, Dr. Primrose's detestation of. *Vicar*, 194. It is only too probable that Goldsmith's practice differed from his precepts in this regard. See Mr. Austin Dobson's *Life*, p. 190.

GARNET, the name of a precious stone. ' The *garnet* is a gem of a middle degree of hardness, between the sapphire and the common crystal. It is found of various sizes. Its colour is ever of a strong red ' (Johnson). *She Stoops*, 131.

GARRICK, DAVID, actor and dramatist (1716–1779). *She Stoops*, 88 (Prologue). Horace Walpole calls this ' a poor prologue ' in more than one letter (see *Letters*, viii. 260, 262). With this opinion may be compared Johnson's observation, ' Dryden has written prologues superiour to any that David Garrick has written ; but David Garrick has written more good prologues than Dryden has done. It is wonderful that he has been able to write such a variety of them ' (Boswell's *Life*, ii. 325, ed. Birkbeck Hill). For Garrick's connexion with the production of Goldsmith's plays see Appendix, pp. 488 seq., 500, and Note 2.

GAY, JOHN (1688–1732), poet and dramatist. *Vicar*, 226. The incident of ' the two lovers so sweetly described by Mr. Gay, who were struck dead in each other's arms ' occurs in a letter written by Gay to a friend, and was published in Pope's *Works*, ed. 1751 (see Appendix, Note 18). In 1729 Gay asked Pope to have these words put upon his tombstone :

'Life is a jest, and all things show it :
I thought so once, but now I know it ;

with what more you may think proper.' Pope fulfilled this request by writing for Gay's memorial in Westminster Abbey one of his best epitaphs (severely criticized by Johnson in his *Life* of Pope):

> Of manners gentle, of affections mild ;
> In wit, a man ; simplicity, a child :
> With native humour temp'ring virtuous rage,
> Form'd to delight at once and lash the age :
> Above temptation, in a low estate,
> And uncorrupted, ev'n among the great :
> A safe companion, and an easy friend,
> Unblamed thro' life, lamented in thy end.
> These are thy honours ! not that here thy bust
> Is mix'd with heroes, or with kings thy dust ;
> But that the worthy and the good shall say,
> Striking their pensive bosoms—*Here* lies GAY.

Gazetteer, The, i.e. *The Gazetteer and London Daily Advertizer.* *Good-Natur'd Man,* 15, 78 ; *Vicar,* 307.

GENTEEL COMEDY, ' sentimental ' or refined comedy as contrasted with ' low ' comedy. *Good-Natur'd Man,* 3. *See also* Sentimental Comedy.

GENUS, a perverted form of ' genius ', a person endowed with genius; applied humorously here. ' O ! my genus, is that you ? ' *She Stoops,* 128.

GHOST. ' We wanted no ghost to tell us that.' *She Stoops,* 101. A reference to *Hamlet,* I. v.

GIBBET, the gallows. *She Stoops,* 158. ' Our possessions are paled up with new edicts every day, and hung round with gibbets to scare every invader.' *Vicar,* 366. Cp. *The Deserted Village,* ll. 318–19 :

> Here, while the proud their long-drawn pomps display,
> There the black gibbet glooms beside the way.

The gallows was a prominent object in the landscape in the eighteenth century. *See* Tyburn.

GO, to risk a sum of money, to wager. ' Go forty guineas on a game of cribbage.' *Good-Natur'd Man,* 37. Cp. Marvell, *Reh. Transp.* i. 283, ' This gentleman would always go half a Crown with me ' (O.E.D.).

Go down, to find acceptance (with the public). 'The only things that go down.' *Vicar*, 295. Cp. Fielding, *Intrig. Chambermaid* (1733) Epil., 'None but Italian warblers will go down.'

Gold and Silver, great scarcity of. *Vicar*, 268.

Good of the House, For the : for the profit or benefit of a landlord, an expression in general use amongst frequenters of public-houses. 'Were you not told to drink freely, and call for what you thought fit, for the good of the house ?' *She Stoops*, 142.

Good-Natur'd Man. The title chosen by Goldsmith for his play had already been used by Fielding for a piece to be produced at Drury Lane in 1742, in which Garrick was to have taken part. But the play, not satisfying the author, was not produced until 1779. See *Fielding*, by Austin Dobson (*English Men of Letters*), 1889, pp. 56 and 94. But the phrase 'good-natur'd man' occurs frequently in Goldsmith's writings. Cp. *Citizen of the World*, Letter 67, 'The discontented being, who retires from society, is generally some good-natured man, who has begun life without experience, and knew not how to gain it in his intercourse with mankind.' See Appendix, pp. 488 seq., and Note 3.

Gooseberry, short for 'gooseberry-wine'. *Vicar*, 212.

Gooseberry-wine. *Vicar*, 207.

Goose-pie. *Vicar*, 216. Cp. Pope, *Rape of the Lock*, iv. 52, 'Here sighs a jar, and there a Goose-pie talks.'

Gosling Green, a pale yellowish colour. 'A waistcoat of gosling green.' *Vicar*, 254.

Gothic, rude, uncouth, in bad taste. 'With his usual Gothic vivacity.' *She Stoops*, 121. See *The Bee*, October 13, 1759, 'A French woman is a perfect architect in dress : she never with Gothic ignorance mixes the orders.' Cp. Fielding, *Tom Jones*, vii. iii, 'Oh more than Gothic ignorance.'

Grass-plot, a piece of ground covered with turf. *Vicar*, 234.

Green, a piece of grassy land situate near a town or village. *Vicar*, 271.

Green Spectacles, Moses and the. *Vicar*, 256.

Gregory, St., on Good Works. *Vicar*, 265.

Groce, an old spelling of 'gross'. *Vicar*, 257.

Groom-porter, 'an officer of the English Royal Household,

abolished under George III ; his principal functions . . . were to regulate all matters connected with gaming within the precincts of the court ' (O.E.D.). *Good-Natur'd Man*, 31.

GROTTO GARDENS, in Clerkenwell. *She Stoops*, 121.

GROUSE. ' The story of ould grouse in the gun-room.' *She Stoops*, 105. ' Grouse is a common name for sporting dogs in Ireland,' wrote Mr. Fitzgerald to Forster (*Life*, Book IV, chap. xv). But ' grouse ' in this sense is not given by the O.E.D. or the *English Dialect Dict.*

GRUB-STREET (now Milton Street, Finsbury). *Vicar*, 310. ' The name of a street in London, much inhabited by writers of small histories, dictionaries, and temporary poems ; whence any mean production is called *grubstreet* ' (Johnson).

Grumbler, The. See Appendix, p. 505.

GRUMBLETONIAN, a grumbler. ' I could be so revenged on the old grumbletonian.' *She Stoops*, 100. The term is adapted from *Muggletonian* and *Grindletonian* (O.E.D.)=the ' country party '. Cp. Macaulay, *History*, chap. xix, ' There was the great line which separated the official men and their friends and dependents from those who were sometimes nicknamed the " Grumbletonians ", and sometimes honoured with the appellation of the *Country party.*'

GUESTS, OBJECTIONABLE, the art of getting rid of. *Vicar*, 189.

GULPH, an old spelling of ' gulf ', a yawning chasm, abyss, the ' bottomless pit '. *Vicar*, 316, 375.

HABUS CORPUS, i.e. the writ of *habeas corpus*. *Good-Natur'd Man*, 42.

HACKNEYED, made trite or commonplace. *Vicar*, 273. Apparently first used in this sense in Hurd's Notes (1749) on Horace's *Art of Poetry*.

HAGGLING, petty squabbling ; literally, bargaining. ' Always haggling and haggling. A man is tired of getting the better before his wife is tired of losing the victory.' *Good-Natur'd Man*, 14. *See* Controversy, and cp. Higgle.

HAND. In phrase ' by the hand of one's body.' *She Stoops*, 166.

HARDCASTLE, MRS. Tony Lumpkin's trick on Mrs. Hardcastle (*She Stoops*, 158-60) was objected to on its first representation as wildly improbable, but a similar imposition had been played on Madame de Genlis by Sheridan. Dr. Birkbeck Hill (*Life of Johnson*, i. 213) considers it possible (and this seems practically certain) that the incidents of Mrs. Hardcastle's drive were suggested by *The Rambler*, No. 34, in which a young gentleman describes a lady's terror on a coach journey : ' Our whole conversation passed in dangers, and cares, and fears, and consolations, and stories of ladies dragged in the mire, forced to spend all the night on a heath, drowned in rivers, or burnt with lightning.'

HARMLESS LITTLE MEN, term applied to children by Mr. Burchell. *Vicar*, 216.

HASPICOL, corrupt form of ' harpsichord ', a stringed instrument with a keyboard. *She Stoops*, 147. See Evelyn's *Diary*, October 5, 1664, ' There was brought a new-invented instrument of music, being a harpsichord with gut strings, sounding like a concert of viols with an organ.'

HAT. 'My hat must be on my head, or my hat must be off.' *Good-Natur'd Man*, 65.

HAWKE. Edward, first Baron Hawke (1705–81), Admiral of the Fleet. He defeated the French off Belle-Ile in 1747, and off Quiberon in 1759. *Good-Natur'd Man*, 41.

HEAD, head-dress; the hair as dressed in some particular manner. ' Pray how do you like this head ? ' *She Stoops*, 121. Cp. Johnson, *Rambler*, No. 191 (1752), ' Ladies asked me the price of my best head.'

HEARTENED, put in good heart, encouraged. ' Heartened by my brother student.' *Vicar*, 319.

HEBE (the personification of eternal youth), Olivia compared with. *Vicar*, 190.

HEDGE-LANE, a narrow but frequented thoroughfare, now Dorset Street. *Good-Natur'd Man*, 67.

HEINEL. Mademoiselle Anna-Frederica Heinel (1752–1808), a famous dancer. *She Stoops*, 170. Horace Walpole wrote : ' There is a finer dancer [than Mademoiselle Guimard], whom Mr. Hobart is to transplant to London ; a Mademoiselle Heinel or Ingle, a Fleming. She is tall, perfectly made, very handsome, and has a set of attitudes copied from the classics ' (*Letters*, viii. 76 : August 25, 1771). See also notes to *Poetical Works*, 221.

HEN. In phrase 'sell one's hen of (or on) a rainy day.' A Scotch proverb: to make a bad bargain. ' I'll warrant we'll never see him sell his hen of a rainy day.' *Vicar*, 256. Lit. 'he will not sell his wares at an unpropitious time' (Hislop). See *English Dialect Dict.*, which cites Kelly's *Scots Proverbs* (1721) 373, and McWard, *Contendings* (1723) 328, ' The Devil is not such a fool as to sell his hen on a rainy day.'

Hermit, The. See *Edwin and Angelina.*

HEYDER ALLY. Haidar Ali, Sultan of Mysore (1717–1782). *She Stoops*, 111. See Macaulay's *Essay on Warren Hastings*, and Walpole's *Letters*, xiii. 27, 38. Haidar Ali dictated peace to England in 1769.

HIGGLE, to haggle over a bargain. 'He always stands out and higgles, and actually tires them till he gets a bargain.' *Vicar*, 254.

HIT, *sb.* (1) a chance, especially a lucky or fortunate chance. ' She was of opinion, that it was a most fortunate hit.' *Vicar*, 213.

HIT, *sb.* (2) in backgammon : 'a game won by a player after his opponent has thrown off one or more men from the board, as distinguished from a *gammon* or a *backgammon*' (O.E.D.). 'I hated all kinds of gaming, except backgammon, at which my old friend and I sometimes took a two-penny hit.' *Vicar*, 194. ' There are two kinds of victory—winning the hit and winning the gammon. The party who has played all his men round into his own table, and by fortunate throws of the dice has borne or played the men off the points first, wins the *hit*. Two hits are reckoned as equal to one gammon in playing matches ' (*Chambers's Information*).

HIT, *v.*, to suit, fit. ' We did not recollect an historical subject to hit us.' *Vicar*, 278.

HOG. ' When she 's with her playmates she 's as loud as a hog in a gate.' *She Stoops*, 124. Cp. similar phrases in O.E.D., s.v. Hog, *sb.* V. 11.

HOIKS (HOICKS), a call used in hunting to incite the hounds. *She Stoops*, 171.

HOLLOW, of sound : not full-toned, sepulchral. ' The deep-mouthed watch-dog at a hollow distance.' *Vicar*, 335.

HOOKER, RICHARD (1554 ?–1600), the divine, author of *Ecclesiastical Polity*; called ' the Judicious '. *Vicar*, 199. See *also* Jewel.

HORATIO, a character in Rowe's *Fair Penitent*. *Vicar*, 306, 323.

HORN, STRAIGHT, a long straight musical instrument such as used by guards on stage-coaches; the post-horn. 'For winding the straight horn . . . he never had his fellow.' *She Stoops*, 99.

HORNPIPE, a dance of English origin, so-called from the instrument to which it was played; all the early hornpipes were in triple time. *Grumbler*, 178. Cp. Spenser, *Shepheardes Calender*, Maye, ll. 22–4:

> Before them yode a lusty Tabrere,
> That to the many a Horne-pype playd,
> Whereto they dauncen, eche one with his mayd.

'Hornpipe, in its present meaning, a step-dance. . . . About 1760 the hornpipe underwent a radical change, for it was turned into common time and altered in character. Miss Anne Catley, Mrs. Baker, Nancy Dawson, and other stage dancers, introduced it into the theatre' (Grove's *Dict. of Music*, ii. 434, ed. 1906).

HORSE, Bishop Jewel's, i.e. his staff. *Vicar*, 199. *See* Jewel.

HORSES, DISEASES OF. *Vicar*, 264. Cp. the Vicar's description of his horse in this passage with the horse on which Petruchio came to his wedding, *Taming of the Shrew*, III. ii. 52: ' Possessed with the glanders and like to mose in the chin; troubled with the lampass, infected with the fashions, full of windgalls, sped with spavins, rayed with the yellows, past cure of the fives, stark spoiled with the staggers, begnawn with the bots, swayed in the back and shoulder-shotten.'

HORSE-STEALING. 'He who deprives the other of his horse shall die.' *Vicar*, 366. Capital punishment for stealing horses, sheep, and other cattle was abolished in 1832 (2 & 3 Will. IV. c. 62).

HORSE-WAY, a way or road by which horses may travel. 'I therefore walked back by the horse-way, which was five miles round, though the foot-way was but two.' *Vicar*, 245. Cp. *King Lear*, IV. i. 58, 'Both stile and gate, horse-way and foot-path.'

HOSPITALITY, Dr. Primrose's views of. *Vicar*, 217.

HOT COCKLES, a rustic game in which one player lay face

downwards, or knelt down with his eyes covered, and being struck on the back by the others in turn, guessed who struck him. *Vicar*, 247. See Gay's *Shepherd's Week, Monday*, 99 :

>   As at hot cockles once I laid me down,
>   And felt the weighty hand of many a clown.

Cp. *Low Life* (1764) 83, ' The felons in Newgate . . . playing at hunt-the-slipper, hot-cockles, and blindman's buff.' The game is still played in Ireland and England, with many variations. See Gomme, *Games* (1894) i. 229. The origin of the name is unknown (it is *not* French).

House, For the good of the. *See* Good.

Humour. ' The public think nothing about dialect, or humour, or character.' *Vicar*, 296. Cp. Goldsmith's Essay on Laughing and Sentimental Comedy : ' Humour at present seems to be departing from the stage, and it will soon happen that our comic players will have nothing left for it but a fine coat and a song ' (*Westminster Magazine*, 1773).

Hunt the Slipper, a children's game, still in vogue. *Vicar*, 247. See Gomme, *Games* (1894) i. 242.

Ideot, so commonly spelt in the eighteenth century. *Good-Natur'd Man*, 23 and *passim*.

Improvements, ' a piece of land improved or rendered more profitable by inclosure, cultivation, the erection of buildings, &c.' (O.E.D.). *She Stoops*, 98 ; *Vicar*, 305. Cp. Twiss, *Tour in Ireland* (1776) 66, ' The gardens (termed *improvements* in Ireland and *policies* in Scotland) are not extensive.'

In case, in the event. *Good-Natur'd Man*, 39, 42. See O.E.D., s.v. Case, *sb.*[1] 10.

In face, to be looking one's best (O.E.D.). ' Am I in face to-day ? ' *She Stoops*, 96.

Inns. ' Sure, you ben't sending them to your father's as an inn ? ' *She Stoops*, 103. The incident on which the plot of the play is based is said to have occurred to Goldsmith when a youth. Travelling to Edgeworthstown he lost his way, and was directed by a wag to the ' best house ' at Ardagh, which turned out to be the squire's. (See Forster's *Life*, Book I, chap. i.) Goldsmith at first called his play ' The Old House a New Inn ', but this title was rejected.

INNS, LANDLORDS OF. ' I desired the landlord, in my usual way, to let us have his company, with which he complied, as what he drank would encrease the bill next morning.' *Vicar*, 199. This custom was not always appreciated by landlords, if we may believe Fielding ; see *Tom Jones*, Book VIII, chap. viii, where he speaks of it as a penance, ' which I have often heard Mr. Timothy Harris, and other publicans of good taste, lament as the severest lot annexed to their calling, namely, that of being obliged to keep cômpany with their guests.'

NAMES OF ROOMS IN. In former days each room of an inn had its own name. ' Pipes and tobacco for the Lamb there. . . To the Dolphin ; quick. . . The Angel has been outrageous this half hour.' *Good-Natur'd Man*, 66. See also *She Stoops*, 134. In 1 *Henry IV*, II. iv, in the Boar's Head Tavern, Eastcheap, rooms are called the ' Half-moon ' and ' Pomgarnet '.

WITH GALLERIES. The gallery at Mr. Hardcastle's house (*She Stoops*, 134) was one of the features which made it look like an inn. Such galleries were formerly common : see *The Old Inns of Old England*, by C. G. Harper (1906). They are now rapidly passing away. ' The George, at Southwark, is the only galleried inn remaining in London. Out of fifty-five inns mentioned in *Pickwick*, only five now survive ' (*Athenaeum*, December 22, 1906). In the *Great Bath Road*, by Mr. Harper (pp. 23, 32), the White Bear, Piccadilly, and the Old Bell, Holborn, are mentioned as still possessing galleries. See Appendix, Note 14.

As to the excellence of old English inns, and the reason thereof, see Macaulay's *History of England*, chap. iii.

INOCULATION, ' originally applied, after 1700, to the intentional introduction of the virus of small-pox in order to induce a mild and local attack of the disease, and render the subject immune from future contagion ' (O.E.D.). ' I vow, since inoculation began, there is no such thing to be seen as a plain woman.' *She Stoops*, 121. Small-pox was greatly dreaded on account of the disfigurement to the face which resulted. Inoculation was introduced into England from Turkey by Lady Mary Wortley Montagu. Its first mention in England seems to have been in the *Philosophical Transactions* for 1714, vi. 88, ' An Account of the procuring of the Small Pox by Incision or Inoculation, as it has for some time been practised at Constantinople.' The progress of inoculation was slow, for in its early days, as Walpole writes, it was 'devoutly opposed' (*Letters*, v. 303). However, by the time of Goldsmith's play the practice had become firmly established, and when Jenner announced the discovery of vaccination in 1798 as an improvement on inoculation, the practice had become fairly general.

INS AND OUTS, those in office and those out of office; the Government and the Opposition with their supporters. *Good-Natur'd Man*, 78. Cp. Chesterfield, *Letter* (1764), 'I believe that there will be something patched up between the *ins* and the *outs*.'

INTAGLIO, a figure cut or engraved into any substance. *Vicar*, 320.

ISLINGTON, a London suburb. *Vicar*, 286. Goldsmith for a time resided at Islington, then quite in the country. The Club of Authors, described in *The Citizen of the World*, met at ' The Broom ' in the same locality.

IZE, dialect form of 'I shall'. 'And so ize go about my business.' *She Stoops*, 106.

IZZARD, old name for the letter *z*, still widely used in the dialects. *She Stoops*, 149. See Johnson's *Dictionary*, Grammar, under Z (ed. 1773), ' Z begins no word originally English; it has the sound, as its name *izzard* or *s hard* expresses, of an *s* uttered with closer compression of the palate by the tongue.' See also *English Dialect Dict.*

JAG-HIRE, an hereditary assignment of land and of its rent as annuity. *Good-Natur'd Man*, 30. 'Urdū *jāgīr*; *jā*, place + *gīr*, holding, holder. An assignment of the king's or government's share of the produce of a district to a person or body of persons, as an annuity, either for private use or for the maintenance of a public (especially military) establishment; also the district so assigned, or the income derived from it' (O.E.D.). See Yule and Burnell, *Hobson-Jobson*, s.v. *jaghire*, ' We believe the traditional stage pronunciation is Jag hire (assonant in both syllables to quag mire).' The word had become familiar to politicians owing to a dispute between Lord Clive and the Court of Directors of the East India Company. Lord Clive wrote a letter to the Proprietors of East-India Stock (see *Universal Museum* for 1764, p. 86), in which he summarizes the case against him as presented by the Directors, and the steps they had taken in stopping payment of his jaghire. A later number of the *Museum* contains ' The Opinion of the Hon. Charles Yorke, touching Lord Clive's Jaghire, taken by the Court of Directors, and read to the General Court of Proprietors, held at Merchant-Taylors-Hall, on Wednesday, May 2 ' (*Universal Museum*, 1764, 248–50).

JERICHO, GO TO. A slang phrase, still in use, indicative of a place far away. *Good-Natur'd Man*, 55. Cp. *Mercurius Aulicus* (1648), ' Let them all go to Jericho, And ne're be seen againe.'

JEWEL, JOHN (1522–71), Bishop of Salisbury. *Vicar*, 199. The story of the ' horse ' given to Hooker by Jewel, as told by Izaak Walton in his *Life of Hooker* (1670), had its counterpart in an incident in Goldsmith's own life. He had sought the hospitality of an old college friend, whose welcome proved none of the kindest, and who was anxious for Goldsmith to quit. ' I have bethought myself of a conveyance for you ; sell your horse, and I will furnish you with a much better one to ride on.' Goldsmith readily grasped at this proposal, and begged to see the nag, on which he led him to his bedchamber, and from under the bed he pulled out a stout oak stick. (See letter from Goldsmith to his mother in Forster's *Life*, vol. i, Appendix B.)

Johnny Armstrong's Last Good Night, an old Border ballad. *Vicar*, 207. See letter from Goldsmith to Hodson, December 27, 1757, ' If I go to the opera where Signora Columba pours out all the mazes of melody, I sit and sigh for Lishoy fireside, and "Johnny Armstrong's Last Good Night" from Peggy Golden.' *See also under* Barbara Allen. For the ballad, see Appendix, Note 17.

JONSON, BEN (1574–1637), poet and dramatist. His plays criticized by Dr. Primrose. *Vicar*, 295–6.

JOSEPH, a long cloak, chiefly worn by women in the eighteenth century. When riding, &c., it was buttoned all down the front, and had a small cape (O.E.D.). ' Olivia would be drawn as an Amazon . . . dressed in a green joseph, richly laced with gold, and a whip in her hand.' *Vicar*, 278.

JUMP WITH, to agree, tally with. *Good-Natur'd Man*, 66.

Keep, to reside, dwell, frequent a particular spot. 'Two of the five [highwaymen] that kept here are hanged.' *She Stoops*, 159. Cp. *Love's Labour's Lost*, IV. i. 101, 'This Armado is a Spaniard, that keeps here in court.'

Kick the Straw. 'Let boys play tricks, and kick the straw.' *Good-Natur'd Man*, 82. The allusion is to Mattocks, the balance-master ; see Cunningham's note to *Citizen of the World*, Letter 21 : 'The exhibitions of Mattocks, the celebrated balance-master, were at this time much run after. Among other tricks he would balance a straw with great adroitness, . . . and now and then he would kick it with his foot to a considerable height and catch it upon his nose, his chin, or his forehead.' Cp. *Citizen of the World*, Letter 45, 'A fellow shall make a fortune by tossing a straw from his toe to his nose.'

Kip, a house of ill fame. 'My business was . . . to assist at tattering a kip, as the phrase was, when we had a mind for a frolic.' *Vicar*, 314. S. Baldwin, in his edition, supplies the following note : 'Tattering a kip : we have never heard this expression in England, but are told that it is frequent among the young men in Ireland. It signifies, beating up the quarters of women of ill fame.'

Knit, to effervesce, form froth, as wine or beer. 'If the gooseberry wine was well knit.' *Vicar*, 277. Cp. *London and County Brewer* (1743), 'Then old Malt-Liquor will knit and sparkle in a glass.'

Knock down for a Song, to call upon one by the knock of a mallet on the table. 'The 'squire is going to knock himself down for a song.' *She Stoops*, 98. Cp. *Essays* ('Descriptions of Various Clubs'), 'My speculations were soon interrupted by the grand, who had knocked down Mr. Spriggins for a song.'

Kute, acute. *Good-Natur'd Man*, 56. *See* 'Cuteness.

Ladies' Club, the Albemarle Street Club for ladies and gentlemen, afterwards 'The Coterie'. *She Stoops*, 136, 165. See Walpole's *Letters*, vii. 381, viii. 117, ix. 161. *See also* Biddy Buckskin, above.

Ladies' Memorandum-book. 'I dressed it myself from a print in the Ladies' Memorandum-book for the last year.' *She Stoops*, 121. Possibly intended for the *Ladies' Complete Pocket Book*, one of the Newbery publications, Part II of which (in **1761**) contained ' A methodical Memorandum Book, disposed in 52 weeks, for keeping a regular account with the greatest ease and propriety of all monies received, paid, lent, or expended, and of all Appointments, Engagements, or Visits that have been made, paid, or received ; and a separate Column for Occasional Memorandums, &c.' This publication was issued 'At the request of several Ladies, eminent for their economy, Price 1s., neatly bound, with Cases for Notes and Letters, and adorned with a Frontispiece of a Lady dressed in the present Fashion.' (Welsh, *A Bookseller of the Last Century*, 249.)

Lady's Magazine. ' Your Ladyship should except . . . your own things in the *Lady's Magazine*. I hope you'll say there's nothing low there.' *Vicar*, 249. The *Lady's Magazine* was started in 1759 by Mr. J. Wilkie, at the Bible in St. Paul's Churchyard. Goldsmith was one of the first contributors, and acted as its editor in 1760, when he raised its circulation to 3,300. See Forster's *Goldsmith*, Book III, chap. iv. There had been previously another *Lady's Magazine* (1749–53), edited by Jaspar Goodwill, of Oxford.

LAMBSWOOL, a drink consisting of hot ale, mixed with the pulp of roasted apples, and sugared and spiced (O.E.D.). *Vicar*, 246–7.

LAND-CARRIAGE FISHERY. ' I know nothing of books ; and yet, I believe, on a land-carriage fishery . . . I can talk my two hours without feeling the want of them.' *Good-Natur'd Man*, 30. This was a topic then engaging some attention ; an article appears in the *Universal Museum* for February, 1764, entitled, ' State of the Project for bringing Fish to London by Land-carriage ; as laid before the Society for the Encouragement of Arts, Manufactures, and Commerce, by Mr. Blake.' Before this the herring fishery had been a matter of discussion. Cp. *The Bee*, November 10, 1759 : ' A few years ago, the herring fishery occupied all Grub Street ; it was the topic in every coffee-house and the burden of every ballad. We were to drag up oceans of gold from the bottom of the sea ; we were to supply all Europe with herrings upon our own terms.' Fish machines for carrying fish by land were established in 1761. See Appendix, Note 7.

LAP-DOG, a lady's. *Vicar*, 288.

LAWS. ' Laws govern the poor, and the rich govern the law.'
Vicar, 303. Cp. *Traveller*, l. 386, ' Laws grind the poor, and rich
men rule the law.'

Laws should reward as well as punish. *Vicar*, 365 seq.
Cp. *Citizen of the World*, Letter 72, ' The English laws punish
vice, the Chinese laws do more, they reward virtue.' *See also*
Penal Laws.

LEGHORN, the philosophical vagabond at. *Vicar*, 322.

LETTER, FOLDING A. ' That sister of mine has some good
qualities, but I could never teach her to fold a letter,' *Good-
Natur'd Man*, 26 ; ' I would fain know who taught Clarissa
to fold a letter thus,' *Grumbler*, 176. Before the days of envelopes
considerable ingenuity was bestowed on the folding of the paper.

LEVELLER, one who would level all differences of position or
rank among men. *Vicar*, 301. ' They have given themselves
a new name, viz. *Levellers*, for they intend to set all things straight,
and raise a parity and community in the kingdom,' MS. News-
letter of November 1, 1647, quoted in O.E.D. See Appendix,
Note 22.

LIBERTY. ' Liberty and Fleet-street for ever.' *She Stoops*,
142. The drunken Jeremy's exclamation is a variation on the
popular cry of the day, ' Wilkes and liberty.'

Dr. Primrose's speech on Liberty. *Vicar*, 300-1. Cp. *The
Traveller*, ll. 335-92. See *Citizen of the World*, Letter 50, ' An
attempt to define what is meant by English Liberty.'

LIBERTY-HALL, a place where one may do as one likes. ' This
is Liberty-hall, gentlemen. You may do just as you please
here.' *She Stoops*, 109.

LIEF, willingly ; as lief = as soon ; still in general use. 'He'd
as lief eat that glass.' *Vicar*, 328. Cp. *Merry Wives of Windsor*,
IV. ii. 117, ' I had as lief bear so much lead.'

LIFE. ' Life at the greatest and best is but a froward child,
&c.' *Good-Natur'd Man*, 15. This thought is taken from
Sir William Temple, *Of Poetry* (1690): ' When all is done, Human
Life is, at the greatest and the best, but like a froward Child,
that must be play'd with and Humor'd a little to keep it quiet
till it falls asleep, and then the Care is over.'

' If we compare that part of life which is to come, by that
which we have past, the prospect is hideous.' *Good-Natur'd*

Man, 15. Repeated from Letter 73 of *The Citizen of the World*, ' Life endeared by age.'

LIGHTSOME, permeated with light, well-lighted. *Vicar*, 218.

LIMNER, an artist, painter. *Vicar*, 277. It has been suggested by Mr. Edward Ford that the allusion is to George Romney (*National Review*, May, 1883). It is said that Romney for some years previous to 1762 had travelled through Yorkshire, painting portraits at a very low price.

LISBON, earthquake at : November 1, 1755. *Good-Natur'd Man*, 58. *See* Earthquake.

LIVING JINGO, a mild oath. *Vicar*, 238. Cp. ' By jingo.'

LLOYD, MISS RACHAEL. *See* Biddy Buckskin.

LOCK-A-DAISY, an exclamation of surprise, in general use ; also written ' lawks-a-daisy '. *She Stoops*, 102.

London Chronicle, The. See *Chronicle*.

London Evening, The, i.e. *The London Evening Post*, dating from 1735. *Vicar*, 299.

LONGITUDE. ' We could as soon find out the longitude.' *She Stoops*, 102. The Government of Queen Anne, by a Bill passed in 1714, had offered £20,000 as a maximum reward for a method that determined the longitude at sea to half a degree of a great circle, or thirty geographical miles. For less accuracy smaller rewards were offered. John Harrison (1693–1776) received £7,500 for his chronometer in 1765, eight years previous to the date of the play. According to Boswell, Zachariah Williams made many attempts to discover the longitude, but failed of success, and Johnson wrote for him a pamphlet entitled, ' An Account of an Attempt to ascertain the Longitude at Sea, by an exact Theory of the Variation of the Magnetic Needle ; with a Table of the Variations of the most remarkable Cities in Europe, from the year 1660 to 1680.' See Boswell's *Life*, i. 301, ed. Birkbeck Hill.

LORETTO. ' Our house may travel through air like the house of Loretto.' *Good-Natur'd Man*, 63. The house of Loretto is in the province of Ancona, eastern Italy. In the interior is the Santa Casa, a famous pilgrimage shrine, reputed to be the veritable house of the Virgin, transplanted by angels from Nazareth, and miraculously set down in Italy on December 10, 1294 (*Century Encyc. of Names*). See Appendix, Note 9.

LOTTERY, 'a publick exposing goods, money, estates, annuities, &c., to be got by any adventurer, who upon paying a certain sum receives a lot or ticket numbered, of which there is commonly a large number, some blanks, some prizes,' Dyche and Pardon's *Dictionary*, ed. 1752. 'I protested I could see no reason for it neither, nor why Mr. Simkins got the ten thousand prize in the lottery and we sate down with a blank.' *Vicar*, 213. Lotteries were formerly a means of raising money on behalf of the State. Cp. *Letters of Junius* (1769) i. 7, ed. 1804, 'If it must be paid by Parliament let me advise the Chancellor of the Exchequer to think of some better expedient than a lottery.'

LOURE, a dance, a kind of jig, or waltz. *Grumbler*, 178. Cp. *Explication of Foreign Words* (1724) 42, '*Loure* is the name of a French Dance, or the Tune thereto belonging, always in Triple Time, and the Movement, or Time, very Slow and Grave.'

LOUVAIN, the philosophic vagabond at. *Vicar*, 319, 321. Goldsmith spent some time at the University of Louvain, at which he is supposed to have taken the degree of Bachelor of Medicine. See Forster's *Life*, Book I, chap. v.

Low (1), not high or elevated in thought or sentiment. 'There's nothing comes out [replied our Peeress] but the most lowest stuff in nature; not a bit of high life among them.' *Vicar*, 249. Goldsmith returns to the same subject in *She Stoops to Conquer*: '*Second Fel.* He never gives us nothing that's low. *Third Fel.* O damn any thing that's low, I cannot bear it.' *She Stoops*, 99. In spite of this sarcasm, Horace Walpole wrote to Mason on March 27, 1773: 'Dr. Goldsmith has written a comedy—no, it is the lowest of all farces. It is not the subject I condemn, though very vulgar, but the execution. The drift tends to no moral, no edification of any kind. The situations, however, are well imagined, and make one laugh, in spite of the grossness of the dialogue, the forced witticisms, and total improbability of the whole plan and conduct. But what disgusts me most is, that though the characters are very low, and aim at low humour, not one of them says a sentence that is natural or marks any character at all. It is set up in opposition to sentimental comedy, and is as bad as the worst of them.' This is in the style of the criticism adopted when *The Good-Natur'd Man* was produced. 'When good Mr. Twitch described his love for humanity, and

Little Flannigan cursed the French for having made the beer threepence-halfpenny a pot, Cooke tells us that he heard people in the pit cry out this was " low " (" language uncommonly low ", said the worthy *London Chronicle* in its criticism), and disapprobation was very loudly expressed.' Forster's *Life*, Book IV, chap. i. Cp. *The Bee*, No. 1, October 6, 1759, where Goldsmith anticipates this criticism: ' Had I been merry, I might have been censured as *vastly low.*'

Low (2), mean, vulgar, disreputable. ' A low paltry set of fellows ' [the company at *The Three Pigeons*]. *She Stoops*, 93.

Low COMEDY, contrasted with genteel or sentimental comedy. *Good-Natur'd Man*, 3 ; *She Stoops*, 87. *See* Low (1), *and* Appendix, pp. 490, 500.

LOW-LIVED, of a low, mean, or disreputable character. *Vicar*, 249.

Low POCKETS, pockets with very little money in them. *Good-Natur'd Man*, 58. Cp. Epigram in *Citizen of the World*, Letter 113: ' 'Twas no defect of your's, but pocket low, Which caused his *putrid kennel* to o'erflow.'

LOYALTY, Dr. Primrose on. *Vicar*, 300 seq. Cp. *The Traveller*, ll. 377–93.

LUD, an exclamation or expletive ; a minced form of ' Lord '. *She Stoops*, 96 and *passim.*

LYING IN STATE, laid out by the undertakers for interment. *Good-Natur'd Man*, 22. For a parallel account to that of old Ruggins, the curry-comb maker, see *Citizen of the World*, Letter 12 : ' When a tradesman dies, his frightful face is painted up by an undertaker, and placed in a proper situation to receive company : this is called lying in state.'

MACCARONI, a fop, a dandy. *She Stoops*, 145. See Goldsmith's Epilogue intended for *She Stoops to Conquer*, but not spoken :

> Ye travell'd tribe, ye macaroni train,
> Of French friseurs and nosegays justly vain.

The O.E.D. says, ' An exquisite of a class which arose about 1760 and consisted of young men who had travelled and affected the tastes and fashions prevalent in continental society. . . .

This use seems to be from the name of the Macaroni Club, a designation probably adopted to indicate the preference of the members for foreign cookery, macaroni being at that time little eaten in England.' In a letter to the Earl of Hertford, Horace Walpole speaks of ' The Maccaroni Club (which is composed of all the young men who wear long curls and spying-glasses) ' : *Letters*, v. 450, ed. 1904. Forster writes, ' Besides red-heeled shoes, the macaronis were distinguished in 1772 by an immense knot of artificial hair behind, a very small cocked hat, an enormous walking-stick with long tassels, and extremely close-cut jacket, waistcoat, and breeches. In the following year a very lofty head-dress was added, and an immense nosegay.' *Life of Goldsmith*, Book IV, chap. x.

MAD DOGS : *Elegy on the Death of a Mad Dog. Vicar*, 286. See also *Good-Natur'd Man*, 59 ; *Vicar*, 313. Cp. *Citizen of the World*, Letter 69, ' The Fear of Mad Dogs ridiculed,' and see note in *Poetical Works*, 212. See Appendix, Note 21, for an amusing description by George Selwyn.

MAN. ' An honest man's the noblest work of God.' *Vicar*, 273. Quoted from Pope's *Essay on Man*, iv. 248.

' Every man's man,' one easily led by others. *Good-Natur'd Man*, 7.

' One's own man,' to be one's own master, to be at one's own disposal. *She Stoops*, 168.

' The greatest object in the universe, says a certain philosopher, is a good man struggling with adversity.' *Vicar*, 391. The philosopher here alluded to is Seneca, whose words had been paraphrased by Pope in the Prologue to Addison's *Cato* :

> No common object to your sight displays,
> But what with pleasure Heav'n itself surveys,
> A brave man struggling in the storms of fate,
> And greatly falling, with a falling state.

' Ecce spectaculum dignum, ad quod respiciat, intentus operi suo, Deus ! Ecce par Deo dignum, vir fortis, cum mala fortuna compositus ! Non video, inquam, quid habeat in terris Iupiter pulchrius, si convertere animum velit, quam ut spectet Catonem, iam partibus non semel fractis, nihilominus inter minas publicas erectum.'—Seneca, *De Providentia*, cap. ii. § 6. The quotation was afterwards put on the title-page of the play, with two lines from Pope ('A brave man, &c.'). Seneca's *Works* were among the books in Goldsmith's sale catalogue.

MANAGER. *See* Colman.

MANETHO, an Egyptian priest of the Sebennytus, who lived in the reign of the first Ptolemy. He wrote a *History of Egypt*, but his work is lost. *Vicar*, 354.

MARCASITE, old name for certain crystallized forms of iron pyrites (*Stanford's Dict.*) ; here, an ornament made of crystallized iron pyrites. *She Stoops*, 130.

MARKET. 'To bring one's face to market,' a proverbial expression : to offer for sale. *She Stoops*, 133. Cp. Rosalind's taunt to Phebe in *As You Like It*, III. v. 60, ' Sell when you can : you are not for all markets.' *See also* Marriage market.

MARLBOROUGH, JOHN DUKE OF (1650–1722). *She Stoops*, 109.

MARRIAGE, LAWS OF. ' We shall soon be landed in France, where even among slaves the laws of marriage are respected.' *She Stoops*, 115. Goldsmith had written against the Marriage Bill of 1753 in the *Citizen of the World*, Letters 72 and 114. But this is generally supposed to be an allusion to the Royal Marriage Act of 1772. See Appendix, Note 13.

Marriage by Popish priest, Olivia's. *Vicar*, 331.

Marriage market. *Vicar*, 288.

Marriage superstition, as to white dress at weddings. *Good-Natur'd Man*, 55.

See also Matrimony *and* Scotch Marriages.

MARRY, an exclamation of surprise or indignation; a corruption of ' Mary ', from a former habit of swearing by the Virgin Mary. *Vicar*, 257.

MARSYAS, FABLE OF. *Vicar*, 218. Marsyas, in Greek mythology, a skilful player on the flute, challenged Apollo to a trial of his skill. The god accepted the challenge, and it was agreed that he who was defeated should be flayed by the conqueror : the victory went to Apollo, who tied his antagonist to a tree and flayed him alive.

MATCHES, matrimonial compacts, proposals of marriage. *Vicar*, 305. Cp. *Twelfth Report Hist. MSS. Commission* (1676) App. v. 28, ' 'Twas a match of his friends and not his owne making.'

composed to accompany the dance; *Ariadne* was an opera by Handel, and the minuet comes at the end of the overture.

MISERY. 'The heights of ambition, and the vale of misery.' *Vicar*, 295.

MODERN ELEGIES compared with old ballads. *Vicar*, 288.

MOLE, metaphor from the. *Vicar*, 218.

MONARCHY, Dr. Primrose on. *Vicar*, 300–3. Cp. *The Traveller*, ll. 393 seq.

Monitor, The. Vicar, 299. *The Monitor, or The British Freeholder*, was a political newspaper claiming the credit of impartiality, and was originally planned by the patriotic Alderman Beckford, the first number appearing on August 9, 1755. See *Catalogue of Early Newspapers in the Hope Collection.*

MONOGAMIST, one who maintains that a clergyman of the Church of England should under no circumstances contract a second marriage. *Vicar*, 193, 266. *See also* Whiston.

MONOGAMY, the principle which forbids second marriages. *Vicar*, 311.

MORAL, moral sentiments. *She Stoops*, 89. Cp. Morality, *and see* Low (1).

MORALITY, a moral. *She Stoops*, 162. Cp. *Citizen of the World*, Letter 48, ' Let us have no morality at present; if we must have a story, let it be without any moral.'

MORICE, to decamp, march off ! *She Stoops*, 129. Cp. Dickens, *Oliver Twist*, ch. viii, ' Now then ! Morrice ! ' Still in use; see *English Dialect Dict.*, s.v. Morris.

MOROCCO, BLACK QUEEN OF. ' Little Flannigan . . . was master of the ceremonies to the black Queen of Morocco, when I took him to follow me.' Elkanah Settle's *Empress of Morocco* was acted March, 1681–2. It was very popular, but its success was due to spectacular display. See Scott's *Dryden*, i. 216; p. 226, ' The height of his ambition is, we know, but to be master of a puppet-show.' Little Flannigan may have appeared in this play, or, as Mr. Austin Dobson suggests, have been employed in a puppet-show on the same theme. Cp. *Essays* (Second Letter on the Coronation), ' To go to Sudrick Fair, to see the Court of the Black King of Morocco, which will serve to please children well enough.'

MOURNING SUIT. ' 'Tis not alone this mourning suit.' *She*

Stoops, 88. A quotation from *Hamlet*, I. ii. 770, ' 'Tis not alone my inky cloak.'

MUFF, a lady's. *She Stoops*, 152 ; *Vicar*, 288. Muffs were formerly used by men, as well as ladies. Cp. *The Bee*, October 13, 1759 (On Dress : St. James's Park) : Miss (addressing her male cousin) : ' I knew we should have the eyes of the Park upon us, with your great wig, so frizzled, and yet so beggarly, and your monstrous muff.' Horace Walpole, in 1764, sent George Montagu a muff (*Letters*, vi. 160).

MUN (1), dialect pronunciation of ' man '. *She Stoops*, 125.

MUN (2), dialect form of ' must '. *She Stoops*, 149.

MURRAIN, an infectious disease among animals. Also used as an imprecation or expression of anger. ' A murrain take such trumpery.' *Vicar*, 257.

MUSIC : playing for subsistence. *Vicar*, 320. This is supposed to be autobiographical. See Forster's *Life*, Book I, chap. v, and cp. *The Traveller*, ll. 239–54.

MUSICAL GLASSES, a musical instrument, consisting of a number of glass goblets, played upon with the end of the finger damped. *Vicar*, 238, 242. See Appendix, Note 19.

NAB, to catch suddenly or unexpectedly, to seize. ' If so be a man's nabb'd.' *Good-Natur'd Man*, 42.

NABOB, a person of great wealth, especially one who has returned from India with a large fortune ; primarily, the title of certain Mahommedan officials. *Vicar*, 242. ' The word *Nabob* began to be applied in the eighteenth century, when the transactions of Clive made the epithet familiar in England, to Anglo-Indians who returned with fortunes from the East ; and Foote's play of *The Nabob* (1768) aided in giving general currency to the word in this sense.' *Hobson-Jobson*, 610.

NAIL, *fig.* to hold or fix down tightly in an argument. *Vicar*, 253.

NAKEDNESS. ' The nakedness of the indigent world may be clothed from the trimmings of the vain.' *Vicar*, 208–9. Cp. Hardcastle in *She Stoops*, 94, where this expression is repeated.

NANCY DAWSON. *See* Dawson.

NEWBERY, FRANCIS (1743–1818). *Vicar*, title-page. Francis Newbery, bookseller, of Paternoster Row, was the first publisher of *The Vicar of Wakefield*, and nephew of John Newbery (q.v.). See Welsh, *A Bookseller of the Last Century*, pp. 118–59 ; and, for particulars as to *The Vicar*, ib. pp. 54–62. See also Appendix, pp. 505–7.

NEWBERY, JOHN (1713–67). ' The philanthropic bookseller in St. Paul's church-yard, who has written so many little books for children.' *Vicar*, 294. John Newbery was uncle of Francis Newbery, the first publisher of *The Vicar of Wakefield*. ' It is not perhaps generally known, that to Mr. Griffith Jones, and a brother of his, Mr. Giles Jones, in conjunction with Mr. John Newbery, the public are indebted for the origin of those numerous and popular little books for the amusement and instruction of children, the Lilliputian histories of Goody Two-shoes, Giles Gingerbread, Tommy Trip, &c., &c., which have ever since been received with universal approbation.' (Nichols's *Literary Anecdotes*, iii. 466.) It was to John Newbery's paper, *The Public Ledger*, that Goldsmith contributed the Letters from a Chinese Philosopher, afterwards published collectively as *The Citizen of the World.* Newbery employed Goldsmith on other subjects, and the tribute in the *Vicar* is not the only one placed to his credit, for, as Forster writes, quoting Cooke, ' it seems to have been a favourite topic with [Goldsmith] to tell pleasant stories of Mr. Newbery, who, he said, was the patron of more distressed authors than any man of his time ' (*Life*, Book III, chap. v). He dealt also in medicine, and was the proprietor of Dr. James's Powder. He was playfully satirized by Johnson in *The Idler*, under the name of ' Jack Whirler ', on account of his bustling energy of manner. A full account of his life and publications will be found in *A Bookseller of the Last Century*, by Charles Welsh (London, 1885).

NEWGATE, a prison in the Old Bailey; before 1815 it was used for felons and debtors. *Vicar*, 309.

NICK, ' to hit, touch lightly ; to perform by some slight artifice used at the lucky moment ' (Todd-Johnson). *She Stoops*, 137. Cp. *The Bee*, October 20, 1759, ' He had, as he fancied, just nicked the time of dinner, for he came in as the cloth was laying.'

NONLY, only, contracted from ' an only '. *She Stoops*, 171. Cp. ' nuncle '.

Numbskulls, blockheads. *She Stoops*, 105, 140. Cp.
Humours of the Fleet (1749) 9, 'Law-loving Numsculls, such as toil
and sweat.'

Nut-burning (or cracking). *Vicar*, 206, 246. This was
a custom in Scotland, Ireland, and the north of England, usually
indulged in on Hallowmas Eve, October 31. It is thus depicted
by Burns in *Halloween* :

> The auld guidwife's well hoordit nits
>> Are round and round divided,
> An' mony lads and lasses fates
>> Are there that night decided :
> Some kindle, couthie, side by side,
>> An' burn thegither trimly ;
> Some start awa', wi' saucy pride,
>> An' jump out-owre the chimlie
>>> Fu' high that night.

Burns remarks in a note : 'Burning the nuts is a famous charm.
They name the lad and the lass to each particular nut, as they
lay them in the fire ; and accordingly as they burn quietly
together, or start from beside one another, the course and the
issue of the courtship will be.' Gay has also written of the
same custom in *The Spell* :

> Two hazel-nuts I threw into the flame,
> And to each nut I gave a sweetheart's name :
> This with the loudest bounce me sore amazed,
> That in a flame of brightest colour blazed ;
> As blazed the nut, so may thy passion grow,
> For 'twas thy nut that did so brightly glow !

Hone says, ' In Ireland, when the young women would know
if their lovers are faithful, they put three nuts upon the bars of
the grates, naming the nuts after the lovers. If a nut cracks
or jumps, the lover will prove unfaithful ; if it begins to blaze
or burn, he has a regard for the person making the trial. If the
nuts, named after the girl and her lover, burn together, they will
be married.' *Every-day Book* (October 31), i. 1410, ed. 1826.
The custom is not mentioned by Hone as practised on Michaelmas
Eve. See the *English Dialect Dict.*, s.v. Nut, for the North
Country practice.

OAF, a simple fellow ; a dolt, blockhead, booby. *She Stoops*, 150. Cp. Gay, *Shepherd's Week* (1714), ' When hungry thou stood'st staring, like an oaf I sliced the luncheon from the barley loaf.'

OBSTROPALOUS, an illiterate form of ' obstreperous ', clamorous, noisy, vociferous. *She Stoops*, 136.

OCELLUS LUCANUS, a Pythagorean philosopher ; he wrote on *The Nature of the Whole* ; but the genuineness of the work is disputed. *Vicar*, 267.

ODDS-BOBS, one of a large number of exclamatory expressions beginning with the word ' odd ', a minced form of ' God '. *Good-Natur'd Man*, 57.

ODSO, an asseveration or exclamation of surprise ; a minced form of ' Godso '. *Good-Natur'd Man*, 56 ; *She Stoops*, 137. Cp. Congreve, *Love for Love* (1695) II. v, ' Odso, let me see : Let me see the Paper.'

OFFER, to present itself, to occur. ' I took shelter . . . in the first ale-house that offered.' *Vicar*, 296.

OLD. ' I love every thing that 's old : old friends, old times, old manners, old books, old wines.' *She Stoops*, 92. So ' Dr. Richard Farmer loved before all things old port, old clothes, and old books ' (*D.N.B.* vol. xviii, p. 215). Cp. also Sir W. Temple, ' I shall conclude with a Saying of *Alphonsus*, Sirnamed the Wise, King of *Aragon*, That among so many things as are by Men possessed or pursued in the Course of their Lives, all the rest are Bawbles, Besides Old Wood to Burn, Old Wine to Drink, Old Friends to Converse with, and Old Books to Read.' Sir William Temple's *Works*, in four volumes, appeared in the auction catalogue for the sale of Goldsmith's books.

OMENS of Olivia and Sophia. *Vicar*, 243.

OTWAY, THOMÁS (1651–1685), poet and dramatist, wrote *Venice Preserved* and *The Orphan*. *Vicar*, 295, 310. Goldsmith is said to have considered Otway the greatest dramatic genius which England had produced after Shakespeare (Prior's *Goldsmith*, ii. 160). *The Orphan* and *Venice Preserved* are two of the very best plays of their time. Otway has been called the founder of the domestic drama, and wrote with so much grace and tenderness that the admiration expressed by Goldsmith is quite natural.

OULD GROUSE. *See* Grouse.

OVERSEEN, betrayed into a fault or blunder ; deceived, mistaken. ' Certain it is, we had all been greatly overseen.' *Vicar*, 279.

OVID'S *Acis and Galatea*, compared with Gay's description of two lovers killed by lightning (see Appendix, Note 18). *Vicar*, 226. Acis, in Greek legend, was a shepherd of Sicily, beloved by Galatea. The happiness of the lovers was disturbed by the jealousy of the Cyclops Polyphemus, who crushed his rival to pieces with a fragment of broken rock.

PACK-HORSE, a horse employed in carrying packs or bundles of goods. *Good-Natur'd Man*, 29. See Macaulay's *History of England*, chap. iii, ' On byroads, and generally throughout the country north of York and west of Exeter, goods were carried by long trains of packhorses, . . . strong and patient beasts, the breed of which is now extinct.'

PADUASOY. A fine rich silk originally manufactured at Padua. *Vicar*, 208.

PAINTED RUINS, the painted scenery of the old Vauxhall Gardens. *Good-Natur'd Man*, 17. See *England's Gazetteer*, s.v. Foxhall (1751), ' In the centre of the area, where the walks terminate, is erected the temple for the musicians, which is encompassed all round with handsome seats, decorated with pleasant paintings, on subjects most happily adapted to the season, place, and company.' Cp. also Dodsley's *London* (1760), ' There are several noble vistas through very tall trees, the spaces between being filled up with neat hedges ; and on the inside are planted flowers and sweet-smelling shrubs. Some terminate by paintings representing ruins of buildings, others a prospect of a distant country, and some of triumphal arches.'

PAINTING. The ' tame correct paintings of the Flemish school' compared with the ' erroneous but sublime animations of the Roman pencil.' *Vicar*, 273. *See* Pictures.

The Vicar's large historical family group. *Vicar*, 278. *See* Limner.

PALED UP, enclosed, fenced ; encompassed. *Vicar*, 366.

PANCAKES AT SHROVE-TIDE, an old-established custom of eating pancakes on Shrove Tuesday which is still generally observed. *Vicar*, 206.

PANDER, a procurer, one who ministers to the lust of others ; a go-between. *Vicar*, 217.

PANTHEON, THE, a bazaar for fancy goods on the south side of Oxford Street, built by James Wyatt, and opened in January, 1772. *She Stoops*, 121. Writing to Sir Horace Mann on April 26, 1771, Horace Walpole speaks of it as follows : ' The new winter Ranelagh in Oxford Road . . . is almost finished. It amazed me myself. The pillars are of artificial *giallo antico*. The ceilings, even of the passages, are of the most beautiful stuccos in the best taste of grotesque. The ceilings of the ball-rooms and the panels painted like Raphael's *loggias* in the Vatican. A dome like the Pantheon, glazed. It is to cost fifty thousand pounds ' (*Letters*, viii. 28–9). Others to praise the Pantheon were Gibbon, and Miss Burney in *Evelina*. Dr. Johnson visited it with Boswell, but considered it inferior to Ranelagh ; see Boswell's *Life*, ed. Birkbeck Hill, ii. 168–9.

PAOLI, PASCAL (1726–1807), a Corsican patriot. *Good-Natur'd Man*, 76. Paoli, after his struggles in Corsica, was fêted in England and became acquainted with Goldsmith, to whom he paid a fine compliment when dining together. ' Monsieur Goldsmith est comme la mer, qui jette des perles et beaucoup d'autres belles choses, sans s'en apperçevoir,' at which Goldsmith was highly pleased. Forster's *Life*, Book IV, chap. xvi.

PARADOXES, of the philosophic vagabond. *Vicar*, 310–11.

PARCEL, an indefinite number, a small company, a ' lot ', now generally used contemptuously. ' We have such a parcel of servants.' *She Stoops*, 134.

PARIS, the philosophic vagabond at. *Vicar*, 320–1. Compare Forster's *Life*, Book I, chap. v.

PASSAY, short for ' passemeasure ', Italian *passamezzo*, a slow dance, apparently a variety of the pavan (O.E.D.). *Grumbler*, 178. Cp. *Twelfth Night*, v. i. 208, ' He's a rogue, and a passy-measures pavin.'

PASSING BELL, ' the bell which rings at the hour of departure, to obtain prayers for the passing soul : it is often used for the bell, which rings immediately after death ' (Johnson). *Good-Natur'd Man*, 12.

PASTE, a composition of pounded rock-crystal melted with

alkaline salts and coloured with metallic oxides, used for making spurious gems. *She Stoops*, 130. Cp. Carey, *Hills of Hybla* (1767) 20, ' Behold her sailing in the pink of taste, Trump'd up with powder, frippery and paste.'

PAT, fit, convenient, suiting exactly. ' Miss Livy's feet seemed as pat to the music as its echo.' *Vicar*, 237. Cp. *Hamlet*, III. iii. 73, ' Now might I do it pat '; *Humours of the Fleet* (1749) 29, ' Whose Applications miss the Purpose pat.'

PATAGONIA, the southernmost portion of South America. *Good-Natur'd Man*, 55.

PATCHED, adorned with patches (q.v.). *Vicar*, 208.

PATCHES, small spots of black silk used to place on the face, either to hide a defect or worn as an additional charm. *Vicar*, 255. This was a fashionable custom in the seventeenth and eighteenth centuries, especially among women. Cp. Lady M. W. Montagu, *Town Eclogues* (1715), ' Hours . . . pass'd in deep debate, How curls should fall, or where a patch to place.'

PATCHINGS, the putting of patches (q.v.) on the face by way of adornment. *Vicar*, 208.

Patient Grissel, the story of. *Vicar*, 216. Grissel, or Griselda, was a character in romance, noted for the way in which she submitted to many cruel ordeals. The subject forms one of the stories in the *Decameron*, and was also told by Chaucer in the *Canterbury Tales* (The Clerk of Oxenford's Tale).

PEACEFUL MANSION, Dr. Primrose's. *Vicar*, 335. Cp. Milton, *Il Penseroso*, ll. 168–9, ' And may at last my weary age Find out the peaceful hermitage.'

PENAL LAWS, Dr. Primrose on. *Vicar*, 366–7. Cp. *Citizen of the World*, Letter 80 : ' Penal laws, instead of preventing crimes, are generally enacted after the commission ; instead of repressing the growth of ingenious villainy, only multiply deceit, by putting it upon new shifts and expedients of practising it with impunity.' *See* Laws.

PENSACOLA, a seaport in Florida. *Good-Natur'd Man*, 49. Pensacola was ceded to Great Britain in 1763; it afterwards reverted to Spain, and passed to the United States in 1821.

PEOPLE, the middle order of mankind. *Vicar*, 302.

PERQUISITE, ' something gained by a place or office over and above the settled wages ' (Johnson) ; a garnish, ' tip '. ' I was apprized [on entering the prison] of the usual perquisite required upon these occasions.' *Vicar*, 353. See, as to this custom, *The Humours of the Fleet* (1749) 16:

> Such the Amusement of this merry Jail,
> Which you'll not reach, if Friends or Money fail:
> For ere its three-fold Gates it will unfold,
> The destin'd Captive must produce some Gold:
> Four Guineas at the least, for diff'rent Fees,
> Compleats your *Habeas*, and commands the Keys.
> Which done, and safely in, no more you're led,
> If you have Cash, you'll find a Friend and Bed;
> But that deficient, you'll but Ill betide,
> Lie in the Hall, perhaps the Common Side.

PERUGINO, PIETRO (1446–1524), his works to be praised. *Vicar*, 321. Perugino was a celebrated Italian painter, and had the distinction of being the master of Raphael. *See* Connoisseurship.

PEWTER PLATTER, a plate or dish made of pewter. 'Tom Twist that spins the pewter platter.' *She Stoops*, 93. Tom Twist, one of the 'choice spirits' of *The Three Pigeons*, may be compared with that member of the Club of Choice Spirits described in the *Essays* who 'sung to a plate which he kept trundling on the edges'.

PHILAUTOS, PHILALETHES, PHILELUTHEROS, PHILANTHROPOS, anonymous writers. *Vicar*, 313. See Goldsmith's Preface to his *Essays* (1765): 'I have seen some of my labours sixteen times reprinted, and claimed by different parents as their own. I have seen them flourished at the beginning with praise, and signed at the end with the names of Philautos, Philalethes, Philelutheros, and Philanthropos.' See Appendix, Note 24.

PHILOSOPHER, A CERTAIN, i.e. Seneca. *Vicar*, 391. *See* Man.

PHILOSOPHIC VAGABOND, history of a. *Vicar*, 308 seq. 'It was common talk at the dinner table of Reynolds that the wanderings of the philosophic vagabond in the *Vicar of Wakefield* had been suggested by his [Goldsmith's] own, and he often admitted at that time, to various friends, the accuracy of special details.' Forster's *Life*, Book I, chap. v. It will be noticed that the Vicar does not mention whether he was altogether satisfied with his son's performances, as narrated by himself.

PHILOSOPHY, the weak consolations of. *Vicar*, 381, 383.

PICKERING, gaol at. *See* Prison *and* Appendix, Note 25.

PICTURES, auctions of, *Vicar*, 321 ; the art of judging and buying, ib. Cp. *Citizen of the World*, Letter 34. *See under* Connoisseurship.

Improving the tints. *Vicar*, 321.

One large historical family piece. *Vicar*, 278-9. *See* Limner.

PIG, the animal or its flesh as an article of food. *She Stoops*, 113. Cp. *Citizen of the World*, Letter 74 : 'Excessively fond of egg-sauce with his pig.' See also *Comedy of Errors*, II. i. 66, ' The pig, quoth I, is burn'd.'

PIMPING, acting as pimp or pander (q.v.). *Vicar*, 314.

PINK, *v.*, ' to work in eyelet holes ; to pierce in small holes ' (Johnson). *Vicar*, 251. Cp. Fuller, *Holy and Profane State* (1642), ' The Turks did use to wonder much at our English men for pinking or cutting their clothes, counting them little better than mad for their pains to make holes in whole cloth.'

PINK OF COURTESY, the 'flower' or finest example of good breeding. *She Stoops*, 150. Cp. *Romeo and Juliet*, II. iv. 61, ' Nay, I am the very pink of courtesy.'

PINK OF PERFECTION, the ' flower ' or most perfect condition of excellence. *She Stoops*, 97.

PINKINGS, the operations of decorating cloth, leather, &c., with holes. *Vicar*, 208.

PINWIRE OF NEWCASTLE. *Vicar*, 393.

PIQUET, a card game played by two persons. *Vicar*, 277.

PITT'LESS STORM. ' To 'bide the pelting of this pitt'less storm.' *Good-Natur'd Man*, 83. Quoted from *King Lear*, III. iv. 29.

PLANTATIONS, settlements in new or conquered countries. ' He only designed to sell me to the plantations.' *Vicar*, 318. Plantations were worked in the eighteenth century by indentured labour or by prisoners transported for felony. Cp. Burke, letter of 1760, ' Will the law suffer a felon sent to the plantations to bind himself for life ? '

POCKET-HOLE, the opening in a garment through which the hand is put into the pocket. *Good-Natur'd Man*, 39 ; *Vicar*, 212, 269. Cp. Johnson, *Idler*, No. 15 (1758), ' She walks with her arms through her pocket-holes.'

POETRY, Roman and English, contrasted. *Vicar*, 226.

PRIVY-COUNSELLOR, a member of the Privy Council, one of the private counsellors of the sovereign. *Good-Natur'd Man*, 11.

PRODIGIOUS, abnormal, out of the common. 'A prodigious family.' *Good-Natur'd Man*, 22.

PROLOCUTOR, one who speaks on behalf of others, a spokesman. 'Olivia undertook to be our prolocutor.' *Vicar*, 248.

PROLOGUES : *Good-Natur'd Man*, 4 ; *She Stoops to Conquer*, 88.

PROPERTIUS, the poor scholar's proposals for a new edition of. *Vicar*, 311.

PROVERBS: As sure as eggs is eggs. *Good-Natur'd Man*, 55.— As loud as a hog in a gate. *She Stoops*, 124.—Good company upon the road is the shortest cut. *Vicar*, 295. Cp. Swift, *The Tripos*, Act III, 'A pleasant companion is as good as a coach.'— We'll never see him sell his hen of a rainy day. *Vicar*, 256. —Women and music should never be dated. *She Stoops*, 135.

PROVIDENCE, kinder to the poor than the rich. *Vicar*, 382.

PRUIN SAUCE. 'Pruin' is an old spelling of 'prune', a dried fruit largely used for eating, dried or stewed. *She Stoops*, 113.

PUBLIC, THE, 'a many-headed monster.' *Vicar*, 323.

Public Ledger, The, a daily newspaper. *Vicar*, 299. The first number was published on January 12, 1760, by John New-bery. Goldsmith was one of the first contributors : his arrange-ment was to write twice a week, and to be paid a guinea for each article. Under this arrangement appeared the famous Chinese Letters. When the series of letters was finished the whole were republished in two volumes, without the author's name, as *The Citizen of the World*. For an account of the establishment of the *Ledger*, see Welsh's *A Bookseller of the Last Century*, pp. 41 seq.

PUFFING QUACK, a boastful pretender to medical skill. *Good-Natur'd Man*, 82. Goldsmith had already treated this subject in the *Citizen of the World*, Letter 45.

PUNISHMENTS, how far efficacious. *Vicar*, 365 seq.

PUPPET-SHOW, an exhibition of puppets, figures representing human beings. 'They would make you look like the court of King Solomon at a puppet-show.' *She Stoops*, 130. Cp. *Essays* (Second Letter on the Coronation), 'I had rather see the Court of King Solomon in all his glory, at my ease in Bartholomew fair.'

PURSE, a fragment of coal or a spark which cracks and flies out of the fire, considered an omen of good fortune. 'The girls themselves had their omens ; . . . purses bounced from the fire.' *Vicar*, 243.   See Brockett, *Glossary of North Country Words* (1846), ' If it is of rounded shape and clinks as it cools it is supposed to be a purse with money in it, and it augurs fortune to the person who picks it up.   If, on the contrary, it is an oblong splinter and emits no sound, it is a " coffin ", and portends evil.' See also the *Connoisseur*, March 13, 1755, vol. iii.

Quatre, four (throw of dice).   *Vicar*, 194.

QUESTIONS AND COMMANDS, the name of a game in which one person addressed ludicrous questions and commands to each member of the company : a popular indoor game in the eighteenth century.   *Vicar*, 247.   Cp. *Spectator*, No. 504, October 8, 1712 (' On trivial Pastimes, capping Verses, Punning, Biting '), ' Of this nature is the agreeable pastime in country halls of cross-purposes, questions and commands, and the like.'

QUICK, JOHN (1748–1831), actor ;   took the part of Post-boy in *Good-Natur'd Man* (p. 6) and Tony Lumpkin in *She Stoops to Conquer* (p. 90).   The latter part had been refused by Woodward, but Quick made it one of the successes of the piece and materially raised his own fortunes.   To show his gratitude to Quick, Goldsmith adapted a translation of Sedley's from Brueys's comedy of *Le Grondeur* and allowed it to be played for the actor's benefit. (See Appendix, p. 505.)   Quick died in 1831, at the advanced age of 83.

QUINCY, JOHN, D.M. (d. 1722).   *She Stoops*, 123.   Dr. Quincy was the author of several medical works in the early eighteenth century, including ' Pharmacopœia officinalis ;   or a compleat English Dispensatory ' (1719), and ' The Dispensatory of the Royal College of Physicians in London ' (1721).

RABBIT (also RABBET), an expletive in general dialect use in the southern and midland counties (*English Dialect Dict.*, s.v. Rabbit, *v.*²).   ' Rabbet me ! '   *Good-Natur'd Man*, 40 ;   *She Stoops*, 157.

RACES, THE.   No doubt those at Doncaster.   *Vicar*, 293.

RAKE'S PROGRESS, the famous series of engravings by Hogarth, issued complete in 1735.   *She Stoops*, 143.

RANELAGH, as a home of fashion, *She Stoops*, 120 ;   compared

requisite another bore my nostrils ? Riddle me that.' Dryden, *Juvenal*, ' Riddle me this; and guess him, if you can, Who bears a nation in a single man ? ' (Todd.)

RIGADON (usually Rigadoon), a lively dance for two persons. *Grumbler*, 178. Cp. Eliza Heywood, *Betty Thoughtless* (1751) i. 85, ' The gentleman commoner . . . led her some steps of a minuette, then fell into a rigadoon.'

RINGS IN THE CANDLE, a superstition indicative of an approaching marriage. *Vicar*, 245.

Robinson Crusoe : Controversy on religion with Friday the savage, *Vicar*, 224 ; Robinson's long-boat, ib. 279.

RORATORIO, a perverted form of ' oratorio '. *She Stoops*, 170. The *Dialect Dictionary* cites ' roratory ' from Baker's *Glossary of Northamptonshire Words* ; and the same form also appears in ' *The Ragged Uproar*, or, The Oxford Roratory ; a new Dramatic Satire. . . . In many Scenes and one very long Act.'

ROSE AND TABLE CUT THINGS (spoken of jewels). *She Stoops*, 130. Rose cut = cut with a smooth, round surface, as distinguished from jewels which have numerous facets; table cut = cut with a flat surface.

ROUND, by a circuitous or round-about course. ' The horseway . . . was five miles round, though the footway was but two.' *Vicar*, 245.

ROUND-ABOUT, a kind of round or ring dance. *Vicar*, 237. ' Any dance in which the dancers stood in a circle was formerly called a round or roundel ' : Grove's *Dict. of Music*, s.v. Round, iv. 166, ed. 1908.

ROWE, NICHOLAS (1673–1718), dramatist and poet. Out of fashion, *Vicar*, 295 ; his *Fair Penitent*, ib. 305.

ROYAL MARRIAGE ACT. See Appendix, Note 13.

RUB, a hardship, misfortune, reverse. ' Those little rubs which Providence sends to enhance the value of its favours.' *Vicar*, 189. Cp. Bunyan, *Pilgrim's Progress*, Part II, ' We have met with some notable rubs already, and what are yet to come we know not.'

RUE, a plant of a fetid odour and an acrid taste (*Ruta graveolens*). *Good-Natur'd Man*, 12.

RUFFLINGS, adornments with frills and ruffles. *Vicar*, 208.

RUGGINS, the curry-comb maker. *Good-Natur'd Man*, 22. *See* Lying in state.

smith's views on runaway marriages are set out at length in an essay on 'A Register of Scotch Marriages' which originally appeared in the *Westminster Magazine*, February, 1773. See also Appendix, Note 8.

SCRUBS, dirty, untidy persons, hence persons of inferiority. *Vicar*, 244. Cp. *The Bee*, October 13, 1759 : 'I [observed] that there was no company in the Park to-day. To this she readily assented ; "and yet," says she, "it is full enough of scrubs of one kind or another." '

SEEDY, shabby, in poor condition. *Good-Natur'd Man*, 39.

SENECA ('a certain philosopher'). *Vicar*, 391. *See under* Man.

SENSIBILITY, susceptibility to impressions of emotion or feeling. 'I applauded my perseverance and address at thus giving sensibility to wretches divested of every moral feeling.' *Vicar*, 364. Cp. *Citizen of the World*, Letter 27, 'My addresses to her aunt would probably kindle her into sensibility.'

SENTIMENTAL, artificially or affectedly tender. '*Miss Hard-castle*. Was there ever such a sober sentimental interview ? I'm certain he scarce look'd in my face the whole time.' *She Stoops*, 120. Cp. Chaucer, *Legend of Good Women*, l. 69, 'But helpeth, ye that han conning and might, Ye lovers, that can make of sentement.' This appears to be the earliest known use of the word in English. See also *Poetical Works*, Appendix B.

SENTIMENTAL COMEDY. *Good-Natur'd Man*, 3 ; *She Stoops*, 87. 'Sentimental Comedy in its very name confesses itself a contradiction in terms' (*Athenaeum*). See Goldsmith's Essay, 'Sentimental and Laughing Comedy,' originally contributed to the *Westminster Magazine* : 'Which deserves the preference— the weeping sentimental comedy so much in fashion at present, or the laughing, and even low comedy, which seems to have been last exhibited by Vanbrugh and Cibber ? '

SENTIMENTALS, SENTIMENTS, artificial expressions of emotion or feeling. *She Stoops*, 88.

SET IN CASE, to set in due order, put a case before one. *Good-Natur'd Man*, 39, 42.

SHABBAROON, LADY. *Good-Natur'd Man*, 27.

SHAGREEN CASES. Shagreen is a species of leather or parchment prepared without tanning ; formerly much used for cases for spectacles, &c. *Vicar*, 257.

SHAKE-BAG CLUB. ' The gentlemen of the Shake-bag Club has cut the gentlemen of the Goose-green quite out of feather.' *She Stoops*, 149. A ' shake-bag' was a game-cock of the largest size. See Smollett, *Humphry Clinker* (1771) 70, ed. 1905, ' I would pit her for a cool hundred,' cried Quin, ' against the best shake-bag of the whole main.' Cp. Pegge, *Mem. on Cock-fighting*, in *Notes and Queries* (1882) 6th S. vi. 543, ' The excellency of the broods at that time consisted in their weight and largeness, . . . and of the nature of what our sportsmen call shakebags or turnpokes.'

SHAKESPEAR, WILLIAM (1564-1616). *Vicar*, 238 ; his plays criticized by Dr. Primrose, ib. 295. Cp. *Enquiry into the Present State of Polite Learning*, 58-9, where similar adverse criticisms are passed.

SHAKING PUDDING, a jelly or white-pot. *She Stoops*, 113.

SHARP, smart, able to act for oneself. *Vicar*, 277.

SHARPER, a trickster, swindler, cheat. *Vicar*, 315, 362.

SHAVED, fleeced, pared close. *Good-Natur'd Man*, 57.

She Stoops to Conquer. This title is probably a reminiscence of Dryden's line, ' But kneels to Conquer, and but stoops to Rise.' See Miss Hardcastle's speech, page 146, and with this speech compare Horace Walpole's criticisms : ' Stoops indeed !—so she does, that is the Muse ; she is draggled up to the knees, and has trudged, I believe, from Southwark Fair ; . . . the heroine has no more modesty than Lady Bridget ' (*Letters*, viii. 261-2). See Appendix, pp. 499 seq.

SHREDDING, the act of trimming oneself out. ' I do not know whether such flouncing and shredding is becoming even in the rich.' *Vicar*, 208.

SHRILLING, ear-piercing. *Vicar*, 335.

SHRUG, *sb.* (1) Traditional shrugs on the stage. *Vicar*, 323. (2) As a passport to fashionable society. *Good-Natur'd Man*, 83. Cp. *Citizen of the World*, Letter 34, ' A well-timed shrug, an admiring attitude, and one or two exotic tones of exclamation, are sufficient qualifications for men of low circumstances to curry favour.'

SHRUG, *v.* ' I have known a piece, with not one jest in the whole, shrugged into popularity.' *Vicar*, 296. *See* Shrug, *sb.* (2).

SHUTER, EDWARD (d. 1776), actor. The original Croaker in

the *Good-Natur'd Man* and the original Hardcastle in *She Stoops to Conquer*. What success the first-named play enjoyed was primarily due to Shuter, who threw himself with zest into the part of Croaker. As Forster says, ' The comedy was not only trembling in the balance, but the chances were decisively adverse, when Shuter came on with the " incendiary letter " in the last scene of the fourth act, and read it with such inimitable humour that it carried the fifth act through' (*Life of Goldsmith*, Book IV, chap. i). He is humorously alluded to in Garrick's Prologue (p. 88) as ' Poor Ned '.

SHY-COCK, one who eludes capture. *Good-Natur'd Man*, 40. Cp. Smollett, *Humphry Clinker* (1771) 79, ed. 1905, ' The doctor, being a shy cock, would not be caught with chaff.'

SIDE-BOX, a box or enclosed seat on the side of a theatre. *Good-Natur'd Man*, 17 ; *She Stoops*, 121. As a rule, the gentlemen sat in the side-boxes, the ladies in the front box. It was from a side-box that Dr. Johnson witnessed the latter play on the opening night. See Forster's *Life of Goldsmith*, Book IV, chap. xv, quoting from Cumberland's *Memoirs* : ' All eyes were upon Johnson, who sat in a front row of a side-box ; and when he laughed everybody thought themselves warranted to roar.'

SINEW, to knit together. ' Serve to sinew the state in times of danger.' *Vicar*, 367. Cp. 3 *Henry VI*, II. vi. 91, ' So shalt thou sinew both these lands together.'

SINK, to consign to perdition. *Good-Natur'd Man*, 29.

SLAVES, transportation as. *Vicar*, 317. *See* Plantations.

SMOCK-RACE, a race run by women for a chemise, or by women in their chemises. *Vicar*, 244. This custom is recorded in the *English Dialect Dict.* for Northumberland, West Yorkshire, and North-East Lancashire. Brockett, *North Country Glossary* (1846) says, ' These races were frequent. . . . The prize, a fine Holland chemise, was usually decorated with ribbons.'

SMOKE, to detect, observe ; to quiz. ' Smoke the pocket-holes.' *Good-Natur'd Man*, 39. ' " Very well, Sir," cried the 'Squire, who immediately smoked him.' *Vicar*, 221.

SOAK, to saturate oneself with drink. *Vicar*, 328.

SONGS AND BALLADS :

 Ally Croaker. *She Stoops*, 111.

 Cruelty of Barbara Allen. *Vicar*, 207.

SONGS AND BALLADS (*continued*):

Death and the Lady. *Vicar*, 286.

*Elegy on the Death of a Mad Dog. *Vicar*, 286.

*Hermit of the Dale (Edwin and Angelina). *Vicar*, 227.

Johnny Armstrong's Last Good Night. *Vicar*, 207 (*512).

The Dying Swan. *Vicar*, 286.

*The Three Jolly Pigeons. *She Stoops*, 98.

Water Parted. *She Stoops*, 99.

*When lovely woman stoops to folly. *Vicar*, 346.

* Words are given in the text.

SONGS, as sung at Ranelagh. *Vicar*, 288.

SOUND, a swoon. ' My lady fell into a sound.' *Vicar*, 248. Cp. Spenser, *Faerie Queene*, VI. I. xxxiv. 2, ' Whiles yet his foe lay fast in senceless sound.' This form still survives in several districts ; see *English Dialect Dict.* It may be worth noting that ' swoon' is given in the first edition ; ' sound ' in the second —perhaps in order to emphasize the vulgarity of Miss Carolina Wilhelmina Amelia Skeggs.

SOUSED, immersed, pickled. ' The poor devil soused in a beer-barrel.' *She Stoops*, 142.

SPADILLE, the ace of spades, the first trump at Ombre. *She Stoops*, 170 (Epilogue). See Pope, *Rape of the Lock*, ed. Holden (1909), pp. 94 seq.

SPARK, a lover, beau, gallant. *She Stoops*, 130.

SPAVIN, a disease in horses, affecting the hock-joint, or joint of the hind-leg, between the knee and the fetlock. *Vicar*, 264.

Sperate miseri, &c. Motto on title-page of the *Vicar*. These words form the concluding sentence of Burton's *Anatomy of Melancholy* :—

' SPERATE MISERI,

CAVETE FOELICES.

Vis à dubio liberari ? vis quod incertum est evadere ? Age poenitentiam dum sanus es ; sic agens, dico tibi quod securus es, quod poenitentiam egisti eo tempore quo peccare *potuisti*.—AUSTIN.'

SPORTERS, sportsmen. *Vicar*, 405.

SPORTSMAN, the Chaplain as. *Vicar*, 234. Perhaps the Chaplain, who thus shot a blackbird, was but a beginner in the ' Art of Shooting Flying ', and taking a few shots at birds outside the strict definition of ' game' for the sake of practice.

SPUNGING-house, a house or tavern where persons arrested for debt were lodged for twenty-four hours, to allow their friends an opportunity of paying the debt. *Good-Natur'd Man*, 3. Cp. *Humours of the Fleet* (1749) 11, ' Seiz'd and hurried to a Spunging-House, Where, when they've fleec'd your Purse of ev'ry Souce,' &c.

SPUNK, spark, spirit, mettle ; ' a low and contemptible expression ' (Johnson). ' The 'squire has got spunk in him.' *She Stoops*, 99.

SQUARE, the ' philosopher ' in Fielding's *Tom Jones* (see Book III, chap. iii). *Vicar*, 224. *See* Disputation. The original of Square is said to have been one Chubb, a deist, of Salisbury ; see Mr. Austin Dobson's *Fielding*, 135.

SQUIBS, fireworks ; when ignited the squib throws out a train of fiery sparks, and bursts with a crack. *Vicar*, 406.

SQUILACHI, Marquis of, Prime Minister at Madrid (1766). *Good-Natur'd Man*, 76. Great riots had taken place at Madrid in 1766, in consequence of an attempt to prevent the wearing of slouched hats and long cloaks. Squillaci, an Italian, was supposed to be at the bottom of the trouble, and he was banished by the King. See Walpole's *Letters* (April 6, 1766), vi. 448-9.

'SQUIRE, a contraction of ' esquire ', a title popularly given to a country gentleman. *She Stoops*, 149 and *passim*.

STAGE, traditional shrugs on the. *Vicar*, 323. Cp. *Citizen of the World*, Letter 21, ' I hate to hear an actor mouthing trifles ; neither startings, strainings, nor attitudes affect me, unless there be cause.' See also ' On our Theatres ', in *The Bee*, October 13, 1759 ; and *An Enquiry into the Present State of Polite Learning*, chap. xii.

STANISLAUS. *See* Poniatowski.

STANTON HARCOURT, Inscription at. *See* Appendix, Note 18.

STINGO, a cant name for a landlord. *She Stoops*, 102.

STIVER (Dutch *stuiver*), a small silver coin, worth one-twentieth part of a Dutch gulden, or one penny in English money. *Vicar*, 405.

STOMACHER, an ornamental covering for the breast, forming part of a lady's dress. *Vicar*, 278.

STROLLING COMPANY, itinerant players, travelling about from place to place. *Vicar*, 295, 305, 323. Cp. Dickens, *Pickwick Papers*, chap. iii, ' " He is a strolling actor," said the lieutenant, contemptuously.' Notwithstanding the contempt in which their calling was held, many notable actors and actresses first made their reputations as members of strolling companies. See also Goldsmith's essay, ' Adventures of a Strolling Player.'

STUCK UP, exhibited. ' I shall be stuck up in caricatura in all the print-shops.' *She Stoops*, 145.

SUSSARARA, a violent scolding; a severe blow; a dialect corruption and use of the legal term ' certiorari ' (*English Dialect Dict.*, s.v. Siserary). ' Gentle or simple, out she shall pack with a sussarara.' *Vicar*, 328. Cp. Smollett, *Humphry Clinker* (1771) 90, ed. 1905, ' I have gi'en the dirty slut a siserary.'

SWATH, a line of grass or corn cut down by the mower. *Vicar*, 217. For a full article on this word, see Prof. Skeat's *Etymological Dictionary of the English Language*, where it is dealt with at length.

SWEETING, a term of endearment, ' sweetheart.' *Good-Natur'd Man*, 24. Cp. *Twelfth Night*, II. iii. 43–4, ' Trip no further, pretty sweeting; Journeys end in lovers meeting.'

SYMPATHY, UNIVERSAL. *Vicar*, 202.

TABERNACLE. ' I believe she [Mrs. Croaker] could spread an horse-laugh thro' the pews of a tabernacle.' *Good-Natur'd Man*, 20. Possibly Goldsmith had in his mind Whitefield's new tabernacle in Tottenham Court Road, erected in 1756 and enlarged in 1759. Cp. Goldsmith's Essay on ' Laughing and Sentimental Comedy ' : ' It depends upon the audience whether they will actually drive these poor merry creatures from the stage, or sit at a play as gloomy as at the Tabernacle.' See Appendix, Note 6.

TABOR, a small shallow drum, used to accompany the pipe. *Vicar*, 237.

TAFFETY CREAM, a dish so called from its resemblance to taffeta, or taffety, a light glossy silk. *She Stoops*, 113. Cp. *taffety*, dainty (*English Dialect Dict.*).

TAKE, understand. ' You take me.' *She Stoops*, 154.

TATTERING A KIP. *See* Kip.

TEA. ' Here too we drank tea, which was now become an occasional banquet.' *Vicar*, 210. At Newbery's Tea Warehouse, c. 1761, a small parcel of tea was advertized for sale at 36s. per lb.

TEIZE, an old spelling of ' tease '. *She Stoops*, 115.

TEMPLE, SIR WILLIAM. *See under* Life ; Old.

TÊTE, false hair, a kind of wig worn by ladies. *She Stoops*, 121.

TÊTE-À-TÊTE. See under *Scandalous Magazine*.

THESES, in foreign Universities and convents. *Vicar*, 323.

THIEFTAKER, one who catches thieves. *Vicar*, 360. ' Dundas left thief-takers in Horne Tooke's house for three days,' S. T. Coleridge in note to Poem on ' Verses addressed to J. Horne Tooke'.

THINGS, i.e. things in general, as the sights of the town. *Good-Natur'd Man*, 18.

Thomas Trip, the history of. *Vicar*, 294. One of the books for children published by the philanthropic publisher, John Newbery. The first edition was published in 1762, the ninth in 1767. The title of the latter edition runs : ' A Pretty Book of Pictures for little Masters and Misses ; or Tommy Trip's History of Beasts and Birds, with a familiar description of each in Verse and Prose, to which is prefixed the history of little Tom Trip himself, of his dog Jowler, and of Woglog the great Giant.' This little book has been attributed to Goldsmith himself.

THORNHILL, SIR WILLIAM (' Mr. Burchell '), a type of universal benevolence. *Vicar*, 202-3. Prior passes the following criticism : ' About Sir William Thornhill there is a coldness that wins little of our regard ; possessed of power, wealth, and reputed benevolence, he takes no steps to assist a worthy and benevolent man struggling with poverty, whose hospitality he enjoys, and to whose daughter he exhibits attachment, but leaves the family to the machinations of his nephew, in consequence of an error on their part, arising, as he must have understood, from justifiable indignation towards him whom they conceived guilty of treachery and ingratitude. His disguise near his own estates cannot be reconciled with probability. Neither can we believe that one so avowedly virtuous would entrust a large portion of his fortune to a nephew capable of appropriating it to the worst purposes, and of whose character he could not, from previous admissions and the report of the country, be ignorant.' *Life of Goldsmith* (1837) ii. 114. Mr. Ford (*National Review*, May, 1883) says that the prototype of this character may have been Sir George Savile, M.P. for the county of York, at once a soldier, a statesman, a philanthropist, and eccentric. It is a singular coincidence that Thornhill, six miles from Wakefield, was the former estate and residence of the Saviles.

THORNHILL CASTLE. *Vicar*, 271. Mr. Edward Ford (*National Review*, May, 1883) suggests that Helmsley is intended.

THREE PIGEONS, THE, an alehouse. *She Stoops*, 98-9 and *passim*. The scene in Act I should be compared with a similar gathering of Choice Spirits in Goldsmith's 'Description of Various Clubs' (*Essays*). See Appendix, Note 11.

Three Jolly Pigeons. 'I'll sing you, gentlemen, a song I made upon this alehouse, the Three Pigeons.' *She Stoops*, 98. There is something anomalous in Tony Lumpkin claiming the authorship of this song, when he has been represented as being so illiterate as to be unable to write his own name, and whose incapacity to read a letter in Act IV is so amusingly illustrated. But, as Mr. Austin Dobson writes, 'It was of himself, not Tony Lumpkin, that he [Goldsmith] was thinking, when he attributed to that unlettered humourist the composition of the excellent drinking song' (*Life of Goldsmith*, p. 27: Great Writers). It is on record that Goldsmith sang this song (in April, 1773) at General Ogle-thorpe's, in company with Johnson, when drinking tea with the ladies; see Boswell's *Johnson*, ii. 219, ed. Birkbeck Hill.

THUMB, RULE OF. *See* Rule.

THUNDER AND LIGHTNING : of cloth that is loud and striking in appearance. *Vicar*, 254.

THWACKUM, a disputatious character in Fielding's *Tom Jones* (see Book III, chap. iii). *Vicar*, 224. *See* Disputation. The original of Thwackum is said to have been one Hele, a school-master of Salisbury; see Mr. Austin Dobson's *Fielding*, 135.

To, used to denote motion towards. 'I'll visit to his Grace's.' *Good-Natur'd Man*, 46.

To A T, said of anything closely resembling another. *She Stoops*, 122.

TOBACCO-STOPPER, a little plug for pressing down the burning tobacco in the bowl of a pipe ; a pipe-stopper. *Vicar*, 365, 405. Cp. *Citizen of the World*, Letter 90, 'I shaped tobacco-stoppers, wrote verses, and cut paper.' For pipe-stoppers, see an article in *The Connoisseur* for June, 1909, illustrated by examples from the Collection of Colonel Horace Gray, V.D. Cp. Boswell's poem on the subject; Will Wimble, Sir Roger de Coverley's friend, was, we are there told, the champion collector. His fame is to be found in the *Spectator*, Nos. 108, 119, 122, 126, 131, 269, 329.

Tom Twist, that spins the pewter platter. *She Stoops*, 93. *See also* Pewter Platter.

Top-knot, an ornamental knot or bow worn on the top of the head by women. *Vicar*, 237.

Touch off, to get the better of, overcome. ' I knew you would touch them off.' *Vicar*, 256.

Touchstone, any test or criterion by which qualities are tried. ' I was resolved therefore to bring him to the touchstone.' *Vicar*, 267.

Tower Wharf, in the City, contiguous to the Tower of London. *She Stoops*, 120.

Train, that part of a gown which trails behind the wearer. ' Their trains bundled up in an heap behind.' *Vicar*, 208. Cp. *Citizen of the World*, Letter 81, ' What chiefly distinguishes the sex at present is the train. . . . Women of moderate fortunes are contented with tails moderately long, but ladies of true taste and distinction set no bounds to their ambition in this particular. . . . And yet, to think that all this confers importance and majesty ! to think that a lady acquires additional respect from fifteen yards of trailing taffety ! '

Transport, effusive joy. *Vicar*, 307, 406, 408. The lines on p. 407, ' And shook their chains In transport and rude harmony,' are from Congreve's *Mourning Bride*, Act i, Sc. ii.

Trapesing, slatternly. *She Stoops*, 101.

Trim, attire, clothing. ' If we walk to the church in this trim.' *Vicar*, 208.

Trolloping, slatternly, untidy. ' The daughter, a tall, trapesing, trolloping, talkative maypole.' *She Stoops*, 101. From *trollop*, a slattern. See Milton, *Apology for Smectymnuus*, § 6, ' His old conversation among the viraginian trollops.'

True-love-knot, a double knot, made with two bows on each side interlacing each other, an emblem of affection. *Vicar*, 206, 243. Cp. Herrick, ' I tell of Valentines, and true-loves-knots, Of omens, cunning men, and drawing lots.'

Trumpery, anything of little account ; here spoken of a worthless character. *Vicar*, 329.

TRUTH. 'I'll lay down my life for the truth,' the motto of Rousseau. *She Stoops*, 161. See *Rambler*, No. 34.

TURN'D OFF, to be hanged, executed as a criminal. *Good-Natur'd Man*, 10.

TWO-PENNY HIT, in backgammon. *Vicar*, 194. *See* Hit, *sb.* (2).

TYBURN, a celebrated gallows or public place of execution at the foot of Edgware Road. *Good-Natur'd Man*, 10 ; *Vicar*, 397. See Forster's *Life of Goldsmith*, Book III, chap. xiii : ' An execution came round as regularly as any other weekly show. . . . Men, not otherwise hardened, found here a debasing delight. George Selwyn passed as much time at Tyburn as at White's ; and Mr. Boswell had a special suit of execution-black, to make a decent appearance near the scaffold.' Cp. Johnson's *London*, lines 238-9 :

> Scarce can our fields, such crowds at Tyburn die,
> With hemp the gallows and the fleet supply.

TYRANNY, Dr. Primrose on. *Vicar*, 300. Cp. *The Traveller*, ll. 361 seq.

UNDER-GENTLEMEN, gentlemen of inferior rank. ' We found our landlord, with a couple of under-gentlemen and two young ladies.' *Vicar*, 236.

UNDERSTRAPPERS, subordinates, inferiors ; literally a variant of ' under-spurleathers ' (Swift). *Good-Natur'd Man*, 31.

UNIVERSITIES AND CONVENTS, FOREIGN, philosophical theses maintained at. *Vicar*, 323.

UNTUTORED NATURE, i.e. untaught, obeying the dictates of nature only. *Vicar*, 366.

UPO', upon, denoting contiguity. ' They have lost their way upo' the forest.' *She Stoops*, 100. Cp. Richardson, *Sir Charles Grandison* (1754), Letter 25, ed. 1896, ' Sir Hargrave . . . has a house upon the Forest.'

URCHIN, a familiar, half-chiding name, usually addressed to a child. *Good-Natur'd Man*, 35.

USHER, the miserable life of an. *Vicar*, 309-10. Forster says : ' There is a dark uncertain kind of story, of [Goldsmith] getting a bare subsistence in this way [as an usher] for some few months, under a feigned name' (*Life*, Book I, chap. vi). In 1757 Goldsmith became an assistant at Dr. Milner's academy at Peckham. It may have been these incidents in his career which supplied the bitter experiences narrated by George Primrose, and of which Goldsmith had written previously in a like strain in *The Bee* (November 10, 1759): 'Every trick is played upon the usher; the oddity of his manners, his dress, or his language, is a fund of eternal ridicule; the master himself, now and then, cannot avoid joining in the laugh; and the poor wretch, eternally resenting this ill-usage, seems to live in a state of war with all the family.'

VAGABOND, A PHILOSOPHIC. *See* Philosophic Vagabond.

VALENTINE MORNING, love-knots on. *Vicar*, 206. *See also* True-love-knots.

VARLET, a term of contempt, a rascal, 'ne'er-do-weel'. *She Stoops*, 162.

VARMENT, a corruption of 'vermin', and often applied contemptuously to troublesome persons. *She Stoops*, 157.

VAUXHALL GARDENS, its painted ruins. *Good-Natur'd Man*, 17. *See* Painted Ruins. Vauxhall, situate on the Surrey side of the Thames, had been a place of public resort since the time of Charles II, continuing as a place of fashionable amusement nearly to the end of the reign of George III. A description by Goldsmith of a visit to Vauxhall will be found in the *Citizen of the World*, Letter 71.

VICAR'S FAMILY, THE: (1) *George* (bred at Oxford); (2) *Olivia*; (3) *Sophia*; (4) *Moses* (designed for business); (5) Two sons more (*Dick* and *Bill*). *Vicar*, 189–90.

VICES, opposed to virtues. *Vicar*, 273–4.

WAGES, dissatisfaction as to. *Good-Natur'd Man*, 10.

WAKEFIELD, three strange wants at. *Vicar*, 193. As to the locality of the story, Prior remarks: 'The reason for fixing the scene near Wakefield, is said [by Cradock, in his *Memoirs*] to have arisen from an excursion made into Yorkshire about the period at which it was written; with what view we are unacquainted; but there is reason to believe he spent some months in that county at some previous period. . . . The name of the vicarage is probably fanciful, but by a curious coincidence it has been ascertained from contemporary statements, that the daughter of the actual Vicar of Wakefield, the Rev. Dr. W., married about this period a Captain M., of the militia, without, it is said, having obtained the parental sanction ; hence rumour induced a suspicion, unfounded no doubt, that with such additions as imagination supplied he had touched upon circumstances in real life.' *Life of Goldsmith* (1837) ii. 116. See Appendix, p. 508.

WALLER, EDMUND (1605–1687), the poet. *Good-Natur'd Man*, 29.

WALL-EYED, having an eye the iris of which is streaked, parti-coloured, or different in hue from the other eye ; squinting. *Vicar*, 245.

WAR. ' Like one of those instruments used in the art of war, which, however thrown, still presents a point to receive the enemy.' *Vicar*, 348. The implement called a caltrop is here intended. *Caltrap*, M.E. *calk-*, *kalketrappe* ; also O.E. *colte-træppe*, &c. Orig. perhaps *chauche-trappe* (Littré) ; possibly in *calcitrappe* an association with *calcare*, to tread. The word presents many difficulties.

WARM, in comfortable circumstances, well-to-do, moderately wealthy. A warm man, *Vicar*, 268, 281 ; a warm fortune, ib. 280.

WARWICK-LANE. ' To-night I head our troops in Warwick-lane.' *Good-Natur'd Man*, 82. A reference to a dispute between the Fellows and Licentiates of the College of Physicians. See notes to *Poetical Works*, 215.

WASH, a liquid used for toilet purposes. *Vicar*, 219, 241.

WASTE, UPON THE, extravagant. *Good-Natur'd Man*, 10.

Water Parted, a song in Arne's opera of *Artaxerxes*, produced in 1762. *She Stoops*, 99.

WAUNS, a contracted form of ' God's wounds ', used as an oath or exclamation. *She Stoops*, 105. See Wound, *English Dialect Dict*.

WEALTH, ACCUMULATION OF, Dr. Primrose on. *Vicar*, 301–2. Cp. *The Deserted Village*, ll. 51–2, ' Ill fares the land, to hast'ning ills a prey, Where wealth accumulates, and men decay.' Goldsmith expresses an opposite view in the *Citizen of the World*, Letter 11.

WEASEL-SKIN PURSE, as token of good luck. *Vicar*, 255. This belief is said to be current in King's Co. and Westmeath, Ireland.

WELBRIDGE FAIR: Moses's bargain at, *Vicar*, 254–6; Dr. Primrose's sale of his horse at, ib. 264 seq., 354. Mr. Edward Ford, in the *National Review* for May, 1883, has sought to identify this place with Welburn.

WELL-KNIT. *See* Knit.

WELLS, THE. *Vicar*, 293. Mr. Edward Ford (*National Review*, May, 1883) suggests that Harrogate is no doubt intended.

WESTMINSTER-HALL, the old Hall of the Palace at Westminster, originally built in the reign of William Rufus. *She Stoops*, 111. Our early Parliaments were held in this Hall, and the Law Courts met here until the opening of the present buildings in 1882. The Hall is said to be the largest apartment not supported by pillars in England.

WHISTLE-JACKET, the name of a famous racehorse. *She Stoops*, 146.

WHISTON, THE REV. WILLIAM (1667–1772), monogamist. *Vicar*, 193, 265. *See* Appendix, Note 16.

Whitehall Evening, i.e. *The Whitehall Evening Post, or London Intelligencer*. *Vicar*, 299.

WHY, used as a call or exclamation. ' Constance, why Constance, I say.' *She Stoops*, 152. Cp. *Merchant of Venice*, II. v. 6–7, ' *Shylock*. Why, Jessica, I say ! *Launcelot*. Why, Jessica ! *Shylock*. Who bids thee call ? '

WIG. ' He fastened my wig to the back of my chair,' &c. *She Stoops*, 92. The trick here played by Tony Lumpkin on Mr. Hardcastle was one played on Goldsmith by the daughter of Lord Clare on his last visit to Gosfield (Forster, *Life*, Book IV, chap. xv).

WILDMAN'S, a coffee-house in Bedford Street, under the Piazza in Covent Garden. *Good-Natur'd Man*, 78.

WILD NOTES, i.e. produced without culture or training. *She Stoops*, 123. Mrs. Hardcastle may have had a confused remembrance of Milton's lines, ' Or sweetest Shakespeare, Fancy's child, Warble his native wood-notes wild' (*L'Allegro*, lines 133–4).

WILMOT, MR., his controversy with Dr. Primrose on Monogamy. *Vicar*, 195–6.

WINDGALL, a soft tumour on the fetlock joints of a horse. *Vicar*, 264.

WINE. ' I . . . asked for the landlord's company over a pint of wine.' *Vicar*, 327. A pint of wine was a common measure.

WIVES, markets for. *Vicar*, 288. *See* Fontarabia, Ranelagh.

WOODEN SHOES. ' What ! give up liberty, property, and, as the *Gazetteer* says, lie down to be saddled with wooden shoes ! ' *Vicar*, 304. ' Wooden shoes ' were objects of ridicule and dislike at the time of the story. Goldsmith, by this mixed metaphor, was probably ridiculing the general style of the *Gazetteer*.

WOODWARD, HENRY (1717–1777), actor. *Good-Natur'd Man*, 6 ; *She Stoops*, 88. Woodward, who took the part of Lofty in *The Good-Natur'd Man*, refused the part of Tony Lumpkin in *She Stoops to Conquer*, but spoke the Prologue to that play ; as to which Horace Walpole wrote, ' Woodward speaks a poor prologue, written by Garrick, admirably ' (*Letters*, viii. 260–1). According to the *Dictionary of National Biography* ' he has had few equals in comedy. His figure was admirably formed, and his expression so composed that he seemed qualified rather for tragedy or fine gentlemen than the brisk fops and pert coxcombs he ordinarily played.' See vol. lxii, p. 419. He is in the *Rosciad*.

WOUNDILY, wondrously, excessively, very. ' They look woundily like Frenchmen.' *She Stoops*, 100. Recorded as obsolescent in the *English Dialect Dict*. Cp. Roby, *Traditions of Lancashire* (1829) ii. 301, ed. 1872, ' Body o' me, but you're grown woundily humoursome.'

YEATING, dialect form of ' eating '. *She Stoops*, 104.

YOUR, used indefinitely. ' I detest your three chairs and a bolster.' *She Stoops*, 103. Cp. *As You Like It*, v. i. 47, ' All your writers do consent that ipse is he.'

ZOUNDS, an expletive, ' God's wounds ! ' *Good-Natur'd Man*, 71 and *passim*.

APPENDIX

THE GOOD-NATUR'D MAN

THIS play was originally intended for Covent Garden Theatre, but at the time when it was ready for representation the affairs of that theatre had been thrown into temporary confusion by the death of Rich, the manager. Goldsmith thereupon decided to try the rival house, Drury Lane, which was under the management of Garrick. Financial pressure doubtless forced Goldsmith to seek a favour at Garrick's hands, for the two had not been on good terms for some time; but Sir Joshua Reynolds acted as an intermediary and brought them together. The interview was not altogether successful: sensitive pride on one side, and the arrogance of a successful man on the other, nearly wrecked the negotiations at the outset. However, the manuscript was placed in Garrick's hands for consideration, only to be followed by excuses and delays on the part of the manager. Privately, he was giving his opinion to Johnson and Reynolds that the play could not possibly succeed; to the dramatist himself he suggested several alterations, which Goldsmith indignantly refused to adopt. Mr. Whitehead (the Poet Laureate) was thereupon suggested as an arbitrator: this proposal was declined, Goldsmith believing that condemnation of the play was already decided in that quarter. Another name was suggested, only to be rejected with warmth; and in this spirit manager and dramatist parted. Goldsmith, however, fully realized the defects of his play, and, writing in a chastened spirit to the manager of Drury Lane, undertook to give him a new character in his comedy, 'and knock out Lofty, which does not do, and will make such other alterations as you direct.' This letter was cruelly endorsed by Garrick 'Goldsmith's *Parlaver*'.

Certain events in the interval had occurred at Covent Garden which resulted in renewed negotiations with that house, now under the management of George Colman, and eventually the manuscript was withdrawn from Garrick and handed over to his rival. Dissensions arising among the new proprietors of Covent Garden Theatre the production of the comedy was again retarded. In the meantime Garrick, in opposition to Goldsmith, had brought out a play at Drury Lane, written by Hugh Kelly, entitled *False Delicacy*, which belonged to the then prevailing school of 'sentimental' comedy, and was likely to have an adverse effect on a play constructed on opposite lines and out of harmony with current taste. ' It was with Steele the unlucky notion began,' writes Forster, ' of setting comedy to reform the morals instead of imitating the manners of the age.' Kelly continued this tradition, and in this play ' sounded the depths of sentimentalism '.

The play was produced for the first time on Saturday, January 23, 1768, six nights before *The Good-Natur'd Man* was brought out at Covent Garden. Johnson pronounced it a play of 'no character ', but it had a great stage success. It was backed by the remaining adherents of the ' sentimental ' school of comedy, and Garrick used all his influence to ensure the success of the piece. Through his intervention, *False Delicacy* was received with 'singular favour ', and a great number of copies of the book was sold, Kelly's profits amounting to above £700.

Whilst success was thus attending Kelly's play, affairs at Covent Garden were not proceeding smoothly. The actors were squabbling over their parts : Powell protested he could make nothing of Mr. Honeywood, and the actors generally thought but little of the play's chance of success—with the possible exception of Shuter. The manager himself had lost all faith, and under the circumstances it is not surprising that Goldsmith should have become down-hearted and despondent. Johnson, however, was steadfast in support, attending a rehearsal, and promising to furnish a prologue.

At last, on Friday, the 29th of January, 1768, the comedy was produced. The majority of the members of the Literary Club— including Johnson, Burke, and Reynolds—attended the first performance, to cheer and encourage their fellow member. The opening was not altogether promising : Johnson's prologue proved somewhat ponderous ; and Powell, with his preconceived ideas of failure, did not mend matters in his representation of Honeywood in the first Act. It was left to Shuter, with his inimitable representation of Croaker, to galvanize the play into life, and make the house ring with honest laughter. On the other hand, the bailiffs' scene was unsuccessful: its humour was too broad for the 'sentimentalists', and its language was thought low—'uncommonly low' said the *London Chronicle* in reporting the play. But Shuter again rescued the piece from failure by his mirth-provoking reading of the 'incendiary' letter in the fourth Act, and this carried the play on to its close with a fair amount of success. For further details of the acting it is only necessary to refer to Forster's *Life of Goldsmith*, which is practically exhaustive on the subject of the drama in Goldsmith's time.

On the second night (February 1) the scene with the bailiffs was omitted, and a few minor alterations were made. The third, sixth, and ninth nights were appropriated for the author's benefit, by which he received some £350 to £400 ; the fifth night had been commanded by their Majesties. In all, it ran for ten consecutive nights, and on the 20th of March it was selected by Shuter for his benefit, the author generously adding ten guineas, in recognition of the actor's great services. A few years later, on May 3, 1773, it was again selected for a benefit—this time for Mrs. Green, the original Mrs. Hardcastle in *She Stoops to Conquer*. At this representation the bailiffs' scene was acted, 'by particular desire' : Morris and Quick were the bailiffs, and Lee Lewes took the part of Lofty.

Goldsmith's profits were small compared with those reaped by Kelly with *False Delicacy*, but the sale of the copyright to W. Griffin added somewhat to the sum. The play was immediately printed, with the bailiffs' scene restored, and the first edition published on February 5, which went off with great rapidity. Prior quotes the following trade advertisement: 'The first large impression of the comedy of *The Good-Natured Man*, written by Dr. Goldsmith, being sold off on Saturday last (the 6th, the day after publication) a new edition will be published this afternoon, at three o'clock ; when those ladies and gentlemen that were then disappointed of their books may be supplied by W. Griffin, in Catherine Street in the Strand.'

On February 22 a fourth edition appeared, and a fifth before the end of the year. Qualified, therefore, as its success on the stage may have been, it is evident from these records that the literary merits of the play were recognized from the first. It had been applauded in manuscript by Edmund Burke ; it was now to obtain the appreciation of the reading public, although not without its detractors. Boswell spoke slightingly of the play to Johnson, but the latter declared it to be ' the best comedy that had appeared since *The Provoked Husband*, and that there had not been of late any such character exhibited on the stage as that of Croaker.' Boswell's *Life*, ii. 48, ed. Birkbeck Hill.

But although *The Good-Natur'd Man* has taken an enduring place in the literature of our country, it has seldom been reproduced on the stage, and the presumption is that it is not really a good acting play. By the courtesy of the Editor of the *Athenaeum*, I am permitted to reprint the following article from the pen of the late Mr. Joseph Knight, concerning a representation of this play in October, 1906 :—

CORONET.—*Afternoon Representation : The Good-Natured Man.* By Oliver Goldsmith. Played in Three Acts.

THE general impression of the demerits, as an acting play, of Goldsmith's *Good-Natured Man* will scarcely be removed by the afternoon presentation given under the direction of Mr. William Poel at the Coronet Theatre. The conditions surrounding the performance were scarcely favourable. So amateurish was the whole that the comparatively subordinate part of Sir William Honeywood assumed, in the hands of Mr. Charles Allen, an importance that can rarely have been assigned it. Mr. Poel himself played Croaker, and Mr. Ben Field doubled the part of Lofty with that of the Footman. In one instance no fewer than three characters were assigned to the same actor, Flannigan (the bailiff's follower), Dubardieu, and the postboy being all in the hands of Mr. Edwin H. Wynne. Miss Richland, the heroine, was played by Miss Muriel Currey ; and Olivia (in whom it is possible to trace a sort of predecessor of Constantia Neville in *She Stoops to Conquer*) was presented gracefully by Miss H. B. Potter. Much stress was laid in Goldsmith's second piece upon the improbability of taking Hardcastle's house for an inn. An error of the kind is insignificant beside that of Croaker, who accepts into his house, as his own daughter Olivia, a stranger palmed off upon him as such by his son Leontine, who has brought her home from Paris for the purpose of marrying her. This piece may have been included in the performances of classical comedy which were, under Buckstone's management, a feature of the Haymarket. No record of any presentation during the past half century is traced previous to the first revival by Mr. Poel in Cambridge, of which that at the Coronet was a repetition.— *Athenaeum*, October 20, 1906.

NOTE 1.—HUGH KELLY

Hugh Kelly was born at Killarney in 1739, the son of a Dublin tavern-keeper. He went to London early in 1760 to try literature as a profession, first, in a moment of rashness, describing himself— a passing weakness which he was not speedily permitted to forget—as a staymaker. He afterwards took to journalism and editing, and wrote political pamphlets, one of which was praised by Lord Chesterfield ; took chambers in Middle Temple Lane, and married Mira (his wife's *nom de plume*). Later on he published one or two novels, and worked for John Newbery as editor of the *Public Ledger*. He published *Thespis : or a Critical Examination of all the Principal Performers belonging to Drury Lane Theatre*, but apologized in the second edition for his 'ruffian cruelty'. At this stage of his career he was taken up by Garrick, in rivalry to Goldsmith, who was then on the point of bringing out *The Good Natur'd Man*. Kelly's play, *False Delicacy*, as stated above, proved very successful in London ; it had also a vogue in country towns in Great Britain, and was translated into several foreign languages. Kelly's last five comedies were all unsuccessful ; but he was one of the most deeply affected of the mourners at Goldsmith's burial, and one of the last to leave the grave ; and for this much may be forgiven him. Kelly died in poverty, February 3, 1777.

NOTE 2.—GARRICK'S TREATMENT OF GOLDSMITH AND 'RETALIATION'

Was it partly the recollection of Garrick's treatment of him and his attitude in the matter of the production of *The Good*

Natur'd Man that led Goldsmith to criticize him, not surely too severely, in *Retaliation*? It may be worth while to reproduce the lines in this place :—

Here lies David Garrick, describe me, who can,
An abridgment of all that was pleasant in man ;
As an actor, confess'd without rival to shine ;
As a wit, if not first, in the very first line ;
Yet, with talents like these, and an excellent heart,
The man had his failings, a dupe to his art.
Like an ill-judging beauty, his colours he spread,
And beplaster'd with rouge his own natural red.
On the stage he was natural, simple, affecting ;
'Twas only that when he was off he was acting.
With no reason on earth to go out of his way,
He turn'd and he varied full ten times a day.
Though secure of our hearts, yet confoundedly sick
If they were not his own by finessing and trick :
He cast off his friends, as a huntsman his pack,
For he knew when he pleas'd he could whistle them back.
Of praise a mere glutton, he swallow'd what came,
And the puff of a dunce he mistook it for fame ;
Till his relish grown callous, almost to disease,
Who pepper'd the highest, was surest to please.
But let us be candid, and speak out our mind,
If dunces applauded, he paid them in kind.
Ye Kenricks, ye Kellys, and Woodfalls so grave,
What a commerce was yours, while you got, and you gave !
How did Grub-street re-echo the shouts that you rais'd,
While he was be-Roscius'd and you were be-prais'd !
But peace to his spirit, wherever it flies,
To act as an angel, and mix with the skies :
Those poets, who owe their best fame to his skill,
Shall still be his flatterers, go where he will.
Old Shakespeare, receive him, with praise and with love,
And Beaumonts and Bens be his Kellys above.

NOTE 3.—SUPPOSED ORIGIN OF THE TITLE ' GOOD-NATUR'D MAN '

Mr. Forster reminds us that one of Nash's friends, introduced as ' the celebrated S—,' is mentioned in Goldsmith's *Life of Nash*,

ed. 1762, as having gone by the name of 'The Good-Natur'd Man'.
But 'good nature' seemed then to be in the air, and it is quite
possible that there was no connexion between Croaker and the
celebrated S—, who is otherwise wholly unknown to us. See
also Glossarial Index, p. 440.

NOTE 4.—PROLOGUE BY DR. JOHNSON. Page 5.

Originally, in the fifth line, ' Our *little* Bard ' had been written.
' Don't call me *our* LITTLE *bard* ' said Goldsmith to Johnson, and
' Our anxious bard' was good-naturedly substituted. Malone
used to refer to this eagerly-desired omission as one of the most
characteristic traits he knew of Goldsmith. (Forster's *Life*,
Book IV, chap. i.)

NOTE 5.—CROAKER AND JOHNSON'S ' SUSPIRIUS '. Page 13.

Johnson's sketch of Suspirius in *The Rambler*, No. 59, has
often been put forward as the original from which Goldsmith
copied Croaker, and he is said to have acknowledged his indebted-
ness to Johnson ; but Mr. J. W. M. Gibbs, in his edition of Goldsmith (ii. 193), suggests that Goldsmith may, after all, have
taken the main idea from his own desponding philosopher in
The Citizen of the World, No. 92. Goldsmith was such an in-
veterate repeater of his own good things—often three or four
times within a short space—that a few additional plagiarisms do
not seem to fall from him with an ill grace.

For purposes of reference, a transcript of the number of
The Rambler in question is annexed.

No. 59.   THE RAMBLER.   Price 2*d*.

Tuesday, October 9, 1750.

> Est aliquid fatale Malum per Verba levare,
>   Hoc querulam Prognen Halcyonemque facit:
> Hoc erat in solo quare Poeantius Antro
>   Voce fatigaret Lemnia Saxa sua.
> Strangulat inclusus dolor atque exaestuat intus
>   Cogitur et Vires multiplicare suas.   OVID.

It is common to distinguish Men by the Names of Animals
which they are supposed to resemble. Thus a Hero is frequently
termed a Lion, and a Statesman a Fox, an extortioner gains the

appellation of Vulture, and a Fop the Title of Monkey. There is also among the various Anomalies of Character, which a Survey of the World exhibits, a Species of Beings in human Form, which may be properly marked out as the Screech-Owls of Mankind.

These Screech-Owls seem to be settled in an Opinion that the great Business of Life is to complain, and that they were born for no other Purpose than to disturb the Happiness of others, to lessen the little Comforts, and shorten the short Pleasures of our Condition, by painful Remembrances of the Past, or melancholy Prognostics of the Future, and their only Care is to crush the rising Hope, to damp the kindling Transport, and allay the golden Hours of Gayety with the hateful Dross of Grief and Suspicion.

To those, whose Weakness of Spirits, or Timidity of Temper, subjects them to Impressions from others, and who are apt to suffer by Fascination, and catch the Contagion of Misery, it is extremely unhappy to live within the Compass of a Screech-Owl's Voice ; for it will often fill their Ears in the Hour of Dejection, and terrify them with Apprehensions which their own Thoughts would never have produced, and sadden, by intruded Sorrows, the Day which might have been passed in Amusements, or in Business ; it will fill the heart with unnecessary Discontents, and weaken for a time that Love of Life which is necessary to the vigorous Prosecution of any Undertaking.

Though I have, like the Rest of Mankind, many Failings and Weaknesses, I have never yet, by either Friends or Enemies, been charged with Superstition ; I never count the Company which I enter, and I look at the New Moon indifferently over either Shoulder. I have, like most other Philosophers, often heard the Cuckoo without Money in my Pocket, and have been sometimes reproached for foolhardy for not turning down my Eyes when a Raven flew over my head. I never go home abruptly, because a Snake crosses my Way, nor have any particular dread of a climaterical Year, but confess that, with all my Scorn of old Women, and their Tales, I always consider it as an unhappy Day when I happen to be greeted in the Morning by *Suspirius* the Screech-Owl.

NOTE 6.—WHITEFIELD'S TABERNACLE.   Page 20.

It may be of interest to append the following quotation from the *Westminster Gazette*. The use of the term 'tabernacle' by Goldsmith and others at this period must have been greatly influenced by the success of George Whitefield, as shown in the new building erected for his preaching a few years before in the Tottenham Court Road:—

'One of the historic landmarks of London Nonconformity seems destined to disappear by the coming sale of Whitefield's Tabernacle, not the one in Tottenham Court Road, but the less known original preaching-place of Whitefield in Finsbury. This was at first a huge wooden shed, with a sugar-cask for pulpit, erected by Calvinistic admirers for Whitefield after his separation from Wesley. They called their temporary structure a *tabernacle* from the movable place of worship of the Israelites; and the name became a designation for all chapels of the Calvinistic Methodists. The permanent edifice was rebuilt forty years ago.'— *Westminster Gazette*, May 3, 1907.

See also Wheatley, *London, Past and Present*, iii. 503 seq.

NOTE 7.—LAND-CARRIAGE FISHERY.   Page 30.

Amongst the notable persons who interested themselves in the carriage of fish must be reckoned Sir Richard Steele, who published, in 1718, in conjunction with Mr. Joseph Gillmore, mathematician, a pamphlet bearing the title, 'An Account of the Fishpool: consisting of a Description of the Vessel so called, lately invented and built for the Importation of Fish alive, and in good health, from parts however distant. A Proof of the Imperfection of the *Well-Boat* hitherto used in the Fishing Trade. The true Reasons why Ships become stiff or crank in sailing; with other Improvements, very useful to all Persons concerned in Trade and Navigation. Likewise, a Description of the Carriage intended for the Conveyance of Fish by land, in the same good Condition as in the *Fish-Pool* by Sea.' Annexed to this pamphlet is the patent which his Majesty, King George I, gave for the use of this invention.

Matthew Bramble, the irascible but good-natured squire in Smollett's *Humphry Clinker*, saw little that was good in this

THE DEAF POSTILION

mode of conveyance. ' Of the fish, I need say nothing in this hot weather, but that it comes sixty, seventy, fourscore, and a hundred miles by land carriage ; a circumstance sufficient, without any comment, to turn a Dutchman's stomach, even if his nose was not saluted in every alley with the sweet flavour of " fresh " mackerel, selling by retail.'—*Humphry Clinker* (1771) 149, ed. 1905.

NOTE 8.—SCOTCH MARRIAGES. Pages 20, 37, 50, 55, 67.

A useful little companion to Goldsmith's allusions to Scotch marriages will be found in *Gretna Green and its Traditions*, by ' Claverhouse ', with twenty-two illustrations, facsimiles of hand-writing, &c. It contains as much information as most readers are likely to require on Scottish runaway marriages. A word must be spoken also in favour of a highly interesting article on the subject which appeared in the *Strand Magazine* of December, 1908. When this article was first published a footnote was appended, stating that at that time the Gretna Green registers (1825–57 and ' relative certificates ') were for sale privately. It is understood that they have since passed into official or semi-official hands.

NOTE 9.—THE HOUSE OF LORETTO. Page 63.

An interesting account of Loretto from the point of view of a Roman Catholic traveller in the seventeenth century is to be found in *The Voyage of Italy*, by Richard Lassels, Gent. (London, 1686), from which the following extract is quoted :—

' From hence we went to see the Cellar of the Holy House, which furnished with Wine not only the Governour's House, the Canons and the Churchmen, the College of the *Penitentiaries*, the Convent of the *Capucins*, the *Seminarists*, the *Hospital*, and all those belonging to the Church any way ; but also furnished all Pilgrims, yea, even all Princes, Cardinals, Bishops, Embassadors, and great Men of known quality, with Wine, as long as they stay here upon Devotion. For this reason there belong large revenues to this Church ; and this Cellar is absolutely the best I saw in Italy. The Vessels are hugely great, and not to be removed from hence. They have a way to take out a piece of their broad sides, and so make them clean. They are all hooped with Iron, and some of them are so contrived that they can draw three several sorts of wine out of one Vessel, and by the same tap. The experience is pretty, but the wine is better. Turselinus in his *Hist. of Loreto*, l. 3. c. 25, writes that between Easter and Whitsuntide, there have flocked thither sometimes five sometimes six hundred thousand Communicants ; and in two days' space in September (about the Feast of the Nativity of our Blessed Saviour) there have appeared two Hundred Thousand Communicants, most of which were Pilgrims.

' Having refreshed ourselves in this Cellar, we went to the Apothecaries-shop, belonging to the Holy House also ; and furnishing Physic to sick Pilgrims for nothing. There we saw those famous Pots, which make even Physic itself look sweetly, and draw all curious strangers to visit them. For round about a great inner Shop, stand Pots of a great size painted by *Raphael Urbin's* own hand, and therefore judged by *Virtuosi* to be of great value. Witness these four only, on which are painted the four *Evangelists*, for the which were offered by a French Embassador in his King's name four Pots of Gold of the same bigness, and were refused. Brave *Raphael*, whose only touch of a finger could *Midas* like, turn Gallipots into Gold. But as Phydias his Statues of Clay were as much adored anciently as his Golden ones : so *Raphaels* hand is as much admired in the Apothecaries Shop of *Loreto* as in the Vatican Pallace of *Rome*. These pots were given to the Holy House by a Duke of *Urbin*, whose Subject *Raphael* was, and for whom he had made them with more than ordinary art.'—*Voyage of Italy*, Part II, pp. 213–4.

In 1809, a Guide to the Holy House was printed and published at Loretto, containing an ' Historical Abridgment of the Prodigious translations of the Holy House of Nazareth ', by M. Murri, translated by a member of the order of Cordeliers, and dedicated to his Excellency Lemarois, Governor-General of the three combined departments of Metauro, Musone, and Tronto, Aide de Camp to Napoleon, Emperor and King. It is illustrated with rude wood-cuts, and was no doubt bought in large numbers by pilgrims and others.

In May, 1868, there was some discussion in the *Athenaeum*, No. 2115, on the whole of the alleged miraculous elements of the story.

Note 10.—Supposed Novel founded upon 'The Good-
Natur'd Man'

Goldsmith is said to have contemplated a narrative version
of *The Good-Natur'd Man*: this novel is stated to have been read
by the author to the family of Mr. Bunbury, and there seems
to be sufficient evidence that Goldsmith had another novel in
preparation a little before his death, but no traces of it remain.
The story, as told by Prior, connects itself with Goldsmith's great
dramatic success, *She Stoops to Conquer*. ' Being pressed by
pecuniary difficulties in 1771–2, Goldsmith had at various periods
obtained the advance of two or three hundred pounds from
Newbery under the engagement of writing a novel, which after
the success of *The Vicar of Wakefield* promised to be one of the
most popular speculations. Considerable delay took place in
the execution of this undertaking, and when at length submitted
to the perusal of the bookseller, it proved to be in great measure
the plot of *The Good-Natured Man*, turned into a tale. Objections
being taken to this, the manuscript was returned. Goldsmith
declared himself unable or unwilling to write another, but in
liquidation of the debt now pressingly demanded, said he should
require time to look round for means of raising the money,
unless Mr. Newbery chose to take the chance of a play coming
forward at Covent Garden. " And yet to tell you the truth,
Frank," added the candid poet in making the proposal, " there
are great doubts of its success." Newbery accepted the offer,
doubtful of being otherwise repaid, and the popularity of *She
Stoops to Conquer* gained, according to the recollection of the
narrator, above three hundred pounds more than the sum
advanced to the author.' (Prior's *Life of Goldsmith*, ii. 417.)

SHE STOOPS TO CONQUER

This play was represented at Covent Garden for the first time
on March 15, 1773. As in the case of *The Good-Natur'd Man*,
there was the same period of suspense, and the same dilatory
proceedings on the part of the manager. Goldsmith in vain
implored Colman to ' take the play and let us make the best of it,
and let us have the same measure at least which you have given

as bad plays as mine '. The MS. was returned with some not wholly unjustifiable criticisms, accompanied by a promise that the play should nevertheless be acted. Goldsmith then submitted the manuscript to Garrick, who hesitated to approve. Johnson intervened, and consulted both managers with a view to an arrangement, and eventually Colman consented, although reluctantly, that it should be brought out at Covent Garden.

Johnson's interest in the play was great from the first. On February 22, 1773, he wrote to Boswell : ' Dr. Goldsmith has a new comedy which is expected in the spring. No name is yet given it. The chief diversion arises from a stratagem by which a lover is made to mistake his future father-in-law's house for an inn. This, you see, borders on farce. The dialogue is quick and gay, and the incidents are so prepared as not to seem improbable ' (Boswell's *Life*, ed. Birkbeck Hill, ii. 205–6). And on March 4, eleven days before the representation, Johnson wrote to the Rev. Mr. White : ' Dr. Goldsmith has a new comedy in rehearsal at Covent Garden, to which the manager predicts ill success. I think it deserves a very kind reception ' (*Life*, ii. 208).

Fortune was to prove kinder in this than in his first play. The way was being prepared for the successful revival of a comedy of manners based on real life, as contrasted with that of the ' sentimental ' or French school which had been so long in fashion. The production by Foote at the Haymarket, by means of puppets, of a piece called *The Handsome Housemaid, or Piety in Pattens*, which was intended to show how a maiden of low degree, by the mere effects of morality and virtue, raised herself to riches and honour, struck a blow at sentimental comedy from which it was slow to recover. Garrick was swift to note the change in taste, and sent Goldsmith a Prologue with which to lead off his play.

Colman, however, remained sceptical to the last ; he had set his mind against the play, refused to supply new dresses and fresh scenery, and sent out his dismal forebodings in the most approved manner of Croaker. Then troubles arose with the actors. Smith threw up Young Marlow ; Woodward refused the part of Tony Lumpkin. If there was any conspiracy against poor Goldsmith, he was to have a signal revenge on his enemies.

Nor was this all, for the mere finding a title for the play proved almost insuperable ; but Goldsmith's own suggestion was at last adopted, and the final difficulty was thus surmounted. ' We are all in labour,' wrote Johnson, ' for a name to Goldy's play.' What now stands as the sub-title, ' The Mistakes of a Night,' was the original title fixed on. *The Old House a New Inn* was put forward as an alternative, and Sir Joshua Reynolds suggested *The Belle's Stratagem.* The question was solved by Goldsmith himself, possibly from remembering Dryden's line—' But kneels to Conquer, and but stoops to Rise'—and the play was thus happily named.

When at last the play was produced its reception exceeded the expectation of the author or his friends. The members of the Club were present in force to applaud the play ; but the spontaneous acclamations and enjoyment of the audience were so great as to render extraneous assistance of this kind unnecessary. Even a hostile critic such as Horace Walpole was obliged to admit its success. Writing to Lady Ossory on March 16 he says, ' There was a new play by Dr. Goldsmith last night, which succeeded prodigiously ' (*Letters*, viii. 256). As for his enthusiastic friends, Johnson's opinion may be given : ' I know of no comedy for many years that has so much exhilarated an audience ; that has answered so much the great end of comedy, making an audience merry.'

The *single hiss* which is said to have so painfully startled Goldsmith at the beginning of the fifth Act, and to have caused Colman to remark, ' Pshaw, Doctor, don't be afraid of a squib, when we have been sitting these two hours on a barrel of gunpowder,' related to the trick played off by Tony Lumpkin on Mrs. Hardcastle—an incident which was no doubt based on Madame de Genlis's similar adventure at the hands of Sheridan. It is said that Goldsmith never forgave Colman for his ill-timed jest, if jest it were. But the moderation with which Goldsmith in the Dedication treated Colman's criticisms betrays no such unforgiving resentment. Indeed, as things turned out, there was more need for pity, as may be judged from the account by Prior : ' The fire of squibs, witticisms, and paragraphs against Colman became incessant ; his opinion of the play was attributed to extreme jealousy. . . . So perseveringly was this warfare carried on, in every variety of form, that the manager became at last seriously annoyed ; he wrote what was considered a penitential letter to Goldsmith, requesting he would "*take him off the rack of the newspapers*", and in order to escape the annoyance in London, took flight, in the beginning of the second week, to Bath.'

The first representation, as has been said, took place on March 15, and the new comedy was continued each night the theatre was open until May 31. The author took three nights for his benefit (March 18, April 12, and April 19), by which it is estimated he received four or five hundred pounds. On the 5th of May, the tenth day of performance, it was commanded by the King and Queen. During the summer Foote produced the play at the Haymarket ; and at Covent Garden it was frequently repeated before the following Christmas. From that time forward it took its place as one of the standard and most acceptable pieces of the British Drama.

Goldsmith had now come to the parting of the ways, and, save in point of reputation and undying fame, the future had little more to offer him. The copyright of his play had passed into the hands of Mr. Francis Newbery, under circumstances already narrated (see Note 10) ; by that publisher it was entered at Stationers' Hall on March 26, 1773, and duly issued, reaching a fifth edition in the same year.

NOTE 11.—THE THREE PIGEONS. Page 98.

On November 6, 1882, at a meeting of the Cambridge Antiquarian Society, a communication from Dr. J. B. Pearson was read, in which he suggested that The Three Pigeons, at the point where the road from Thame to Abingdon crosses that from London to Oxford, was possibly the site where Goldsmith laid the scene of *She Stoops to Conquer*. This, however, does not seem probable. The name was often used as the sign of inns and shops in the seventeenth and eighteenth centuries, notably The Three Pigeons at Brentford, an inn which has acquired celebrity owing to its being one of the few haunts of Shakespeare now remaining. Cp. Ben Jonson's *Alchemist*.

NOTE 12.—GREEN AND YELLOW DINNERS. Page 113.

Horace Walpole, in a letter written April 7, 1765, describes a dinner at Northumberland House at which he was present, and where, after long waiting, the guests 'sat down to a table for four-teen covers ; but, instead of substantials, there was nothing but a profusion of plates striped red, green, and yellow, gilt plate, blacks, and uniforms! My Lady Finlater, who had never seen these embroidered dinners, nor dined after three, was famished.' (See *Letters*, vi. 212–13, ed. Mrs. Paget Toynbee.)

George Selwyn also narrates his experience at the *French Ambassador's*, some four years after such dinners had been ridiculed in *She Stoops to Conquer* : ' [*February*, 1777] I dined on Sunday at the French Ambassador's ; a splendid and wretched dinner, but good wine ; a quantity of dishes which differed from one another only in appearance ; they had all the same taste, or equally wanted it. The middle piece, the *demeurant*, as it is called, a fine Oriental arcade, which reached from one end of the table to the other, fell in like a *tremblement de terre*. The wax, which cemented the composing parts, melted like Icarus's wings, and down it fell. Seventy *bougies* occasioned this, with the numbers all adding to the heat of the room. I had a more private and much better dinner yesterday at Devonshire House.' From *George Selwyn, his Letters and his Life*, edited by E. S. Roscoe and Helen Clergue (London, Fisher Unwin, 1899, p. 116).

NOTE 13.—ROYAL MARRIAGE ACT (12 GEO. III), III. cap. 11.
Page 115.

This Act was passed in consequence of the marriage of William Henry, Duke of Gloucester, the King's brother, to the Dowager Lady Waldegrave, and that of William Augustus, Duke of Cumberland, to the widow of Colonel Horton. The latter marriage was formally announced to George III, and duly authenticated (see Walpole's *Letters*, i. p. li, viii. 167, 205, and *passim*). The Duke of Gloucester was present at the representation on the first night of *She Stoops to Conquer*, and the allusion in Hastings's speech to ' the laws of marriage ' in France directed the applause of the audience to the Duke. See Forster's *Life*, Book IV, chap. xvi. Boswell, at a dinner at General Paoli's, endeavoured to obtain from Goldsmith an admission that the marriage of the Duke was in his mind, but without any decided success. After all, it may have been a random shot which happened to hit the mark. That no offence was taken at Court is shown by the fact that George III commanded a performance on the tenth night of the play, and again in the following season.

It will be remembered that Johnson strongly disapproved of the Royal Marriage Bill (see Boswell's *Life*, edited by Dr. Birkbeck Hill, vol. ii, p. 152): 'Because, said he, I would not have the people think that the validity of marriage depends on the will of man, or that the right of a King depends on the will of man. I should not have been against making the marriage of any one of the royal family, without the approbation of King and Parliament, highly criminal.'

A very curious complication arose through the careless drafting of the Act. This was drawn by Mansfield, Thurlow, and Wedderburne, who had unluckily made all parties present at the marriage guilty of felony; and as nobody could prove the marriage except a person who had been present at it, there could be no prosecution, because nobody present could be compelled to be a witness. This put an end to the matter.

Note 14.—Inns with Galleries. Page 134.

A miniature book on *Old English Inns* has been written by Mr. George T. Burrows and published by Mr. Werner Laurie, which will be of use to the hasty traveller; but Mr. C. G. Harper, by his many publications on *Our Old Inns* and *The Great Main Roads*, has fairly made this branch of the subject his own. The illustrations to Mr. Harper's numerous works from his own pen add much to their value and interest.

Note 15.—Embroidery and Needlework as occupation for Ladies. Pages 137, 242, 251.

There are several interesting records in literature concerning household industry similar to that displayed by Miss Hardcastle and the Vicar's daughters, Olivia and Sophia. Cp. Shakespeare, *Titus Andronicus*, II. iv. 39–40:

> Fair Philomela, she but lost her tongue,
> And in a tedious sampler sew'd her mind.

Midsummer Night's Dream, III. ii. 203–8:

> We, Hermia, like two artificial gods,
> Have with our needls created both one flower,

Both on one sampler, sitting on one cushion,
Both warbling of one song, both in one key,
As if our hands, our sides, voices, and minds,
Had been incorporate.

See also Milton, *Comus*, 750–3 :

It is for homely features to keep home,
They had their name thence ; coarse complexions,
And cheeks of sorry grain, will serve to ply
The sampler, and to tease the housewife's wool,

with the Lady's lofty reply to this false reasoning.

SCENE FROM ' THE GRUMBLER '
Page 173.

Of this piece little need be said. It was produced for the
benefit of Quick (to whom Goldsmith was deeply grateful for
the successful way in which he had acted the part of Tony
Lumpkin) at Covent Garden Theatre, May 8, 1773, and this
seems to have been its only representation. It is merely an
adaptation of Sir Charles Sedley's *The Grumbler*, itself a translation of Brueys's French comedy, *Le Grondeur*. The scene here
given was first printed by Prior in his edition of 1837, and has
appeared in several editions of the plays since that time, but it
cannot be said to add anything to Goldsmith's reputation.

THE VICAR OF WAKEFIELD

In March, 1766, the following advertisement appeared in *The
St. James's Chronicle* : ' In a few days will be published, in two
volumes, twelves, price six shillings bound, or five shillings
sewed, *The Vicar of Wakefield*. A tale, supposed to be written
by himself. Printed for F. Newbery at the Crown in Paternoster
Row.' On the 27th of March the book was issued. It had been
practically finished, in all probability, as early as 1762, for in the
account books kept by Benjamin Collins of Salisbury, Mr. Charles
Welsh discovered the following entry : ' Vicar of Wakefield,
2 vols. 12mo, $\frac{1}{3}$rd. B. Collins, Salisbury, bought of Dr. Gold-

smith, the author, October 28, 1762, £21.' (*A Bookseller of the Last Century*, 1885, pp. 58–9.) Collins, it will be observed by reference to the facsimile title, was ultimately the printer of the book. This discovery has given rise to some doubts as to the reliance to be placed on certain details in Boswell's account of Johnson's connexion with the publication. 'Johnson informed me,' says Boswell, 'that he had made the bargain for Goldsmith, and the price was sixty pounds. "And, Sir, (said he), a sufficient price too, when it was sold; for then the fame of Goldsmith had not been elevated, as it afterwards was, by his *Traveller*; and the bookseller had such faint hopes of profit by his bargain, that he kept the manuscript by him a long time, and did not publish it till after *The Traveller* had appeared. Then, to be sure, it was accidentally worth more money." Mrs. Piozzi and Sir John Hawkins have strangely mis-stated the history of Goldsmith's situation and Johnson's friendly interference when this novel was sold. I shall give it authentically from Johnson's own exact narration:—I received one morning a message from poor Goldsmith that he was in great distress, and as it was not in his power to come to me, begging that I would come to him as soon as possible. I sent him a guinea and promised to come to him directly. I accordingly went as soon as I was drest, and found that his landlady had arrested him for his rent, at which he was in a violent passion. I perceived that he had already changed my guinea, and had got a bottle of Madeira and a glass before him. I put the cork in the bottle, desired he would be calm, and began to talk to him of the means by which he might be extricated. He then told me that he had a novel ready for the press, which he produced to me. I looked into it, and saw its merit; told the landlady I should soon return, and having gone to a bookseller, sold it for sixty pounds. I brought Goldsmith the money, and he discharged his rent, not without rating his landlady in a high tone for having used him so ill.' [1] (Boswell's *Life*, i. 415–6, ed. Birkbeck Hill.)

---

[1] A sentence in *The Vicar of Wakefield* (p. 391) furnishes an apt commentary on this story: 'The greatest object in the universe, says a certain philosopher, is a good man struggling with adversity; yet there is still a greater, which is the good man that comes to relieve it.'

To a certain extent the entry in Collins's account-book bears out Boswell's narrative: the sums of money are identical, if we allow that ' sixty pounds' was a slip for ' sixty guineas ', or, as some say, that 'guineas' and 'pounds' were convertible terms. But are we to accept the statement 'bought of Dr. Goldsmith' with literal exactness ? May it not have happened that Johnson interviewed Francis Newbery, nephew of the ' philanthropic bookseller ', John Newbery, and actually received the whole of the money on Goldsmith's behalf ? Newbery would then approach Collins, the Salisbury printer, to offer him a share, which seems a more likely proceeding than that Johnson or Goldsmith should do so. But if the manuscript was in the hands of the booksellers in 1762, why was publication deferred until 1766 ? At the earlier period, it must be remembered, as Boswell points out, that Goldsmith ' had published nothing with his name ' : he was known in some degree as an essayist, his fame as a poet was not yet. The booksellers, in thinking the matter over, may have come to the conclusion that Goldsmith's reputation would grow, and that when he had become known to the public by the issue of some of his works under his own name the novel would stand a better chance of acceptance. Even Johnson was doubtful, as appears from a statement made after Goldsmith's death. ' His *Vicar of Wakefield*,' he said, ' I myself did not think would have much success. It was written and sold to a bookseller before his *Traveller*, but published after, so little expectation had the bookseller from it. Had it been sold after the *Traveller*, he might have had twice as much money for it, though sixty guineas was no mean price. The bookseller had the advantage of Goldsmith's reputation from *The Traveller* in the sale, though Goldsmith had it not in selling the copy ' (*Life*, iii. 321). It may also be urged, in substantiation of Johnson's statement, that if the author had not been already paid for his work he would have been more eager to see it published.

That the novel was written as early as 1762 may be deduced from the following facts : (1) *The Auditor*, which is spoken of in chapter xix as though living, was started on June 10, 1762, and ceased to exist February 8, 1763 ; (2) the musical glasses (see pages 238, 242) were all the craze in 1761–2 ; (3) in chapter xviii Goldsmith speaks of ' the philanthropic bookseller in St. Paul's

Churchyard . . . compiling materials for the history of one Mr. Thomas Trip': this book appears on John Newbery's List for 1762; (4) Boswell did not make Johnson's acquaintance until 1763, and it will be noted that he does not tell of what passed under his own eyes, but 'authentically from Johnson's own exact narration'. Additions were made later to the novel—such as *The Hermit* and the *Elegy on a Mad Dog*; but these, admirable in themselves, were mere padding to help the volumes out to the required length, and do not carry the story forward in any way.

But reluctant as all concerned seem to have been to bring *The Vicar of Wakefield* to life, once published it began to make its way. Issued on March 27, 1766, a second edition was called for by the end of May; on the 25th of August a third edition appeared. There were also in the same year two unauthorized reprints—one at Dublin, the other at London. A fourth edition came out in 1770, a fifth in 1773, a sixth in 1779. These were all small editions, according to the booksellers' accounts, so that the success of the book was not at first overwhelming. In 1792 an edition appeared with plates after Stothard's design, and by this time the twenty-second edition had been reached. There is no need to further enumerate the successive editions of what has proved to be one of the most popular books of English literature. Those interested in pictorial art may be referred to an article by Mr. Austin Dobson entitled, 'The *Vicar of Wakefield* and its illustrators,' in *Side-walk Studies*, pp. 130–47.

The question has been asked and partially answered, 'Why did Goldsmith call his masterpiece "The Vicar of WAKEFIELD"?' The place itself plays only a small part in the story. In the first chapter its name is merely mentioned; in chapter ii we are told that there were three strange wants there: ' a parson wanting pride, young men wanting wives, and ale-houses wanting customers'; in the third chapter the Vicar and his family migrate to a distant neighbourhood. There is probably no trace of any direct connexion between Goldsmith and Wakefield now discoverable; but Mr. Ford in his interesting and persuasive article published in the *National Review* of May, 1883, shows how the somewhat puzzling topography may be accounted for on the basis of Goldsmith's own hints and figures. See also under *Wakefield*, p. 484.

SUPPRESSED OR ALTERED PASSAGES

Chapter III

Page 204, lines 19–22. ' I could not but smile . . . make us more happy.' 1766 *edition reads*—' I could not but smile to hear her talk in this strain : one almost at the verge of beggary thus to assume language of the most insulting affluence, might excite the ridicule of ill-nature ; but I was never much displeased with those innocent delusions that tend to make us more happy.'

Chapter V

Page 212, line 30. *After* ' for which he had the satisfaction of being laughed at ' 1766 *edition has*—' for he always ascribed to his wit that laughter which was lavished at his simplicity.' This may have been struck out by Goldsmith from self-conscious motives, as the passage conveys a striking image of his own character as seen by his intimates.

Page 213, lines 12–14. *For* ' nor why Mr. Simkins got the ten thousand prize in the lottery, and we sate down with a blank ' 1766 *edition reads*—' nor why one got the ten thousand prize in the lottery, and another sate down with a blank. " But those," added I, " who either aim at husbands greater than themselves, or at the ten thousand pound prize, have been fools for their ridiculous claims, whether successful or not." '

Chapter VII

Page 224, lines 9–11. *After* ' The vice does not lie in assenting to the proofs they see ; but in being blind to many of the proofs that offer ' 1766 *has*—' Like corrupt judges on a bench, they determine right on that part of the evidence they hear ; but they will not hear all the evidence. Thus, my son, though, &c.'

Chapter XV

Page 275, lines 30–3. ' Thus my children . . . still remaining.' 1766 *edition reads*—' Thus, my children, after men have travelled through a few stages in vice, they no longer continue to have shame at doing evil, and shame attends only upon their virtues.'

Chapter XVI

Page 277, lines 18-19. *For* ' in the composition of a pudding, it was her judgment that mixed the ingredients' 1766 *edition reads* ' in the composition of a pudding, her judgment was infallible.'

Chapter XXVIII

Page 377, lines 31-2. *After* ' I must suffer, my life is forfeited, and let them take it' 1766 *edition adds*—' it is my last happiness that I have committed no murder, tho' I have lost all hopes of pardon.'

Page 378, lines 34 seq. *For* ' I have sent a challenge, and as I am the first transgressor upon the statute, I see no hopes of pardon' 1766 *edition reads*—' I have sent a challenge, and that is death by a late act of parliament.'

Mr. Burchell might here have 'ingeminated' *Fudge* with good reason ; there was no such enactment on the statute-book. See Note 26.

Other Imputed Suppressions.

Johnson, in conversation with Boswell, mentions other passages as having been deleted :—

' *Johnson.* I remember a passage in Goldsmith's *Vicar of Wakefield*, which he was afterwards fool enough to expunge: " I do not love a man who is zealous for nothing." Boswell. That was a fine passage. Johnson. Yes, Sir : There was another fine passage too, which he struck out: " When I was a young man, being anxious to distinguish myself, I was perpetually starting new propositions. But I soon gave this over ; for, I found that generally what was new was false." ' (Boswell's *Life*, iii. 375-6, ed. Birkbeck Hill.)

With respect to the second instance Johnson's memory (he was speaking in 1779) may have misled him, for the same thought occurs, in rather different words, in chapter xx, pp. 310-11.

Note 16.—Goldsmith and Dr. Whiston. Page 193.

William Whiston, from whom Goldsmith borrowed several traits—more especially as regards the Vicar's views on monogamy in *The Vicar of Wakefield*—and who was a thorn in the side of many authorities, ecclesiastical, scientific, and academical, during his stormy life played many parts, and stirred up many hornets' nests. In the *Memoirs of his Life and Writings written by himself* (London, ed. 2, 1749), he expresses his views on monogamy and other subjects with a plain-spoken asperity which can scarcely have failed to raise him up many powerful enemies, as did Dr. Primrose when he trampled Mr. Wilmot under foot, and would not allow him to be a husband in any sense of the word. The pith of the Vicar's remarks on monogamy, by which he meant in brief the remarriage of a clergyman of the Church of England, will be found at p. 540 of Whiston's *Memoirs*. At p. 197 there is an obvious reference to Archbishop Tenison's harsh treatment of him, likewise mentioned in *The Vicar* (p. 265) in almost identical terms. Sir Leslie Stephen contributed a full life of Whiston to volume lxi of the *Dictionary of National Biography*. Whiston identified the Lost Ten Tribes with the Tartars ; claimed to have identified Mary Tofts, the ' rabbit woman ', with the woman mentioned in the book of Esdras ; claimed to have predicted an earthquake of about the same date ; and assured Prince Eugène on the general's famous visit to Queen Anne that he had fulfilled some of the prophecies of the Apocalypse, whereto the Prince replied that ' he had not been aware that he had the honour of being known to St. John '. It is only fair to the Prince to say that he presented Dr. Whiston with an honorarium of fifteen guineas in recognition of the ' dedication of his first imperfect Essay on the Revelation of St. John '.

Whiston was buried near his wife, who died in January, 1750–1, at Lyndon, Rutlandshire. I have not found any record of the alleged inscription on her tomb (*Vicar of Wakefield*, p. 193) ; it is, no doubt, a simple fabrication of Goldsmith's, who is fond of similar mystifications, even when they can be dismissed by a moment's comparison of facts. Whiston is now remembered chiefly, if at all, by his translation of Josephus, now itself happily superseded by that of Prof. Margoliouth. His *Memoirs* still retain distinct value as a picture of the state of religion and manners in the seventeenth and early eighteenth centuries. Whiston's learning was certainly vast in bulk and many-sided, but he lacked common-sense and critical power, so that very few of his numerous writings can be read to-day. The trail of forgotten controversies is over them all; but it is not amiss perhaps that a few readers should now and then linger over their dusty pages. He would doubtless have been a far happier man if he had abjured his own strange theology for the mathematical studies in which he might have made a great and unassailable reputation.

NOTE 17.—JOHNNY ARMSTRONG'S LAST GOOD-NIGHT. Page 207.

Goldsmith more than once shows his keen regard for this old ballad. 'The music of the most accomplished singer,' he says in his *Essays*, 'is dissonance to what I felt when an old dairymaid sang me into tears with *Johnnie Armstrong's Last Good-Night*.' The verses are said to have been composed by one of the Armstrongs, executed for the murder of Sir John Carmichael of Edrom, Warden of the Middle Marches. Two stanzas are printed by Scott in *The Minstrelsy of the Scottish Border* (vol. ii, p. 123) :—

> This night is my departing night,
>   For here nae langer must I stay;
> There's neither friend nor foe o' mine
>   But wishes me away.

> What I have done thro' lack of wit
>   I never, never can recall;
> I hope ye're a' my friends as yet;
>   Good-night, and joy be with you all!

NOTE 18.—TWO LOVERS STRUCK DEAD BY LIGHTNING. Page 226.

The story of 'the two lovers so sweetly described by Mr. Gay, who were struck dead in each other's arms' was told by Gay in a letter to Mr. F[ortescue], written from Stanton Harcourt, where he was staying with Pope, on August 9, 1718, and published in 1737. It runs thus in Pope's *Works*, viii. 115, ed. 1751 :—

'The only news that you can expect to have from me here, is news from heaven, for I am quite out of the world, and there is scarce any thing can reach me except the noise of thunder, which undoubtedly you have heard too. . . A cock of barley in our next field has been burned to ashes. Would to God that this heap of barley had been all that perished! for unhappily beneath this little shelter sat two more such constant lovers than ever were found in Romance under the shade of a beech tree. John Hewet was a well-set man of about five and twenty. Sarah Drew might be called rather comely than beautiful, and was about the same age. They had pass'd thro' the various labours of the years together, with the greatest satisfaction ; if she milk'd, 'twas his morning and evening care, to bring the cows to her hand ; it was but last fair he bought her a present of green silk for her hat, and the posies on her silver ring was of his chusing. . . It was that very morning that he had obtained the consent of her parents, and it was but till the next week that they were to be happy. Perhaps in the intervals of their work they were now talking of the wedding cloaths. . . . While they were thus busied, (it was on the last day of July between two or three in the afternoon) the clouds grew black, and such a storm of thunder and lightning ensued, that all the labourers made the best of their way to what shelter the trees and hedges afforded. Sarah was frightened, and fell down in a swoon on a heap of barley. John, who never separated from her, sat down by her side, having raked together two or three heaps, the better to secure her from the storm. Immediately there was heard so loud a crack, as if heaven had split asunder ; every one was now solicitous for the safety of his neighbour, and called to one another throughout the field. No answer being returned to those who called for our Lovers, they stept to the place where they lay ; they perceived the barley in a smoke, and then spied this faithful pair : John with one arm about Sarah's neck, and the other held over her, as to skreen her from lightning. They were struck dead, and stiffen'd in this tender posture. . . My Lord Harcourt, at Mr. Pope's and my request, has caused a stone to be placed over them, upon condition that we furnish'd the Epitaph, which is as follows :—

> When Eastern lovers feed the fun'ral fire,
> On the same pile their faithful fair expire :
> Here pitying Heav'n that virtue mutual found,
> And blasted both, that it might neither wound.
> Hearts so sincere th' Almighty saw well pleas'd,
> Sent his own lightning, and the victims seiz'd.

But my Lord is apprehensive the country people will not understand this, and Mr. Pope says he'll make one with something of Scripture in it, and with as little of poetry as Sternhold and Hopkins.'

The Epitaph which Pope wrote was this :—

Near this place lie the bodies of
JOHN HEWET and SARAH DREW,
an industrious young Man
and Virtuous Maiden of this Parish ;
Who being at Harvest-Work
(with several others)
Were in one instant killed by Lightning
the last day of July 1718.

It would appear that the letter was written jointly by Gay and Pope, as the latter, with very little variation, told the same tale in a letter to Mrs. Mary Blount, dated August 6, 1718, three days before Gay's letter. Pope also told the story in nearly identical language to Lady Mary Wortley Montague on September 1, 1718, sending the poetical inscription as in Gay's letter, and adding the following :—

I

Think not, by rig'rous judgment seiz'd,
  A pair so faithful could expire ;
Victims so pure Heav'n saw, well pleas'd,
  And snatch'd them in celestial fire.

II

Live well, and fear no sudden fate ;
  When God calls virtue to the grave,
Alike 'tis justice, soon or late,
  Mercy alike to kill or save.
Virtue unmov'd can hear the call,
And face the flash that melts the ball.

Pope adds, ' Of the epitaphs which I made, the critics have chosen the godly one: I like neither . . . Upon the whole, I cannot think these people unhappy. The greatest happiness, next to living as they would have done, was to die as they did.'

Thackeray, in his *Lectures on the English Humourists* (Lecture IV : Prior, Gay, and Pope), came to the conclusion that Gay's letter was the original, and that ' the great Mr. Pope admired it so much that he thought proper to steal it ' ; but it is clear from a letter written to Pope by Lord Bathurst on August 14, 1718 (first published in Elwin and Courthope's *Pope's Works*, viii. 324), that it was a joint production, for the writer acknowledges the receipt of the story in these words : ' I must now return my thanks to Mr. Gay and you for your melancholy novel you sent me of the two unhappy lovers ; but why unhappy after all ? . . . I will only say that their names would never have been recorded to posterity but for this accident.'

NOTE 19.—MUSICAL GLASSES. Pages 238, 242.

The power of producing musical sounds from glass basins or drinking-glasses by the application of the moistened finger, and of tuning them so as to obtain concords from two at once, was known as early as the middle of the eighteenth century. Gluck, when in England, played at the Little Theatre in the Haymarket, 1746, a concerto on 26 drinking glasses tuned with spring water. Horace Walpole, writing to Sir. H. Mann (March 28, 1746), says : ' He [Gluck] is to have a benefit, at which he is to play on a set of drinking-glasses, which he modulates with water ' (*Letters*, ii. 184). But it was not until 1761 and 1762 that musical glasses became a craze of ' genteel ' life. Private letters and newspapers teem with references to them at that date. Thus Gray to Mason (December 8, 1761), ' Dear Mason,—Of all loves come to Cambridge out of hand, for here is Mr. Delaval and a charming set of glasses that sing like nightingales ; and we have concerts every other night, and shall stay here this month or two.' See Gray's *Letters*, ed. Tovey, ii. 246 *note* ; also Thomas Campbell, *A Philosophical Survey of the South of Ireland, in a series of Letters to John Watkinson, M.D.*, p. 452 ; and the article on Pockrich in the *Dictionary of National Biography*. For further information on the scientific side, see Grove's *Dictionary of Music*, ii. 296 (ed. 1906), s.v. Harmonica.

The same idea had occurred to the Chinese hundreds of years before this time. Musical cups were known to them in the tenth century A.D. They put a greater or less quantity of water in each, and thus produced modulation.

NOTE 20.—CUTTING PAPER. Page 251.

As an additional illustration to this once fashionable custom the following poem by Pope is given :—

On the Countess of Burlington cutting paper.

PALLAS grew vapourish once, and odd,
　　She would not do the least right thing,
Either for goddess or for god,
　　Nor work, nor play, nor paint, nor sing.

Jove frown'd, and ' Use,' he cried, ' those eyes
　　So skilful, and those hands so taper ;
Do something exquisite and wise—'
　　She bow'd, obey'd him,—and cut paper.

This vexing him who gave her birth,
　　Thought by all heaven a burning shame ;
What does she next, but bids on earth
　　Her BURLINGTON do just the same.

PALLAS, you give yourself strange airs ;
　　But sure you'll find it hard to spoil
The sense and taste of one that bears
　　The name of Saville and of Boyle.

Alas ! one bad example shown ;
　　How quickly all the sex pursue !
See, madam, see the arts o'erthrown
　　Between JOHN OVERTON [1] and you.

NOTE 21.—THE FEAR OF MAD DOGS. Pages 286-7.

Notwithstanding the ridicule which Goldsmith poured upon those who stood in dread of mad dogs, both in this Elegy and in his paper on the subject in the *Public Ledger* for August 29, 1760 (afterwards reprinted in the *Citizen of the World*), people still went in fear of hydrophobia, an example of which appears in *George Selwyn's Letters* (ed. Roscoe and Clergue, 1899), pp. 274-5 :—

' [1790, *August* 12, *Richmond*] Now *à d'autres choses.* I have in my last fright forgot one where there were better grounds for it. The day I wrote to you last, as you know, I was at Isleworth.

[1] Principal vendor of mezzotints of his day (*D.N.B.*).

Coming from thence, and when I landed, the first thing I heard was that people with guns were in pursuit of a mad dog, that he had run into the Duke's garden. Mie Mie [Maria Fagniani] came the first naturally into my thoughts; she is there sometimes by herself reading. My impatience to get home, and uneasiness till I found that she was safe and in her room, *n'est pas à concevoir.* The dog bit several other dogs, a bluecoat boy, and two children, before he was destroyed. John St. John, who dined with me, had met him in a narrow lane, near Mrs. Boverie's, him and his pursuers. John had for his defence a stick, with a heavy handle. He struck him with this, and for the moment got clear of him; *il l'a culbuté.* It is really dreadful; for ten days to come we shall be in a terror, not knowing what dogs may have been bitten. Some may now have *le cerveau qui commence à se troubler.*'

NOTE 22.—THE LEVELLERS. Page 301.

Clarendon, in his *History of the Rebellion*, x. 140, thus speaks of the Agitators, a name given to the agents or delegates of the private soldiers in the Parliamentary army of 1647-9: ' They entered into new associations, and made many propositions to their officers and to the Parliament to introduce an equality into all conditions, and a parity amongst all men; from whence they had the appellation of *Levellers*.'

Goldsmith does not seem to have altogether grasped the aims and intentions of the Levellers. Mr. Alfred Beesley, in his admirable *History of Banbury*, reprints a pamphlet containing the Levellers' *Declaration*, which gives a summary of their programme. It is entitled: ' England's Standard Advanced in Oxfordshire, or a declaration from Mr. Wil. Thomson, and the oppressed People of this Nation now under his conduct in the said County. Dated at their Randez-vous May 6, 1649. Whereunto is added an Agreement of the Free People of England, as the Grounds of their Resolutions. Printed in the Yeer 1649.' In this, the Levellers enumerated the wrongs under which the nation suffered, calling upon all who had any sense of the bonds and miseries of the people ' to help a miserable nation to break the bands of cruelty, and set the people free '.

On Friday, May 11, the House took into consideration the ' business of the Levellers ' and declared Thomson's adherents rebels and traitors. On Saturday, May 12, it was reported that ' It hath pleased God to bring this great Bubble of the Levellers about Banbury to a sudden breaking, and that Thomson had escaped with a party of about 300.' The end of the abortive rising was that Capt. Thomson was taken prisoner and shot together with his brother, whereon the insurrection collapsed. The two Thomsons were shot in Burford churchyard, having refused quarter.

With these documents should be compared the correspondence of the Levellers with Charles II in 1656, through their spokesman, William Howard (printed in Macray's edition of Clarendon's *History of the Rebellion*, vol. vi, pp. 67 seq.), one sentence of which will serve to show its general purport. It runs: 'What can we do more worthy of Englishmen, as we are by nation, or of Christians, as we are by profession, than every one of us to put our hand to an oar, and try if it be the will of our God that such weak instruments as we may be in any measure helpful to bring it at last into the safe and quiet harbour of justice and righteousness ! '

Note 23.—Eastern Tales. Page 313.

A very valuable contribution to the *History of the Oriental Tale in England in the Eighteenth Century* has been made recently by Miss Martha Pike Conant, Ph.D., of the Columbia University, U.S.A. This interesting book may be cordially recommended to all students of Goldsmith, especially of that phase of his work in which he was so deeply interested—possibly in spite of himself—in tales more or less oriental. Miss Conant has dealt with the subject very sympathetically, and her book will interest many readers in England as well as in the United States.

Note 24.—Philautos, Philalethes, &c. Page 313.

The Catalogues of the Bodleian and other great Libraries teem with such strange compounds as those here glanced at by Goldsmith, and many others like them. Perhaps the most interesting among those enumerated is a work by *Eugenius Philalethes* (Thomas Vaughan), entitled *The Man-Mouse taken in a Trap, and tortur'd to death for gnawing the Margins of Eugenius Philalethes* (1650). This book is a reply to Dr. Moore, who is styled in the Dedication ' a simple Bedlam ', ' a certain Master

of Arts of Cambridge ', and ' a Poet in the Loll and Trot of
Spencer ', ' a very Elf in Philosophie '.

NOTE 25.—PICKERING AS THE SUPPOSED SCENE OF DR. PRIMROSE'S IMPRISONMENT. Page 353.

Visitors to Pickering, which has been suggested as the site
of the prison which was the scene of the Vicar's sufferings and
final triumph over his enemies, may be safely advised to read *The
Evolution of an English Town*, by Gordon Home (Methuen & Co.).
This book contains much information as to the peculiarly rich folk-
lore of the district and the history of the Castle and Vale of
Pickering, together with many other interesting details, including
a sketch-map of the district.   A sketch of the Black Hole of
Thornton-le-Dale shows an underground cell beneath some
cottages which was formerly the village prison, and has been
supposed to have sheltered the Vicar and his family.   See an
article by Mr. Edward Ford in the *National Review* for May, 1883.

NOTE 26.—DUELLING.   Pages 378, 391.

The statement of George Primrose, that by sending a challenge
to 'Squire Thornhill he had laid himself open to the extreme
punishment of the law, has no real warrant in fact.   Curiously,
a similar statement is made by Sheridan in *The Rivals* (Act v,
sc. 1), where Faulkner exclaims to Julia, ' You see before you
a wretch, *whose life is forfeited.* . . I left you fretful and passionate
—an untoward event drew me into a quarrel—the event is, that
I must fly this kingdom instantly.'   The law on the subject at
that time is thus stated in Burn's *Law Dictionary* (ed. 1792) :—

' Although upon the single combat no death ensue, nor blood
be drawn, yet the very combat for revenge is an affray, and a
great breach of the king's peace ;   an affright and terror to the
king's subjects ;   and is to be punished by fine and imprisonment,
and to find sureties for the good behaviour.   3 *Inst.* 157.

' And where one party kills the other it comes within the
notion of murder, as being committed by malice aforethought ;
where the parties meet avowedly with an intent to murder,
thinking it their duty, as gentlemen, and claiming it as their
right, to wanton with their own lives, and the lives of others,
without any warrant for it, either human and divine ;   and

therefore the law hath justly fixed on them the crime and punishment of murder.   4 *Black.* 199.

' But if two persons fall out upon a sudden occasion, and agree to fight in such a field, and each of them goeth to 'fetch his weapon, and they go into the field, and therein fight, and the one killeth the other, this is no malice prepensed; for the fetching of the weapon, and going into the field, is but a continuance of the sudden falling out, and the blood was never cooled : but if there were deliberation, as that they meet the next day, nay, though it were the same day, if there were such a competent distance of time, that in common presumption they had time of deliberation, then it is murder.   1 *Hale's Hist.* 453.'

Goldsmith has evidently tried to put himself right, for the first edition contained certain passages which he afterwards changed. See Note on Suppressed Passages (Chapter XXVIII), p. 510.

Note 27.—Early Drama in America.

In view of Goldsmith's admiration for Otway, it may be of interest to note that this dramatist was one of the first to be represented on the American stage.

The *New York Nation* of January 28, 1909, contained a highly interesting article on ' The First Play in America '.   It is there decided, on very strong evidence, that the first playhouse in America dates from *circa* 1750, when a performance of Otway's *Orphan* was given in a Boston Coffee House.   In 1866, Ireland wrote a circumstantial account of a company of actors that reached New York in February, 1750, under the management of ' a certain Kean and Murray '.   The Philadelphia records of the Murray and Kean Company have been brought to light. An entry in John Smith's *Journal* gives the name of what was probably the first play acted by them :—

' Sixth Month (August 22d, 1749).   Joseph Morris and I happened in at Peacock Bigger's, and drunk tea there, and his daughter, being one of the company who were going to hear the tragedy of *Cato* acted, it occasioned some conversation, in which I expressed my sorrow that anything of the kind was encouraged.'